Non-Traditional Security Issues in ASEAN

Non-Traditional Security Issues in ASEAN

Agendas for Action

EDITED BY

MELY CABALLERO-ANTHONY
LINA GONG

 YUSOF ISHAK
INSTITUTE

First published in Singapore in 2020 by
ISEAS Publishing
30 Heng Mui Keng Terrace
Singapore 119614

E-mail: publish@iseas.edu.sg
Website: <http://bookshop.iseas.edu.sg>

ISEAS Library Cataloguing-in-Publication Data

Names: Anthony, Mely Caballero-, editor. | Gong, Lina, editor.
Title: Non-traditional security issues in ASEAN : agendas for action / edited by Mely Caballero-Anthony and Lina Gong.
Description: Singapore : ISEAS – Yusof Ishak Institute, 2020. | Includes bibliographical references.
Identifiers: ISBN 978-981-4881-08-1 (paperback) | 978-981-4881-09-8 (PDF)
Subjects: LCSH: National security—Southeast Asia. | Human security—Southeast Asia.
Classification: LCC UA832.8 N81

Typeset by International Typesetters Pte Ltd

CONTENTS

ABOUT THE CONTRIBUTORS

Mely CABALLERO-ANTHONY is Professor of International Relations and Head of the Centre for Non-Traditional Security (NTS) Studies at the S. Rajaratnam School of International Studies (RSIS), Nanyang Technological University (NTU), Singapore. Prof Anthony teaches courses on Non-Traditional Security in Asia and Security Governance. She is also currently Chair of the RSIS Committee on Promotion and Tenure.

Prof Anthony's research interests include regionalism and multilateralism in the Asia Pacific, human security and non-traditional security, conflict prevention and global governance. She has published extensively on a broad range of security issues in the Asia Pacific in peer-reviewed journals and international academic press. Her latest books, both single-authored and co-edited, include: *Negotiating Governance on Non-Traditional Security in Southeast Asia and Beyond* (2018), *An Introduction to Non-Traditional Security Studies* (2016), *Asia on the Move* (2015), and *Human Security and Climate Change* (2014).

Rini ASTUTI is Research Fellow in the Inter-Asia Engagements cluster of Asia Research Institute (ARI), National University of Singapore. She obtained her PhD in Geography from Victoria University of Wellington, New Zealand. Prior to joining ARI, Dr Astuti was a Research Fellow with the S. Rajaratnam School of International Studies, Nanyang Technological University, Singapore. Her research interests focus on sustainable governance of transboundary environmental problems in Southeast Asia.

Christopher CHEN is an Associate Research Fellow at the Centre for Non-Traditional Security (NTS) Studies at the S. Rajaratnam School of International Studies (RSIS), Nanyang Technological University (NTU), Singapore. He obtained a Master of International Relations and a Bachelor of Arts (Media & Communication and Politics & International Studies) from the University of Melbourne (UniMelb), Australia. He currently specializes in the area of humanitarian assistance and disaster relief. His research interests include Humanitarian Assistance and Disaster Relief (HADR) in the Asia Pacific; institutional memory; human rights in Asia; forced migration; politics and conflicts in the Asia Pacific.

Alistair D.B. COOK is Coordinator of the Humanitarian Assistance and Disaster Relief Programme and Senior Fellow at the Centre for Non-Traditional Security (NTS) Studies at the S. Rajaratnam School of International Studies (RSIS), Nanyang Technological University (NTU), Singapore. His research interests focus on the Asia Pacific, and Myanmar in particular, on humanitarian affairs, foreign policy and regional cooperation. He has recently authored or co-authored "Achieving the ASEAN 2025 Vision for Disaster Management: Lessons from a Worthy Journey", *ASEAN Risk Monitor and Disaster Management Review* (2019); "Integrating Disaster Governance in Timor-Leste: Opportunities and Challenges", *International Journal of Disaster Risk Reduction* (2019); "Negotiating Access to Populations of Concern in Southeast Asia", *Pacific Review* (2018); "An Assessment of International Emergency Disaster Response to the 2015 Nepal Earthquakes", *International Journal of Disaster Risk Reduction* (2018); "Humanitarian Technology Survey", *RSIS Policy Report* (2017); and co-edited *Irregular Migration and Human Security in East Asia* (2017); *Civilian Protection in the Twenty-First Century: Governance and Responsibility in a Fragmented World* (2016); and *Non-Traditional Security in Asia: Issues, Challenges and Framework for Action* (2013).

Yen Ne FOO is a National Project Coordinator at the International Labour Organization (ILO). She has a Masters in International Relations from the S. Rajaratnam School of International Studies (RSIS), Nanyang Technological University (NTU), Singapore. Her areas of expertise include labour migration, gender equality and elimination of violence against women. Prior to her work at the ILO, she was a Senior Analyst at the Centre for Non-Traditional Security Studies, RSIS, researching on humanitarian assistance and disaster relief in the ASEAN region.

Lina GONG is Research Fellow at the Centre for Non-Traditional Security (NTS) Studies at the S. Rajaratnam School of International Studies (RSIS), Nanyang Technological University (NTU), Singapore. She received her PhD from RSIS, NTU. Her PhD thesis is on China's engagement with the UN peacekeeping. Her research interests include non-traditional security studies in East Asia, China and global governance, peace and conflict. She currently focuses on China-ASEAN cooperation in non-traditional security issues and disaster management in Southeast Asia and the broad Asia-Pacific region.

Jose Ma. Luis ("Louie") MONTESCLAROS is Associate Research Fellow at the Centre for Non-Traditional Security (NTS) Studies at the S. Rajaratnam School of International Studies (RSIS), Nanyang Technological University (NTU), Singapore. He holds a Master's Degree in Public Policy from the Lee Kuan Yew School of Public Policy, National University of Singapore (Full ASEAN Scholar) and a BS Economics degree from the University of the Philippines, Diliman. Louie conducts policy analysis using dynamic models of food security, climate change and urban agriculture in Singapore and Southeast Asia, and was also one of the two modellers in a major project with the Singapore government's Inter-Ministerial Committee on Food Security. He also co-developed (First Inventor) a preliminary commercial viability assessment tool for climate-adaptive agricultural technologies, contributing to NTU's pool of copyrighted intellectual property. He has, in the past, consulted with the World Bank Group on agriculture, small and medium enterprise development and ASEAN's inclusive growth. He has also co-facilitated the development and assessment of long-term plans of over ten cities, two municipalities and a national association of cities in the Philippines, using the Performance Governance System, an adaptation of the Balanced Scorecard.

Margareth SEMBIRING is an Associate Research Fellow at the Centre for Non-Traditional Security (NTS) Studies at the S. Rajaratnam School of International Studies (RSIS), Nanyang Technological University (NTU), Singapore. Her focus is on transboundary environmental and climate change-related issues, particularly in Southeast Asia. She examines regional and national mechanisms put in place to address these issues. At the same time, she is undertaking a PhD study that assesses energy transition from fossil fuels to renewable energy sources in the Philippines and Indonesia.

Julius Cesar I. TRAJANO is Research Fellow with the Centre for Non-Traditional Security (NTS) Studies at the S. Rajaratnam School of International Studies (RSIS), Nanyang Technological University (NTU), Singapore. His research interests are in non-traditional security issues in the Asia Pacific, particularly nuclear security governance, peacebuilding in the southern Philippines, marine environmental protection, and human trafficking. He has recently authored or co-authored "A Policy Analysis of Nuclear Safety Culture and Security Culture in East Asia", *Nuclear Engineering and Technology* (2019); "Peacebuilding from the Grassroots: Resolving Conflicts in Mindanao", *Asia Dialogue* (2019); and "Enhancing Nuclear Energy Cooperation in ASEAN: Regional Norms and Challenges", in *Learning from Fukushima: Nuclear Power in East Asia* (2017). He is presently the coordinating chair for the Asia Working Group as well as the Working Group 2 vice chair, both within the International Nuclear Security Education Network, and is a member of the Council for Security Cooperation in the Asia-Pacific Nuclear Energy Experts Group.

1

BEYOND SECURITIZATION: GOVERNING NTS ISSUES IN SOUTHEAST ASIA

Mely Caballero-Anthony and Lina Gong

1.1   Introduction

The Southeast Asian region provides a good test bed to examine how non-traditional security (NTS) issues have been governed. Over the past two decades, the region had experienced a number of crises that have had significant impact on the security agenda of states and the nature of multilateral security and development cooperation that have evolved within and beyond Southeast Asia. Among the most consequential crises that have occurred were the Asian financial crisis in 1997, the health emergencies caused by SARS epidemic in 2003 and H5N1 highly pathogenic avian influenza in 2005, the catastrophic devastations brought on by large-scale natural disasters like Typhoon Haiyan in 2013, the multi-faceted impact of the transboundary haze in 2015 and the escalation of the Rohingya refugee issue in 2017. While these security problems are typically non-military in nature, they are referred to as NTS issues since they are found to gravely threaten the survival and well-being of states and societies.[1] There is increasing and disquieting evidence that the impact of NTS issues like climate change and its attendant threats, forced migration, and emerging infectious diseases, among others, threatens the lives of countless vulnerable communities and risks the future progress upon which societies across the world depend on. To be sure, these kinds of issues have seriously challenged regional stability, peace and security. More importantly, these concerns have raised questions on how security is governed from the national, regional and even to the global level, and consequently brought to scrutiny the kinds of policies and institutions that have been developed to address them.

The impact of NTS has led a number of scholars in Southeast Asia and other subregions in Asia to examine why and how certain issues should be securitized, and analyse how they pose a threat to state and human security. Many of these studies have also proposed measures on how governments and regional institutions like the Association of Southeast Asian Nations (ASEAN) could deal with NTS threats more effectively. [2] But beyond the academic institutions, it is also useful to note that since the early 2000s, NTS has started to find traction among the policy community in the region. Moreover, NTS has started to appear in the security lexicon of ASEAN. One of the early documents that reflects this is the Joint Declaration on Cooperation in the Field of Non-traditional Security Issues adopted by ASEAN and China in 2002.[3]

More than ten years on, the NTS language is now widely used in the official documents in ASEAN and the broader East Asia. Beyond official pronouncements, progress can also be seen in the way the region has responded to NTS challenges, evidenced by a variety of regional arrangements that were established in ASEAN and with its dialogue partners. For example, in July 2005, ASEAN adopted the ASEAN Agreement on Disaster Management and Emergency Response (AADMER) to better respond to catastrophic natural disasters. In 2007, the ASEAN+3 Emerging Infectious Diseases Programme was initiated to enhance regional cooperation in dealing with emerging infectious diseases. An array of related agreements was reached to combat the chronic problem of transboundary haze, like the 2002 ASEAN Agreement on Transboundary Haze Pollution, the 2003 ASEAN Peatland Management Initiative, and the 2005 ASEAN Peatland Management Strategy.[4]

In spite of the progress made in establishing relevant regional mechanisms and spending efforts at better policy planning and coordination to deal with NTS issues, the changing dynamics in managing these threats as well as the emergence of new NTS challenges have put more pressures on finding better ways to govern NTS. For instance, there are increasing demands to protect the marine environment against the effects of climate change and increasing use of the regional seas including maritime traffic. This has led to the adoption of the ASEAN-China Declaration for A Decade of Coastal and Marine Environmental Protection in the South China Sea in 2017 and the East Asia Summit Leaders' Statement on Combating Marine Plastic Debris in 2018. However, the unresolved territorial disputes in the South China Sea have been hampering regional coordination and cooperation. Meanwhile, the cross-cutting impact of other NTS threats are also becoming more apparent and increasingly affecting many vulnerable communities. For example, rising sea levels and increasing frequency of extreme weather events from climate change have aggravated food and water insecurities in parts of Asia. Health security is also seriously challenged by the expansion of slums in Asia's mega-cities. As a consequence of rising urbanization, new health problems arise as critical infrastructure for sewage and waste management are not adequately in place.

Against this background, the main objective of this book is to examine the current state of governance of NTS challenges confronting the ASEAN region. By presenting selected NTS issues such as climate change, food security, environmental protection, humanitarian assistance and disaster response, health security, nuclear security, and human trafficking and forced displacement, the book aims to identify some of the major gaps and challenges in the governance of these issues. Given the growing complexity of NTS issues, we argue that the governance of NTS issues becomes even more compelling. Going beyond securitization, governing NTS must now focus on building capacity and improving mechanisms that deal with NTS. Within the context of Southeast Asia, this further means deepening regional cooperation and strengthening regional institutions. All these are the critical agendas that call for action in ASEAN.

We begin this introductory chapter with a short overview of the development of NTS as a concept and an approach and draw the linkages between NTS and security governance. We examine these linkages within the Southeast Asian context. The chapter concludes by highlighting some of the key findings of the case studies in this book and their implications on crafting the NTS agenda for action in ASEAN.

1.2   Non-Traditional Security in Asia

Revisiting NTS as a Concept and Approach

A question often asked with regard to non-traditional security is how this concept sits with the other familiar concepts of security in Asia like comprehensive security, cooperative security and human security. For a start, it is useful to note that for many post-colonial, developing states in Asia, the organizing concept of security has been comprehensive security. It is an expanded security concept that goes beyond the traditional preoccupation with military threats to national security to include political, economic and socio-cultural issues. Since the mid-1990s, however, there have been many scholars who have criticized the state-centric focus of comprehensive security contending that it was no longer reflective nor adequate to address the kinds of security challenges to states and societies brought on by a significantly changed international environment. It was during this period, when the concept of human security emerged that challenged the state-centric approach to security and laid an important foundation for the emergence of the NTS discourse.[5]

The human security concept pays particular attention to the security threats faced by individuals, communities and societies, which were often lost in the state-centric analysis of security. By recasting the security referent to individuals/communities instead of the state, and reframing the questions from "what is security" to "who is to be secured and from what?"—human security highlights the kinds of issues, insecurities and vulnerabilities faced by people from all walks of life, and sheds light on the nature of security practices that could be detrimental to ensuring human security for all. The human security approach also problematizes the role of the state as the only provider of security since there are times when the state and/or state action causes human insecurities. It is in safeguarding and guaranteeing human security where cooperative security approaches not only among state actors but also non-state actors become even more important.[6]

NTS shares the conceptual space of human security, in that it does not confine the remit of security to traditional, state-centric threats which are often military in nature. However, NTS does not privilege only individuals as the main security referent, but regards both referents—state and individuals—as not mutually exclusive. Both security referents need to feel secure since a state that is insecure will not be able to provide for the well-being and security of its people. NTS therefore recognizes the role of the state as the primary provider of human security while, at the same time, is mindful of how state apparatuses when misused can be a threat and/or detrimental to human security. Like human security, NTS helps to broaden and deepen the understanding of security and the role that actors, both state and non-state, can play in providing and ensuring security.[7]

NTS and the Process of Securitization

The development of NTS scholarship has drawn from the securitization theory of the Copenhagen School in understanding why and how certain issues become security threats to states and individuals/communities. The securization theory of Barry Buzan, Ole Waever and Jaap de Wilde points to the critical role of the speech act in framing an issue as an existential threat to a referent's survival and well-being. The purpose of the speech act is to convince an audience about an existential threat and construct an inter-subjective understanding within and among constituencies about the implications of a particular threat and to agree on the necessary policies and emergency measures needed to address it.[8] In the domestic domain, particularly liberal democracies, the general public's acceptance that an issue poses an existential threat to a referent object is an important criteria for a securitization process to succeed. This also includes getting the public's support for certain policies and measures to be adopted. Even in non-liberal states, the public's response to securitization matter especially when urgent policy responses to an existential threat requires not only rapid mobilization of resources but also introducing extraordinary measures like compulsory quarantine during an epidemic outbreak. Securitization constitutes a key step to gaining legitimacy and public support, which in turn become bases for maintaining public trust and accountability.

The nature and extent of securitization are also context specific, heavily influenced by the kind of political and security environment at the national, regional and international levels. Quite often, the process(es) of securitization is easier to do for countries belonging to the same region that face common security threats. Geographic proximity and close socio-economic ties enable states and communities to present their case for securitizing a particular issue—environmental protection, population displacement, health emergency, etc., convince their constituencies and persuade the relevant authorities to take immediate action to respond to such a threat. The appropriation of the language of security, through the securitization process, therefore allows for designating an issue/or sets of issues as security challenges, elevating them to high politics and into the national and regional security agenda.

There have been abundant examples of countries in Southeast Asia and the wider region invoking the language of NTS at the national and regional levels. Many state leaders in ASEAN and East Asia declared the SARS epidemic as an issue of national and international security. At the height of its outbreak in 2003, then Chinese Premier Wen Jiabao declared that the situation in China remained "grave", and that "the health and security of the people, overall state of reform, development, and stability, and China's national interest and international image [were] at stake".[9] Similarly, then Chinese President Hu Jintao referred to environmental pollution, major natural disasters and pandemics as NTS issues in his address at the 2008 APEC summit in Peru after the Wenchuan earthquake earlier that year.[10] President Benigno Aquino declared a state of calamity after Typhoon Haiyan landed in the central Philippines on 7 November 2013 and left a trail of devastation resulting in huge human casualties and destruction of properties. In brief, the securitization of NTS issues has in effect laid the foundation for exploring pathways of improving security governance in the region.

Growing Complexity of NTS Challenges

As noted above, many NTS issues are often interlocking, with one being the cause or multiplier of another. Climate change, which is considered a threat multiplier, is a good example to illustrate this. In the 2018 Global Risks Report by the World Economic Forum, climate change was ranked highest in the list of global risks in terms of likelihood and impact. It is also noteworthy that failure of climate mitigation and adaptation is among the top five global risks. Further, the latest report released in October 2018 by the UN Intergovernmental Panel on Climate Change (IPCC), titled *Global Warming of 1.5°C*, has warned that our planet is on the way to the 1.5°C limit and that the sustained trend of global warming has shown no sign of relenting. Effects of climate change like the increase of the frequency of extreme weather events have serious implications for public health, water and food availability and the ecosystem. The impact of climate change on the environment such as desertification of land, drying up of rivers and bleaching of corals are extremely consequential to humanity but are proving difficult to reverse or repair. Rising sea levels threaten the future of states in low-lying areas, not to mention the very existence and identity of people living in these states. The UN Secretary General Antonio Guterres has warned that the interconnection of megatrends like food insecurity and water crises with climate change and people's movements are becoming more acute and creating situations where more people are displaced and more tensions and conflicts can emerge.

Aside from climate change, infectious diseases are a serious threat to global security. In 2000, the UN Security Council adopted Resolution 1308 which recognized the HIV/AIDS as a threat to international peace and security. The resolution expressed concern that the spread of HIV/AIDS constituted a potential risk to the health of UN peacekeepers and the support personnel. The threat became more vivid recently with the outbreak of Ebola virus disease in West Africa between 2014 and 2015 that took away over 11,000 lives. These cases show that non-military issues of global concern can be as destructive as military conflicts.

Compounding the complexity of NTS issues is their transborder impact. A number of transboundary crises in recent years has shown that it is difficult to contain the impact of an NTS problem within national borders. For instance, transboundary haze has been a chronic problem that has affected several Southeast Asian countries. The recent major episode that occurred in 2013 saw the Pollutant Standards Index (PSI) reading in Singapore reaching a record high of 401. The haze was caused by large-scale forest fires in Kalimantan and Sumatra in Indonesia and in some parts of Malaysia, often started by the unregulated slash and burn practices of farmers and worsened by dry weather conditions.[11] The same is true for cases of forced migration and violence-induced displacement. The recent exodus of Rohingya people from the Rakhine state of Myanmar has increasingly become a regional concern as neighbouring countries like Malaysia, Indonesia and Thailand became destinations for refugees.[12] It is estimated that over 700,000 Rohingya has sought refuge in Bangladesh since violence drastically escalated in Rakhine in August 2017. Apart from the fact that the security of the refugees is seriously threatened, the receiving countries have had to face various challenges, like the financial burden of hosting them and the possible threats to social cohesion. For these kinds of complex problems with transborder impact, finding solutions is often beyond the capacity of any single government.

There is also the scale and magnitude of many NTS challenges, which further push the limits of state capacity to handle. Catastrophic disasters like Typhoon Haiyan are good examples. Haiyan is considered to be one of the most intense tropical cyclones on record. While the Philippine authorities had prepared in advance, they found themselves woefully under-resourced to respond to the cataclysmic impact of the disaster of such scale. Severely damaged infrastructure made it very difficult for aid workers to reach the affected areas and deliver timely humanitarian relief goods. Moreover, the country's military that had been expected to help provide transport and airlift facilities did not have adequate capacity. Similarly, when Indonesia was hit by several earthquakes in the second half of 2018 which occurred almost successively in a short span of time, the government found itself having to accept international aid and assistance against its strained capacity and limited resources.[13] In brief, transnationality and the scale of the impact of NTS have significantly altered the way these threats are addressed.

NTS Challenges Facing the Region

What are some of the critical NTS challenges that threaten the security of the ASEAN and the wider region? It is beyond the scope of this book to discuss all NTS problems in ASEAN. Instead, we highlight some key challenges to emphasize their importance to the peoples' security.

Top of the list is climate change that increases the frequency of natural disasters and have thus put significant stress on Southeast Asian countries. According to the statistics of UNESCAP, Southeast Asia is among the most severely-impacted regions in the world. Between

2000 and 2016, natural disasters caused the death of 362,000 people and affected over 250 million.[14] The Philippines, Indonesia, Myanmar, Thailand and Vietnam are the most affected states in Southeast Asia. The Indian Ocean tsunami in 2004 caused casualties over 200,000, with Indonesia as the most affected. Cyclone Nargis that hit Myanmar in 2008 resulted in 70,000 people dead or missing and affected over 1.5 million. In addition, natural disasters also caused serious economic losses. Typhoon Haiyan caused damages amounting to 3.72 per cent of the Philippines' GDP in 2013.[15] What is worrying is that the UN predicts that the risk of floods and droughts in Southeast Asia will increase significantly by 2030 as a result of climate change, leading to economic losses amounting to 3 per cent of the GDP of the Philippines, 2 per cent of Laos, and over 1.5 per cent of Cambodia.[16] Other NTS issues will also be exacerbated by climate change, like food security and health security. A representative of FAO pointed out that agricultural and fishery outputs in the Philippines will decrease by 25 per cent and 40 per cent. The percentage of malnutrition among children under five increased from 30.3 per cent in 2013 to 33.4 per cent in 2017.[17]

Environmental degradation both on land and below water presents another serious challenge to Southeast Asian countries. With a total population of over 600 million and having enjoyed rapid economic development for decades, the tension between economic growth and environmental sustainability has become more pronounced in recent years. The ASEAN Secretariat pointed out in 2006 that major environmental stresses in the region include deforestation for agriculture and excessive exploration of natural resources like water, timber and fishery.[18] The forest coverage of Indonesia dropped from 65.4 per cent in 1990 to 50.2 per cent in 2015, as a result of deforestation for plantation of palm oil, which is a key source of revenue for Indonesia.[19] Because many people still use the slash and burn practice to deforest, transboundary haze has been a major environmental threat that emanates primarily from Indonesia but had also seriously affected the neighbouring countries. Marine environmental pollution in the regional seas is another manifestation of environmental degradation in the region. It has been shown that China, Indonesia, the Philippines, Thailand and Vietnam together produced over half of plastic waste in the world's oceans.[20] The threat of marine plastic waste is increasingly getting the attention of governments in the region.

Movement of people is another serious and difficult issue facing the region, particularly irregular migration like people smuggling and trafficking as well as forced displacement. In the latter, the Rohingya refugee crisis did not only raise security concerns for the affected people and the destination countries, but it also caused tensions in relations among member states of ASEAN. In September 2017, Malaysia decided to withdraw from the ASEAN Chairman's statement on the Rakhine situation since it disagreed with the omission of the Rohingyas in its content. Trafficking in persons is another major problem plaguing Southeast Asia. According to the United Nations, East Asia, including Southeast Asia, is a major source for human trafficking, with victims found in more than sixty countries across the globe.[21] Thailand and the Philippines were the key countries of origin for the trafficking flows to North America.[22] Within the region, domestic and intra-regional trafficking is also prevalent in ASEAN. For instance, 90 per cent of the four million migrants in Thailand in 2015 were from Cambodia, Lao PDR and Myanmar, and up to 23 per cent of these migrant workers could be classified as victims of trafficking.[23]

Southeast Asian countries are only too aware of the security implications of infectious diseases having experienced the outbreaks of a string of virulent diseases like Severe Acute Respiratory Syndrome (SARS) and Zika virus disease since the early 2000s. China and Southeast Asian countries were at the forefront of the battle against SARS in 2003, reporting 7,760 of the world's total 8,096 cases.[24] South Korea saw in 2015 the biggest outbreak of Middle East Respiratory Syndrome (MERS) out of Saudi Arabia where the disease was first diagnosed in 2012. 186 infections were diagnosed in the country during the outbreak, with 36 deaths associated with the disease.[25] Zika was the most recent infectious disease that has affected Southeast Asia with cases reported in regional countries like Singapore, Malaysia and Thailand. Moreover, nearly 3.5 million people in Southeast Asia have been living with HIV/AIDS in 2015, with Thailand, Myanmar and Indonesia representing the high burden countries from Southeast Asia.[26]

As noted above, the implications to security from these NTS threats often go beyond any single sector and national border. Unilateral responses are therefore inadequate, necessitating bilateral and multilateral actions. Moreover, as many Southeast Asian countries are developing countries with limited resources and capacity, technical and financial assistance are acutely needed to strengthen their capacity in dealing with various NTS threats. In this regard, it becomes even more critical to examine how best to strengthen multilateral cooperation and coordination and explore how multiple actors from different sectors contribute to the governance of NTS.

1.3   Governance of NTS in Southeast Asia: Beyond Securitization

The region's experiences in dealing with NTS issues show that these issues can escalate and become more complex unless they are dealt with decisively and effectively. But given that NTS issues are inter-related and have cross-cutting effects, governance is not a straightforward process, to say the least. It can be multi-faceted too and can be viewed as an on-going set of processes, generating different types of responses in the different stages of managing or solving the problems.

Mindful of the intricacies of NTS governance, we present here a rather simplified way of understanding how these set of processes can unfold. This is by no means the only way to chart NTS governance. But we think it is useful to start with the process of securitization to understand why and how an issue is and has become NTS threat. We then track how policies are crafted and even re-crafted including after the process of desecuritization, and what mechanisms are established to address the challenges as they come. The institutionalization that follows are also meant to build and strengthen the capacities of affected states and communities to respond. This continuing process(es) is depicted in Figure 1.1 and discussed briefly below.

FIGURE 1.1
Process of NTS Governance

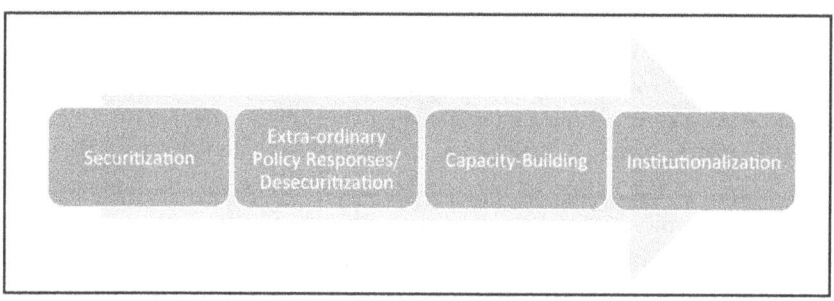

Securitization/Desecuritization and High-level Policy Response

While NTS governance may be similar to "normal" governance which includes the processes of agenda setting, negotiation, decision-making and implementation, what distinguishes it from others are the securitization/desecurization steps and the extra-ordinary policy responses taken at the highest level to address the issues which includes emergency measures.[27] As noted in the earlier section, securitization is a precondition for NTS threats to receive immediate attention and sufficient resources. It is based on consent and legitimacy rather than by force, which means that the securitizing actors, the audience and other stakeholders are able to agree that an issue in question is existentially threatening.[28]

High-level policy responses following securitization generally consists of rapid mobilization of resources and increasing capabilities, introducing emergency measures as needed, speedy implementation and monitoring. In cases where the impact of an NTS threat is transboundary and beyond the capacity of a single country affected, the responses unfold at multiple levels—national, bilateral, regional and international. For example, during major outbreaks of forest fires in Indonesia in the past, neighbouring countries responded immediately in deploying firefighters and dispatching helicopters at the request of the Indonesian government. After the onset of Typhoon Haiyan, the UN expeditiously deployed their emergency response team to the worst affected city, in less than a day, to help the government's massive search and rescue operations.

Securitization often makes for rapid policy responses including the introduction of extraordinary measures. During the outbreak of SARS in 2003, the WHO declared the epidemic a public health emergency of international concern (PHEIC). As a consequence, the WHO issued travel alerts to affected countries with major outbreaks, and publicly criticized China where the largest number of cases was reported for withholding information and issuing travel warnings.[29] Such actions would have been regarded as a transgression or interference in national health policies but this was tolerated by governments concerned due to the serious transboundary impacts and cross-sectoral repercussions of the epidemic. Amid the outbreak of the Ebola disease in West Africa in 2014 and 2015, the WHO decided that experimental drugs which had not yet been tested on humans can be used to treat Ebola patients given the race against time to contain the disease. In ordinary cases, it is deemed unethical to use experimental drugs or treatment on patients without prior human tests.[30]

One would also note that the use of military force in dealing with certain NTS challenges is not uncommon. While deployment of foreign militaries to a sovereign state is often associated with external intervention, their deployment/involvement during times of emergencies are tacitly accepted by affected countries. For example, countries like the United States, China and the United Kingdom sent military personnel and equipment to countries that were hit by the Ebola outbreak in 2014 and 2015 to assist in the treatment and control of the disease. Given its strong capability in search and rescue as well as logistics and transport, the US military forces played a critical role in many post-disaster search and rescue and research operations in Asia, such as the Great East Japan earthquake in 2011 and Typhoon Haiyan in 2013.[31] When parts of the Attapeu province in southern Laos were hit by severe floods in late July 2018 after a hydroelectric dam collapsed, China sent a fully equipped medical team from the People's Liberation Army (PLA) to Laos, which arrived at the disaster site two days after the collapse. Given the sensitiveness of foreign military presence in a sovereign state, having strong military involvement is usually based on strong bilateral ties. The United States is able to speedily deploy its military forces in Japan and the Philippines during humanitarian emergencies since they are allies of the United States. Japan also hosts a US military base in its territory. In the case of Laos, the PLA rescue team could be speedily deployed because the two countries' militaries were having a joint humanitarian rescue and medical drill in Vientiane when the tragedy happened.

While extraordinary measures are accepted in times of emergencies however, they cannot and should not be continued when the threat level goes down. Continuing them often comes with negative and/or unintended consequences. For instance, the Chinese government imposed border control, quarantine of foreign visitors and trade restrictions in 2009 to prevent the spread of the H1N1 influenza. While such measures reduced the risk of the transmission in China, it affected its bilateral relations with some American countries that were affected by H1N1.[32] Military response by one state to an emergency situation in another sovereign state is sensitive and delicate due to the Westphalian sovereignty, so extreme caution is often necessary to avoid setting precedents. It is therefore necessary to end the emergency status or desecuritize when ordinary measures are sufficient for governing the issue. Desecuritization, therefore, is to bring issues back to normal politics.

Institutionalization and Capacity Building

The governance of NTS issues, however, does not stop with desecuritization. As many NTS challenges now are more complex and often recur in different forms like the case of emerging infectious diseases, more efforts must be spent to improve governance through capacity building and institutionalization.[33] This also means designating and/or establishing national agencies to deal specifically with particular issues and become focal points for inter-agency coordination while putting in place clear procedures and policy instruments.[34]

We do see institutionalization already taking place in Asia. With the frequency of natural disasters in the region, many countries like Indonesia, Philippines and China have instituted national plans for disaster response and risk reduction. These national plans cover most aspects of disaster response, from financing to application of technologies, from information sharing to early warning, from coordination to accountability.[35] Mechanisms for communication and coordination are laid out in the national plans to guide the flow of information and coordinate activities of different actors. Such plans are supported by enacting domestic laws and regulations on relevant issue areas. The national plan for disaster response is just one example of a structured and even institutionalized national response to NTS issues. At the regional level, countries enter into various arrangements to demonstrate political will and commit resources for regional efforts. ASEAN member states signed AADMER in July 2005 and ratified it in December 2009. This was further strengthened by the "Declaration on One ASEAN One Response: ASEAN Responding to Disasters as One in the Region and Outside the Region" signed in Vientiane in September 2016. The two documents represent the aim of member states to improve the capacity of the region as a whole in responding to disasters and humanitarian emergencies by harnessing strengths from different sources. Supporting these regional efforts is the ASEAN Coordinating Centre for Humanitarian Assistance on disaster management (AHA Centre) established in 2011 to facilitate disaster relief efforts in the region. Institutionalization must go hand-in-hand with capacity building. Building capacity translates in many forms from raising awareness, increasing competence and technical expertise, knowledge sharing, and building financial resources. Lack of funding is usually a major constraint facing many developing countries in dealing with NTS challenges. Financing support therefore should also be strengthened. Japan has been funding the Disaster Emergency Logistics System for ASEAN project since 2012. The project aims to strengthen the capacity of regional countries in emergency logistics, which is an important component of disaster management.[36] The European Union (EU) reached an agreement with the AHA Centre in October 2018 to provide 10 million euro to support ASEAN's effort in disaster response.[37]

1.4   The State of NTS Governance in Southeast Asia

Having outlined the framework of NTS governance, we now highlight below some of the key observations and governance challenges based on the findings of the respective chapters of this book.

Climate Change

Climate change induces and compounds other non-traditional issues. Climate change has certainly increased the frequency of extreme weather events in Southeast Asia, which has caused greater numbers of people to be forcibly displaced and have put great pressures on carrying out humanitarian assistance and disaster relief. These challenges are discussed at length in Chapter 5 on complex disasters and Chapter 8 on forced migration. In addition to extreme weather events, studies have shown that even small changes in the climate like subtle increase of temperature can have important impacts on food security and the marine environment like decrease of crop yields and loss of coral reef. These effects are discussed in Chapter 3 on food security and Chapter 4 on marine environmental protection.

As one of the global hotspots for disaster risk, it is imperative for Southeast Asia to build its climate resilience through climate change adaptation. While there are a wide range of interventions that can contribute to climate change adaptation efforts in the region, there is a need to establish a centralized mechanism that can coordinate different policies across different sectors. At present, approaches toward climate adaptation have been sporadic and done mainly at sectoral levels.

An important issue for climate change governance is the critical role of technology in building capacity for climate adaptation and mitigation. Given the different levels of economic development among ASEAN member states, ASEAN can look into collectively developing the region's own technological capability for climate mitigation and adaptation purposes. Crafting innovative financing mechanism should also be explored to reduce reliance on foreign aid and assistance in building up capacity for climate mitigation and adaptation.

Food Security

A key indicator of food security is eradicating hunger and malnutrition. Although Southeast Asia has started to see a reversal in addressing hunger which saw the number of hungry people decreasing from 101.7 million in 2005 to 60.5 million in 2014, this increased for the first time to 63.5 million by 2016. The rise in Southeast Asia's undernourishment figures has been mostly driven by a large increase in the number of undernourished in Indonesia, leading one to think that this increase in hunger may just be a "one-country" phenomenon, or a false alarm. However, other Southeast Asian countries are now seeing similar trends of slowing progress in addressing undernourishment, with a few countries having very slow progress of less than 1 per cent reduction in hunger over the recent years. These countries can potentially follow Indonesia's pattern, and eventually enter a period of increasing undernourishment as well.

A systemic trend observed across the region is a slowdown in cereal yield growth, which is alarming given spatial constraints to food production, and that cereals make up the majority of regional food consumption. This contributes to increasing food scarcity; higher food prices; and ultimately, more limited access to food. Governments, the private sector, academia and other sectors will therefore need to work together to address these challenges. A critical gap to fill will be in providing information on climate impacts on crop production and food security, that are downscaled to the national and subnational levels, and which can be translated into advice on policy and technological innovations to adopt. Generating relevant data, including financial analysis, will therefore be crucial steps in addressing challenges to food security.

Marine Environmental Protection

Protecting the marine environment is a key component of environmental security. This has in fact received increasing attention at regional and international levels, as evidenced by the inclusion of an ocean-related goal in the 2030 Sustainable Development Goals (Goal 14: Life below water) and the convening of the first Ocean Conference by the UN in 2017.

As discussed in the chapter on marine environment protection (MEP) which examines the state of marine environment in the South China Sea (SCS), the rate of degradation of the environment is at an alarming rate as a result of both human activities and climate change. The degradation has serious security implications for the littoral states and their population as the marine environment is important for food security, health security, economic security and environmental security. Degradation of the marine environment can worsen the situation in the SCS as the littoral states are competing for various marine resources that are depleting.

Marine environmental protection has been viewed as an important avenue for building mutual trust and confidence among the littoral states of the SCS. Measures to advance this agenda include establishing marine protected areas, strengthening relevant laws and regulations, engaging multiple stakeholders and encouraging scientific and technical collaboration. As ASEAN and China have been negotiating the Code of Conduct (COC) since 2013, more balanced attention should be given to both maritime disputes and the marine ecosystem as the latter is no less important for national and human securities in the region. In addition, ASEAN member states and China can initiate new collaborative efforts based on their Declaration for the Decade of Coastal and Marine Environmental Protection in the South China Sea (2017–2027). MEP should also incorporate into ASEAN member states' efforts to achieve Sustainable Development Goals.

Complex Disasters

Since Southeast Asian leaders signed the AADMER in 2005, the region has prioritized developing national and regional disaster management capabilities to respond to disasters. However, the back-to-back disasters that occurred between July and August 2018 in Lombok Island, West Nusa Tenggara, Indonesia tested the response capacities of the national government and the humanitarian community. The gap between regional and national disaster management capacity suggests that AADMER is largely seen and implemented as a regional project, with more limited impact on national disaster risk management frameworks. There is room for National Disaster Management Organisations (NDMOs) to consider how it can align national disaster management goals with regional ones and better leverage regional resources for national capacity building in technical and operational aspects of disaster management.

Local organizations could also benefit from more support—in the form of resources, media coverage and training as they strive to develop more robust policies and systems. Climate change adaptation initiatives also need to be better incorporated into disaster preparedness efforts. The huge economic losses stemming from the multiple disasters also necessitate a drastic re-evaluation of the way financial risk is managed in the region. Engagement with the private sector, particularly with insurers and reinsurers, should be a policy imperative.

Nuclear Security

Nuclear security has become a new concern for the region given the growing interests and possibility of using nuclear energy in Southeast Asia. Aside from nuclear energy, nuclear security matters given the use of radioactive materials across the region for medical and other purposes. The recent cases of missing radioactive materials in Southeast Asia in 2019 alone vividly highlight the significance of enhancing nuclear security in the region.

One evident gap in nuclear security governance in Southeast Asia is weak nuclear security culture, accentuating the significance of human factors, such as attitudes, awareness and behaviours. Given that not all Southeast Asian states are parties to important global nuclear conventions, including nuclear security treaties, it is essential for countries with nuclear activities and radioactive sources for non-power applications to ratify all treaties.

The ASEAN Network of Regulatory Bodies on Atomic Energy (ASEANTOM) has been driving regional cooperation on civilian nuclear capacity-building among ASEAN member states. The network has been conducting regular exchanges of best practices, capacity-building efforts, and assistance to member states to implement key international agreements. Apart from regional bodies such as the ASEANTOM, nuclear security training and support centres of excellence (COEs) can potentially play a key role in establishing a regional nuclear security architecture. A collaborative network of COEs in Southeast Asia can complement the work of ASEANTOM in terms of sharing good practices, resources, expertise and information.

Trafficking in Persons

Despite the ratification of global and regional anti-trafficking frameworks and enactment of relevant national laws, human trafficking remains an endemic security problem in Southeast/East Asia, threatening states and societies. Two-thirds or 25 million of global trafficking victims were identified to be in the region. The lack of effective law enforcement efforts, as a primarily tool to implement states' robust legal frameworks, remains a challenge. Inadequate institutional resources, funding and training for frontline officers and law enforcers impede the investigation of human trafficking cases. Corruption and trafficking are also deeply intertwined in the region. The failure of governments to run after and prosecute complicit officials and law enforcers exacerbates the corruption-trafficking nexus in the region.

Drawing the crime of human trafficking out of the shadows of law is made difficult by (i) the ambiguous definition of human trafficking in persons in international law; and (ii) the disjuncture between human trafficking contexts in East Asia and what international anti-trafficking legal regimes seek to address. If the law is to be the bedrock of counter-trafficking measures in the region, human trafficking terminologies and definitions must be clearly defined and understood by law enforcers and responsive to the region's human trafficking context and emerging trends. Government agencies, while assuming primary responsibility, would need to deepen their cooperation with the civil society and humanitarian organizations that assist and provide support services for victims of trafficking in order to promote a victim-centred, trauma-informed approach to counter trafficking.

Displaced Persons

Globally there are three main drivers for displacement—disasters, development and conflict. Within Southeast Asia regional governance has focused on disasters but there are recent attempts to extend this governance framework to conflict displacement. Disaster impacts have remained localized areas of vulnerability. The impacts of development on the displacement of people are harder to monitor with the main driver being rapid urbanization and large-scale infrastructure projects. But most significantly, conflict as a driver tends to lead to more protracted displacement both within countries and across international borders.

Indonesia, Malaysia, the Philippines and Thailand have either offered sanctuary to populations displaced by conflict in neighbouring countries or been the source of internal conflict generating displacement for fellow ASEAN member states. While presently only the Philippines is a signatory to the UN Refugee Convention, all have offered some form of sanctuary to displaced persons. Within the broader Asia and Pacific, the top four hosting countries are Bangladesh, Malaysia, Thailand and Indonesia. Bangladesh hosts 907,199 refugees and asylum-seekers the vast majority of which are Rohingya from Myanmar.

ASEAN has moved towards a networked regional grouping that demonstrates a greater potential to work collaboratively, across different levels of governance. The shift towards a network approach sees ASEAN member states working together to aid local communities. Through this approach fellow ASEAN member states provide surge capacity to national government agencies to provide its affected population with relief items. However, the absence of a regional humanitarian champion within ASEAN and the present dominance of a state-led approach to the regional humanitarian mechanism offer pause for thought and the need to moderate expectations. While state-led humanitarianism lends itself to disasters, the same cannot be said for conflict given that states themselves are parties directly involved in conflicts making it impossible at present for regional governance to offer anything more than short-term relief to those displaced at best.

Health Security

The threats of new and re-emerging infectious diseases and the speed of change in the burden of diseases have raised concerns about the ability of states in Southeast Asia to adequately and effectively deal with challenges to health security. People in the developing world, like Southeast Asia, suffer a disproportionate burden of infectious diseases compared to the rest of the world. Past experiences of Asian countries show that regional approaches have been essential for effective response to epidemics like SARS, H5N1 and H1N1. Moreover, the focus of ASEAN health cooperation has seen a visible shift from pandemic preparedness to broader approach to health security as threats also arise from problems like Anti-Microbial Resistance (AMR), non-communicable diseases and climate-related health issues.

Moving forward, greater efforts should be made both at the national and regional levels to strengthen public health systems. This means that at the ASEAN level, there should be more time and resources invested in helping build the capacity of public health systems of ASEAN countries that are in need of support. It should be noted that the success and the quality of governance of health security is largely dependent on efforts at the national level to build strong health systems and have the capacity and adequate resources to detect, prevent, and control the spread of infectious diseases. Strong national health systems continue to be the foundation of regional and global efforts to promote health and human security. The resources of non-state actors and the private sector should also be mobilized in order to provide quality health care and inclusive access to health provision.

1.5 Conclusion

Since the Asian financial crisis in 1997 and the outbreak of SARS in 2003, NTS has been established as an important policy discourse and approach to security governance in Asia. While countries in the region have started to develop some capacity in addressing a variety of NTS issues over the years, the new dynamics of existing issues and emerging challenges further highlight the need for constant improvement in governance. Apart from setting priorities and adopting exceptional measures in times of crises, NTS governance needs to adopt a long-term approach that values institutionalization and capacity building. Moreover, given the transnationality of NTS, the thrust for stronger institutionalization and capacity building can no longer be limited at the national level. Efforts at enhancing regional multilateral cooperation and building strong regional institutions are essential if effective management of transnational NTS challenges were to be achieved.

We conclude this chapter by emphasizing three core themes that emerged from the case studies in this book. One of the themes that came out from all the chapters is the need to engage multiple actors in the governance of NTS issues. Apart from government officials, civil society groups and non-governmental organizations have become critical actors in dealing with problems like trafficking in person, marine environmental protection, complex disaster management, and health security. They play important roles in education, awareness-raising, monitoring and assistance.

Similarly, the private sector has also become an indispensable partner. Private companies are great resources for technical expertise and innovation. They have also become an important partner in addressing financing gaps and generating creative approaches to build human capital through skills training and development.

Another theme is the need to push for effective enforcement of national and regional laws and regulations to deal with NTS challenges. Building robust legal frameworks and implementing them remain a challenge but can no longer be ignored if problems like human trafficking and other transnational crimes, environmental protection, health security and many others were to be addressed.

The last but certainly not least, is the need to seriously put more efforts in improving coordination across different sectors and at multiple levels in dealing with NTS challenges. This can be done in tandem with deepening regional multilateral cooperation and strengthening regional institutions to achieve the goals of ensuring human security for all.

NOTES

1. Mely Caballero-Anthony, "Understanding Non-Traditional Security", in *An Introduction to Non-Traditional Security Studies: A Transnational Approach*, edited by Mely Caballero-Anthony (London: Sage, 2016), p. 6.
2. Mely Caballero-Anthony, "Combating Infectious Diseases in East Asia: Securitisation and Global Public Goods for Health and Human Security", *Journal of International Affairs* 59, no. 2 (2006): 105–27; Mely Caballero-Anthony, Ralf Emmers, and Amitav Acharya, eds., *Non-Traditional Security in Asia: Dilemmas in Securitization* (London: Ashgate, 2006).
3. Stéphanie Martel, "From Ambiguity to Contestation: Discourse(s) of Non-Traditional Security in the ASEAN Community", *Pacific Review* 30, no. 4 (2017): 554.
4. Shahar Hameiri and Lee Jones, *Governing Borderless Threats: Non-Traditional Security and the Politics of State Transformation* (Cambridge, UK: Cambridge University Press, 2015), p. 95.

5. Caballero-Anthony, "Understanding Non-Traditional Security", in *An Introduction to Non-Traditional Security Studies*, pp. 7–10.

6. Surin Pitsuwan and Mely Caballero-Anthony, "Human Security in Southeast Asia: 20 Years in Review", *Asian Journal of Peacebuilding* 2, no. 2 (2014): 199–215; Amitav Acharya, "Human Security – East Versus West", *International Journal* 56, no. 3 (2001): 442–60.

7. Caballero-Anthony, "Understanding Non-Traditional Security", in *An Introduction to Non-Traditional Security Studies*, pp. 14–15.

8. Barry Buzan, Ole Waever, and Jaap de Wilde, *Security: A New Framework for Analysis* (Boulder, US: Lynne Rienner Publishers, Inc, 1998), pp. 23–26.

9. Huang Yanzhong, "Pursuing Health as Foreign Policy: The Case of China", *Indiana Journal of Global Legal Studies* 17, no. 1 (2010): 116.

10. Hu Jintao, "Speech at the Second Session of the 16th APEC Economic Leaders' Meeting", Lima, Peru, 22 November 2008, http://www.gov.cn/ldhd/2008-11/23/content_1156875.htm (in Chinese).

11. Euston Quah, "Transboundary Pollution in Southeast Asia – The Indonesian Fires", *World Development* 30, no. 3 (2002): 429–41.

12. Shakeeb Asrar, "Rohingya Crisis Explained in Maps", *Aljazeera*, 28 October 2017, https://www.aljazeera.com/indepth/interactive/2017/09/rohingya-crisis-explained-maps-170910140906580.html.

13. Sheany, "Indonesia Weighs Foreign Aid Offers; Resists Declaring National Disaster in C. Sulawesi", *Jakarta Globe*, 1 October 2018, https://jakartaglobe.id/news/indonesia-weighs-foreign-aid-offers-resists-declaring-national-disaster-in-c-sulawesi/.

14. UNESCAP, *Disaster Resilience for Sustainable Development: Asia-Pacific Disaster Report 2017* (Bangkok: United Nations Publication, 2018), p. 10.

15. Asian Development Bank, "Recent Significant Disasters in the Asia and Pacific Region", Infographic, 27 September 2016, https://www.adb.org/news/infographics/recent-significant-disasters-asia-and-pacific-region.

16. UNESCAP, *Disaster Resilience for Sustainable Development*, p. 13.

17. Karen Bermejo, "Climate Change Will Impact Philippines' Ability to Feed its People", *Eco-Business*, 17 October 2017, http://www.eco-business.com/news/climate-change-will-impact-philippines-ability-to-feed-its-people/.

18. ASEAN Secretariat, "ASEAN Regional Security: The Threats Facing it and the Way Forward", 2006, https://asean.org/?static_post=asean-regional-security-the-threats-facing-it-and-the-way-forward-by-asean-secretariat.

19. World Bank Data, "Forest Area (% of land area)", undated, https://data.worldbank.org/indicator/AG.LND.FRST.ZS (accessed 21 January 2019).

20. "Asian Nations Pledge to Fight Plastic Pollution", *Straits Times*, 9 June 2017, https://www.straitstimes.com/asia/australianz/asian-nations-pledge-to-fight-plastic-pollution.

21. United Nations Office on Drugs and Crime (UNODC), *Global Report on Trafficking in Persons* (New York: UNODC, 2018), p. 69.
22. Ibid., p. 74.
23. UNODC, *Trafficking in Persons from Cambodia, Lao PDR and Myanmar to Thailand* (Bangkok: UNODC, 2017), p. 2.
24. World Health Organization (WHO), "Summary of Probable SARS Cases with Onset of Illness from 1 November 2002 to 31 July 2003", 31 December 2003, https://www.who.int/csr/sars/country/table2004_04_21/en/ (accessed 22 January 2019).
25. WHO, "Middle East Respiratory Syndrome Coronavirus (MERS-CoV) – Republic of Korea", Disease Outbreak News, 7 July 2015, https://www.who.int/csr/don/07-july-2015-mers-korea/en/ (accessed 22 January 2019).
26. According to the geographic definition of the WHO, South-East Asia include Southeast Asia and South Asia. See, WHO, *Progress Report on HIV in the WHO South-East Asia Region 2016*, http://apps.searo.who.int/PDS_DOCS/B5282.pdf (accessed 22 January 2019).
27. Deborah D. Avant, Martha Finnemore, and Susan K. Sell, "Who Governs the Globe?" in *Who Governs the Globe?*, edited by Deborah D. Avant, Martha Finnemore, and Susan K. Sell (Cambridge: Cambridge University Press, 2010).
28. Mark Webber, "Security Governance", in *Handbook of Governance and Security*, edited by James Sperling (Cheltenham, UK: Edward Elgar, 2014), pp. 21–22.
29. Tine Hanrieder and Christian Kreude-Sonnen, "WHO Decides on the Exception? Securitization and Emergency Governance in Global Health", *Security Dialogue* 45, no. 4 (2014): 332.
30. Anne Roemer-Mahler and Stefan Elbe, "The Race for Ebola Drugs: Pharmaceuticals, Security and Global Health Governance", *Third World Quarterly* 37, no. 3 (2016): 487–506.
31. Thomas Lum and Rhoda Margesson, "Typhoon Haiyan (Yolanda): U.S. and International Response to Philippines Disaster", Congressional Research Service Report, 10 February 2014, https://fas.org/sgp/crs/row/R43309.pdf.
32. Huang, "Pursuing Health as Foreign Policy", pp. 140–44.
33. James Sperling, "Governance and Security in the Twenty-first Century", in *Handbook of Governance and Security*, p. 9.
34. Buzan, Waever, and Wilde, *Security*, p. 28.
35. "China Issues Emergency Plan for National Disasters", The State Council of the People's Republic of China, Latest Releases, 24 March 2016, http://english.www.gov.cn/policies/latest_releases/2016/03/24/content_281475313714102.htm.
36. AHA Centre, "Press Release: Japan Continues to Support Disaster Management Programme in ASEAN", 25 January 2018, https://ahacentre.

org/press-release/japan-continues-support-disaster-management-programme-in-asean/.
37. European Commission, "ASEAN: EU to Support Disaster Management in One of the World's Most Disaster-Prone Regions", International Cooperation and Development, 18 October 2018, https://ec.europa.eu/europeaid/news-and-events/asean-eu-support-disaster-management-one-worlds-most-disaster-prone-regions_en.

REFERENCES

Acharya, Amitav. 2001. "Human Security – East Versus West". *International Journal* 56, no. 3: 442–60.

AHA Centre. 2018. "Press Release: Japan Continues to Support Disaster Management Programme in ASEAN", 25 January 2018. https://ahacentre.org/press-release/japan-continues-support-disaster-management-programme-in-asean/.

ASEAN Secretariat. 2006. "ASEAN Regional Security: The Threats Facing it and the Way Forward". https://asean.org/?static_post=asean-regional-security-the-threats-facing-it-and-the-way-forward-by-asean-secretariat.

Asian Development Bank. 2016. "Recent Significant Disasters in the Asia and Pacific Region". Infographic, 27 September 2016. https://www.adb.org/news/infographics/recent-significant-disasters-asia-and-pacific-region.

"Asian Nations Pledge to Fight Plastic Pollution". *Straits Times*, 9 June 2017. https://www.straitstimes.com/asia/australianz/asian-nations-pledge-to-fight-plastic-pollution.

Asrar, Shakeeb. 2017. "Rohingya Crisis Explained in Maps". *Aljazeera*, 28 October 2017. https://www.aljazeera.com/indepth/interactive/2017/09/rohingya-crisis-explained-maps-170910140906580.html.

Avant, Deborah D., Martha Finnemore, and Susan K. Sell. 2010. "Who Governs the Globe?" In *Who Governs the Globe?*, edited by Deborah D. Avant, Martha Finnemore and Susan K. Sell. Cambridge: Cambridge University Press, pp. 1–31.

Bermejo, Karen. 2017. "Climate Change Will Impact Philippines' Ability to Feed its People". *Eco-Business*, 17 October 2017. http://www.eco-business.com/news/climate-change-will-impact-philippines-ability-to-feed-its-people/.

Buzan, Barry, Ole Waever, and Jaap de Wilde. 1998. *Security: A New Framework for Analysis*. Boulder, US: Lynne Rienner Publishers, Inc.

Caballero-Anthony, Mely. 2006. "Combating Infectious Diseases in East Asia: Securitisation and Global Public Goods for Health and Human Security". *Journal of International Affairs* 59, no. 2: 105–27.

————., ed. 2016. *An Introduction to Non-Traditional Security Studies: A Transnational Approach*. London: Sage.

Caballero-Anthony, Mely, Ralf Emmers, and Amitav Acharya, eds. 2006. *Non-Traditional Security in Asia: Dilemmas in Securitization*. London: Ashgate.

"China to Form Ministry of Emergency Management". *Xinhua*, 13 March 2018. http://www.xinhuanet.com/english/2018-03/13/c_137035514.htm.

European Commission. 2018. "ASEAN: EU to Support Disaster Management in One of the World's Most Disaster-Prone Regions". International Cooperation and Development, 18 October 2018. https://ec.europa.eu/europeaid/news-and-events/asean-eu-support-disaster-management-one-worlds-most-disaster-prone-regions_en.

Hameiri, Shahar and Lee Jones. 2015. *Governing Borderless Threats: Non-Traditional Security and the Politics of State Transformation*. Cambridge, UK: Cambridge University Press.

Hanrieder Tine and Christian Kreude-Sonnen. 2014. "WHO Decides on the Exception? Securitization and Emergency Governance in Global Health". *Security Dialogue* 45, no. 4: 331–48.

Hu, Jintao. 2008. "Speech at the Second Session of the 16th APEC Economic Leaders' Meeting", Lima, Peru, 22 November 2008. http://www.gov.cn/ldhd/2008-11/23/content_1156875.htm (in Chinese).

Huang, Yanzhong. 2010. "Pursuing Health as Foreign Policy: The Case of China". *Indiana Journal of Global Legal Studies* 17, no. 1: 105–46.

"Indonesia's Latest Tsunami Raises Global Questions over Disaster Preparedness". *Straits Times*, 30 December 2018. https://www.straitstimes.com/asia/se-asia/indonesias-latest-tsunami-raises-global-questions-over-disaster-preparedness.

Lum, Thomas and Rhoda Margesson. 2014. "Typhoon Haiyan (Yolanda): U.S. and International Response to Philippines Disaster". Congressional Research Service Report, 10 February 2014. https://fas.org/sgp/crs/row/R43309.pdf.

Martel, Stéphanie. 2017. "From Ambiguity to Contestation: Discourse(s) of Non-Traditional Security in the ASEAN Community". *Pacific Review* 30, no. 4: 549–65.

Moroney, Jennifer D.P., Stephanie Pezard, Laurel E. Miller, Jeffrey Engstrom, and Abby Doll. 2013. *Lessons from Department of Defense Disaster Relief Efforts in the Asia Pacific Region*. Rand Corporation.

Pitsuwan, Surin and Mely Caballero-Anthony. 2014. "Human Security in Southeast Asia: 20 Years in Review". *Asian Journal of Peacebuilding* 2, no. 2: 199–215.

Quah, Euston. 2002. "Transboundary Pollution in Southeast Asia – The Indonesian Fires". *World Development* 30, no. 3: 429–41.

"Relief Agencies Struggle to Cope with Scale of Sulawesi Disaster". *Asia Times*, 1 October 2018. http://www.atimes.com/article/criticism-rising-over-indonesias-disaster-response/.

Roemer-Mahler, Anne and Stefan Elbe. 2016. "The Race for Ebola Drugs: Pharmaceuticals, Security and Global Health Governance". *Third World Quarterly* 37, no. 3: 487–506.

Sapiie, Marguerite Afra. 2019. "New BNPB Head Wants TNI to Guard Disaster Warning Devices". *Jakarta Post*, 15 January 2019. https://www.thejakartapost.com/news/2019/01/15/new-bnpb-head-wants-tni-to-guard-disaster-warning-devices.html.

Sheany. 2018. "Indonesia Weighs Foreign Aid Offers; Resists Declaring National Disaster in C. Sulawesi". *Jakarta Globe*, 1 October 2018. https://jakartaglobe.id/news/indonesia-weighs-foreign-aid-offers-resists-declaring-national-disaster-in-c-sulawesi/.

Sperling, James, ed. 2014. *Handbook of Governance and Security.* Cheltenham, UK: Edward Elgar.

United Nations Economic and Social Commission for Asia and the Pacific (UNESCAP). 2018. *Disaster Resilience for Sustainable Development: Asia-Pacific Disaster Report 2017.* Bangkok: United Nations Publication.

United Nations Office on Drugs and Crime (UNODC). 2017. *Trafficking in Persons from Cambodia, Lao PDR and Myanmar to Thailand.* Bangkok: UNODC.

———. 2018. *Global Report on Trafficking in Persons.* New York: UNODC.

World Bank Data. Undated. "Forest Area (% of land area)". https://data.worldbank.org/indicator/AG.LND.FRST.ZS (accessed 21 January 2019).

World Health Organization (WHO). 2003. "Summary of Probable SARS Cases with Onset of Illness from 1 November 2002 to 31 July 2003", 31 December 2003. https://www.who.int/csr/sars/country/table2004_04_21/en/ (accessed 22 January 2019).

———. 2015. "Middle East Respiratory Syndrome Coronavirus (MERS-CoV) – Republic of Korea". Disease Outbreak News, 7 July 2015. https://www.who.int/csr/don/07-july-2015-mers-korea/en/ (accessed 22 January 2019).

———. 2016. *Progress Report on HIV in the WHO South-East Asia Region 2016.* http://apps.searo.who.int/PDS_DOCS/B5282.pdf (accessed 22 January 2019).

2

CLIMATE CHANGE AND REGIONAL COOPERATION IN SOUTHEAST ASIA

Margareth Sembiring

2.1 Dedicated Mechanisms for Regional Cooperation on Climate Change

Introduction

Climate change adaptation, alongside with climate change mitigation, is often regarded as a means to dealing with the potential devastating effects of climate change. The Intergovernmental Panel on Climate Change (IPCC) defines mitigation as "an anthropogenic intervention to reduce the sources or enhance the sinks of greenhouse gases".[1] Climate change adaptation is referred to as an "adjustment in natural or human systems in response to actual or expected climatic stimuli or their effects, which moderates harm or exploits beneficial opportunities".[2] In other words, while climate change mitigation has the general objective of reducing carbon emission, climate change adaptation aims to increase resilience against possible future climate events. Unlike its climate change mitigation counterpart, however, climate change adaptation often receives lesser attention from policymakers.[3]

The uncertain nature of future climate events contributes significantly to the lagging behind of climate change adaptation initiatives vis-à-vis climate change mitigation. Furthermore, while carbon emission reduction can be measured with relative ease thanks to the availability of tools such as the Greenhouse Gas Protocol,[4] estimating the level of climate resilience built upon climate change adaptation interventions is not as straightforward. "Timeframe, uncertainty and reverse logic of adaptation, messiness and complexity of adaptation, lack of baseline data, no defined yardsticks for success, and lack of resources and coordination"[5] are some of the identified challenges that render climate change adaptation a less favourable option for policymakers.

Despite an apparent lack of preferences for climate change adaptation, its relevance will become more pronounced as disaster events are increasingly attributed to the changing climate. Working on pre-emptive measures to respond to climate eventualities will result in community preparedness and resilience against potential attendant disasters. As climate change impacts various aspects of human lives in different ways, building climate resilience is key to ensuring the continuity and sustainability of the society.

One way of operationalizing climate change adaptation is through the applications of technology. The concept is not entirely new as local communities have long incorporated traditional practices to deal with climate-induced events such as flooding.[6] With technological advancement, options for adaptation measures become wider and solutions for building climate resilience in specific sectors can be better crafted.

In its report, the Asian Development Bank (ADB) listed down the different climate change adaptation technologies that can be applied in agriculture, coastal resources, human health, transportation, water resources and disaster risk management sectors.[7] It also identified the types of technologies that can answer various cross-sectoral needs as seen in Table 2.1.

TABLE 2.1

Types of climate Change Adaptation Technologies and Their Potential Cross-sector Uses

Multi-need Technology	AGRICULTURE NEEDS					
	New Crop Varieties with Greater Heat Tolerance	New Crop Varieties with Lower Water Requirements	Improved Water Collection, Storage, and Distribution Techniques	Improved Irrigation Efficiency	New Crop Varieties with Higher Moisture Tolerance	Improved Drainage Techniques
Agriculture						
Crop breeding	✓	✓			✓	
Floating agriculture			✓			
Fungal symbionts	✓	✓			✓	
Laser land levelling			✓	✓		✓
Pressurized irrigation			✓	✓		✓
Coastal and water resources						
Accommodation to flooding						✓
Structural barriers						
Coastal engineering						
Beach nourishment and dune construction						
Constructed wetlands and artificial reefs						
Geosynthetics						
Water Resources						
Aquifer recharge			✓			
Desalination			✓			
Interbasin water transfer			✓			
Nonstructural barriers to flooding						
Rainwater harvesting			✓	✓		✓
Reservoirs			✓			
Stormwater management and bioswales						✓
Water demand reduction			✓	✓		✓
Water loss reduction			✓	✓		✓
Water storage			✓	✓		
Disaster risk management						
Early-warning systems						
Light detection and ranging (LIDAR)				✓		✓
Monitoring systems						
Social media in disaster response						

Source: ADB (2014).

AGRICULTURE NEEDS						
New Crop Varieties with Improved Pest and Disease Resistance	Improved Pest and Disease Management Techniques	Barriers to Saltwater Intrusion	Increased Sustainable Aquifer Recharge	New Crop Varieties with Greater Salinity Tolerance	Improved Extreme Weather Prediction and Early Warning Systems	Improved Crop and Livestock Protection from Extreme Weather Events
✓	✓			✓		✓
		✓				✓
✓	✓			✓		✓
						✓
		✓				✓
		✓				✓
		✓				✓
		✓				✓
			✓			
						✓
						✓
		✓				✓
						✓
						✓
						✓
						✓
						✓
					✓	✓
						✓
	✓				✓	✓
					✓	✓

While the table provides options for technological solutions in building climate resilience, the final choices will depend on various factors including climate risk assessment, available funding, and actors' preferences, among others. In light of technological development, it is important to note whether the technologies used in climate change adaptation are considered new technologies, or leading to new technological innovations, or they are essentially a reuse and an improved version of existing technologies.

A number of climate change adaptation strategies based on sectoral approach have been planned at the national level.[8] From a resilience-building perspective, however, climate adaptation initiatives that look into the ecosystems as a whole are far more effective than those on a sectoral basis. A "geographically-focused perspective"[9] that possibly needs to be implemented across shared national borders is better able to address climate vulnerability more holistically. Drafting regional climate adaptation blueprints is therefore key, especially because they are currently less common than national-level policies. In Southeast Asia, for example, a regional climate adaptation plan is still absent,[10] although at subregional level the Mekong River countries have got their climate adaptation acts together under the leadership of the Mekong River Commission.

Climate adaptation cooperation at the Mekong River presents a good point for review not only because it is one of the areas in Asia-Pacific that are most vulnerable to climate change impacts,[11] but also because Lower Mekong River Basin region already has a mechanism to deal with climate change adaptation in place. Kranz et al. (2010) even observed that its climate change adaptation initiatives are likely to stand on solid ground thanks to the Mekong River regime's high effectiveness in managing the transboundary river basins.[12]

Against this backdrop, taking the Lower Mekong River as a case study, this chapter aims to provide a preliminary assessment of the role of regional cooperation in effecting technological solutions for climate change adaptation in member countries. It examines the processes involved, identifies practices and potential gaps, and assesses the contribution of such cooperation to national initiatives on climate change adaptation. This study argues that having a dedicated regional mechanism for climate change adaptation will lead to more effective implementations of technologies for climate change adaptation and recommends the Association of Southeast Asian Nations (ASEAN) to look into establishing a similar mechanism at Southeast Asia level.

The Mekong River Basin and Climate Change

The Mekong River runs for 4,800 km across six different countries namely China, Myanmar, Lao PDR, Thailand, Cambodia, and Vietnam (see Figure 2.1a). Out of the 795,000 km² of the total Mekong River basin area, Lao PDR, Thailand, Cambodia, and China are endowed with the largest share while much smaller parts are located in Vietnam and Myanmar as shown in Figure 2.1b.

FIGURE 2.1a
Mekong River Basin Area

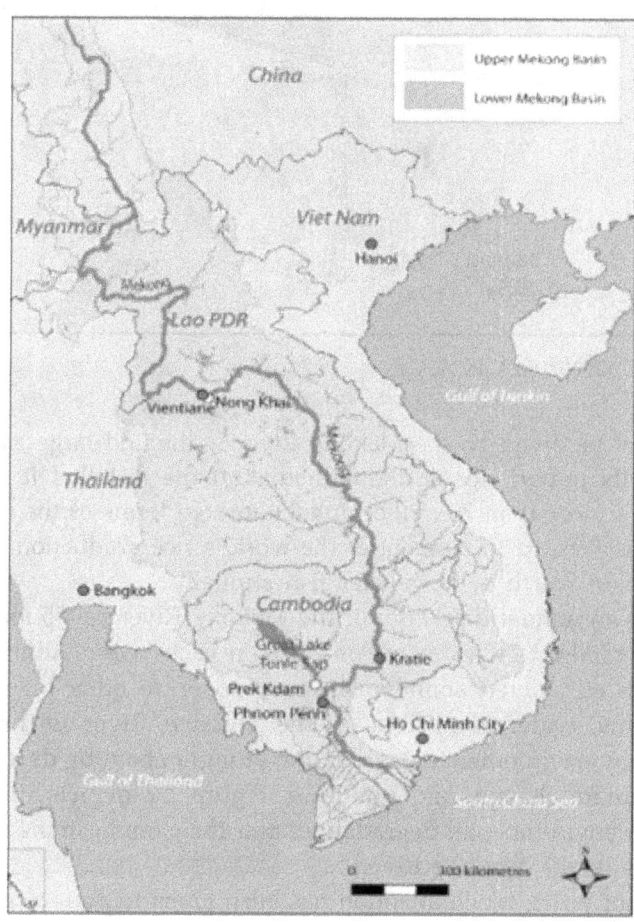

Source: MRC (2009); FAO (2011).

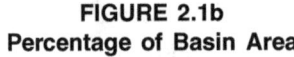

FIGURE 2.1b
Percentage of Basin Area

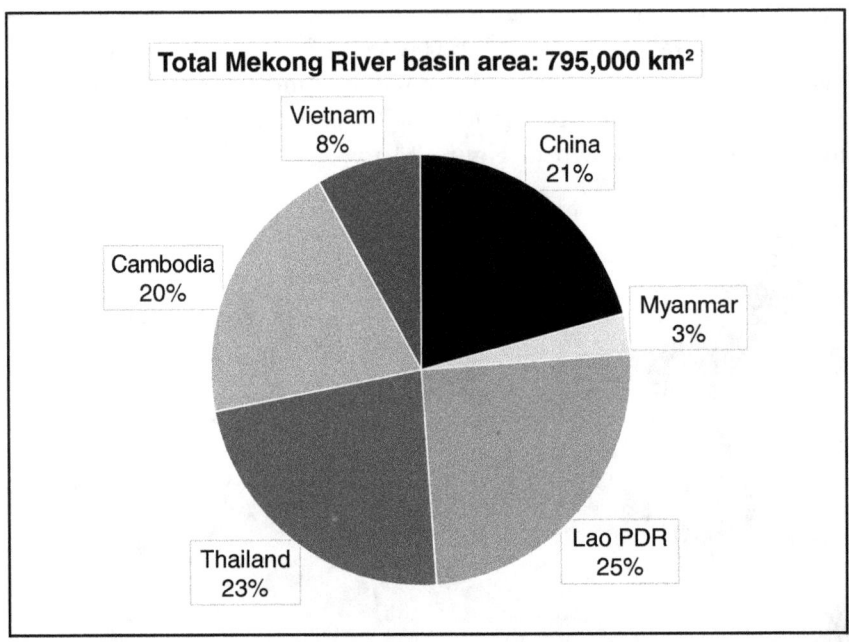

Source: MRC (2009); FAO (2011).

In terms of biodiversity, the Mekong River is the 2nd largest after the Amazon. Its importance is highlighted with the fact that it supports the lives of more than 70 million inhabitants. In terms of the economy, the basin makes up 15 per cent of the world's rice production and sees US$17 billion worth of freshwater fish annually.[13]

The mean annual discharge of the Mekong River is 475 km³ and it provides 8,500 m³ of water for one person each year.[14] Although this quantity is considered abundant in comparison to other international river basins, water conditions in the Mekong River is threatened primarily by environmental degradation brought about by development needs, climate change, and pollution. Figure 2.2 depicts the factors leading to environmental degradation, and their implications on water conditions in the Mekong River.

In recent years, much attention has been given to dam construction activities along the main Mekong River and their implications on people's livelihoods and displacement. Considering that the use of water in the Mekong River is mainly for irrigation-related purposes

FIGURE 2.2
Factors Leading to Environmental Degradation and Implications on Water Condition

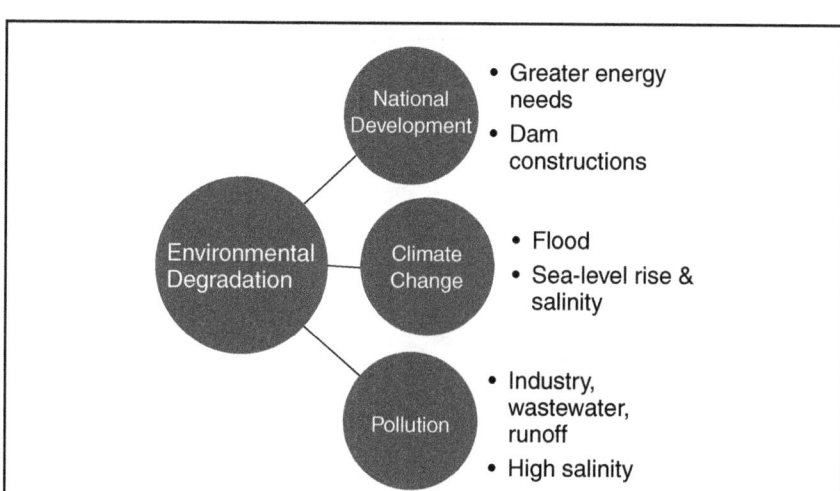

Source: Author.

as seen in Figure 2.3, it is not surprising that concerns surrounding the Mekong River are primarily on livelihoods including agriculture and fisheries.

While dam constructions driven by national development and greater needs for energy sources dominate the discussions surrounding the Lower Mekong River basin, climate change is also an issue that warrants attention. The major risks coming from climate change are increased frequency and intensity of floods during the wet season. Eastham et al. (2008)[15] predicted that the river runoff would increase by 21 per cent and this may lead to a decrease in floodplain fish productivity by 18 per cent.

Another climate-induced phenomenon is sea level rise and attendant increased salinity intrusion. Smajgl et al. (2015) estimated that sea level rise would stand at 30 cm by 2050, and this will bring significant detrimental impacts on agricultural production.[16] It may also cause some parts of the land to disappear due to permanent inundation. Västilä et al. (2010) further suggested that the increasing severity of flood events will not only damage food crops, but also affect infrastructure, floodplain vegetation and reduce the fertile area.[17]

FIGURE 2.3
Water Use Along the Mekong River Basin

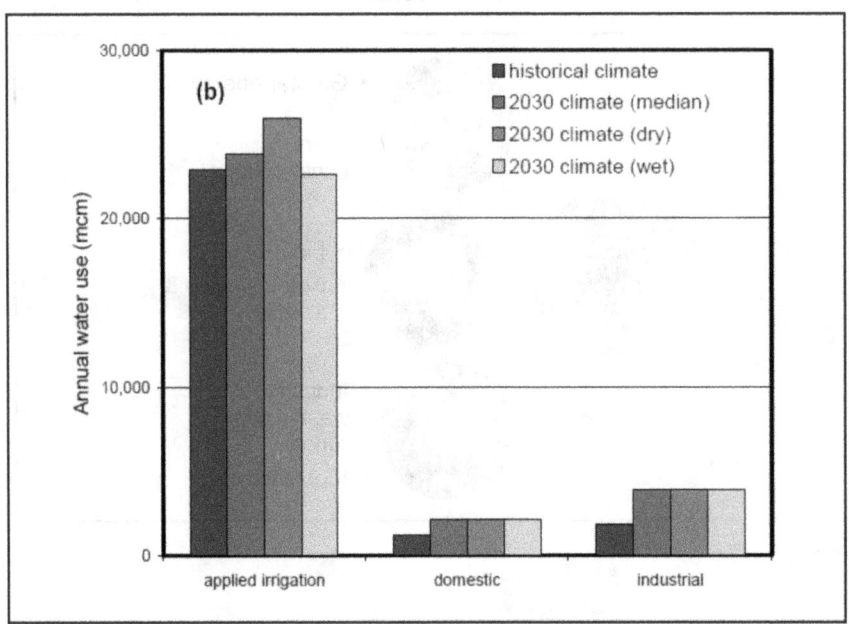

Source: Eastham et al. (2008).

Given the potentially devastating consequences arising from climate change, countries in the Lower Mekong River have drafted their respective national climate change policies. Cambodia formulated its National Adaptation Programme of Action to Climate Change (NAPA) in 2006 and Lao PDR in 2009. Vietnam has multiple climate change-related policies incorporating climate change adaptation framework such as the Central Party Committee's Resolution 24/NQ/TW (2013) on Responding to Climate Change,[18] National Climate Change Strategy 2011,[19] National Action Plan on Climate Change 2012–2020,[20] National Green Growth Strategy 2012,[21] and National Action Plan on Green Growth 2014.[22] Thailand's climate adaptation outlook is reflected in the National Adaptation Plan 2015–2023.

Additionally, these countries have established a regional mechanism for climate change initiatives under the Mekong River Commission (MRC). As it is argued that the existence of a dedicated regional framework on climate change adaptation may lead to better interventions in individual member countries, the next section examines the interactions between national and regional processes more closely.

Climate Change Adaptation Mechanism in the Lower Mekong River

The United Nations Framework Convention on Climate Change (UNFCCC) suggested a mechanism for climate change adaptation as seen in Figure 2.4, and climate change adaptation in the Lower Mekong River Basin generally follows the proposed model. It starts with a management, i.e. the MRC, that looks at the potential impacts of climate change in certain areas, and uses the findings to design relevant climate change adaptation policies and solutions. The MRC provides the institutional and financial supports for climate change adaptation efforts in the Lower Mekong River to take place. The subregional grouping then established the Climate Change and Adaptation Initiative (CCAI) as a platform for Cambodia, Lao PDR, Thailand and Vietnam to formulate and share adaptation strategies. It has been instrumental in assessing the impacts of climate change on the Lower Mekong Basin.

The CCAI has implemented one demonstration project in each of the MRC member country and the extent of the climate adaptation work ranged from vulnerability assessment, awareness raising, capacity building, to actual implementations including irrigation extension, alternative livelihood activities and the use of flood-tolerant rice.[23] Through its findings and studies, the CCAI aspires to complement existing national climate adaptation policies of the MRC member countries and guides their climate adaptation efforts. The CCAI recognizes that climate change adaptation will need continuous efforts. As such, monitoring progress and keeping track of trends are factored in as a key factor in ensuring suitable adaptation measures.

The presence of the CCAI serves as a good starting point for the MRC member countries to come together to work on climate change adaptation. Although specific adaptation strategies may differ from one place to another, the MRC member countries are essentially facing similar climate risks. These include the occurrence of more frequent drought and flooding and their impacts on agriculture and fishing productivity. By working on climate change adaptation collaboratively, countries can have better awareness of the challenges facing their neighbouring countries and better appreciation of the impacts of their neighbours' climate change adaptation initiatives, or the lack of such,

FIGURE 2.4
Steps to Plan for Climate Change Adaptation Measures

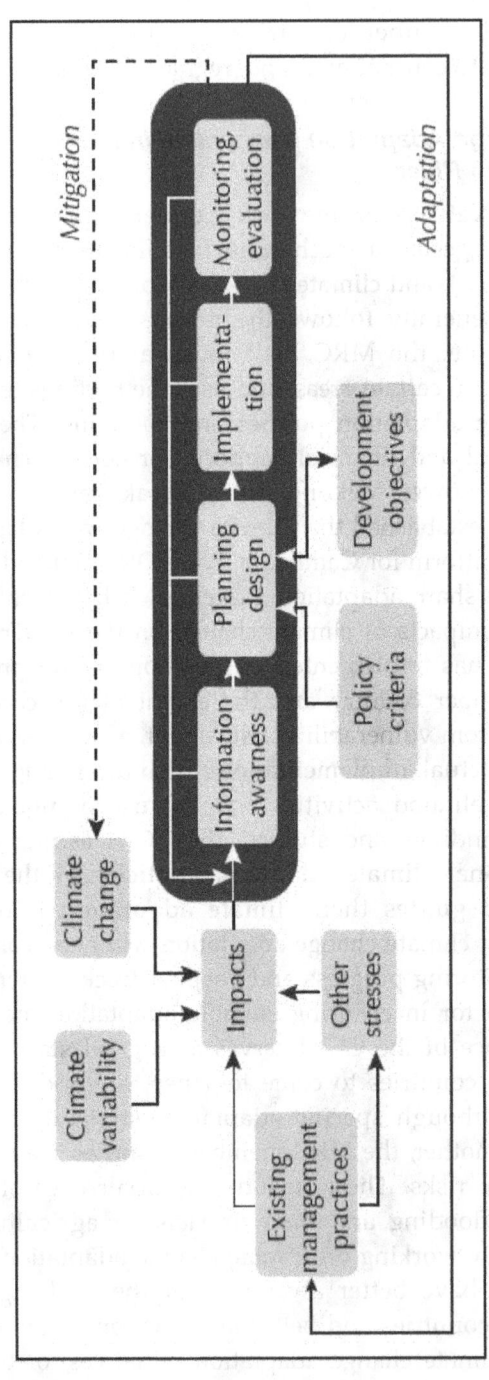

Source: UNFCCC (2006).

on their own state of climate vulnerability. After all, climate change impacts recognize no borders and there is a need to respond to the issues from an ecosystem rather than a sectoral perspective. Having a regional mechanism that directly informs national initiatives is therefore likely to result in the strengthening of the resilience of the Lower Mekong Basin as a whole.

To operationalize its cooperation, the MRC has drafted the Mekong Adaptation Strategy and Action Plan (MASAP) and taken into account existing relevant initiatives including the 2016–2020 Integrated Water Resources Management-based Basin Development Strategy (BDS), the 2016–2020 Strategic Plan, and the 2009–2025 Climate Change and Adaptation Initiative (CCAI) Framework Document. The MRC adopts a holistic two-pronged approach by formulating policy-based and vulnerability-based adaptation measures.[24] The former creates enabling environments, such as policy and institution, financial and information system, human resource capacity, among others, whereas the latter addresses water, resources and socio-economic vulnerability through technical and infrastructure solutions. The MASAP focuses on seven priority areas namely the mainstreaming of climate change into national policies, cooperation and partnership, transboundary and gender sensitive adaptation framework, adaptation finance, monitoring, data collection and sharing, capacity building, and communication and outreach.[25] The comprehensive approach to climate adaptation initiatives is also reflected in the MRC's strategy to engage external partners such as ASEAN, the Lancang-Mekong Cooperation (LMC), donors, international financial institutions and the wider climate change stakeholders. The presence of regional policies and a vision to adopt technological solutions for climate change adaptation provide a strong building block for regional climate-resilience building processes to take place.

Donors and Climate Change Adaptation Technology

Guided by policies that determine adaptation strategies and priorities, countries then carry out risk and vulnerability assessments to identify potential problems and present a range of possible solutions, including technology interventions. Although solutions are already on the table, the uptake of such recommendations appears to be very much dependent on donor support. This can be observed from several planned activities under MASAP strategic priorities that suggest a heavy reliance on external financing. Examples include the identification of the need to foster partnerships especially for the purpose of securing funding for the project formulations and implementations, the acknowledgment of the need to identify funding sources and develop proposal for submission to funding source, and the emphasis on securing access to adaptation financing.[26] Such extent of reliance on donor interventions may significantly influence the workings of the regional mechanism, including the choice of technology solutions for climate change adaptation.

Donors have indeed been playing significant roles in supporting many climate change adaptation initiatives in the Lower Mekong River Basin. In fact, 96 per cent of the total US$15,901,305 budget plan that the CCAI estimated for the years 2011–2015 was funded by donors[27] as seen in Table 2.2.

TABLE 2.2
CCAI Funding for 2011–2015 Agreed and Committed

Funding Agreed, Committed and Pledged	USD
Australia, agreement	2,260,000
Denmark, agreement	900,000
Germany, committed	1,950,000
Luxembourg, agreement	2,600,000
Sweden, agreement with EP	545,000
Finland, agreement with IKMP, ICBP	600,000
EU, pledged	6,500,000
Total	15,335,000
Funding gap	545,000

Source: MRC (2011).

While donors' involvements serve as an important enabling factor, their influence may extend to the choice of intervention measures. The ADB, for example, carried out climate change impacts assessments in Kien Giang and Ca Mau provinces and came up with a set of climate change adaptation recommendations. Of the long list of options encompassing various technological solutions such as the construction of irrigation and drainage systems, clean water supply system and environmental sanitation, the building of dykes and roads, the upgrading of canals, and drainage sewage and wastewater treatment in various cities and provinces, the ADB proposed a shorter list of climate adaptation actions in which the ADB priority was part of the evaluation criteria.[28]

German development agency GIZ has also contributed to climate change adaptation efforts in Lower Mekong River Basin. Focusing on flood management, one pilot project was conducted in each of the MRC member states. In Lao PDR's Khammouane province, the initiative has led to technological applications in the construction of new bore wells, communal water storage and filtration systems.[29] In Vietnam, the project carried out in Dong Thap province has focused more on non-structural interventions. The structural, technological intervention was reflected in the provision of water storage tanks and filters.[30] The extent to which GIZ had influence over the choices of such technologies needs to be further examined.

The USAID also conducted similar climate change adaptation projects in Thailand's Chiang Rai and Sakon Nakhon provinces, Lao PDR's Khammouane province, Cambodia's Kampong Thom province and Vietnam's Kien Giang province.[31] Risks of flooding and drought were identified in Thailand, Lao PDR and Cambodia, whereas the threats of sea level rise, coastal erosion and salinity intrusions were highlighted in Vietnam. Of the various climate adaptation initiatives that the USAID implemented, technology applications were mostly evident in the water, agriculture, and livestock management sectors. On water-related concerns in Lao PDR, technological solutions were seen in the constructions of gravity-fed water harvesting systems, storage tanks, pipelines and taps, and wash platforms. In a bid to conserve water, they installed taps that only discharge water when in demand in some small-scale household pig productions.

Aside from these measures, the USAID also tried to improve climate resilience through non-technological solutions such as awareness raising, the introduction of black pigs and more robust crops such as fruit trees, Assam tea, pepper, bamboos, and edible rattan, the construction of fish ponds and compost pits, and the establishment of community forests.

Fundamental to the debates on donors influence is that their choices may not exactly match the priorities of recipient countries.[32] Although the observation is not completely unfounded, it also cannot be concluded definitively. Many of the climate change adaptation interventions begin with climate risk and vulnerability assessments and they provide the basis and justification for the choice of climate adaptation actions technologies. Any possible interventions in the final choices will warrant further examinations.

MRC's Regional Climate Change Adaptation Initiatives

The MRC has carried out pilot projects in some demonstration sites between 2010 and 2013. In Cambodia, the climate change adaptation project was implemented in Prey Veng province, an area of high vulnerability to flood and drought, as seen in Figure 2.5.[33] The technology intervention implemented was the rebuilding of a reservoir. The reservoir was reconstructed to provide water to nearby communities

FIGURE 2.5
The Estimated Area within Prey Keng Province where the 1st Batch of MRC's Demonstration Projects were Carried Out in Cambodia

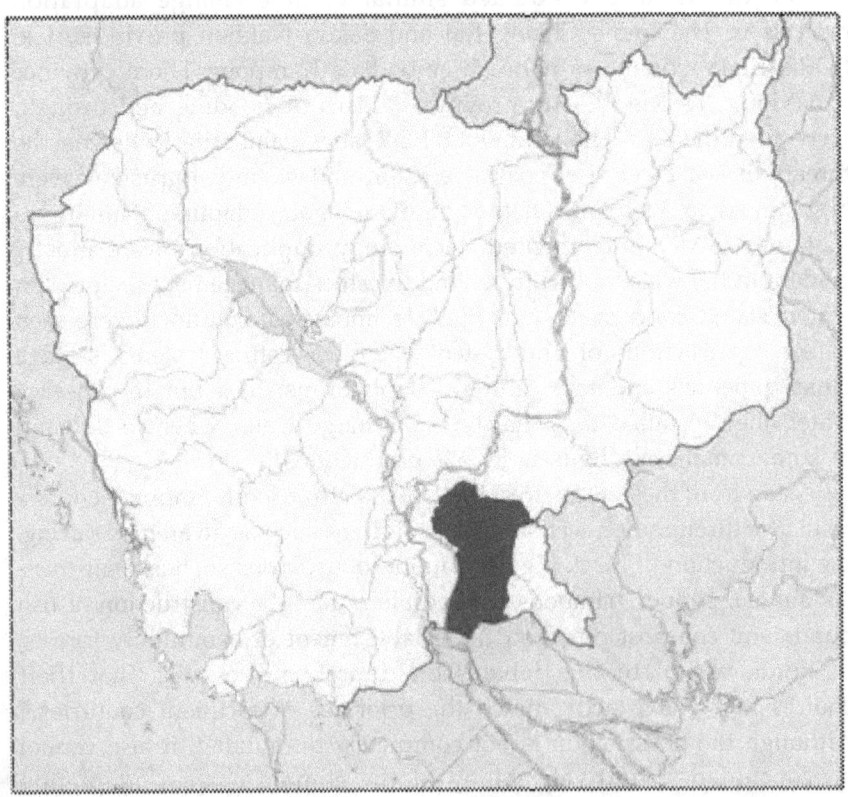

Source: MRC (2014), p. 16.

in times of drought. Subsequently, climate adaptation interventions in the province focused on crop planting strategies, water management-related measures including encouraging responsible and efficient use of water, and other technological solutions such as the building and repairing of flood protection dikes, the upgrading of water gates and the building of culverts among others.

In Lao PDR, the climate change adaptation activities were carried out in Champhone district of Savannakhet province seen in Figure 2.6.[34] Climate adaptation measures mainly aimed to increase resilience against worsening flood and drought. Technological measures applied included the extension of irrigation canal, the use of flood-tolerant rice varieties, and the possible use of sandy soils for agricultural crops.

FIGURE 2.6
The Estimated Area within Champhone District of Savannakhet Province where the 1st Batch of MRC's Demonstration Projects were Carried Out in Lao PDR

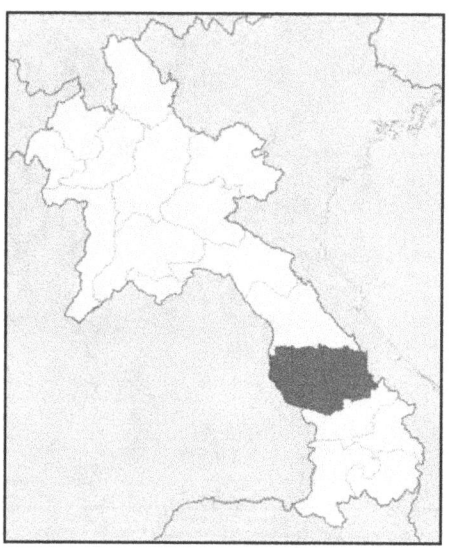

Source: MRC (2014), p. 22.

In Thailand, the MRC's climate adaptation demonstration projects were carried out in Sai Na Wang community of Kalasin province at the upper catchment of Young River Basin and Wang Luang communities of Roi-Et province at the lower end of the Yang River Basin as seen

FIGURE 2.7
The Estimated Area where the 1st Batch of MRC's Demonstration
Projects were Carried Out in Thailand

Source: Warnset and Inmuong (2014), p. 47.

in Figure 2.7.[35] The former was selected due to its susceptibility to drought and the latter due to its history of heavy floods.

The activities carried out in the project sites were mostly on assessments and awareness raising through stakeholder meetings, surveys, research, and database building. The only climate adaptation initiative having technological spin in it was the devising and the installation of a low-cost climate telemetering system at four riverside stations of the Young River Basin. It functions as a data collection tool as the sensors gather climate data, rainfall wind speed and direction, temperature and humidity. It then transmits the information that has been stored in a data-logger to a server at the RMUTI via GPRS module internet network.

Although the low-cost telemetering system seems to be the only technological solution being introduced, the project uncovered existing local-based climate-resilient farming practices that include the applications of integrated farming, smart water management in the paddy, animal manure instead of chemical fertilizer, climate-tolerant native seed, farmland resource recycling, soil moisture conservation through the planting of fruits and trees, and fish and poultry farming in the paddy pond. Such discovery resonates with studies by Nyong et al. (2007)[36] and Anik and Khan (2012),[37] among others, that showcase local communities' capability to design their own adaptation methods. The identification of existing local knowledge signifies that solutions may not necessarily be designed from scratch and technology applications may only need to complement and optimize the outputs of existing adaptation practices. Regional cooperation can document and process such wisdom and experiences systematically, and utilize them to develop the region's own technological solutions to climate change adaptation in Southeast Asia.

In Vietnam, the pilot project was carried out in Binh Giang commune of Kien Giang province seen in Figure 2.8. Just like other Mekong River states, the main climate-related concerns in Binh Giang commune are flood and drought.[38] Based on the findings, a combination of structural and non-structural measures is deemed to provide the best avenues for climate change adaptation. Structural measures entail technological interventions, for example in the construction of sea dykes and hydraulic works such as canals, sluices and embankments. Indeed, the project recommended that there is a need for more sluices, digging of some existing and new canals, and expansion of flood discharge areas. Non-structural measures emphasize on the social elements including forecasting capability, awareness raising, and warning system among others.

FIGURE 2.8
Geographical Location of Binh Giang Commune

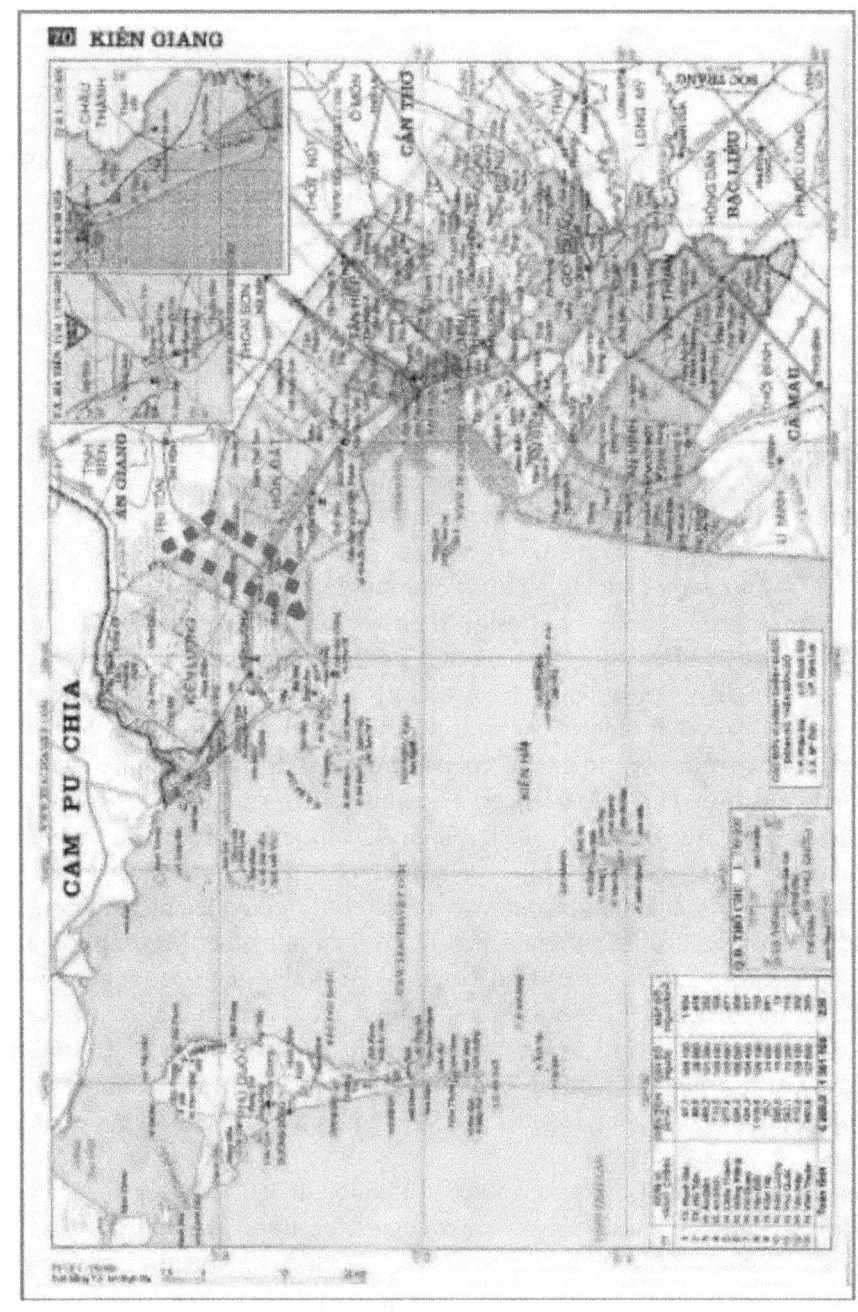

Source: Truong and Nguyen (2014), p. 107.

At this juncture, it can be observed that the MRC's CCAI has indeed complemented national adaptation plans through pilot projects in MRC member states. Through the projects, it has also facilitated the use of different types of technology in building climate adaptation capacity. The regional framework, therefore, provides a good platform to implement climate adaptation initiatives on the ground.

Climate Change Adaptation in Regional Setting—Challenges and Way Forward

Although the CCAI has successfully administered its functions to complement national adaptation efforts, the regional grouping is yet to exercise its full potential as the approach appears to focus on individual countries. It has neither adopted an ecosystem lens in assessing the vulnerability of the overall Lower Mekong River Basin nor has it come up with joint projects where member states can share resources and work collaboratively to build climate change adaptation. There has yet, for example, climate change adaptation project that is designed along shared borders among MRC member states. Doing so is critical to ensure that climate adaptation is achieved in the Lower Mekong River Basin and not only in some select sites within member states.

In addition to the suggested regional-level ecosystem approach, building regional resilience can also be done by replicating similar projects in other areas. The USAID suggested that this can be done through "ground-up pathways, knowledge products, financing pathways, and thematic scaling".[39] Ground-up pathways broadly refer to the efforts to influence national planning by local stakeholders whereas knowledge products mean the documentation of lessons learned in a way that can be relevant and applicable in other areas. Financing pathways are particularly challenging because even if funding sources like international agencies, multilateral development organizations and multilateral climate funds can be relatively easy to identify, meeting the conditions stated by the sources can serve as barriers to accessing the funding. Thematic scaling is another form of packaging the lessons learned from a particular site into broad themes that can be applied elsewhere.

In terms of institutional framework, aside from providing the institutional and financial space for climate change adaptation projects to operate, the extent to which such cooperation has resulted in increased regional climate resilience remains uncertain. Indeed, measuring the level of increased resilience brought about by adaptation initiatives is not a straightforward undertaking. The USAID report referred to it as "an emerging science, with new models arising from experiences around the world".[40] The efforts to develop climate adaptation indicators are essentially a recent phenomenon and there is yet a standardized guideline to follow. Similarly, although there are a number of attempts to theorize and formulate the indicators to measure resilience, consensus on measurement is yet to materialize. The absence of such standardized measurements makes evaluating the effectiveness of regional adaptation initiatives challenging.

In terms of technological applications, this study reveals that the technologies used for climate change adaptation in the Lower Mekong Basin are not entirely new. In fact, the majority of technology use is found in civil engineering or infrastructural applications such as the building or upgrading of embankments, dykes, and water storage and filter. This is in line with a range of technological solutions suggested by the ADB that are mainly on infrastructure except for agriculture and disaster risk management. The real question therefore appears to be whether or not existing infrastructure is sufficient in number and quality to face future climate stresses. Technology applications are frequently labelled as hard policy options and often face competitions from soft policy options like land use change, introduction of salinity-tolerant rice varieties and crops.[41] While civil engineering solutions seem to dominate the applications of technology in climate change adaptation, the emergence of modern technologies characterized by digitization, lightweight, and mobility, may bring about the development of more innovative and effective technologies for climate change adaptation.

The insights from climate change adaptation initiatives in the Lower Mekong Basin provide a few important pointers for other regions to learn from. Institutional support from the subregional MRC grouping in the form of dedicated structure, functions and policies on climate change adaptation seems to act as a key enabler that allows member states to carry out concerted efforts to assess climate risks and obtain funding. Although the MRC has yet to fully utilize the full potential of its mechanism to bring all member states to work collaboratively, establishing a dedicated regional mechanism for climate change adaptation provides the right platform for various region-wide climate adaptation cooperation to flourish.

Additionally, it has also been observed that technologies used for climate change adaptation need not necessarily be the ones that are too advanced or futuristic. Countries can tap into existing technologies, and this will potentially reduce the costs incurred to acquire such technologies. The regional mechanism will enable countries to come together and work collaboratively to perfect existing technologies, benefit from technology transfers and their spin-offs, and develop new technologies that better respond to the needs at the local level. Lastly, although measuring climate adaptation and resilience is still a work-in-progress, an institutionalized regional approach to climate change adaptation is likely to be more effective in building overall resilience compared to individual country's efforts. It will also make room for joint climate change adaptation initiatives along shared borders between countries in the region in the future.

2.2 The Case for a Dedicated Regional Mechanism for Climate Change: A Comparative Assessment

Given the utility of a dedicated mechanism for climate change adaptation in regional cooperation as evidenced in the Lower Mekong Basin case, it is argued that centralization at the regional level is critical to effective and implementable climate actions. Regional cooperation aimed at addressing climate concerns have sprung up in the last decade following the relevant developments at the international level. Regions, however, differ in their approach and conceptualization of such cooperation. Koremanos et al. (2001)[42] posited that the design of international institutions vary based on membership, scope, centralization, control and flexibility.

To further assess the argument of the need to establish a dedicated regional mechanism for climate change, it is important to examine climate change cooperation across different regions. The questions that guide the assessment of existing climate cooperation models include: (1) has it been able to go beyond conducting studies, dialogues, knowledge sharing and other confidence-building measures?, and (2) has it been able to formulate regional-level interventions grounded on a holistic assessment of the region as an ecosystem? The study looks into regional cooperation in Europe, North America, Africa, Middle East, South Asia, and South America.

Comparative Assessments of Regional Cooperation on Climate Change

The configurations of multilateral cooperation vary across regions. Some organizations like the European Union (EU) and the South Asian Association for Regional Cooperation (SAARC) enjoy a dominant presence in their respective region. Others like the League of Arab States (LAS) and the African Union (AU) stand side by side with other important regional platforms such as the Gulf Cooperation Council (GCC) and the Regional Economic Communities respectively. On the other hand, the regional arrangements in North America and South America contrast starkly as the former has no regional organization whereas the latter has myriad regional groupings that look into environment and climate change issues. Despite varying arrangements, each region has its own way to deal with climate change. The assessment of these different regional mechanisms leads to the following observations:

1) A dedicated regional mechanism facilitates more comprehensive climate interventions

As a supranational body, the EU is in the position of offering the best case study for a centralized regional mechanism. The EU established the European Environment Agency (EEA) that specifically looks into environment-related issues including climate change. The presence of EEA, supported by the European Commission (EC), enables a comprehensive approach that covers the necessary enabling factors for the implementation of regional climate actions at the national level. These include funding, technical and policy support tools, knowledge-sharing platform, meteorological services body, and research institution.[43] A dedicated "LIFE" funding that currently runs for the period of 2014 to 2020 can be tapped into for climate change adaptation and mitigation efforts. Copernicus Climate Change Services was established to monitor and analyse weather and climatic data. Joint Research Centre-Institute for Environment and Sustainability (JRC-IES) was instituted to serve as the science and technological arm of EU's environment-related policymaking processes.

In addition to laying down the supporting building blocks, the EU also demonstrates its reliance on technology to solve climate concerns. The EU conducted an assessment of climate adaptation gaps within member states, and integrated them into €80 billion worth of region-wide Horizon 2020 research and innovation programme from 2014 to 2020.[44] The incorporation of research, and science and technology elements into the adaptation approach shows that EU is ready and confident to find its own solutions to the problems it identifies in the vulnerability assessments. It is observed that the dedicated regional mechanism has also enabled the creation of an informative web-based knowledge-exchange platform called Climate-ADAPT.[45] The sharing of best practices and experiences is an important component in climate change adaptation, and a platform of a similar scale is yet to be found in other regional arrangements.

Beyond capacity building, the EU is also capable of formulating region-focused measures as evidenced in the establishment of various transnational cooperation such as, among others, in the Adriatic-Ionian, Alpine Space, Atlantic Area, Balkan-Mediterranean, and Baltic Sea subregions[46] that look into certain climate concerns more specifically. As climate considerations will be incorporated into existing regional policies such as the Common Agricultural Policy (CAP), the Cohesion Policy and the Common Fisheries Policy (CFP), the influence of climate actions will also be extended regionally.[47] It is evident, therefore, that the whole-of-Europe approach provides a seamless machinery for effective regional climate change actions. The EU model affirms the earlier observation on the Lower Mekong Basin cooperation[48] which noted that a dedicated regional mechanism for climate change leads to better coordination, planning and implementation of relevant initiatives.

2) A dedicated regional arrangement is likely to formulate implementable interventions at the national level although they do not necessarily have an ecosystem perspective in their project design

The second observation made in the Lower Mekong Basin case study was the absence of an ecosystem approach to project design although climate interventions are implementable at the national level.[49] An examination into the regional cooperation in North America confirms this argument. Despite not having a regional institution, North American countries namely the United States, Canada and Mexico signed the North American Agreement for Environmental Cooperation in 1993 and established the Commission for Environmental Cooperation (CEC) following the agreement.[50] The CEC focuses on sustainable development and environmental and economic policies and makes climate change as one of its priority areas. Although it is unclear whether the CEC has conducted a region-wide climate vulnerability assessment, it has implemented a number of climate mitigation and adaptation pilot projects in the three countries. An example will be a current project on the syndromic surveillance (SyS) systems to monitor extreme heat events implemented in some pilot sites in the United States, Canada, and Mexico.[51]

3) A dedicated regional mechanism for climate change may rely on other existing regional institutions for implementations

The AU model provides another example of the importance of a dedicated mechanism for climate change. The AU Commission, together with the United Nations Economic Commission for Africa (ECA) and the African Development Bank (AfDB), established the Climate for Development in Africa (ClimDev-Africa) Programme.[52] Unlike the CEC, ClimDev-Africa Programme does not formulate and directly implement projects. Generally, rather, it functions as a support system for national climate initiatives through capacity building, knowledge exchanges, studies and assessments. It is the leading climate change initiative among several other regional arrangements such as the Framework of Southern and Northern Africa Climate Change Programmes and the East African Community Climate Change.[53] The centrality of ClimDev-Africa Programme is reflected in the support it enjoys from the Africa Climate Policy Centre (ACPC), the Climate Change and Desertification Unit (CCDU), and ClimDev Special Fund (CDSF), and a web of entities including Africa's Regional Economic Communities, River Basin Organizations, national governments, among others,[54] that are encouraged to take up and implement its work outputs. Additionally, other regional institutions were set up to execute climate actions such as Regional Climate Centres, Regional Climate Research Partnership, and Regional Outlook Forum.[55] At this junction, it can be observed that while a dedicated regional institution for climate change may provide an avenue for effective interventions, it may not necessarily bear the responsibility to implement them. In such instances, monitoring and evaluation become a critical component to ensuring effective coordination and project implementation.

4) The absence of a dedicated regional mechanism for climate change limits the extent of climate actions to assessments and knowledge exchanges

Thus far, the case for a dedicated regional mechanism for effective climate actions has been well demonstrated. The contrary, therefore, suggests that the absence of such a mechanism will inhibit the extent of climate interventions in the region. An examination into regional cooperation in the Middle East and South Asia seems to conform to this argument. In the Middle East, the LAS and GCC are important regional organizations. Despite their presence, it is the international organizations that are taking the lead in regional climate efforts. This is evidenced in the formulation of Arab Climate Resilience Initiative by the UNDP Regional Bureau for Arab States (UNDP-RBAS),[56] a report on Regional Cooperation for Climate Change Adaptation in the Arab Region by the United Nations Economic and Social Commission for Western Asia (UN ESCWA),[57] and a report on Adaptation to a Changing Climate in the Arab Countries by the World Bank.[58] The UN ESCWA is particularly pivotal in galvanizing climate actions, bringing regional actors together, and assisting the LAS in climate change impact assessments, capacity development, and technical cooperation. Some important documents that the UN ESCWA has come up with include the Arab Strategy for Water Security in the Arab Region to Meet the Challenges and Future Needs for Sustainable Development 2010–2030, the Arab Framework Action Plan on Climate Change (AFAPCC) 2010–2020, and the Arab Strategy for Disaster Reduction 2020.[59] These external parties-supported initiatives generally target implementations at the national level. The establishment of the Regional Initiative for the Assessment of Climate Change Impacts on Water Resources and Socio-Economic Vulnerability in the Arab Region (RICCAR),[60] which seems to be the most prominent regional arrangement on climate-related matters to date, was also supported by the UN ESCWA. The RICCAR's Arab Climate Change Assessment Report[61] launched in 2017, which was supported by multiple partners and donors, seems to be the first intervention that took on a regional perspective. At this junction, it can be observed that thus far the climate actions taken in the Middle East are limited to information collection and knowledge sharing. Although the AU's ClimDev-Africa Programme shares similar functions, the absence of a dedicated regional institution potentially renders little coordination, monitoring and evaluation for climate actions among the LAS members.

A similar observation is made in South Asia. The SAARC pronounced their commitments to address climate change in the 2008 Dhaka Declaration and the 2010 Thimpu Silver Jubilee Declaration. Such commitments were further manifested in the numerous regional centres and policy documents that ensued. In fact in comparison to ASEAN, the SAARC has more dedicated regional centres that look into specific environmental issues. These include SAARC Disaster Management Centre (SDMC) in Delhi, SAARC Forestry Centre in Bhutan, SAARC Energy Centre in Islamabad, SAARC Meteorological Research Centre (SMRC) in Dhaka, and SAARC Coastal Zone Management Centre (SZMC) in Male.[62] The SAARC also gives access to the SAARC Development Fund to finance climate-related interventions.[63] It was observed, however, that these initiatives are mainly focused on capacity building and knowledge producing and sharing, and there remains a lack of joint planning and project implementation.[64] Regional political constellation and deep-seated mistrust among SAARC member states were identified as some of the potential causes,[65] although it may also be argued that the absence of a dedicated regional mechanism for climate change could also potentially contribute to a lack of joint implementable projects.

5) An all-inclusive dedicated mechanism is critical despite numerous existing climate-related regional arrangements

Cooperation in South America is characterized by a web of regional groupings that vary according to membership and focus areas. The regional arrangements that look into climate-related issues alone include Community of Latin American and Caribbean States (CELAC), Summit of Latin America and the Caribbean on Integration and Development (CALC) and the Rio group, Bolivarian Alliance for the Peoples of Our America (ALBA), Ibero-American Forum of Ministers of Environment, Organization of American States (OAS), Amazon Cooperation Treaty Organization, Andean Community of Environmental Authorities (CAAAM), Caribbean Community (CARICOM), Association of Caribbean States (ACS) and the Caribbean Sea Commission (CSC), and Central American Commission for Environment and Development (CCAD).[66]

The CARICOM even has a dedicated Caribbean Community Climate Change Centre (CCCC).[67] The existence of these myriad regional arrangements suggests that environmental and climate-related issues receive considerable attention in South America. At the same time, however, it also reflects a lack of coordination at the regional level. [68] It was noted that the various groupings make it difficult to prioritize climate actions in the region, and there is a possibility of effort overlapping and resource over-stretch as a result.

The critical need for a centralized structure for climate change matters at the regional level was realized relatively recently with the signing of the Cartagena Declarations in 2016. It brought all thirty-three Latin and America and Caribbean (LAC) countries to work on climate change collectively, and it envisioned the establishment of a Regional Cooperation Platform.[69] The effectiveness of this new regional mechanism on climate change remains to be seen; however, learning from the insights from other regions, the establishment of such a dedicated institution may prove to be a step in the right direction for climate change actions in South America.

2.3 Conclusion

The empirical study on regional arrangements for climate change in Europe, North America, Africa, the Middle East, South Asia, and South America has affirmed the observation on the Southeast Asia's Lower Mekong River Basin about the importance of having a dedicated regional mechanism to handle climate concerns. Laying down the necessary foundations for a special regional climate change institution, such as funding sources, research institutional support, climate services support, among others, is critical to ensure its operational and functional sustainability.

Among the different regional groupings, the EU appears to be the only institution that is able to formulate plans and projects from a regional perspective. Other regions, despite having numerous regional policy documents and action plans, tend to apply a country-focused lens as they concentrate more on building national capacity and implementing projects at the national level. A dedicated regional climate mechanism may be established by various means including a multilateral agreement, a commitment from the larger regional organization and support from donors or external partners. A dedicated regional arrangement for climate change may not function as the implementing body as it may tap on to other existing groupings in the region to carry out plans and projects as seen in the case of AU. In regions where climate change is still being handled in a more decentralized manner, the extent of cooperation seems to be limited to assessments, capacity building and knowledge sharing.

As climate change becomes a more pressing concern that needs urgent solutions to, the establishment of a dedicated regional mechanism is therefore critical. It will enable the application of an ecosystem approach in the formulation, management, and implementation of regional interventions, which in turn will lend itself to facilitating technological cooperation for climate change adaptation and mitigation in the region.

NOTES

1. Intergovernmental Panel on Climate Change (IPCC), *Glossary of Terms used in the Third Assessment Report*, 2001, p. 379, https://www.ipcc.ch/pdf/glossary/tar-ipcc-terms-en.pdf (accessed 15 March 2018).
2. Ibid., p. 365.
3. Climate Change Secretariat (UNFCCC), *Technologies for Adaptation to Climate Change* (Bonn: UNFCCC, 2006).
4. Greenhouse Gas Protocol, undated, http://www.ghgprotocol.org/ (accessed 19 December 2017).
5. Jennifer Ellis, *Climate Resilience Indicator Literature Review: Prepared as part of "Using Columbia Basin State of the Basin Indicators to Measure Climate Adaptation"*, Columbia Basin Trust, 2014, http://www.cbrdi.ca/wp-content/uploads/ClimateAdaptation_LitReview_15-03-15.pdf (accessed 19 December 2017).
6. Climate Change Secretariat (UNFCCC), *Technologies for Adaptation to Climate Change*.
7. Asian Development Bank (ADB), *Technologies to Support Climate Change Adaptation* (Mandaluyong City, Philippines: Asian Development Bank, 2014), https://www.adb.org/sites/default/files/publication/149400/technologies-climate-change-adaptation.pdf (accessed 21 December 2017).
8. See, for examples, the 2006 National Adaptation Programme of Action to Climate Change of Cambodia and the 2009 National Adaptation Programme of Action to Climate Change of Lao PDR.
9. USAID, *Asia-Pacific Regional Climate Change Adaptation Assessment Final Report: Findings and Recommendations* (Washington, D.C.: International Resources

Group, 2010), http://pdf.usaid.gov/pdf_docs/pnads197.pdf (accessed 20 December 2017).

10. Emmanuel de Guzman, "How Asean Could Pave Way for a Climate-resilient Southeast Asia", *Inquirer.net*, 10 November 2017, http://opinion. inquirer.net/108609/asean-pave-way-climate-resilient-southeast-asia (accessed 20 December 2017).

11. USAID, *Asia-Pacific Regional Climate Change Adaptation Assessment Final Report*.

12. Nicole Kranz, Timo Menniken, and Jochen Hinkel, "Climate Change Adaptation Strategies in the Mekong and Orange-Senqu Basins: What Determines the State-of-Play?" *Environmental Science & Policy* 13, no. 7 (2010): 648–59.

13. The Economist Intelligence Unit, "New EIU Report: Mekong River Basin Water Security", 16 March 2017, http://foodsecurity.dupont.com/2017/03/16/new-eiu-report-mekong-river-basin-water-security/ (accessed 20 June 2018).

14. Mekong River Commission (MRC), *IWRM-Based Basin Development Strategy for the Lower Mekong Basin*, 2009, http://archive.iwlearn.net/mrcmekong. org/download/programmes/bdp/IWRM-based-Basin-Dev-Strategy-1st-Incomplete-Con-Draft6Oct09.pdf.

15. J. Eastham et al., *Mekong River Basin Water Resources Assessment: Impacts of Climate Change* (Canberra: Commonwealth Scientific and Industrial Research Organisation, 2008), http://www.clw.csiro.au/publications/waterforahealthycountry/2008/wfhc-MekongWaterResourcesAssessment.pdf.

16. A. Smajgl et al., "Responding to Rising Sea Levels in the Mekong Delta", *Nature Climate Change* 5 (2015): 167–74.

17. K. Västilä et al., "Modelling Climate Change Impacts on the Flood Pulse in the Lower Mekong Floodplains", *Journal of Water and Climate Change* 1, no. 1 (2010): 67–87, http://jwcc.iwaponline.com/content/1/1/67?utm_source=TrendMD&utm_medium=cpc&utm_campaign=Journal_of_Water_and_Climate_Change_TrendMD_1 (accessed 22 December 2017).

18. Central Executive Committee of Vietnam Communist Party, "Resolution No.: 24-NQ/TW Active in Response to Climate Change, Improvement of Natural Resource Management and Environmental Protection", 2013, http://www.climatechange.vn/en/wp-content/uploads/sites/2/2017/04/Resolution-24NQ-TW-on-proactive-response-to-climate-change.pdf (accessed 15 March 2018).

19. The Prime Minister of Vietnam, "Decision 2139/QĐ-TTg on National Strategy on Climate Change", 2011, http://chinhphu.vn/portal/page/portal/English/strategies/strategiesdetails?categoryId=30&articleId=10051283 (accessed 16 March 2018).

20. The Prime Minister of Vietnam, "Decision No. 1474/QĐ-Ttg on Issuance of National Action Plan on Climate Change Period 2012–2020", 2012, https://

thuvienphapluat.vn/van-ban/Tai-nguyen-Moi-truong/Decision-No-1474-QD-TTg-on-issuance-of-national-action-plan-on-climate-change-182078.aspx (accessed 16 March 2018).

21. The Prime Minister of Vietnam, "Decision No. 1393/QĐ-TTg on Approval of the National Green Growth Strategy", 2012, https://www.giz.de/en/downloads/VietNam-GreenGrowth-Strategy.pdf (accessed 16 March 2018).

22. The Prime Minister of Vietnam, "Decision No. 403/QĐ-TTg on Approval of the National Action Plan on Green Growth in Vietnam for the Period of 2014–2020", 2014, http://cfovn.mpi.gov.vn/Portals/0/Upload/Decision_403-2014-TTg_EN.pdf (accessed 16 March 2018).

23. MRC, "Climate Change and Adaptation Initiative", undated, http://www.mrcmekong.org/assets/Posters-leaflets/CCAI-leaftlet-final.pdf (accessed 4 December 2017).

24. MRC, *Mekong Adaptation Strategy and Action Plan Version 3.0*, 2017, p. 42, http://www.mrcmekong.org/assets/Uploads/MASAP-Ver-3.0.pdf (accessed 19 April 2018).

25. Ibid., p. v.

26. Ibid., pp. 48–50.

27. MRC, *Climate Change Adaptation Initiative 2011-2015 Programme Document* (Vientiane: MRC, 2011), http://www.mrcmekong.org/assets/CCAI-2011-2015-documentFinal.pdf.

28. Philip Buckle, *Climate Change Impact and Adaptation Study in the Mekong Delta TA7377-VIE Vietnam Final Report, an ADB Technical Assistance Consultant's Final Report*, 2013, https://www.adb.org/sites/default/files/project-document/80872/43295-012-tacr-04.pdf.

29. "Mekong River Commission and GIZ Conclude Adaptation Pilot Project in Khammouane", *GIZ*, 23 May 2016, https://www.giz.de/en/worldwide/38683.html (accessed 15 December 2017).

30. "GIZ Conclude Adaptation Pilot Project in Mekong Delta", *VOV/GIZ, MRC*, 5 May 2016, http://english.vov.vn/society/mrc-giz-conclude-adaptation-pilot-project-in-mekong-delta-318937.vov (accessed 15 December 2017).

31. DAI, *USAID Mekong Adaptation and Resilience to Climate Change (USAID Mekong ARCC) Final Report*, 2016, http://mekongarcc.net/sites/default/files/usaid_mekong_arcc_final_report_rev_2.pdf (accessed 22 December 2017).

32. See for example, Jessica M. Ayers and Saleemul Huq, "Supporting Adaptation to Climate Change: What Role for Official Development Assistance?" presented at DSA Annual Conference 2008 "Development's Invisible Hands: Development Futures in a Changing Climate", Church House, Westminster, London, 8 November 2008, https://www.iied.org/supporting-adaptation-climate-change-what-role-for-official-development-assistance (accessed 21 December 2017).

33. MRC, *Results and Lessons Learnt from the First Batch of Local Demonstration Projects 2010-2013, Demonstration Project Series No. 1* (Vientiane: MRC, 2014).

34. Ibid.

35. Prasit Warnset and Yanyong Inmuong, *Local Demonstration Projects on Climate Change Adaptation Final Report of the First Batch Project in Thailand* (Vientiane: Mekong River Commission, 2014), http://www.mrcmekong.org/assets/Publications/Reports/Local-demonstration-projects-on-CCA-final-report-of-1st-batch-project-in-Thailand.pdf (accessed 21 December 2017).

36. A. Nyong, F. Adesina, and B. Osman Elasha, "The Value of Indigenous Knowledge in Climate Change Mitigation and Adaptation Strategies in the Africa Sahel", *Mitigation and Adaptation Strategies for Global Change* 12, no. 5 (2007): 787–97.

37. Sawon Istiak Anik and Mohamed Abu Sayed Arfin Khan, "Climate Change Adaptation through Local Knowledge in the North Eastern Region of Bangladesh", *Mitigation and Adaptation Strategies for Global Change* 17, no. 8 (2012): 879–96.

38. Hong Tien Truong and Nguyen Anh Duc, *Local Demonstration Projects on Climate Change Adaptation Final Report of the First Batch Project in Viet Nam* (Vientiane: Mekong River Commission, 2014), http://www.mrcmekong.org/assets/Publications/Reports/Local-demonstration-projects-on-CCA-final-report-of-1st-batch-project-in-Vietnam.pdf (accessed 21 December 2017).

39. DAI, *USAID Mekong Adaptation and Resilience to Climate Change (USAID Mekong ARCC) Final Report*, p. 69.

40. Ibid., p. 94.

41. Smajgl et al., "Responding to Rising Sea Levels in the Mekong Delta", pp. 167–74.

42. Barbara Koremanos, Charles Lipson, and Duncan Snidal, "The Rational Design of International Institutions", *International Organization* 55, no. 4 (2001): 761–99.

43. European Commission, "Strengthening Europe's Resilience to the Impacts of Climate Change", undated, https://ec.europa.eu/clima/sites/clima/files/docs/eu_strategy_en.pdf (accessed 20 June 2018).

44. Ibid.

45. European Climate Adaptation Platform, undated, https://climate-adapt.eea.europa.eu/ (accessed 20 June 2018).

46. European Climate Adaptation Platform, "Transnational Regions and Other Regions and Countries", undated, https://climate-adapt.eea.europa.eu/countries-regions/transnational-regions (accessed 20 June 2018).

47. European Commission, "Strengthening Europe's Resilience to the Impacts of Climate Change".

48. See Margareth Sembiring, "Examining Cooperation for Climate Change Adaptation in Southeast Asia: The Case of Lower Mekong River Basin",

NTS Insight, No. IN18-03 (Singapore: RSIS Centre for Non-Traditional Security Studies (NTS Centre), 2018), http://www.rsis.edu.sg/wp-content/uploads/2018/04/NTS-insight-Technology-Applications-in-Climate-Change-Adaptation-Regime-LMB-Case.pdf (accessed 20 June 2018).

49. Ibid.

50. Commission for Environmental Cooperation, undated, http://www.cec.org/ (accessed 20 June 2018).

51. Commission for Environmental Cooperation, "Monitoring Health Impacts from Extreme Heat Events", undated, http://www.cec.org/our-work/projects/monitoring-health-impacts-extreme-heat-events (accessed 20 June 2018).

52. ClimDev-Africa, undated, http://www.climdev-africa.org/ (accessed 20 June 2018).

53. Estherine Lisinge-Fotabong et al., *Climate Diplomacy in Africa* (Berlin: Adelphi, 2017), https://www.climate-diplomacy.org/file/2566/download?token=0ttwy308 (accessed 20 June 2018).

54. ClimDev-Africa, *Annual Report 2015: Supporting Africa's Response to Climate Change*, 2015, http://www.climdev-africa.org/sites/default/files/DocumentAttachments/ClimDev-Africa%202015%20Annual%20Report.pdf (accessed 20 June 2018).

55. ClimDev-Africa, *Annual Report 2016: Supporting Africa's Response to Climate Change* (Addis Ababa: Africa Climate Policy Center, 2016), http://www.climdev-africa.org/sites/default/files/DocumentAttachments/ClimDev%20annual%20report%202016--%20Final.pdf (accessed 20 June 2018).

56. UNDP Regional Bureau for Arab States (UNDP-RBAS), Arab Climate Resilience Initiative, undated, http://www.arabclimateinitiative.org/index.html (accessed 20 June 2018).

57. United Nations Economic and Social Commission for Western Asia (ESCWA), *Regional Cooperation for Climate Change Adaptation in the Arab Region E/ESCWA/SDPD/2017/IG.1/5*, 2017, https://www.unescwa.org/sites/www.unescwa.org/files/events/files/regional_cooperation_for_climate_change_adaptation_eng.pdf (accessed 20 June 2018).

58. Dorte Verner, *Adaptation to a Changing Climate in the Arab Countries: A Case for Adaptation Governance and Leadership in Building Climate Resilience* (Washington, D.C.: The World Bank, 2012), https://openknowledge.worldbank.org/handle/10986/12216 (accessed 20 June 2018).

59. ESCWA, *Regional Cooperation for Climate Change Adaptation in the Arab Region*, E/ESCWA/SDPD/2017/IG.1/5, 2017.

60. ESCWA, *The Regional Initiative for the Assessment of Climate Change Impacts on Water Resources and Socio-Economic Vulnerability in the Arab Region (RICCAR)*, undated, https://www.unescwa.org/climate-change-water-resources-arab-region-riccar (accessed 20 June 2018).

61. ESCWA et al., *Arab Climate Change Assessment Report – Main Report, E/ESCWA/SDPD/2017/RICCAR/Report* (Beirut: RICCAR, 2017), https://www.unescwa.org/publications/riccar-arab-climate-change-assessment-report (accessed 20 June 2018).

62. UNISDR/SDMC, *Integration of Disaster Risk Reduction and Climate Change Adaptation in SAARC Region: Implementation of the Thimphu Statement on Climate Change – A Comprehensive Study of the Policy, Institutional Landscape, and Resource Allocation for Disaster Risk Reduction and Climate Change Adaptation in South Asia*, 2014, https://www.researchgate.net/publication/299430726_Integration_of_Disaster_Risk_Reduction_and_Climate_Change_Adaptation_in_SAARC_Region (accessed 21 June 2018).

63. Arabinda Misha et al., *Climate Risks in the SAARC Region: Ways to Address the Social, Economic & Environmental Challenges*, 2014, https://www.researchgate.net/publication/283436395_Climate_risks_in_the_SAARC_region_ways_to_address_the_social_economic_environmental_challenges (accessed 21 June 2018).

64. Ibid.

65. Ibid.

66. United Nations Environment Programme, *Review of Existing Intergovernmental Priorities on Sustainable Development, with an Emphasis on Environment, in Latin America and the Caribbean, UNEP/LAC-IGWG.XIX/8*, 2014, http://www.pnuma.org/forodeministros/19-mexico/documentos/Regional%20and%20subregional%20priorities%2023%20August%202013%20_3_.pdf (accessed 21 June 2018).

67. Caribbean Community Climate Change Centre, undated, http://www.caribbeanclimate.bz/ (accessed 21 June 2018).

68. Alessandra Lazzari, "Climate Cooperation in Latin America and Caribbean Countries", *International Climate Policy* 41 (2016): 14–15, http://www.iccgov.org/iccgstudies/international-climate-policy-n-41/ (accessed 21 June 2018).

69. Ibid.

REFERENCES

Anik, Sawon Istiak and Mohamed Abu Sayed Arfin Khan. 2012. "Climate Change Adaptation through Local Knowledge in the North Eastern Region of Bangladesh". *Mitigation and Adaptation Strategies for Global Change* 17, no. 8: 879–96.

Asian Development Bank (ADB). 2014. *Technologies to Support Climate Change Adaptation*. Mandaluyong City, Philippines: ADB. https://www.adb.org/sites/default/files/publication/149400/technologies-climate-change-adaptation.pdf (accessed 21 December 2017).

Ayers, Jessica M. and Saleemul Huq. 2008. "Supporting Adaptation to Climate Change: What Role for Official Development Assistance?" Presented at DSA Annual Conference 2008 "Development's Invisible Hands: Development Futures in a Changing Climate", Church House, Westminster, London, 8 November 2008. https://www.iied.org/supporting-adaptation-climate-change-what-role-for-official-development-assistance (accessed 21 December 2017).

Buckle, Philip. 2013. *Climate Change Impact and Adaptation Study in the Mekong Delta TA7377-VIE Vietnam Final Report, an ADB Technical Assistance Consultant's Final Report.* https://www.adb.org/sites/default/files/project-document/80872/43295-012-tacr-04.pdf.

Caribbean Community Climate Change Centre. Undated. http://www.caribbeanclimate.bz/ (accessed 21 June 2018).

Central Executive Committee of Vietnam Communist Party. 2013. "Resolution No.: 24-NQ/TW Active in Response to Climate Change, Improvement of Natural Resource Management and Environmental Protection". http://www.climatechange.vn/en/wp-content/uploads/sites/2/2017/04/Resolution-24NQ-TW-on-proactive-response-to-climate-change.pdf (accessed 15 March 2018).

Climate Change Secretariat (UNFCCC). 2006. *Technologies for Adaptation to Climate Change.* Bonn: UNFCCC.

ClimDev-Africa. Undated. http://www.climdev-africa.org/ (accessed 20 June 2018).

———. 2015. *Annual Report 2015: Supporting Africa's Response to Climate Change.* http://www.climdev-africa.org/sites/default/files/DocumentAttachments/ClimDev-Africa%202015%20Annual%20Report.pdf (accessed 20 June 2018).

———. 2016. *Annual Report 2016: Supporting Africa's Response to Climate Change.* Addis Ababa: Africa Climate Policy Center. http://www.climdev-africa.org/sites/default/files/DocumentAttachments/ClimDev%20annual%20report%202016--%20Final.pdf (accessed 20 June 2018).

Commission for Environmental Cooperation. Undated. http://www.cec.org/ (accessed 20 June 2018).

———. Undated. "Monitoring Health Impacts from Extreme Heat Events". http://www.cec.org/our-work/projects/monitoring-health-impacts-extreme-heat-events (accessed 20 June 2018).

DAI. 2016. *USAID Mekong Adaptation and Resilience to Climate Change (USAID Mekong ARCC) Final Report.* http://mekongarcc.net/sites/default/files/usaid_mekong_arcc_final_report_rev_2.pdf (accessed 22 December 2017).

Eastham, J., Freddie Mpelasoka, Mohammed Mainuddin, Catherine Ticehurst, Peter Dyce, Geoff Hodgson, Riasat Ali, and Mac Kirby. 2008. *Mekong River Basin Water Resources Assessment: Impacts of Climate Change.* Canberra: Commonwealth Scientific and Industrial Research Organisation. http://

www.clw.csiro.au/publications/waterforahealthycountry/2008/wfhc-MekongWaterResourcesAssessment.pdf.

Ellis, Jennifer. 2014. *Climate Resilience Indicator Literature Review: Prepared as part of "Using Columbia Basin State of the Basin Indicators to Measure Climate Adaptation"*. Columbia Basin Trust. http://www.cbrdi.ca/wp-content/uploads/ClimateAdaptation_LitReview_15-03-15.pdf (accessed 19 December 2017).

European Climate Adaptation Platform. Undated. https://climate-adapt.eea.europa.eu/ (accessed 20 June 2018).

————. Undated. "Transnational Regions and Other Regions and Countries". https://climate-adapt.eea.europa.eu/countries-regions/transnational-regions (accessed 20 June 2018).

European Commission. Undated. "Strengthening Europe's Resilience to the Impacts of Climate Change". https://ec.europa.eu/clima/sites/clima/files/docs/eu_strategy_en.pdf (accessed 20 June 2018).

FAO Aquastat. 2011. "Mekong River". http://www.fao.org/nr/water/aquastat/basins/mekong/index.stm (accessed 20 June 2018).

"GIZ Conclude Adaptation Pilot Project in Mekong Delta". *VOV/GIZ, MRC*, 5 May 2016. http://english.vov.vn/society/mrc-giz-conclude-adaptation-pilot-project-in-mekong-delta-318937.vov (accessed 15 December 2017).

Greenhouse Gas Protocol. Undated. http://www.ghgprotocol.org/ (accessed 19 December 2017).

de Guzman, Emmanuel. 2017. "How Asean Could Pave Way for a Climate-resilient Southeast Asia". *Inquirer.net*, 10 November 2017. http://opinion.inquirer.net/108609/asean-pave-way-climate-resilient-southeast-asia (accessed 20 December 2017).

Intergovernmental Panel on Climate Change (IPCC). 2001. *Glossary of Terms used in the Third Assessment Report*. https://www.ipcc.ch/pdf/glossary/tar-ipcc-terms-en.pdf (accessed 15 March 2018).

Koremanos, Barbara, Charles Lipson, and Duncan Snidal. 2001. "The Rational Design of International Institutions". *International Organization* 55, no. 4: 761–99.

Kranz, Nicole, Timo Menniken, and Jochen Hinkel. 2010. "Climate Change Adaptation Strategies in the Mekong and Orange-Senqu Basins: What Determines the State-of-Play?" *Environmental Science & Policy* 13, no. 7: 648–59.

Lazzari, Alessandra. 2016. "Climate Cooperation in Latin America and Caribbean Countries". *International Climate Policy* 41: 14–15. http://www.iccgov.org/iccgstudies/international-climate-policy-n-41/ (accessed 21 June 2018).

Lisinge-Fotabong, Estherine, Mamadou Diakhité, Kwame Ababio, and Cheikh Tidjane N'dongo. 2017. *Climate Diplomacy in Africa*. Berlin: Adelphi. https://

www.climate-diplomacy.org/file/2566/download?token=0ttwy308 (accessed 20 June 2018).

Mekong River Commission (MRC). Undated. "Climate Change and Adaptation Initiative". http://www.mrcmekong.org/assets/Posters-leaflets/CCAI-leaftlet-final.pdf (accessed 4 December 2017).

———. 2009. *IWRM-Based Basin Development Strategy for the Lower Mekong Basin*. http://archive.iwlearn.net/mrcmekong.org/download/programmes/bdp/IWRM-based-Basin-Dev-Strategy-1st-Incomplete-Con-Draft6Oct09.pdf.

———. 2011. *Climate Change Adaptation Initiative 2011-2015 Programme Document*. Vientiane: MRC. http://www.mrcmekong.org/assets/CCAI-2011-2015-documentFinal.pdf.

———. 2014. *Results and Lessons Learnt from the First Batch of Local Demonstration Projects 2010-2013, Demonstration Project Series No. 1*. Vientiane: MRC.

———. 2017. *Mekong Adaptation Strategy and Action Plan Version 3.0*. http://www.mrcmekong.org/assets/Uploads/MASAP-Ver-3.0.pdf (accessed 19 April 2018).

"Mekong River Commission and GIZ Conclude Adaptation Pilot Project in Khammouane". *GIZ*, 23 May 2016. https://www.giz.de/en/worldwide/38683.html (accessed 15 December 2017).

Misha, Arabinda, Yvani Deraniyagala, Dorji L., Khan S.R., Rahma A., Roy J., Kelkar U., Karky B.S., Mohan Munasinghe, Sharef M., Neer Shrestha Pradhan, and Vaidya R.A. 2014. *Climate Risks in the SAARC Region: Ways to Address the Social, Economic & Environmental Challenges*. https://www.researchgate.net/publication/283436395_Climate_risks_in_the_SAARC_region_ways_to_address_the_social_economic_environmental_challenges (accessed 21 June 2018).

Nyong, A., F. Adesina, and B. Osman Elasha. 2007. "The Value of Indigenous Knowledge in Climate Change Mitigation and Adaptation Strategies in the Africa Sahel". *Mitigation and Adaptation Strategies for Global Change* 12, no. 5: 787–97.

Sembiring, Margareth. 2018. "Examining Cooperation for Climate Change Adaptation in Southeast Asia: The Case of Lower Mekong River Basin". *NTS Insight*, No. IN18-03. Singapore: RSIS Centre for Non-Traditional Security Studies (NTS Centre). http://www.rsis.edu.sg/wp-content/uploads/2018/04/NTS-insight-Technology-Applications-in-Climate-Change-Adaptation-Regime-LMB-Case.pdf (accessed 20 June 2018).

Smajgl, A., T.Q. Toan, D.K. Nhan, J. Ward, N.H. Trung, L.Q. Tri, V.P.D. Tri, and P.T. Vu. 2015. "Responding to Rising Sea Levels in the Mekong Delta". *Nature Climate Change* 5: 167–74.

The Economist Intelligence Unit. 2017. "New EIU Report: Mekong River Basin Water Security", 16 March 2017. http://foodsecurity.dupont.com/2017/03/16/new-eiu-report-mekong-river-basin-water-security/ (accessed 20 June 2018).

The Prime Minister of Vietnam. 2011. "Decision 2139/QĐ-TTg on National Strategy on Climate Change". http://chinhphu.vn/portal/page/portal/English/strategies/strategiesdetails?categoryId=30&articleId=10051283 (accessed 16 March 2018).

———. 2012. "Decision No. 1393/QĐ-TTg on Approval of the National Green Growth Strategy". https://www.giz.de/en/downloads/VietNam-GreenGrowth-Strategy.pdf (accessed 16 March 2018).

———. 2012. "Decision No. 1474/QĐ-Ttg on Issuance of National Action Plan on Climate Change Period 2012–2020". https://thuvienphapluat.vn/van-ban/Tai-nguyen-Moi-truong/Decision-No-1474-QD-TTg-on-issuance-of-national-action-plan-on-climate-change-182078.aspx (accessed 16 March 2018).

———. 2014. "Decision No. 403/QĐ-TTg on Approval of the National Action Plan on Green Growth in Vietnam for the Period of 2014–2020". http://cfovn.mpi.gov.vn/Portals/0/Upload/Decision_403-2014-TTg_EN.pdf (accessed 16 March 2018).

Truong, Hong Tien and Nguyen Anh Duc. 2014. *Local Demonstration Projects on Climate Change Adaptation Final Report of the First Batch Project in Viet Nam.* Vientiane: Mekong River Commission. http://www.mrcmekong.org/assets/Publications/Reports/Local-demonstration-projects-on-CCA-final-report-of-1st-batch-project-in-Vietnam.pdf (accessed 21 December 2017).

UNDP Regional Bureau for Arab States (UNDP-RBAS). Arab Climate Resilience Initiative. Undated. http://www.arabclimateinitiative.org/index.html (accessed 20 June 2018).

United Nations Economic and Social Commission for Western Asia (ESCWA). Undated. *The Regional Initiative for the Assessment of Climate Change Impacts on Water Resources and Socio-Economic Vulnerability in the Arab Region (RICCAR).* https://www.unescwa.org/climate-change-water-resources-arab-region-riccar (accessed 20 June 2018).

———. 2017. *Regional Cooperation for Climate Change Adaptation in the Arab Region. E/ESCWA/SDPD/2017/IG.1/5.* https://www.unescwa.org/sites/www.unescwa.org/files/events/files/regional_cooperation_for_climate_change_adaptation_eng.pdf (accessed 20 June 2018).

——— et al. 2017. *Arab Climate Change Assessment Report – Main Report. E/ESCWA/SDPD/2017/RICCAR/Report.* Beirut: RICCAR. https://www.unescwa.org/publications/riccar-arab-climate-change-assessment-report (accessed 20 June 2018).

United Nations Environment Programme. 2014. *Review of Existing Intergovernmental Priorities on Sustainable Development, with an Emphasis on Environment, in Latin America and the Caribbean. UNEP/LAC-IGWG.XIX/8.* http://www.pnuma.org/forodeministros/19-mexico/documentos/Regional%20and%20subregional%20priorities%2023%20August%202013%20_3_.pdf (accessed 21 June 2018).

UNISDR/SDMC. 2014. *Integration of Disaster Risk Reduction and Climate Change Adaptation in SAARC Region: Implementation of the Thimphu Statement on Climate Change – A Comprehensive Study of the Policy, Institutional Landscape, and Resource Allocation for Disaster Risk Reduction and Climate Change Adaptation in South Asia.* https://www.researchgate.net/publication/299430726_Integration_ of_Disaster_Risk_Reduction_and_Climate_Change_Adaptation_in_SAARC_ Region (accessed 21 June 2018).

USAID. 2010. *Asia-Pacific Regional Climate Change Adaptation Assessment Final Report: Findings and Recommendations.* Washington, D.C.: International Resources Group. http://pdf.usaid.gov/pdf_docs/pnads197.pdf (accessed 20 December 2017).

Västilä, K., M. Kummu, C. Sangmanee, and S. Chinvanno. 2010. "Modelling Climate Change Impacts on the Flood Pulse in the Lower Mekong Floodplains". *Journal of Water and Climate Change* 1, no. 1: 67–87. http://jwcc. iwaponline.com/content/1/1/67?utm_source=TrendMD&utm_medium= cpc&utm_campaign=Journal_of_Water_and_Climate_Change_TrendMD_1 (accessed 22 December 2017).

Verner, Dorte. 2012. *Adaptation to a Changing Climate in the Arab Countries: A Case for Adaptation Governance and Leadership in Building Climate Resilience.* Washington, D.C.: The World Bank. https://openknowledge.worldbank.org/ handle/10986/12216 (accessed 20 June 2018).

Warnset, Prasit and Yanyong Inmuong. 2014. *Local Demonstration Projects on Climate Change Adaptation Final Report of the First Batch Project in Thailand.* Vientiane: Mekong River Commission. http://www.mrcmekong.org/assets/ Publications/Reports/Local-demonstration-projects-on-CCA-final-report-of- 1st-batch-project-in-Thailand.pdf (accessed 21 December 2017).

3

SOUTHEAST ASIA'S FOOD SECURITY: INFLECTION POINT?

Jose Ma. Luis Montesclaros

3.1 Introduction

Over the past decade, Southeast Asia was close to halving its under-nourishment from 18.1 per cent of its population in 2005 to 9.7 per cent in 2014,[1] or a reduction of 41 million people undernourished from as much as 101.7 million undernourished in 2005.[2] This was largely from the successful initiatives that increased per capita income and reduced poverty across the ASEAN member states (AMSs). However, regional statistics show a potential reversal in these trends: over the past three years, Southeast Asia's undernourishment increased by 3 million from 2014 to 2016.[3]

This coincides with the global situation, wherein global under-nourishment increased for the first time in a decade from 2015 to 2016, by 19.8 million people, followed by an increase of 20.2 million from 2016 to 2017.[4] It runs counter to the trend of falling global undernourishment which the world achieved in pursuit of the Millennium Development Goals, from 14.2 per cent in 2005 to 10.6 per cent in 2015.[5]

These statistics are fuelling fears that the region, and the world over, could be seeing a new era of increasing food insecurity. This chapter therefore critically reviews the state of the region's food insecurity, focusing on the issue of increasing undernourishment, alongside an assessment of the national and regional gaps in addressing this issue. It then provides recommendations on how these mechanisms can be tweaked to better respond to this non-traditional security (NTS) threat.

3.2 Food Security Framework and Measurement of Undernutrition

Food security is defined by the Food and Agriculture Organization of the United Nations (FAO) as a "situation that exists when all people, at all times, have physical, social and economic access to sufficient, safe and nutritious food that meets their dietary needs and food preferences for an active and healthy life".[6] Following this definition, the framework adopted by the NTS Centre in studying food security distinguishes four key facets.[7] The first is food availability, whether there is sufficient food to meet demand, at the global, regional, country, and subregional/subcountry levels. This is primarily affected by factors which affect the production side, in terms of crop yields and land allocation for agricultural purposes.

The next facet is physical food access, wherein disruptions can prevent food produced in farms from reaching consumers, such as trade embargoes and transport route blockage from extreme weather events. The third facet is economic food access, wherein individuals may not be able to afford food. This is linked to physical access, because in times of shortage, prices for commodities can increase,[8] as in the 2007–8 food price crisis when prices for certain grains more than doubled.[9] The fourth is food utilization, or whether there is "sufficient, safe and nutritious food that meets dietary needs...". This refers to nutrition outcomes from food consumption, and can be measured by malnourishment. Malnourishment can take the form of undernourishment, or having less than the recommended calories per day per person, which can lead to wasting and stunting; on the other extreme, one can have too many of the calories, leading to obesity and being overweight, which may also lead to adverse health outcomes (e.g. diabetes, hypertension).

This chapter's focus on undernourishment is in line with the second Sustainable Development Goal (SDG) that is related to global hunger,[10] and falls under the food utilization facet. This is a critical NTS concern to states, given the potential for political instability when left unchecked. Riots in more than sixty countries[11] occurred alongside the 2007–8 food price crisis mentioned above, wherein income levels of more than 100 million people fell below the poverty line, among which, 63 million were re-classified as undernourished.[12]

Food utilization is linked to the first three facets. Hence, government interventions have been in providing incentives for food production so that there is sufficient food produced (e.g. to motivate farmers to plant a sufficient number of seeds, India guarantees farmers that they will buy grains at a pre-identified price);[13] monitoring trade routes; maintaining food banks or stockpiles where food can be stored for future use; and guiding consumers on proper storage and consumption habits to avoid food poisoning and spoilage.

It will be useful to note the manner by which undernourishment is measured by the FAO, in order to understand the trends above. A key challenge faced in measuring undernourishment is that it is expensive to conduct nationwide household surveys on an annual basis; hence, comparable undernourishment figures are derived mathematically from two proxies. The first is based on perception surveys on inequalities in access to food, along a spectrum of regular access to food (best case), to severe food insecurity (worst case). The FAO uses the "Food Insecurity Experience Scale" to detect changes in inequality of food access, which require a smaller number of individuals/households to be surveyed. (This data is not yet made available on the FAO web page for this tool, though.)[14]

As the use of the perception survey is rather limited and may lack an objective basis for determining undernourishment levels, the FAO complements this with empirical data on the total caloric availability from food, measured in terms of dietary energy consumption per person (DEC). This is derived from the total quantity of food items available ("food supply"), and the caloric content of each food item. The quantity of food items available is based on three subfactors, namely: domestic production, food stocks, and imports (see Figure 3.1). When the computed DEC per person is less than the minimum required level of DEC per person, a particular country or area is classified as having a certain level of undernourishment.[15] Hence, undernourishment is calculated as the result of factors shaping both food availability and access.

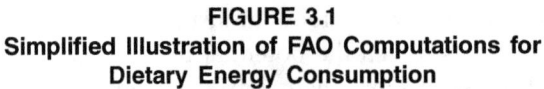

FIGURE 3.1
Simplified Illustration of FAO Computations for
Dietary Energy Consumption

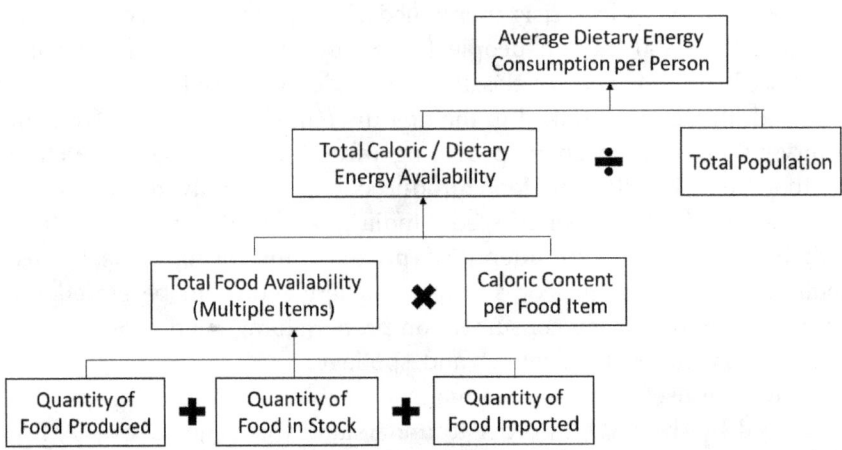

Note: The figure illustrates how the DEC is computed. First, total food available is the sum of all food products produced, imported, or kept in stock. This is then multiplied by the amount of calories per item, to derive the total number of calories available. Finally, this is divided by the population, to derive the dietary energy consumption per person.
Source: Author.

3.3   Inflection Point in Southeast Asia?

Undernourishment in Recent Years: False Alarm?

Since the start of the millennium, Southeast Asia saw substantive progress in addressing undernourishment, given increasing per capita income in the region. This can be credited to the vision of the ASEAN Economic Community, with its economic policies for improving industry and labour productivity, creating more employment opportunities, and developing greater connectivity across AMSs.[16] The region's GDP in turn increased from less than US$500 billion in 1998, to US$2.4 trillion by 2013 (current US$).[17]

Poverty, measured by the share of people living under $2 per day, fell in all countries where data was available (i.e. Cambodia, Indonesia, Lao PDR, the Philippines, Thailand and Vietnam).[18] This points to an increase in the share of people that can afford a decent meal on a daily basis, addressing the inequality/accessibility component of undernourishment. In turn, this also impacts on the food availability aspect, as the larger market of paying consumers leads farmers to increase their production targets, given the increase in revenues they could gain from intensified farm activity.

The turning point in Southeast Asia's undernourishment was apparently reached in the recent years, when 3 million more people were computed to be undernourished, from 2014 to 2016.[19] This may be a false alarm, though, given that the summarized regional statistics can be misleading when broken down into individual countries. One finds that increasing undernourishment in recent years applies only to Indonesia, from 2015 to 2017.[20] Otherwise, undernourishment either did not change (i.e. in Brunei, Cambodia, Lao PDR, the Philippines), or was reduced, as can be seen in Myanmar (400,000), Thailand (100,000) and Vietnam (500,000) (see Table 3.1).

Even if only Indonesia suffered an increase in undernourishment, it still makes up the largest share (40 per cent) of the region's total population. For this reason, even a miniscule increase in the prevalence or share of undernourished within Indonesia can have a large impact on the region's food statistics (2.5 million), outweighing improvements in other countries where undernourishment decreased.

TABLE 3.1
Undernourishment in Southeast Asia (millions), 2015–17

	2015	2016	2017
Brunei Darussalam	< 0.1	< 0.1	< 0.1
Cambodia	2.9	2.9	2.9
Indonesia	17.7	18.8	20.2
Lao PDR	1.1	1.1	1.1
Malaysia	0.9	0.9	0.9
Myanmar	6	5.7	5.6
Philippines	14.2	14.2	14.2
Singapore	No data	No data	No data
Thailand	6.3	6.3	6.2
Vietnam	10.7	10.4	10.2

Notes: 1) Figures are based on three-year averages as of that year. For instance, the 2015 figure is based on the three-year average from 2013 to 2015.
2) The FAO website reports country data only in three-year averages, while it reports regional data on an annual basis; as a result, the summed up country figures by year may differ from the regional data reported. (accessed 17 December 2018).
Source: Adapted from FAO, "Suite of Food Security Indicators", http://www.fao.org/faostat/en/#data/FS (accessed 17 December 2018).

Long-Term View: A Credible Risk

From a longer-term viewpoint, one can nonetheless observe a slow-down in the rate at which undernourishment is addressed in individual countries. In fact, what Indonesia experienced in recent years could be foreboding of potential undernourishment outcomes that can be faced by other Southeast Asian countries in the future. The long-term pattern that concluded in this outcome for Indonesia was: first, a stage of slowing progress, followed by an inflection point of zero or minimal progress, and subsequently, negative progress, or an increase in undernourishment (see Figure 3.2).

Other ASEAN countries could potentially follow this pattern in the long-term (in fact, some have already gone through it). Based on the prevalence or share (per cent) of undernourished, in fact, one can observe three batches of countries (see Figure 3.3).

- Slowing progress can be observed in Lao PDR, Myanmar and Vietnam:
  - Lao PDR: undernourishment decreased by 6.3 per cent from 2007 to 2012, but only by 3 per cent, from 2012 to 2017.
  - Myanmar: undernourishment decreased by 13.2 per cent from 2007 to 2017, but only by 4.8 per cent from 2012 to 2017.
  - Vietnam: undernourishment decreased by 4.6 per cent from 2007 to 2012, but only by 2.2 per cent from 2012 to 2017.
- Zero or minimal progress can be observed in Cambodia and Malaysia:
  - Cambodia: undernourishment decreased by less than 1 per cent (0.2 per cent) from 2012 to 2017.
  - Malaysia: undernourishment decreased by less than 1 per cent (0.6 per cent) from 2012 to 2017.
- Negative progress, or already increasing undernourishment, can be observed in the Philippines and Thailand.
  - Philippines saw an increase in undernourishment from 13 per cent in 2010 to 14.2 per cent in 2015.
  - Thailand saw an increase in undernourishment from 8.8 per cent in 2013 to 9 per cent in 2017.

FIGURE 3.2
Number of People Undernourished (million) and Share of Undernourished (three-year average)

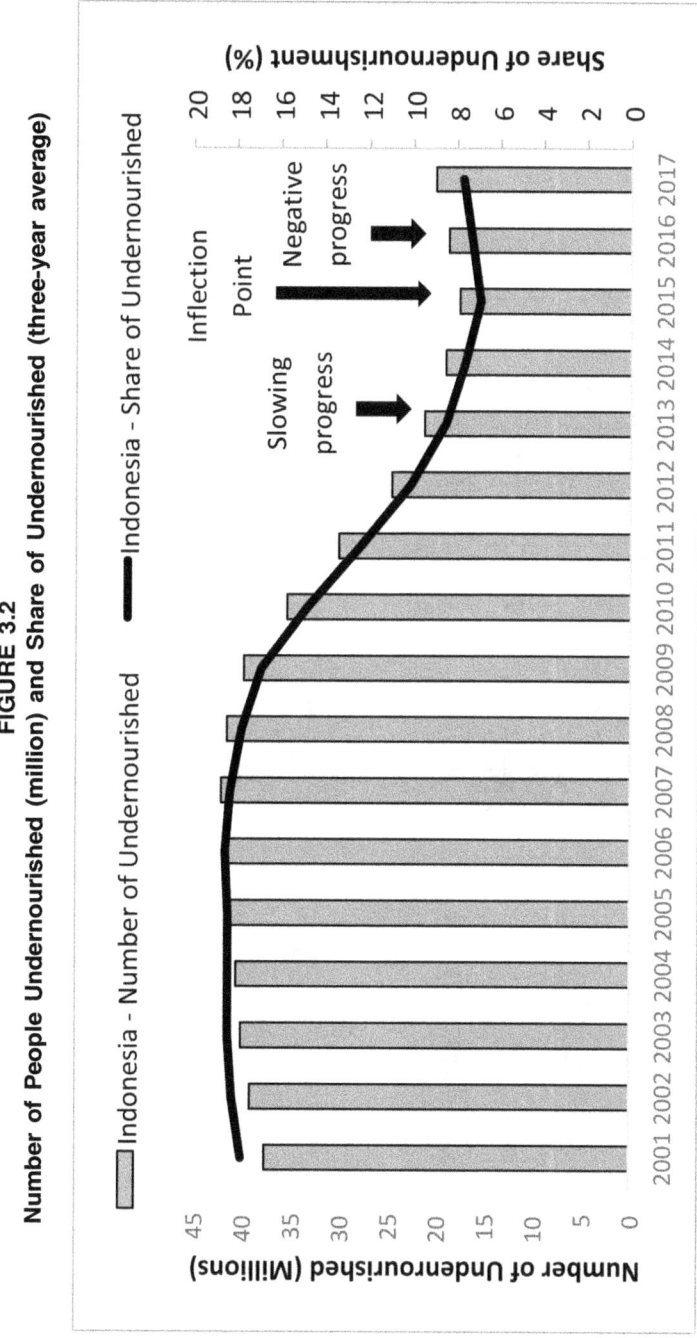

Note: Figures are based on three-year averages as of that year. For instance, the 2002 figure is based on the three-year average from 2000 to 2002.
Source: Adapted from FAO, "Suite of Food Security Indicators", http://www.fao.org/faostat/en/#data/FS (accessed 17 December 2018).

FIGURE 3.3

Changes in the Number and Share of Undernourished in Southeast Asia, 2001–17

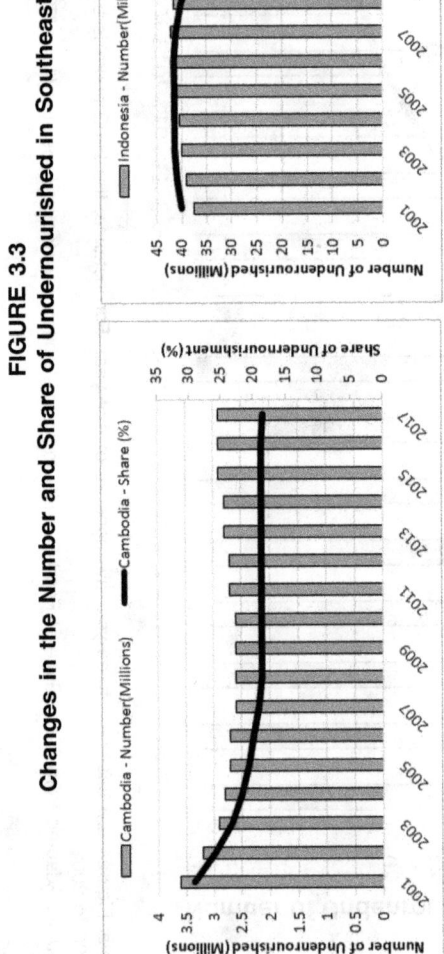

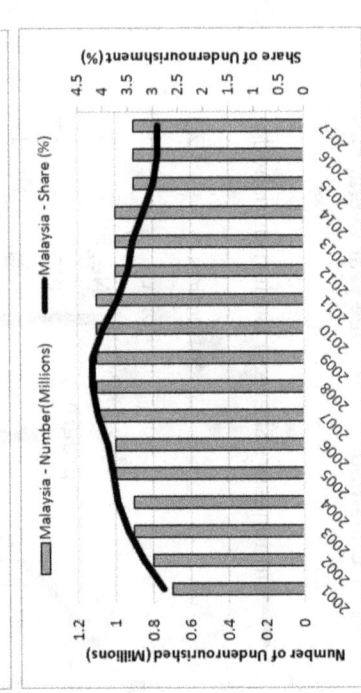

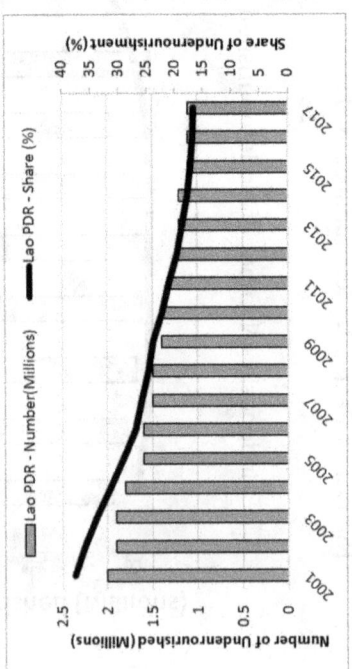

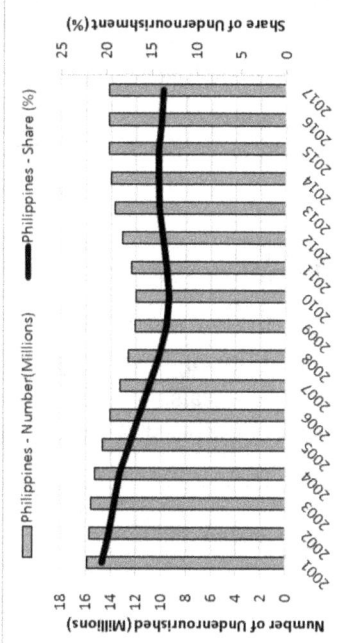

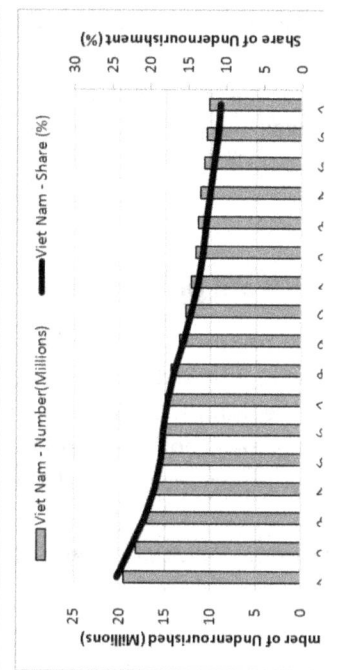

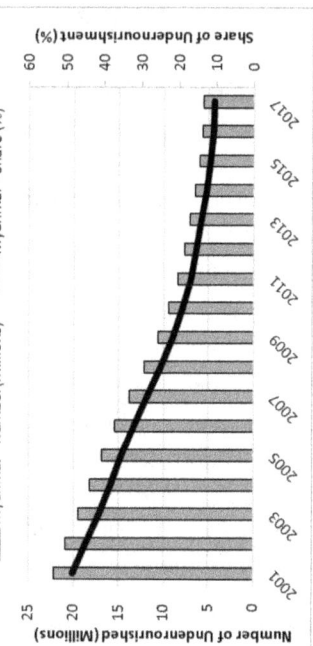

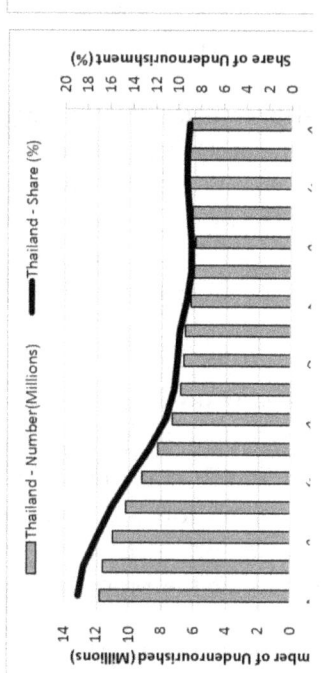

Note: Figures are based on three-year averages as of that year. For instance, the 2002 figure is based on the three-year average from 2000 to 2002. Data for Singapore is not available.

Source: Adapted from FAO, "Suite of Food Security Indicators", http://www.fao.org/faostat/en/#data/FS (accessed 17 December 2018).

These observations make an inflection point in undernourishment a credible risk to the region. In fact, if one looks at the number of undernourished (rather than the percentage), one can observe that an inflection point was already reached in earlier periods, in Cambodia (2007), Thailand (2013), the Philippines (2009), and as earlier mentioned, Indonesia (2015).

3.4   Climate Effects on Regional Undernourishment

To understand the undernourishment outcomes in Southeast Asia, it is important to look at the factors affecting the supply of food products consumed in the region. This section focuses on cereals, which make up the majority (58 per cent) of calorie-intake in Southeast Asia,[21] and the climate as an important factor shaping this.

Importance of Cereal Production in Southeast Asian Food Security

Table 3.2 shows the quantity of cereal imports as a share of the total domestic supply of cereals. A value of 1 indicates total dependence on imports, and a value of 0 indicates that the country depends totally on domestic production.[22]

One can find that majority of the region is dependent on domestic cereal production, rather than imports, with the exception of Brunei, Malaysia and Singapore.[23] Moreover, majority of rice imported by these three importing countries is also sourced from producers within the region, namely, Cambodia, Thailand and Vietnam.[24] Thus, production plays an important part of meeting consumption needs in the region.

Slower Cereal Yield Growth

Three key crops relevant to the region's cereal consumption are rice, maize and wheat, which make up 75 per cent, 13 per cent and 12 per cent of cereal consumption, respectively.[25] Given Southeast Asia's high dependence on production for meeting consumption needs, it is important to look at the production levels of farmers in producing these critical crops.

TABLE 3.2
Share of Cereal Imports out of Total Domestic Cereal Supply

	2000	2005	2010	2013
Brunei Darussalam	1.07	1.00	1.03	0.94
Cambodia	0.05	0.02	0.02	0.03
Indonesia	0.14	0.10	0.13	0.15
Lao PDR	0.02	0.03	0.02	0.01
Malaysia	0.82	0.84	0.76	0.77
Myanmar	0.01	0.01	0.01	0.01
Philippines	0.25	0.22	0.22	0.16
Singapore	1.00	1.00	1.00	1.00
Thailand	0.08	0.10	0.14	0.13
Vietnam	0.05	0.07	0.16	0.12

Notes: 1) For Singapore, a value of 1 was used given that the country does not have any
domestic rice production, although this could be more than 1 in cases when
the country re-exports its rice.
2) 2013 was the latest year available on the FAO website.
3) Figures were derived from total imports and total domestic supply, in the
FAO's Commodity Balance Sheets.

Source: Adapted from FAO, "Commodity Balances – Crops Primary Equivalent, 2013",
2018, http://www.fao.org/faostat/en/#data/BC (accessed 17 December 2018).

Domestic production depends on the land area (hectares) allocated
for food production, and the yields or amount of food produced for
every unit of land planted (tonnes per hectare). Given that farmers
cannot simply keep clearing forests to make way for more agricultural
land, farming yields have been given more emphasis than land area,
in the field of agriculture.

If we compare yields from the past three decades in the key grains
in Southeast Asia (see Figure 3.4), from 1961 to 1990, to the next decade
beginning 1990, we find that the annualized growth rates have slowed
down in Southeast Asia for cereals in general. Whereas rice yields in
the previous three decades grew by 2.1 per cent per year, they grew
by only 1.4 per cent per year in the next three decades.[26]

FIGURE 3.4
Slowing Yield Growth in Southeast Asia
(Annualized Yield Growth, for 1961–90 in comparison to 1990–2016)

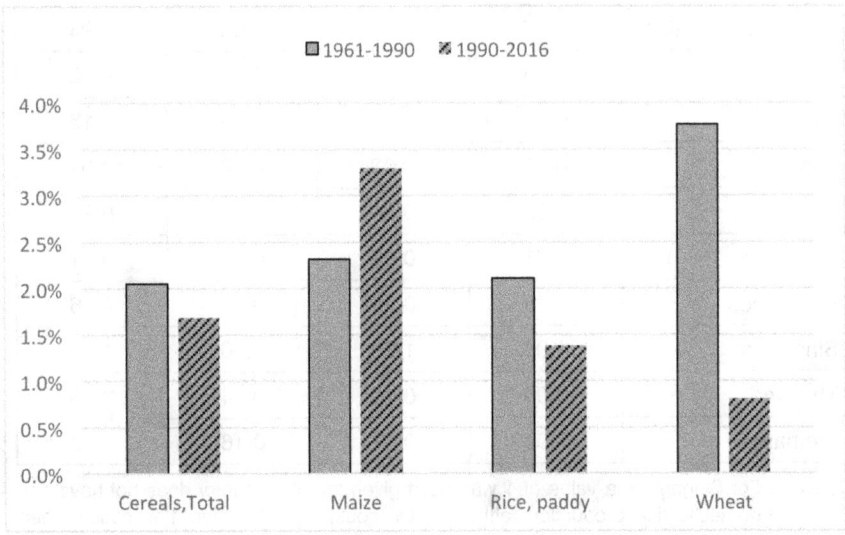

Source: Adapted from FAO, "Crops (Production), 1961–2016", 2018, http://www.fao.org/faostat/
en/#data/QC (accessed 17 December 2018).

Contributions of Changing Environments to Yield Growth Slowdowns

A number of factors can explain the change in the performance of cereal yields. Van Ittersum et al. (2013) differentiate these into yield reducing factors, such as weeds, pests/diseases and pollutants; water and nutrient supply; and factors impacting yield potential, such as carbon dioxide, radiation, temperature and features of the cultivars.[27]

1) Extreme Conditions and Disruptions

ASEAN data shows that indeed, these factors have significant impacts on farmland in the region. ASEAN Food Security Information System (AFSIS) statistics show that for the crop year 2016/17, a total of 559,724 hectares, or 1.1 per cent of the 51.2 million hectares of harvested area for rice in the region, were damaged by floods, droughts, pests, diseases and other causes.[28] Impacts are disproportionately felt by a few countries which are randomly hit by crop disruptions. For instance,

Thailand alone suffered 62.3 per cent of the total damage in crop land, at 349,082 hectares, which made up 3.6 per cent of its total rice planted areas in 2016/17.[29] Moreover, the duration of the impact is not recorded by AFSIS, such that areas which are damaged may take a long time to recover, thus causing a larger impact on food production activity.

The most critical across these factors, in the case of Southeast Asia, were water and nutrient factors, which made up 71.1 per cent of the total damaged areas, followed by pests and diseases which made up 22.4 per cent of the total damaged areas.[30] Episodes of extreme weather events have shown trends of increasing frequency. For instance, the number of floods ranged from 47 to 104 events globally from 1990 until 1999, whereas since the year 2000, this has not fallen below 106 floods, and the maximum were 196 floods (see Table 3.3).[31]

TABLE 3.3
Number of Extreme Disasters in Low- and Middle-Income in 1990–2016 (classified by FAO as "Climate-Related")

	1990–99		2000–16	
	Lowest	**Highest**	**Lowest**	**Highest**
Floods	47	104	106	196
Storms	29	51	44	80
Droughts	5	19	7	26
Extreme Temperature	2	7	6	29

Source: Adapted from FAO, "State of Food Insecurity in the World 2018 (website interface)", 2018, http://www.fao.org/state-of-food-security-nutrition/en/ (accessed 17 December 2018).

2) Long-Term Changes

Apart from extreme weather events, subtle changes in growing environments may also have important impacts on yields. The highest potential growth that can be achieved by a crop depends on whether ideal temperatures, nutrients and water supply are provided to the crops.[32] Findings of the Inter-Governmental Panel on Climate Change's (IPCC) Fifth Assessment Report (AR5) by the Second Working Group (WGII) show that Southeast Asia's temperatures have increased by an average of 0.14°C to 0.20°C per decade since the 1960s, alongside an increase in hot days and warm nights, and less days of cooler weather.[33] Annual precipitation in the average wet-day has also been observed to increase by 22 mm per decade, and in the case of extreme wet days, an increase of 10 mm per decade has been observed, although these changes differ depending on which part of Southeast Asia the farm is located. In fact, Peninsular Malaysia saw a decline in total rainfall and in the frequency of wet days during the southwest monsoon season.[34]

The impacts on rice production vary by area and by season. For instance, across seasons, the March to June rice growing season shows high risk of heat stress in Myanmar, Thailand, Laos and Cambodia, while the periods of vulnerability differ in the case of the Philippines (April or June), Vietnam (April or August) and Indonesia (August). [35] Furthermore, these growing seasons apply to different parts of the rice producing countries. Moreover, sea level rise could have an impact on cereal growing activity in coastal areas along the Mekong River Delta. As a result, the IPCC AR5 WGII notes that shifts in rice growing areas can be expected in different areas of the region. [36]

In addition to direct impacts of environmental changes on crop production, they may also affect the distribution of weeds, pests and diseases, which further reduce yields. The Asia section of the Fourth Assessment Report (AR4) of the IPCC shows that areas with cooler climates would favour the increase in insect populations.[37] These insects in turn may serve as carriers or vectors for diseases. Furthermore, while enriched carbon dioxide content in the soil stimulates further plant growth in general, a side effect of this is that weeds are provided with more nutrients to grow as well.[38]

3) Implications on Availability and Access

As the previous section has shown, yield declines brought about by changes in the environments for food production may lead to a lower DEC, unless producers are able to adapt their farming systems and technologies to minimize these impacts.

The other factor to consider is that yield declines may translate to lower incomes received by farmers, thereby reducing their own economic access to food. Moreover, extreme weather events can wipe out entire batches of crops for harvest, leading to disruptive food price inflation, as seen in the 2007–8 crisis that led to millions made undernourished, as food became less accessible to them. In fact, along a spectrum ranging from the ideal scenario, of regular access to food, to the worst case scenario, of severe food insecurity, regional estimates show that Asia saw an increase in both moderate and severe food insecurity from 2014 to 2016,[39] thus contributing to the undernourishment outcomes.

Furthermore, there are other implications of climate change on undernourishment (see Figure 3.5). For instance, extreme weather events can cause the transport of food to be delayed, so that even if there is enough produced, it may not reach consumers in urban or other rural areas. Moreover, in the absence of controlled temperatures in food storage, there is also a risk that, going beyond cereals, one can see spoilage of perishable products like eggs, fruits and vegetables, and meat.[40]

FIGURE 3.5
Mapping Out Adaptation Options

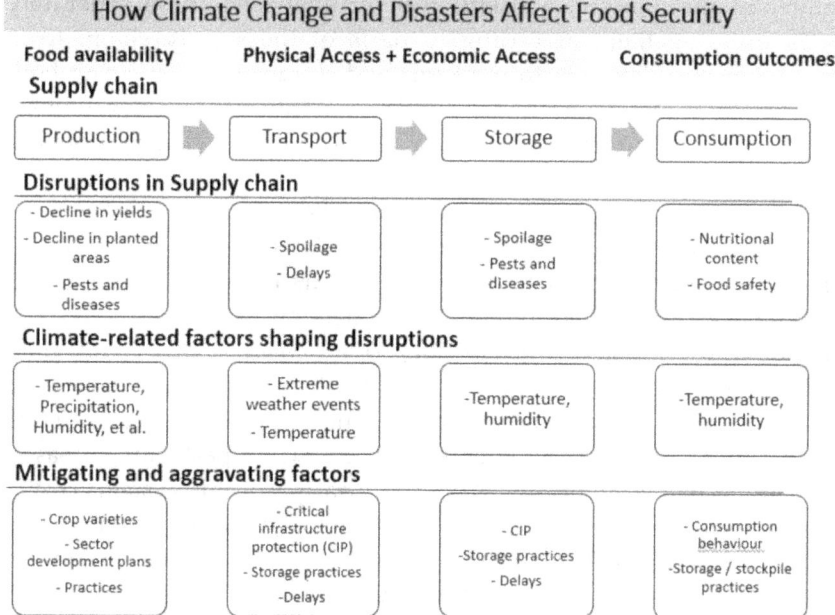

Note: "Mitigating" refers here to minimizing the impacts on agricultural yields and food security, and does not refer to minimizing emissions, which are outside the scope of this chapter.

Source: Mely Caballero-Anthony, Jose Ma. Luis Montesclaros, and Margareth Sembiring, "Evaluating the Distributional Impacts of Disasters and Climate Change and Development of Adaptation Road Maps: Rethinking ASEAN Strategy, Policies and Actions", presented at the Workshop on Roadmaps for Disaster Resilience and Climate Change Adaptation, hosted by the Economic Research Institute for East Asia and the Pacific (ERIA), Siem Reap, Cambodia, September 2018.

3.5   National and Regional Imperatives in Addressing Adaptation Gaps

Key Interventions Needed

There is no shortage in adaptation options for farmers. Figure 3.5 shows that climate change can impact on production, transport, storage, and even food consumption outcomes, through variations in temperature, humidity, precipitation, and extreme weather events. To address these, it is important to understand which factors can aggravate or mitigate the impact of climate change on the supply chain, and in turn, on consumption outcomes. Potential interventions are listed, first on the basis of facets of food security, from food availability, to physical access and economic access, and finally, food utilization (consumption outcomes). Because the food security aspects are interrelated and influence one another, a useful way of analysing these separately is by dividing them according to parts of the supply chain, from production (availability), to transport and storage (each affecting both physical and economic access), and consumption. The interventions are in relation to challenges in the face of climate change, on each supply chain stage.

A critical priority is on the production side, by halting the slowdown in yield growth in cereals, at the minimum, and ideally, to boost yield growth in order to compensate for prior years of poorer performance. This involves providing guidance to farmers on the appropriate seeds and farming systems to implement, given changes in soil (erosion; salt-water intrusion; over-fertilization which can allow weeds to spread),[41] temperatures, precipitation, and the potential eco-system changes in the form of emergence of plant-related pests and diseases. Infrastructure investments in establishing early warning systems (EWS) can also allow farmers to forecast extreme weather disruptions, while advanced crop analytics can provide farmers with advice on how to time their planting and harvesting activities.[42]

A further priority is on the side of transport and storage, through critical infrastructure protection and improvement,[43] or ensuring that transport routes (ports, roads, bridges) and storage areas for food are kept in good condition. This should be complemented by guidance to consumers in determining appropriate storage and consumption practices to minimize food spoilage, which can lead to food poisoning, as well as minimize food wastage. Similarly, guidance will be needed so that states are able to maintain sufficient food stocks to buffer against extreme weather disruptions, and in the case of ASEAN, regional stockpiles for staple commodities can be useful tools minimizing the impacts on consumption.

3.6 Regional and National Gaps in Implementing Prescribed Interventions

One of the challenges that governments may face in providing farmers with appropriate guidance, is the insufficiency of climate projections (e.g. temperature, precipitation), which form the basis for said guidance. These environmental projections are commonly available at the national level, or at the multi-country level of agro-climatic zones as categorized by the IPCC. However, impacts can vary significantly within countries, from one subnational area to another, with cooler areas benefitting from warmer growing environments, and *vice versa*. As such, presently available IPCC assessments can be too broad to be relevant to governments and communities at the subnational level.

Furthermore, even if data is available on such downscaled climate impacts, more work needs to be done in translating these into accurate and actionable advice to give to farmers.[44] This is because of the eco-system impacts of changes in temperature and humidity can go beyond just the direct impact on plants, but also touch on indirect impacts, through the growth of weeds, pests and diseases; these factors may disproportionately impact on specific crops as well, and should thus feed into subnational vulnerability assessments. Thus, another problem is the lack of research capacity to translate downscaled climate impacts into specific impacts on yields of plants, from both direct and indirect factors. A further problem is the lack of capacity to translate subnational yield assessments into vulnerability assessments, in terms of both acute and long-term undernourishment implications. If these gaps are filled, governments could be able to prioritize interventions according to their effectiveness, feasibility and viability, and focus on areas where they can make the biggest impacts in addressing undernourishment.[45]

A further gap is related to funding, as prescribed interventions can be too expensive for individual farmers to purchase, and may even fall beyond the grasp of governments. For instance, at the Workshop on Roadmaps for Disaster Resilience and Climate Change Adaptation, hosted by the Economic Research Institute for East Asia and the Pacific (ERIA), in Siem Reap, Cambodia, September 2018, government officers in Mekong countries (Cambodia, Lao PDR, Myanmar and Vietnam) shared funding gaps that prevent them from taking advantage of new technologies for adaptation. In fact, the gap was more than 92 per cent of the total budget required in Cambodia alone, and delegates and experts at the conference agreed this situation was not unique to Cambodia, but applied to other developing countries as well.[46]

At the root of the capacity gaps highlighted are gaps in national and regional policies. The first is that no specialized body exists that can be made accountable for minimizing climate impacts on agricultural yields and on food security.[47] Heading up to the 2015 Vision of the ASEAN community, agriculture had been placed under the ambit of the ASEAN Economic Community (AEC), while climate adaptation and ensuring all people across socio-economic classes are able to access food, had been under the ASEAN Socio-Cultural Community (ASCC).[48] These were somehow addressed in the AEC 2016–2025 Blueprint, where objectives were added to make agriculture more resilient to extreme weather conditions.[49] Moreover, the ASCC 2025 Blueprint now has sections focusing on social safety nets that help vulnerable populations access food. However, based on existing research output and national and regional policies, no comprehensive downscaled assessments exist. This is important because this information forms the logical starting point for diagnosing climate vulnerabilities of food supply chains in the region, from farm to fork.

3.7   Potential Improvements in Regional Approaches

A potential regional initiative is to develop a specialized body or centre, which is accountable for ensuring comprehensive downscaled climate assessments across subnational areas in all ASEAN states. This centre can also take the lead in conducting assessments on crop yield impacts per area; identifying the appropriate interventions to apply for every area; and assessing vulnerable areas, based on their poverty levels, population trends, consumption patterns, and food stocks.[50] In other words, an assessment similar to the one captured in Figure 3.5. It can be a research and coordinating centre which plays a turnkey role in drawing support from related bodies, such as private sector firms in agriculture, farming cooperatives, and government bodies, in upgrading the capacity to scale up climate adaptation initiatives in agriculture. This reduces information asymmetry among the actors, and allows the suppliers of agricultural machinery, technology, and inputs (e.g. seeds) to match the services they provide to the most pressing needs at the local level.

Apart from actors which are directly involved in production and extension services, the proposed centre may also be given a role in engaging the financial community. Financiers already provide crop insurance to a few farmers, to cushion them against the impacts of pest/disease- and weather-related disruptions to their own incomes. However, the reach of these initiatives is still limited because not all farmers are keen to take this up. Farmers may not know if the price of insurance products is fair in relation to the risk that they face. An intermediating role can thus be played by the centre, in developing a better understanding of crop insurance policies, to increase the trust of farmers, and in turn, lead to their adoption of these crop insurance products.

This centre can likewise help develop the eco-system of firms, farmers, financiers, and governments, in implementing the recommended interventions. New industries may be developed locally, for instance, in diverting information communications technology (ICT) capacities of the region, towards developing sensors that track weather and other changes, or locally-developed EWSs which monitor pertinent factors relevant to the subnational areas and crops. For instance, apart from the IPCC assessments on climate impacts, these locally developed EWSs can focus on warning indicators for factors linked to the emergence of diseases.

The envisioned centre can also conduct financial assessments of cooperative endeavours, whether it be producing downscaled assessments, or developing new agricultural technologies, to ensure that stakeholders will have sufficient incentive to buy into these, while at the same time ensuring these are financially viable by themselves, based on normal market operations. This assessment can be done by applying the same "farm-to-fork" logic which has been envisioned by the FAO. The only difference will be that in conducting such financial assessments, an important element will be to trace back the value to be acquired, from "fork-to-farm", or from the final demand for food products (consumers themselves) to the producers of crops (farmers). These assessments can help assess the potential value of interventions that help bridge adaptation gaps. Financial metrics such as the internal rate of return (IRR) of an investment, as well as land and other asset pricing assumptions, will be key to structuring these cooperative endeavours. Insights from these assessments may likewise help identify the types of inputs to supply to farmers that will be responsive to the unique challenges they face in their respective areas, in the present, and in the foreseeable future, based on downscaled assessments.

3.8 Conclusion

Southeast Asian countries face a credible risk of a reversal of their progress in addressing undernourishment. Many of AMSs are seeing a slow-down in the rate at which they are addressing this issue, and can potentially follow the example of Indonesia which, for the first time in a decade, started to see more people undernourished in 2014 (in fact, some have already gone through this).

Given the region's reliance on internally (i.e. within the region) produced cereals for majority of its consumption and daily calorie requirements, a critical issue is the slowdown in growth yields in cereals, especially in rice which makes up three-fourths of total cereal consumption. Yet, there is an insufficient information base that can allow governments to advise farmers on the appropriate interventions to implement, because most climate impact assessments available today focus on environmental changes at the national or even broader cross-national climatic areas only. Governments likewise face funding shortages in this regard.

A critical regional imperative is thus to establish a specialized body that can allow for a focused and functional multi-stakeholder approach, drawing support from farmers, companies, financiers and governments, in conducting downscaled assessments. Such assessments form the basis for identifying appropriate interventions to implement in light of projected risks and changes in environments and eco-systems. Furthermore, this body will benefit from a "fork-to-farm" analysis which assesses the total financial value which can be captured by stakeholders who participate in cooperative endeavours, thus providing them with the financial rationale to sustain their contributions to regional climate adaptation.

NOTES

1. Food and Agriculture Organisation of the United Nations (FAO), *State of Food Insecurity in the World 2018* (Rome: FAO, 2018), http://www.fao.org/3/I9553EN/i9553en.pdf.
2. Ibid.
3. Ibid.
4. Ibid.
5. Ibid.
6. FAO, International Fund for Agricultural Development (IFAD), and World Food Programme (WFP), "Glossary of Selected Terms", in *The State of Food Insecurity in the World 2015* (Rome: FAO, 2015), http://www.fao.org/hunger/glossary/en/.
7. For further reference, the reader is directed to Paul Teng and Jonatan Lassa, "Food Security", in *An Introduction to Non-Traditional Security Studies: A Transnational Approach*, edited by Mely Caballero-Anthony (Los Angeles, London, New Delhi, Singapore, Washington, D.C.: SAGE Publications, 2016).
8. Irene A. Kuntjoro, Sofiah Jamil, and Arpita Mathur, "Food", in *Non-Traditional Security in Asia: Issues, Challenges and Framework for Action*, edited by Mely Caballero-Anthony and Alistair D.B. Cook (Singapore: Institute of Southeast Asian Studies, 2013).
9. Derek Headey, "Rethinking the Global Food Crisis: The Role of Trade Shocks", *Food Policy* 36, no. 2 (2011): 136–46, https://www.sciencedirect.com/science/article/abs/pii/S0306919210001065.
10. United Nations General Assembly, "Transforming Our World: The 2030 Agenda for Sustainable Development", Resolution A/RES/70/1, adopted by the General Assembly on 25 September 2015, https://www.unfpa.org/sites/default/files/resource-pdf/Resolution_A_RES_70_1_EN.pdf.
11. *The Economist*, "Whatever Happened to the Food Crisis?" The Economist Group, 2 July 2009, http://www.economist.com/node/13944900.
12. The World Bank Group, *The World Bank Group and The Global Food Crisis: An Evaluation of the World Bank Group Response* (Washington, D.C.: The World Bank Group, 2013), http://ieg.worldbankgroup.org/evaluations/world-bank-group-and-global-food-crisis (accessed 28 August 2017).
13. Ashok Gulati, Tirtha Chatterjee, and Siraj Hussain, "Supporting Indian Farmers: Price Support or Direct Income/Investment Support?" *Working Paper No. 357* (New Delhi: Indian Council for Research on International Economic Relations, 2018), http://icrier.org/pdf/Working_Paper_357.pdf.
14. Carlo Cafiero, Sara Viviani, and Mark Nord, "Food Security Measurement in a Global Context: The Food Insecurity Experience Scale", *Measurement* 116 (February 2018): 146–52, https://doi.org/10.1016/j.measurement.2017.10.065.

15. FAO, "Suite of Food Security Indicators", 2018, http://www.fao.org/faostat/en/#data/FS (accessed 17 December 2018).
16. Mely Caballero-Anthony and Richard Barichello, *Balanced Growth for Inclusive and Equitable ASEAN Community* (Singapore: NTS Centre, RSIS, NTU, 2015), https://www.rsis.edu.sg/wp-content/uploads/2015/09/ASEAN-Canada_Balanced-Growth-for-Inclusive-and-Equitable-ASEAN-Community.pdf.
17. Andrew Beath, Yumeka Hirano, and Jose Ma Luis P. Montesclaros, *Bridging the Development Gap: ASEAN Equitable Development Monitor 2014 (English)* (Washington, D.C.: World Bank Group, 2014), http://documents.worldbank.org/curated/en/352061468232750667/Bridging-the-development-gap-ASEAN-equitable-development-monitor-2014.
18. Ibid.
19. FAO, *State of Food Insecurity in the World 2018*.
20. For each country, the average level of undernourishment over the past three years is used, based on data availability in the FAO website.
21. FAO, "Food Balance Sheet, 2013", 2018, http://www.fao.org/faostat/en/#data/FBS (accessed 17 December 2018). Note: Latest available data on share of total calories from cereals is for 2013.
22. Definition of cereal import dependency is available in FAO, "Suite of Food Security Indicators".
23. FAO, "Commodity Balances – Crops Primary Equivalent, 2013", 2018, http://www.fao.org/faostat/en/#data/BC (accessed 17 December 2018). Note: Latest available data is for 2013.
24. International Trade Centre, "International Trade in Goods – Imports 2001–2017", undated, http://www.intracen.org/itc/market-info-tools/statistics-import-product-country/ (accessed 1 February 2019).
25. FAO, "Food Balance Sheet, 2013".
26. FAO, "Crops (Production), 1961–2016", 2018, http://www.fao.org/faostat/en/#data/QC. Note: Latest available data is for 2016.
27. van Ittersum et al., "Yield Gap Analysis with Local to Global Relevance—A Review", *Field Crops Research* 143 (2013): 4–17, http://www.yieldgap.org/documents/10180/35397/2013%20FCR%20vanIttersumetal%20Yield%20Gap%20Analysis%20Review.pdf.
28. ASEAN Food Security Information System (AFSIS), *Report on Early Warning Information, No. 19* (Bangkok: AFSIS, 2017), http://www.aptfsis.org/uploads/normal/EWI%20Report%2019/EWI%2019%20-%20Sep%202017.pdf.
29. Ibid.
30. Ibid.
31. FAO, "State of Food Insecurity in the World 2018 (website interface)", 2018, http://www.fao.org/state-of-food-security-nutrition/en/.
32. van Ittersum et al., "Yield Gap Analysis with Local to Global Relevance—A Review".

33. Hijioka et al., "Asia", in *Climate Change 2014: Impacts, Adaptation, and Vulnerability. Part B: Regional Aspects. Contribution of Working Group II to the Fifth Assessment Report of the Intergovernmental Panel on Climate Change*, edited by V.R. Barros et al. (Cambridge, United Kingdom and New York, NY, USA: Cambridge University Press, 2014): 1327–70, https://www.ipcc.ch/site/assets/uploads/2018/02/WGIIAR5-Chap24_FINAL.pdf.

34. Ibid.

35. Ibid.

36. Ibid.

37. Cruz et al., "Asia", in *Climate Change 2007: Impacts, Adaptation and Vulnerability. Contribution of Working Group II to the Fourth Assessment Report of the Intergovernmental Panel on Climate Change*, edited by M.L. Parry et al. (Cambridge, UK: Cambridge University Press, 2017): 469–506, https://www.ipcc.ch/report/ar4/wg2/.

38. Ibid.

39. Cafiero, Viviani, and Nord, "Food Security Measurement in a Global Context".

40. Mely Caballero-Anthony, Jose Ma Luis Montesclaros, and Margareth Sembiring, "Evaluating the Distributional Impacts of Disasters and Climate Change and Development of Adaptation Road Maps: Rethinking ASEAN Strategy, Policies and Actions", presented at the Workshop on Roadmaps for Disaster Resilience and Climate Change Adaptation, hosted by the Economic Research Institute for East Asia and the Pacific (ERIA), Siem Reap, Cambodia, September 2018.

41. Nimai Senapati, Hamish E. Brown, and Mikhail A. Semenov, "Raising Genetic Yield Potential in High Productive Countries: Designing Wheat Ideotypes Under Climate Change", *Agricultural and Forest Meteorology* 271 (June 2019): 33–45, https://doi.org/10.1016/j.agrformet.2019.02.025.

42. Felix Rembold et al., "ASAP: A New Global Early Warning System to Detect Anomaly Hot Spots of Agricultural Production for Food Security Analysis", *Agricultural Systems* 168 (January 2019): 247–57, https://doi.org/10.1016/j.agsy.2018.07.002.

43. Cristina Alcaraz and Sherali Zeadally, "Critical Infrastructure Protection: Requirements and Challenges for the 21st Century", *International Journal of Critical Infrastructure Protection* 8 (January 2015): 53–66, https://doi.org/10.1016/j.ijcip.2014.12.002.

44. Andrew Challinor et al., "Improving the Use of Crop Models for Risk Assessment and Climate Change Adaptation", *Agricultural Systems* 159 (January 2018): 296–306, https://doi.org/10.1016/j.agsy.2017.07.010.

45. Ibid.

46. Jose Ma Luis Montesclaros, Suresh Babu, and Paul Teng, "IoT-enabled Farms and Climate-adaptive Agriculture Technologies: Investment Lessons from

Singapore", *IFPRI Discussion Paper 01805* (Washington, D.C.: International Food Policy Research Institute, 2019), http://ebrary.ifpri.org/utils/getfile/collection/p15738coll2/id/133079/filename/133287.pdf (accessed 1 March 2019).

47. Ibid.

48. Mely Caballero-Anthony et al., "Linking Climate Change Adaptation and Food Security in ASEAN", *ERIA Discussion Paper Series 2015-74* (November 2015), http://www.eria.org/ERIA-DP-2015-74.pdf.

49. Caballero-Anthony, Montesclaros, and Sembiring, "Evaluating the Distributional Impacts of Disasters and Climate Change and Development of Adaptation Road Maps".

50. Ibid.

REFERENCES

Alcaraz, Cristina and Sherali Zeadally. 2015. "Critical Infrastructure Protection: Requirements and Challenges for the 21st Century". *International Journal of Critical Infrastructure Protection* 8 (January): 53–66. https://doi.org/10.1016/j.ijcip.2014.12.002.

ASEAN Food Security Information System (AFSIS). 2017. *Report on Early Warning Information, No. 19*. Bangkok: AFSIS. http://www.aptfsis.org/uploads/normal/EWI%20Report%2019/EWI%2019%20-%20Sep%202017.pdf.

Beath, Andrew, Yumeka Hirano, and Jose Ma Luis P. Montesclaros. 2014. *Bridging the Development Gap: ASEAN Equitable Development Monitor 2014 (English)*. Washington, D.C.: World Bank Group. http://documents.worldbank.org/curated/en/352061468232750667/Bridging-the-development-gap-ASEAN-equitable-development-monitor-2014.

Caballero-Anthony, Mely, Jose Ma. Luis Montesclaros, and Margareth Sembiring. 2018. "Evaluating the Distributional Impacts of Disasters and Climate Change and Development of Adaptation Road Maps: Rethinking ASEAN Strategy, Policies and Actions". Presented at the Workshop on Roadmaps for Disaster Resilience and Climate Change Adaptation, hosted by the Economic Research Institute for East Asia and the Pacific (ERIA), Siem Reap, Cambodia, September 2018.

Caballero-Anthony, Mely, Paul Teng, Goh Tian, Maxim Shrestha, and Jonatan Lassa. 2015. "Linking Climate Change Adaptation and Food Security in ASEAN". *ERIA Discussion Paper Series 2015-74* (November). http://www.eria.org/ERIA-DP-2015-74.pdf.

Caballero-Anthony, Mely and Richard Barichello. 2015. *Balanced Growth for Inclusive and Equitable ASEAN Community*. Singapore: NTS Centre, RSIS, NTU. https://www.rsis.edu.sg/wp-content/uploads/2015/09/ASEAN-

Canada_Balanced-Growth-for-Inclusive-and-Equitable-ASEAN-Community. pdf.

Cafiero, Carlo, Sara Viviani, and Mark Nord. 2018. "Food Security Measurement in a Global Context: The Food Insecurity Experience Scale". *Measurement* 116 (February): 146–52. https://doi.org/10.1016/j.measurement.2017.10.065.

Challinor, Andrew J., Christoph Müller, Senthold Asseng, Chetan Deva, Kathryn Jane Nicklin, Daniel Wallach, Eline Vanuytrecht, Stephen Whitfield, Julian Ramirez-Villegas, and Ann-Kristin Koehler. 2018. "Improving the Use of Crop Models for Risk Assessment and Climate Change Adaptation". *Agricultural Systems* 159 (January): 296–306. https://doi.org/10.1016/j. agsy.2017.07.010.

Cruz, R.V., H. Harasawa, M. Lal, S. Wu, Y. Anokhin, B. Punsalmaa, Y. Honda, M. Jafari, C. Li, and N. Huu Ninh. 2017. "Asia". In *Climate Change 2007: Impacts, Adaptation and Vulnerability. Contribution of Working Group II to the Fourth Assessment Report of the Intergovernmental Panel on Climate Change*, edited by M.L. Parry, O.F. Canziani, J.P. Palutikof, P.J. van der Linden, and C.E. Hanson. Cambridge, UK: Cambridge University Press, pp. 469–506. https://www.ipcc.ch/report/ar4/wg2/.

Food and Agriculture Organisation of the United Nations (FAO). 2018. "Commodity Balances – Crops Primary Equivalent, 2013". http://www. fao.org/faostat/en/#data/BC.

———. 2018. "Crops (Production), 1961–2016". http://www.fao.org/faostat/ en/#data/QC.

———. 2018. "Food Balance Sheet, 2013". http://www.fao.org/faostat/en/#data/ FBS.

———. 2018. *State of Food Insecurity in the World 2018*. Rome: FAO. http:// www.fao.org/3/I9553EN/i9553en.pdf.

———. 2018. "State of Food Insecurity in the World 2018 (website interface)". http://www.fao.org/state-of-food-security-nutrition/en/.

———. 2018. "Suite of Food Security Indicators". http://www.fao.org/faostat/ en/#data/FS.

FAO, International Fund for Agricultural Development (IFAD), and World Food Programme (WFP). 2015. "Glossary of Selected Terms". In *The State of Food Insecurity in the World 2015*. Rome: FAO. http://www.fao.org/ hunger/glossary/en/.

Gulati, Ashok, Tirtha Chatterjee, and Siraj Hussain. 2018. "Supporting Indian farmers: Price Support or Direct Income/Investment Support?" *Working Paper No. 357*. New Delhi: Indian Council for Research on International Economic Relations. http://icrier.org/pdf/Working_Paper_357.pdf.

Headey, Derek. 2011. "Rethinking the Global Food Crisis: The Role of Trade Shocks". *Food Policy* 36, no. 2: 136–46. https://www.sciencedirect.com/ science/article/abs/pii/S0306919210001065.

Hijioka, Y., E. Lin, J.J. Pereira, R.T. Corlett, X. Cui, G.E. Insarov, R.D. Lasco, E. Lindgren, and A. Surjan. 2014. "Asia". In *Climate Change 2014: Impacts, Adaptation, and Vulnerability. Part B: Regional Aspects. Contribution of Working Group II to the Fifth Assessment Report of the Intergovernmental Panel on Climate Change*, edited by V.R. Barros, C.B. Field, D.J. Dokken, M.D. Mastrandrea, K.J. Mach, T.E. Bilir, M. Chatterjee, K.L. Ebi, Y.O. Estrada, R.C. Genova, B. Girma, E.S. Kissel, A.N. Levy, S. MacCracken, P.R. Mastrandrea, and L.L. White. Cambridge, United Kingdom and New York, NY, USA: Cambridge University Press, pp. 1327–70. https://www.ipcc.ch/site/assets/uploads/2018/02/WGIIAR5-Chap24_FINAL.pdf.

International Trade Centre. Undated. "International Trade in Goods – Imports 2001–2018". http://www.intracen.org/itc/market-info-tools/statistics-import-product-country/ (accessed 1 February 2019).

Kuntjoro, Irene A., Sofiah Jamil, and Arpita Mathur. 2013. "Food". In *Non-Traditional Security in Asia: Issues, Challenges and Framework for Action*, edited by Mely Caballero-Anthony and Alistair D.B. Cook. Singapore: Institute of Southeast Asian Studies.

Montesclaros, Jose Ma. Luis, Suresh Babu, and Paul Teng. 2019. "IoT-enabled Farms and Climate-adaptive Agriculture Technologies: Investment Lessons from Singapore". *IFPRI Discussion Paper 01805*. Washington, D.C.: International Food Policy Research Institute. http://ebrary.ifpri.org/utils/getfile/collection/p15738coll2/id/133079/filename/133287.pdf (accessed 1 March 2019).

Rembold, Felix, Michele Meroni, Ferdinando Urbano, Gabor Csak, Hervé Kerdiles, Ana Perez-Hoyos, Guido Lemoine, Olivier Leo, and Thierry Negre. 2019. "ASAP: A New Global Early Warning System to Detect Anomaly Hot Spots of Agricultural Production for Food Security Analysis". *Agricultural Systems* 168 (January): 247–57. https://doi.org/10.1016/j.agsy.2018.07.002.

Senapati, Nimai, Hamish E. Brown, and Mikhail A. Semenov. 2019. "Raising Genetic Yield Potential in High Productive Countries: Designing Wheat Ideotypes Under Climate Change". *Agricultural and Forest Meteorology* 271 (June): 33–45. https://doi.org/10.1016/j.agrformet.2019.02.025.

Teng, Paul and Jonatan Lassa. 2016. "Food Security". In *An Introduction to Non-Traditional Security Studies: A Transnational Approach*, edited by Mely Caballero-Anthony. Los Angeles, London, New Delhi, Singapore, Washington, D.C.: SAGE Publications.

The Economist. 2009. "Whatever Happened to the Food Crisis?" The Economist Group, 2 July 2009. http://www.economist.com/node/13944900.

The World Bank Group. 2013. *The World Bank Group and The Global Food Crisis: An Evaluation of the World Bank Group Response*. Washington, D.C.: The World Bank Group. http://ieg.worldbankgroup.org/evaluations/world-bank-group-and-global-food-crisis (accessed 28 August 2017).

United Nations General Assembly. 2015. "Transforming Our World: The 2030 Agenda for Sustainable Development". Resolution A/RES/70/1, adopted by the General Assembly on 25 September 2015. https://www.unfpa.org/sites/default/files/resource-pdf/Resolution_A_RES_70_1_EN.pdf.

van Ittersum, Martin K., Kenneth G. Cassman, Patricio Grassini, Joost Wolf, Pablo Tittonell, and Zvi Hochman. 2013. "Yield Gap Analysis with Local to Global Relevance—A Review". *Field Crops Research 143*: 4–17. http://www.yieldgap.org/documents/10180/35397/2013%20FCR%20vanIttersumetal%20Yield%20Gap%20Analysis%20Review.pdf.

4

MARINE ENVIRONMENTAL PROTECTION IN THE SOUTH CHINA SEA

Lina Gong, Julius Cesar I. Trajano,
Margareth Sembiring and Rini Astuti

4.1   Marine Environmental Degradation: An Increasing NTS Threat

The importance of oceans and seas for mankind is increasingly recognized by the international community. The inclusion of an ocean-related goal into the Sustainable Development Goals (SDGs), namely SDG 14 "Life below Water", is a move to this end. Further development of this momentum has been seen in 2019, with important international meetings convened to discuss necessary policies and initiatives for saving the marine environment. Among the many meetings, the first Ocean Conference convened by the United Nations (UN) in June 2017 in New York was the most high-profile.[1] This was followed by the High-level Political Forum (HLPF) for Sustainable Development in July 2017, during which the protection of marine biodiversity in the high seas was discussed amidst a host of sustainable development issues.[2] These high-level events have successfully shaped the perspectives of the policymakers, increasing global attention towards the health of our oceans. During the Ocean Conference this year, the UN, governments, non-governmental organizations (NGOs), regional institutions, the private sector, the scientific community, and other stakeholders offered more than 1,400 voluntary commitments, pledging to take action in saving our shared marine environment.[3]

In Southeast Asia, where water bodies account for over two thirds of the region's area, these voluntary commitments, if translated into policies, may have important implications. The South China Sea (SCS), an important body of water in the region, has attracted growing international attention in recent years for maritime disputes involving several claimants, which include Brunei, the People's Republic of China, Taiwan, Malaysia, Indonesia, the Philippines, and Vietnam. Marine environmental protection has been overshadowed by maritime disputes in regional and international security discourses. For instance, between 2009 and 2016, the number of news reports that covered the maritime disputes was 8,795 as compared to 25 news reports on environmental protection.[4]

The same tendency to prioritize territorial disputes was also observed in official discourse. For instance, in the Chairman's Statement of the 30th ASEAN Summit in Manila in April 2017, the SCS was the first issue of the section on regional and international issues, followed by maritime security and cooperation that included maritime environment. It was only in November 2017, at the 20th ASEAN-China Summit in Manila, when state leaders agreed to pay attention to the marine environment in the SCS with the issuance of the Declaration for the Decade of Coastal and Marine Environmental Protection in the South China Sea (2017–2027).[5] This joint declaration may hopefully jumpstart the cooperation needed to prevent the deterioration of the marine environment in the SCS. It indicates the realization among SCS states that urgent cooperative actions are necessary despite the unresolved territorial disputes among them.

As mentioned earlier, the international will to protect marine environments is evidently growing. The translation of such commitments into effective policies, actions, and cooperation in the SCS will be examined in this study. This non-traditional security (NTS) insight is one of a series of two that evaluates the current marine environmental challenges facing the Southeast Asian nations around the SCS. It examines the environmental risks induced by human activities and climate change, and explores collaborative opportunities and mechanisms to enhance regional governance and protection of the SCS and other seas in the region.

The debate on maritime security has been framed as a sovereignty dilemma as opposed to environmental protection. This is also the case in the SCS. The question remains whether littoral states can cooperate on marine environmental protection despite nationalist rhetoric and overlapping territorial claims. Moving away from thorny sovereignty issues, we seek to engage in the debate on maritime security from a NTS perspective, which is non-state centric and collaborative. We are offering a different framing on maritime security while recognizing that a NTS perspective is not the only non-state centric framework that can be used in examining this multifaceted issue. Using a NTS perspective, we call for balanced attention to both traditional and non-traditional security issues identified in the 2002 Declaration of Conduct of the Parties in the South China Sea, such as maritime scientific research, maritime search and rescue, transnational crimes, and marine environmental protection. This balance may facilitate and advance collaboration in these contested waters. Furthering the discussion, this section examines the security implications of marine environmental degradation for Southeast Asia, especially how they are magnified by climate change.

Importance of Marine Environment from a NTS Perspective

The ramifications of ocean-related problems are not limited to the sphere of economic development but also felt in the realm of security. NTS issues refer to non-military challenges that pose imminent threats to state security and people's well-being. The emergence of the NTS notion in the international, particularly East Asian, security discourse is a result of broadening security agendas. Environmental concerns have been viewed as a security issue by many people in the international community since the 1987 Brundtland Report that explicitly acknowledges the threat posed by environmental crisis to national security and human security.[6] In 1992, the UN Conference on Environment and Development lifted the environmental discourse to a higher level by bringing it to a more influential audience.[7] Environmental security issues made further headways into the international security agenda as the UN Security Council convened meetings in 2007 and 2011 to discuss the implications of climate change for international peace and security.

Ocean-related problems should be part of the environmental security discourse. The oceans play a critical role in ensuring human security as challenges to the marine environment have important implications for food security, health security, economic security and environmental security. In 2015, the World Wildlife Fund (WWF) estimated that oceans were worth US$24 trillion, a value equal to the 7th largest economy in the world.[8] According to the Food and Agriculture Organization of the United Nations (FAO), the value of exports of fishery products, inedible fish by-products and aquatic plants was US$130.6 billion in 2012.[9] The ocean economy that includes sectors like fishery, aquaculture, and marine and coastal tourism creates hundreds of millions of jobs, with more than 10 per cent of the world's population relying on the marine economic sectors for livelihoods, most of whom are in developing countries.[10] In East Asia, a majority of regional countries are either island states or have long coast lines. Hence, the importance of the seas is even more evident in the region. Marine economy accounted for 9.5 per cent of China's national GDP in 2016 and created 35.5 million jobs. China's fishery output accounted for one third of the world's total in 2013, generating a trade surplus in fishery of US$11.6 billion.

Fish is also a major source of protein for people in Southeast Asia. For instance, nearly 40 per cent of the animal protein supply in the Philippines comes from fish and seafood, and over 50 per cent in Indonesia. The consumption of seafood is projected to grow in the future as more countries in the region are reaching middle-income levels. The quality and safety of seafood and aquacultural products have important bearings on people's health security. Accumulation and concentration of toxic matters and heavy metals in sea creatures threaten the health of people who consume contaminated seafood. Apart from enhancing various components of human security, oceans are also essential regulators of the global climate, absorbing about 30 per cent of carbon dioxide generated by human activities.[11] Marine and coastal ecosystems are rich in biodiversity, housing over 200,000 identified species and millions of unidentified ones.[12] Marine plants play a critical role in protecting shorelines in the face of extreme weather events that are becoming more frequent as a result of climate change. Sea level rise, induced by global warming, translates to flooding and salt intrusion. Increased salinity means death of mangroves and reduced agricultural productivity. In Vietnam, for instance, 85 per cent of flooding will occur in the Mekong River Delta affecting mainly agriculture and aquaculture lands, and a one-metre sea level rise will impact six million people. In Malaysia, sea level rise may inundate 1,000 km^2 of agricultural lands and displace more than 0.05 million people in 2100. Therefore, protecting the marine environment is vital for global efforts to combat the impacts of climate change.

In addition, it is argued in some research that illegal, unreported and unregulated (IUU) fishing breeds other NTS threats such as human trafficking, slavery, piracy, other organized transnational crimes and even terrorism. Marine environments can become a challenge to traditional security in the sense that depletion of marine resources like fish stocks fuels competition between states and strains interstate relations. For instance, fishing boats from some countries are confiscated for poaching by their neighbours. Indonesia destroyed 81 fishing boats from Vietnam, the Philippines, Malaysia and China in April 2017. Malaysia burned two fishing boats from a neighbouring country in August 2017. Such cases add complications to efforts addressing maritime disputes, and even instigate tensions between agents of traditional/state security. It is thus imperative to carry out effective protection of the seas, like curbing IUU and promoting sustainable exploitation of marine resources, so as to prevent the issue from becoming more threatening to human security and regional peace.

Causes of Environmental Degradation in the SCS

SCS is one of the world's most diverse marine ecosystems, hosting 76 per cent of the world's coral species and 37 per cent of reef-fish species.[13] It is home to more than 8,600 species of marine plants and animals.[14] However, the marine environment in the SCS is without an overarching environmental regime. Environmental degradation in the SCS has reached an alarming point. According to the Southeast Asian Fisheries Development Centre in Bangkok, 30 per cent of seagrass, 16 per cent of mangroves, and 16 per cent of live coral cover are lost every ten years since 2007.[15]

Human-induced Pollution

The targets of SDG 14 identify land-based activities as the main sources of marine pollution. Marine biologists estimate that human activities have destroyed 16,200 hectares of coral reefs, nearly 10 per cent of the total reefs in the SCS.[16] The current rate of reef destruction translates to the SCS littoral states suffering a US$6 billion a year in potential economic loss.[17] Human-induced pollution includes discharge of untreated domestic and industrial waste, port and harbor operations, agricultural and aquaculture production, and mining activity. For instance, it is common in countries bordering the SCS to convert coastal areas to aquaculture farms, particularly for shrimp farming.[18] The resulting contaminants include pathogenic bacteria, nutrient and organic matter, heavy metals and toxic particles, which cause pollution in a variety of forms like red tide, algal bloom, and poisoning and death of marine creatures.[19] Such practices are detrimental to mangrove habitats, resulting in the loss of 16 per cent of mangroves in the SCS every ten years, according to an estimate in 2007.[20]

Unsustainable exploitation of resources constitutes another major stressor on the marine environment in the SCS. It includes overfishing and IUU fishing. Southeast Asia and China together account for around 25 per cent of the world's total population, many of whom have improved living conditions brought about by the region's fast economic development.[21] Unsustainable fishing in the region is driven by the growing appetite for seafood. As domestic consumption expands, China's fishermen tend to overfish, depleting China's own fish resources. Surging market demands have driven Chinese fishing fleets to explore oceans afar, which is criticized by experts as threatening the global fishery.[22] However, the depletion of fish stocks is not a unique problem of China, but is also seen in Southeast Asian countries. Ninety per cent of fishing vessels in Indonesian waters have no permits. Ten out of 13 designated fishing grounds in the Philippine waters are overfished.[23] Moreover, destructive fishing practices like bottom trawling and the use of poison and explosives pose a serious threat to coral reefs in the SCS. Sixteen per cent of coral reefs will be lost every ten years based on an estimate in 2007.[24]

Other forms of anthropogenic pollution include land reclamation, plastic waste, and unsustainable tourism. Among the top ten countries in the world that throw plastic waste into the oceans, five are around the SCS—China, Indonesia, the Philippines, Vietnam and Malaysia.[25] Plastic waste pollutes the seas, releasing toxins in the dissolving process. The toxic chemicals can enter human food chains via fish that consume the toxins.[26] Plastic waste can be life-threatening to sea creatures swallowing big pieces of plastic debris.[27] Such hazardous waste can alter the marine ecosystems, having a ripple effect across the global hydrospheric environment. In view of the detrimental impacts of human activities in the SCS, these unsustainable practices should be targeted in the efforts to protect the sea.

Climate Change Effects in the SCS

Climate variability poses an even more pressing challenge to marine protection. Marine environments play an important role in mitigating climate change impacts. Bodies of water, for example, are capable of absorbing carbon dioxide from the air while coral reefs and mangroves can provide natural breaks against storm surges. At the same time, however, the marine habitats are "victims" of the changing climate itself as warming sea surface temperatures, increasing sea salinity, rising sea levels, and other climate-related changes pose threats to marine ecosystem.

Broad assessments at global and regional levels have identified the general trends of climate change impacts on the marine environment. The Intergovernmental Panel on Climate Change (IPCC), however, points out that these assessments alone are not enough. This point is clearly demonstrated by the large variations of sea level rise from one region to another.[28] As such, there is a need to downscale these studies to a local level in order to enable better understanding of future climate-related scenarios and consequences at more specific locales.

This observation applies to the SCS as well. The SCS, although often referred to as a single body of water, is not a uniform entity. Different parts of the SCS are impacted differently by climate variability.[29] For example, changes in water temperature and salinity vary across the SCS, and also between coastal and offshore areas (as illustrated in Figures 4.1a and 4.1b). As indicated in Figure 4.1a, the circled region has experienced varying surface temperature changes ranging from approximately 0.2 to 1 degree Celsius between 1958 and 2014 illustrating differential heating of surface waters of the SCS. Similarly, Figure 4.1b illustrates salinity level changes within the SCS ranging from around −0.4 to −0.8 between 1958 and 2008.[30]

Another indication of the different effects of climate change on the SCS is in the concentrations of chlorophyll-a.[31] As shown in Figure 4.2, between 1958 and 2014 the concentrations of chlorophyll-a increased by up to 0.2 mg/m-3 along the coastal lines of Vietnam but decreased by close to 0.2 mg/m-3 along coastal lines of northwestern Borneo island. The changes of chlorophyll-a concentrations appear to range from −0.05 to 0.05 mg/m-3 in different offshore areas of the SCS. These concentrations will be affected by increased rainfall brought about by rising sea surface temperatures.[32]

FIGURE 4.1

Different Parts of the South China Sea Experience Different Degrees of Changes in Sea Surface Temperature between 1958 and 2014 and Sea Surface Salinity between 1958 and 2008

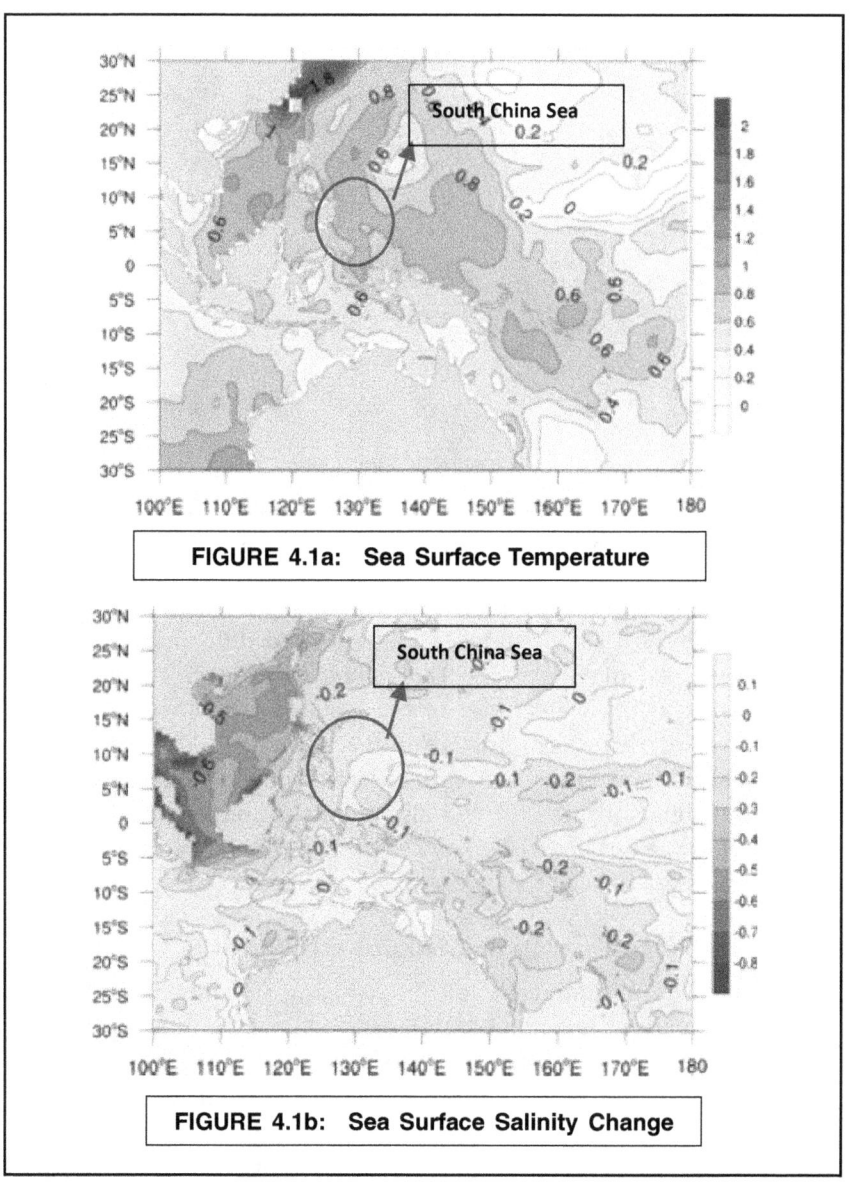

FIGURE 4.1a: Sea Surface Temperature

FIGURE 4.1b: Sea Surface Salinity Change

Note: The circled South China Sea area is an approximate illustration.
Source: Cai et al. (2017), p. 165.

FIGURE 4.2
Changes in Chlorophyll-a Concentrations are Not Uniform within the South China Sea area

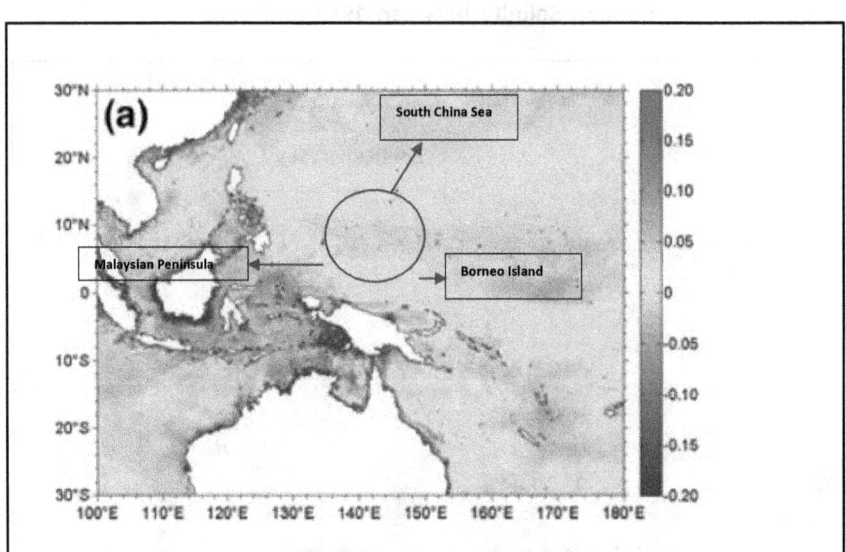

Note: The circled South China Sea area is an approximate illustration.
Source: Cai et al. (2017), pp. 163–76.

Additionally, sea level rise will be experienced differently across the SCS as illustrated in Figure 4.3. The estimated changes range from 2 to 4 mm/year at the waters east of the Malaysian peninsula to 4 to 6 mm/year off northwestern coast of Borneo island.

Due to differences in distinct variables mentioned above, the impacts on marine habitats in the SCS will also vary. Possible effects of climate variability on mangroves, fisheries, seagrass and coral reefs are briefly described below.

1) Climate Change Impacts on Mangroves in the SCS

Mangroves have a significant role in reducing flooding risk, as they provide protection against coastal erosion and inundation. Their underground root networks and complex vegetation structure are capable of reducing waves by 75 per cent.[33] Mangroves along the margins of the SCS basin are important as they make up 11 per cent of world's mangroves.[34] While the distribution of mangroves seem to cover most areas surrounding the SCS basin as shown in Figure 4.4,

FIGURE 4.3
The Different Degrees of Sea Level Changes in the South China Sea

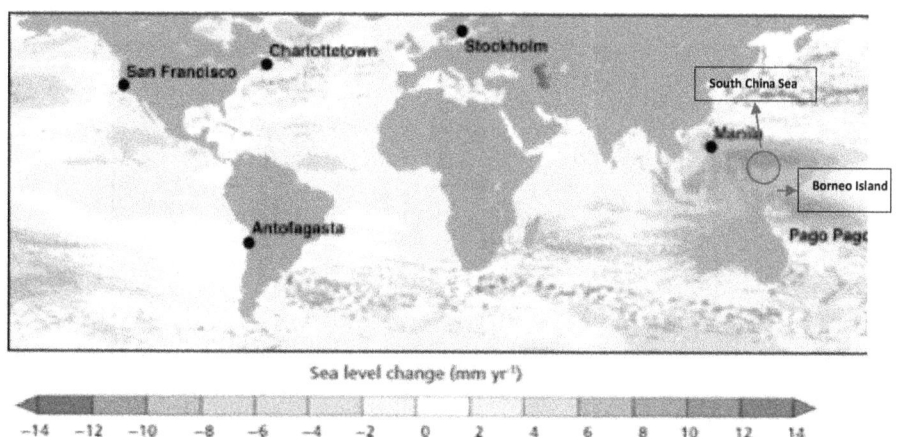

Note: The illustration is taken from the original report by Ove Hoegh-Guldberg et al. where they used the cities of Manila, Pago Pago, Stockholm, Charlottetown, San Francisco and Antofagasta in their study. The circled South China Sea area is an approximate illustration.

Source: Hoegh-Guldberg et al. (2014), pp. 1655–731.

the decreasing mangrove population at an annual rate of 1.61 per cent between 1990 and 2000, which was higher than the rate of the world average at 1.04 per cent during the same period,[35] poses a cause for concern. Such reduction signifies reduced natural barriers against flood risk in coastal areas of littoral states in the SCS.

Climate change-induced sea level rise, warming sea surface temperatures, precipitation and storminess would affect mangroves in a significant way. Increased salinity also affects mangrove growth and has the potential to damage plant life.[36] Sea level rise and attendant coastal inundation are the biggest threats to mangrove ecosystems, although certain types of mangroves can be more resilient.[37] It is broadly projected that more resilient mangrove species would be able to adapt to sea-level rise by moving landwards. However, their pathways may be blocked by natural or artificial hard structures.[38] Additionally, global warming brought about by greenhouse gas emission, which is also responsible for climate change, has resulted in mangroves expanding polewards worldwide.[39] Due to the large variants and wide distribution of mangroves species,[40] effects of climate change may vary from one

FIGURE 4.4
Mangrove Distribution in Asia, 2010–15

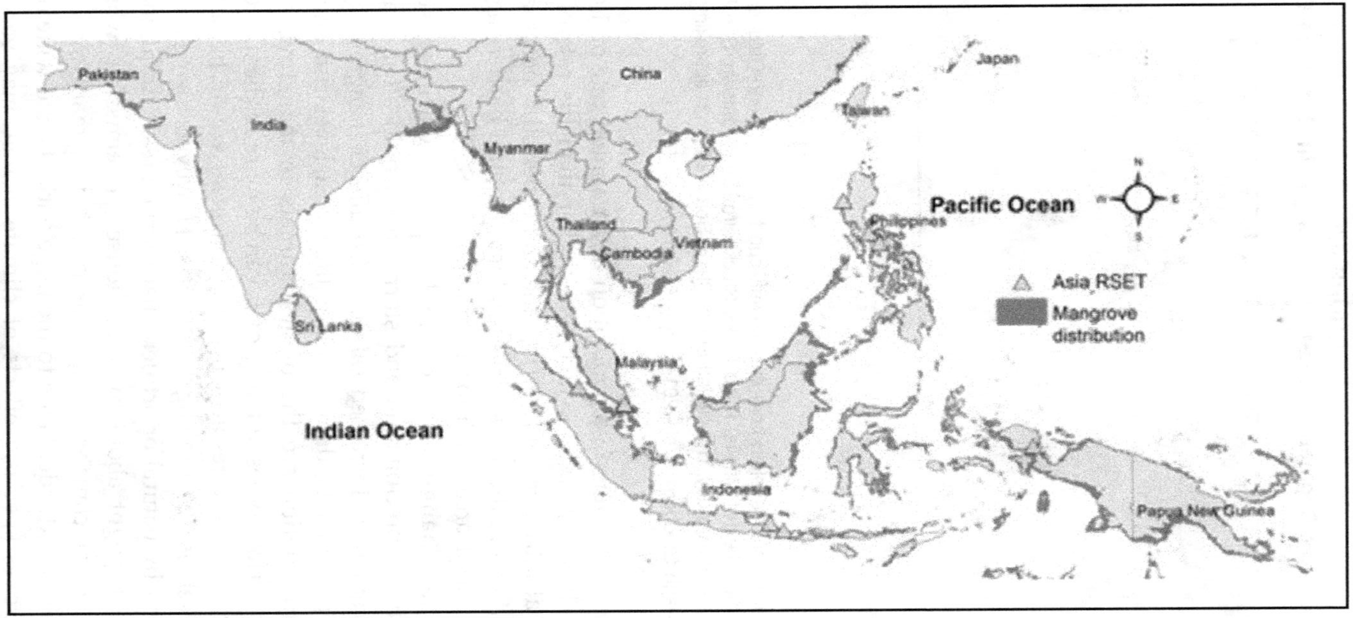

Source: Giri et al. (2011), pp. 154–59.

region to another. There is a dearth of regional and localized studies on these effects.[41]

2) Climate Change Impacts on Fisheries in the SCS

A study on terrestrial habitats' response to climate change found that terrestrial animal and plant species have been moving away from the equator at around 20 cm per hour in the last forty years. In addition, it is projected to continue doing so until at least the end of this century.[42] It appears that several marine species are exhibiting similar behaviour. A study by the US Navy confirmed fish migration northwards.[43] This is further observed in the projections of catch potential which show an overall decrease particularly in tropical areas. Figure 4.5 illustrates temperature increases and corresponding fish stock depletion. In tropical waters, where the SCS is located, subtropical fish species have already decreased significantly, following a change in average sea surface temperatures between 1970 and 2000. With a projected continuous rise in temperature, even the typically tropical or warm-water fish species may leave tropical waters, causing severe fish stock depletion along the tropical areas.

The impacts on fish stock in tropical waters can further be illustrated in the projected change in catch potential. Figure 4.6 shows that between 2005 and 2055, parts of the SCS will experience a wide range of changes in maximum catch potential (with some areas losing 5 to 16 per cent while others experiencing an increase of up to 16 to 30 per cent).[44] The sizes of fish are projected to shrink as well. A study suggests that increasing sea temperatures may reduce fish size by 14 to 24 per cent globally from 2000 to 2050.[45]

3) Climate Change Impacts on Seagrass in the SCS

Eighteen out of the 60 seagrass species in the world are found in or adjacent to SCS.[46] It is broadly predicted that seagrass is heading towards extinction due to anthropogenic activities such as irrigation, coastal developments, wastewater discharge and fisheries development.[47] About 30 to 40 per cent of seagrass beds have disappeared in Indonesia, while the figures stand at 20 to 30 per cent in Thailand and 30 to 50 per cent in the Philippines.[48] Patchy seagrass has been severely damaged in Singapore due to landfill activities.[49] The destruction of seagrass habitats is damaging not only to marine biodiversity, but also to the economy and food security. This is because seagrass beds provide

FIGURE 4.5
Fish Stocks from Tropical Waters, including the South China Sea, May Reduce in the Future as They Move Toward More Temperate or Cooler Seas

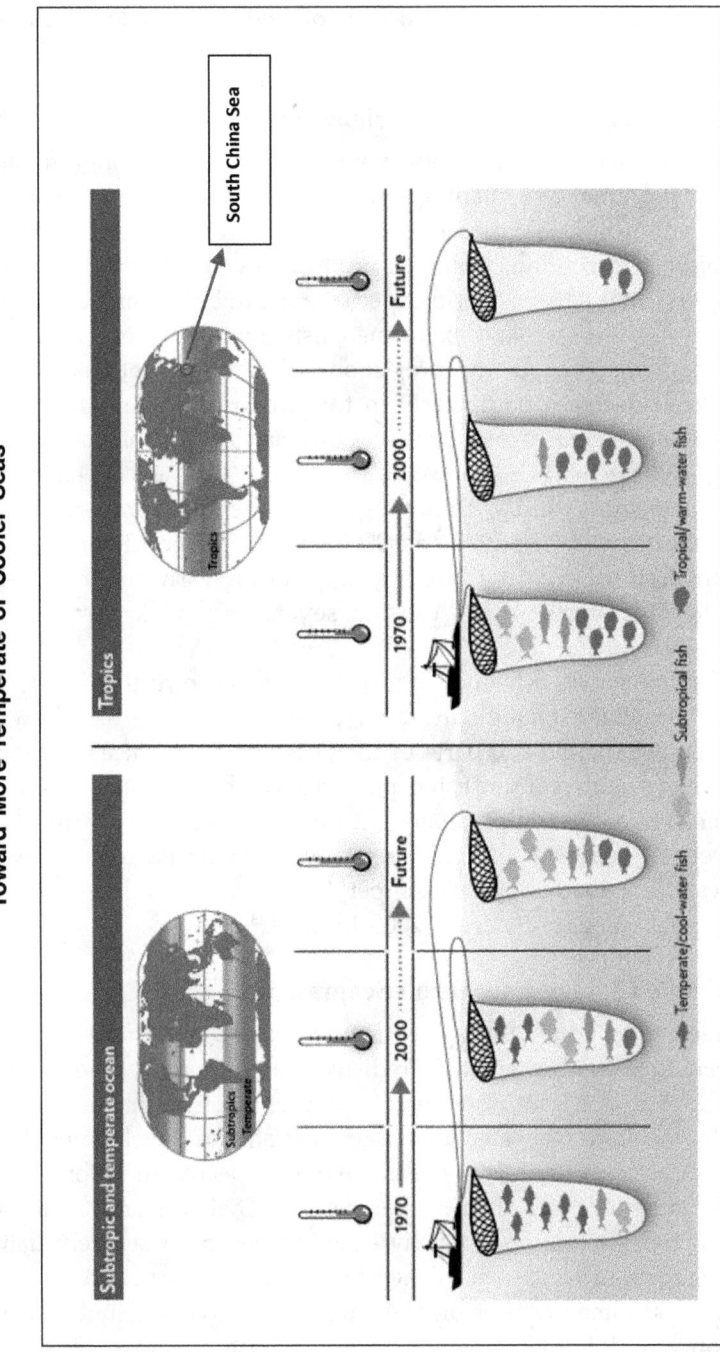

Source: The Pew Charitable Trusts (2013).

FIGURE 4.6
Change in Maximum Catch Potential between 2005 and 2055 based on a Climate Change Scenario in the Special Report on Emission Scenarios A1B

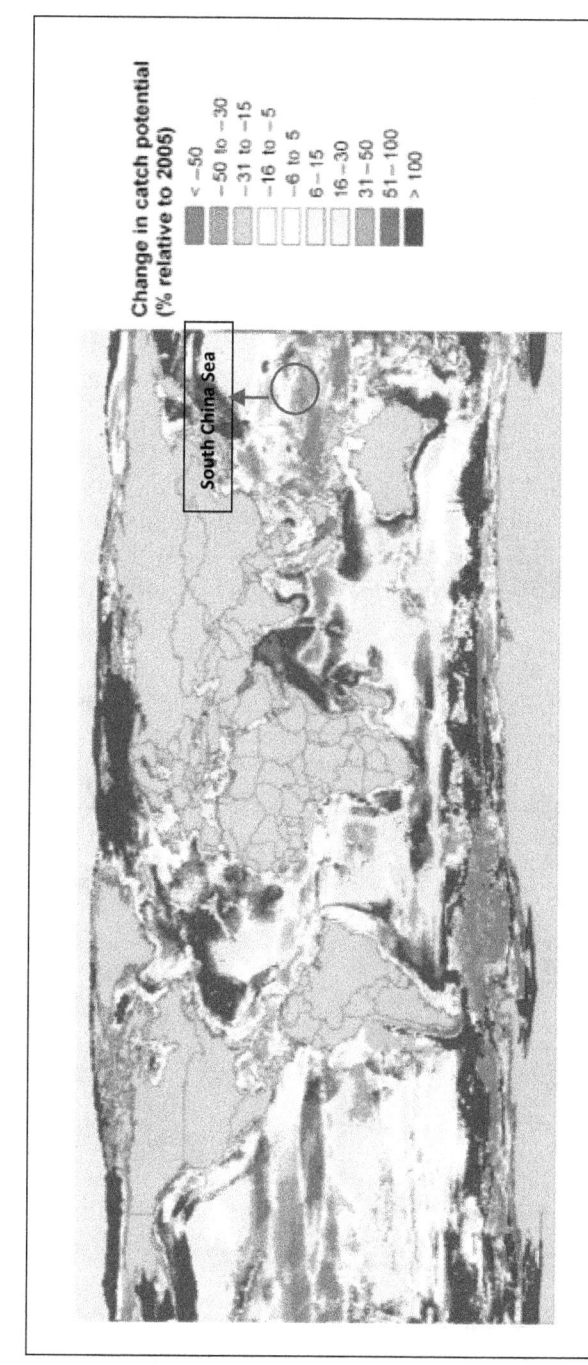

Note: The circled South China Sea area is an approximate illustration.

Source: Cheung et al. (2013a).

spawning spaces for fish.[50] As seagrass also serves as food to certain types of fishes (such as rabbitfish and wrasse), depleting seagrass means reducing fish stocks for human consumption.

4) Climate Change Impacts on Coral Reefs in the SCS

Coral reefs in SCS have been subject to warming sea surface temperatures and ocean acidification since the early 1980s.[51] It was estimated that coral reefs in SCS decreased by 16 per cent between 1994 and 2004.[52] In fact, 40 per cent of corals were bleached on Dongsha Atoll in the northern part of SCS due to a two degree Celsius sea surface temperature rise during the 2015 El Niño event—a mass coral bleaching phenomenon unseen in the last forty years.[53]

On the subject of ocean acidification, a study suggests that the surface of the SCS will become 0.3 to 0.35 pH levels more acidic, and this acidification will somewhat be uniform throughout the SCS as shown in Figure 4.7.[54] However, little is known about the ability of coral reefs and other calcifying reef organisms to adapt to acidifying sea waters.[55]

FIGURE 4.7
The South China Sea Will Become More Acidic, and the Study Suggests that the Degree Would be Somewhat Uniform throughout the South China Sea area

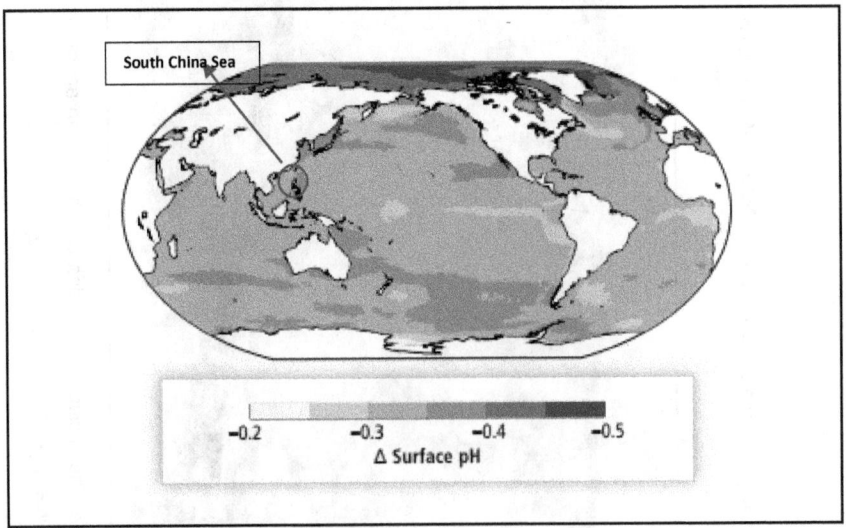

Note: The circled South China Sea area is an approximate illustration.
Source: Hoegh-Guldberg et al. (2014).

4.2   The Need for Marine Environmental Governance

The alarming state of the environment in the SCS indicates the urgency for enhancing cooperation among countries concerned, as effective governance of the waters is beyond the capacity of any individual country. Nevertheless, maritime disputes that have heightened tensions among littoral states have significantly shifted attention and resources from arising non-traditional insecurities. As China and the Philippines restart bilateral talks in the SCS and ASEAN and China are currently negotiating a legally binding Code of Conduct (COC) in these waters, we should push for more attention to be given to the natural marine environment in these dialogues. Marine environmental protection, viewed as a "soft security" issue, might hold the key to building mutual trust and confidence among littoral states. Instead of further militarizing troubled waters, ASEAN, together with China, should form a cooperative management framework in the SCS with marine environmental protection as one of its main pillars.

Cooperative avenues highlighted in both the SDGs and the *ASEAN Community Blueprint 2025* include protection of marine environment and biodiversity, scientific research and technology transfer, sustainable use of marine resources and collective response to threats to the seas.[56] This section will assess the region's performance in the aforementioned areas of interest by (1) examining various national and regional mechanisms, (2) canvassing lessons and practices of other regions in transboundary marine governance, and (3) putting forward recommendations for initiating and enhancing cooperation.

Key Areas for Effective Marine Environmental Protection

A key dimension of marine environment protection (MEP) is to remove stressors on the marine environment. The international arbitral ruling at The Hague on the SCS acknowledged the irreparable destruction of the coral reef ecosystem due to clam-coral poaching, overfishing, land reclamation and illegal fishing activities in the SCS.[57] Land-based activities like industrial and household discharge of untreated waste and marine debris are a major source of pollution. Moreover, according to the United Nations Educational, Scientific and Cultural Organization (UNESCO), degradation and unsustainable exploitation affect over 60 per cent of the world's marine ecosystems.[58] For instance, surging demands for seafood drive overfishing. There is a need to strike a balance between the capacity of the marine environment and exploitation of marine resources. Sustainability in production should therefore be promoted, which is also recommended by the SDG Goal 12: Responsible Consumption and Production. To encourage sustainable practices in development, economic incentives can be provided to developing countries as well as small stakeholders, who are more likely to be vulnerable to the possible short-term economic losses resulting from promoting more sustainable growth patterns in the marine economy.

Apart from the removal of stressors, strengthened protection and conservation are essential. The establishment of marine protected areas (MPAs) is a widely adopted approach for that purpose. According to the International Union for Conservation of Nature (IUCN), an MPA refers to *"a clearly defined geographical space, recognised, dedicated and managed, through legal or other effective means, to achieve the long-term conservation of nature with associated ecosystem services and cultural values"*.[59] Essentially, an MPA is set up to ensure greater protection and better management of marine fauna and flora like coral reefs, mangrove forests and seagrass. Existing research has shown that MPAs can prevent further deterioration in, and even increase, biodiversity.[60] The effectiveness of MPAs depends on clear definitions of goals of protection, specification of restricted activities, sustainable funding, and strict enforcement.[61]

Availability of accurate and updated data is critical for effective MEP. This must be primarily done at the national level through monitoring the status of marine and coastal environments, assessing the effectiveness of protection, and analysing the causes of degradation. Various scientific research projects have been undertaken by littoral states to monitor the status of the marine environment in the SCS.[62] What is more important now is for them to advance sharing of scientific information and data, given that marine environmental challenges are often transboundary and defy unilateral solutions. Apart from collaboration in scientific research, cooperation and coordination in law enforcement also need to be strengthened. While littoral states have put in place a variety of national marine policies and laws like fishing moratorium and coastal patrols, overarching policies and cooperation frameworks at the regional level are essential as unsustainable and even illegal practices often cross maritime boundaries.

Marine Environmental Protection in the SCS: National and Regional Efforts

1) Protection and Conservation: Marine Protected Areas

One of the earliest MEP efforts of ASEAN member states was the establishment of a national system of MPAs. A peaceful marine park or MPA is not a new concept in ASEAN. Individually, Southeast Asian states have designated MPAs along their coastlines since the 1990s. They also signed the ASEAN Declaration on Heritage Parks and Reserves in 1984 and the updated ASEAN Declaration on Heritage Parks in 2003, in which they all agreed to designate protected areas to be inscribed as the ASEAN Heritage Parks. Several MPAs have been labelled as ASEAN Heritage Parks—areas of particular biodiversity importance that require conservation and protection initiatives.[63]

However, despite signing the two declarations in 1984 and 2003, no littoral state bordering the SCS and adjoining the Gulf of Thailand had more than 6 per cent of its territorial waters protected in 2014 (see Figure 4.8). The coverage rate of MPAs in the SCS (0.31 per cent) was

FIGURE 4.8
Coverage Rate (in per cent) of MPA in China and some ASEAN Member States in 2014

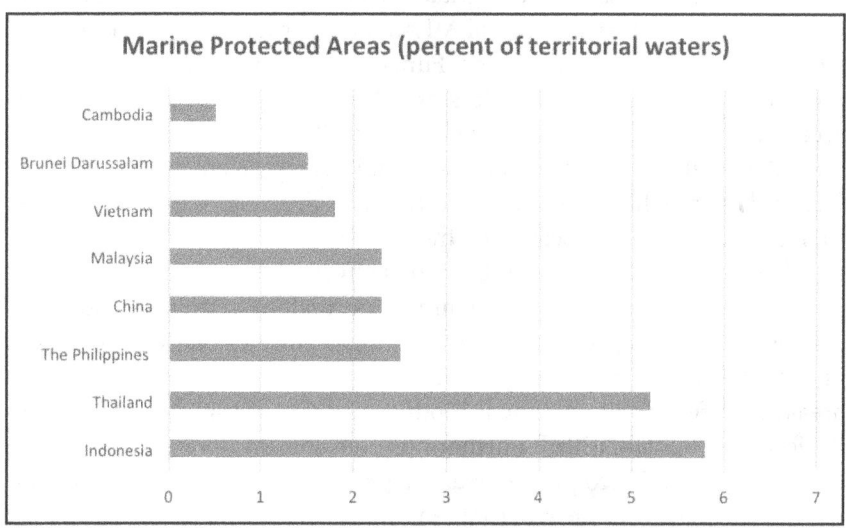

Source: United Nations Environmental Program and the World Conservation Monitoring Centre, as compiled by the World Resources Institute (2014).

negligible based on a study in 2014.[64] Apart from the limited coverage of existing MPAs, management gaps in the identified MPAs have yet to be addressed.[65] Based on the 2010 gap analysis of the ASEAN Centre for Biodiversity (ACB), 35 out of 152 coastal and marine key biodiversity areas identified by ASEAN member states were managed as MPAs, 20 were partly protected, and the rest were not protected at all.[66] The UN Environment Programme (UNEP) and the Global Environment Facility launched a project to protect coral reefs in the SCS between 2002 and 2008. The project designated 83 target coral reef sites, amounting to 29 per cent of the total area in the SCS.[67] Only 5 per cent of the designated area was considered to be under effective management.[68] Management effectiveness for 29 per cent of coral reef sites was very low, while around 13 per cent of the sites were not even covered by any form of protective management.[69]

The management effectiveness of existing MPAs in individual countries remains inadequate. The Philippines has the highest number of MPAs in Southeast Asia, but only 100 of its 1,557 MPAs were properly managed[70] and only 541 had geographical coordinate information, which was needed to determine the coverage of MPAs for monitoring and law enforcement purposes.[71] In Vietnam, only five among 16 established MPAs were being managed.[72] Considered as the largest littoral state in the SCS,[73] China has also designated 266 MPAs along its coastlines.[74] China began establishing special MPAs and marine parks in the 1980s.[75] Under China's National Marine Functional Zoning Plan (2011–2020), 5 per cent of its territorial waters and 11 per cent of nearshore marine areas will be under MPA designation by 2020.[76] By the end of 2014, only 2.65 per cent of China's territorial waters were under MPAs.[77] Nearly half of China's MPAs are located in the Yellow Sea, while only four small MPAs are located in the SCS.[78]

There are various reasons behind ineffective management of MPAs nationally and regionally. In China, for instance, there is no well-organized planning for MPAs at a national scale as the establishment of many existing MPAs does not correspond to the priority marine areas identified in the National Biodiversity Conservation Strategy and Action Plan (2011–2030).[79] Furthermore, ecological connectivity, which has been globally recognized as a key principle in the conservation and management of marine environments, has never been incorporated in the designation criteria for MPAs and MPA networks design in China.[80] In terms of protection objectives, inter-tidal ecosystems, mangroves, rare and endangered species, and islands are the main targets, while coral reefs have not been receiving enough attention.[81] The lack of funding also hinders the effectiveness of MPAs in China as well as other littoral states.[82] In China, the central government provides limited funds to cover the cost of infrastructure in newly established national MPAs and human resources for management of these areas. Hence, just a minority group of MPAs in China is able to afford an independent and long-term monitoring programme.[83] Moreover, the existing MPAs of littoral states are not integrated regionally (e.g., a regional MPA network) or even bilaterally, while the integration of MPAs may have fostered MEP cooperation among the littoral states.

2) Strengthening Relevant Laws and Regulations

There are indeed challenges to MEP measures in the region. One such challenge is the lack of effective legal frameworks at the national level, hampering the institutionalization of compliance and enforcement mechanisms in the region. The ineffective levels of management of MPAs are partly caused by inconsistent and incoherent marine environmental laws and regulations.[84] For instance, Vietnam's Law on Environmental Protection does not have enough provisions on the protection of the marine environment and its general principles are not strong and sound enough to establish an MEP legal regime.[85] China's 1994 Regulations on Nature Reserves and the 1995 Regulations on Marine Nature Reserves have relatively weak legal prowess and do not have specific guidelines for implementation, monitoring and evaluation.[86] China does not have an overarching legal framework to coordinate efforts in managing MPAs more broadly given that it is the local governments that oversee the daily management and enforcement of individual MPAs.[87]

In the Philippines, there is also a need to integrate and coordinate existing MEP measures so as to strengthen the implementation of a national law on protected areas. This need is supposed to be addressed by a proposed legislation, the Expanded National Integrated Protected Area System Act, which will amend the twenty-five-year-old National Integrated Protected Areas System Act.[88] However, the proposed bill is still pending in the Philippine Congress[89] as it is not among the legislative priorities of the government.[90] The new bill will widen the coverage of protected areas and will provide a regular annual budget for the upkeep and protection of the MPAs. But more importantly, if enacted into law, local communities and other stakeholders will have the legal basis and incentives to participate in the management and protection of the areas.[91] Major incentives include direct financial benefits from participating in the management of MPAs, employment opportunities for local stakeholders, increased fish catches for coastal communities, and prevention of illegal fishing activities in marine areas with strong tourism potentials.[92]

3) Involvement of Local Stakeholders

Collaborative management is vital for effective management of MEP as this model of management is more likely to attract sustainable funding. A multiple-stakeholder approach that engages national and local authorities, communities, the private sector and other resource users is needed. Clear delineation of roles, responsibilities and benefits needs to be laid out.[93] It is very important that local stakeholders have a sense of ownership to be able to contribute to the effective management of MPAs. Weak involvement and resistance from relevant local stakeholders can affect the implementation of relevant marine environmental laws and undermine the effectiveness of existing national MPAs.

Some of Thailand's coastal communities were reported to have negative perceptions about MPAs because of the restrictive implications on their fishing activities.[94] They thought that it is only the tourism sector that would stand to benefit from protecting coral reef sites.[95] In Indonesia's Wakatobi National Park, in an MPA near south Sulawesi, most of the locals believe that their traditional activities (fishing, coral gleaning, etc.) have insignificant impact on the ecosystem and should not be restricted by any conservation efforts.[96] Instead, they blame big commercial fishing vessels that use destructive fishing methods.[97] In the Philippines, local communities near some of the MPAs complain that they were excluded from MPA management meetings and that their views were not taken into account in decision-making.[98] Their perceived level of their involvement in the management of the MPAs was very low.[99] Filipino coastal communities negatively viewed many of the country's MPAs as barriers to their ability to fish in front of their homes.[100] This is because most MPAs have been designed to merely protect marine biodiversity rather than to replenish fish stocks and support local economies.[101]

4) Scientific and Technical Collaboration

Given that certain aspects of the marine ecosystem are mobile, collaboration among littoral states is therefore fundamental. However, traditional security concerns constitute a major barrier to collaborative efforts. No littoral state of the SCS has so far extended its MPAs to contested waters.[102] There is a need to create a regional MPA network that will cover even the overlapping territorial claims in the SCS. Scientific cooperation among experts and environmental NGOs can offer a mutually acceptable path to ecological solutions in the SCS, avoiding nationalist rhetoric and sensitive sovereignty issues. There were earlier proposals to do so, through bilateral and multilateral scientific cooperation, such as the 1996–2007 Philippines-Vietnam Joint Oceanographic and Marine Scientific Research Expedition in the SCS (JOMSRE-SCS).[103] By 2008, scientists and experts from this expedition proposed that the Philippines and Vietnam must collaborate for the establishment of trans-border peace parks or MPAs in the contested Spratlys, with 30 per cent of the total area to be designated as "no-take" zones for any marine resources to allow build-up of marine life.[104]

They also recommended to include all SCS states, including China, in establishing MPAs in the SCS.[105] Hence, in 2009, three negotiation meetings were conducted to include China in JOMSRE-SCS.[106] Vietnam, the Philippines and China agreed on the goals of the joint project, scientific activities, surveyed data/information, and specimen sharing with the view of creating a network of MPAs.[107] However, the proposed joint initiatives were never implemented.[108] Rising geopolitical tensions among littoral states at that time[109] may have prevented the implementation.

ASEAN and China also attempted to create a regional network of marine scientists and a platform for sharing of scientific data through the UNEP's South China Sea project, Reversing Environmental Degradation in the South China Sea and Gulf of Thailand (2002–2008).[110] Its overall objective was to serve as a platform for scientific collaboration and partnership in addressing environmental problems of the SCS.[111] The project involved government scientists from focal ministries and specialized agencies, marine experts from universities, NGOs, and local community groups from six participating countries (Cambodia, China, Indonesia, Malaysia, the Philippines, and Thailand). It achieved some positive outcomes, particularly the increased collaboration among the scientists of participating countries, but heightened tensions among littoral states prevented the momentum of scientific cooperation, which would have positively contributed to tangible regional policies on MEP in the SCS.[112]

Lessons from Other Regions

Considering the relatively low effectiveness and cooperation in MEP in the SCS, it is helpful to understand how other regions protect their seas, particularly in disputed waters, so as to draw lessons for better protection of the SCS. This section examines MEP efforts in the Mediterranean Sea, North America and Central America in two focal areas: the implementation of regional cooperative frameworks and the involvement of multiple actors.

1) Stronger Framework for Cooperation

One crucial lesson from the Mediterranean Sea region is the importance of an institutional framework for cooperation. In 1975, sixteen Mediterranean countries and the European Community adopted the Mediterranean Action Plan, with the aim of protecting the marine and coastal environments, controlling pollution, preserving biodiversity, and promoting sustainable development within the Mediterranean Region.[113] In 1976, the Convention for the Protection of the Mediterranean Sea against Pollution (Barcelona Convention) was adopted to address pollution caused by waste dumping from ships and aircraft.[114] It also mandates state parties to forge cooperation in combating pollution in case of maritime emergency. There are now twenty-two contracting state parties to the two legally binding conventions.[115] They are determined to protect the marine and coastal environments of the Mediterranean Sea through boosting coordinated regional and national plans of action.[116] As a result, through large-scale national and regional conservation efforts, there are now 1,231 MPAs covering 7.14 per cent of the Mediterranean Sea.[117]

Countries in the Americas have established a number of regional initiatives for MEP. Various commitments for marine-related regional cooperation have been sealed with formal declarations and agreements, thereby giving them a solid foundation for related subsequent initiatives. The Mesoamerican Barrier Reef Initiative, for example, is a transboundary collaboration among Mexico, Belize, Guatemala and Honduras aimed at promoting the conservation and sustainable use of the Mesoamerican

Barrier Reef System.[118] The multilateral cooperation began with the signing of the Tulum Declaration in 1997. The Declaration also gave rise to other initiatives such as the Mesoamerican Barrier Reef System (MBRS) Project and the Reef Eco-Regional Plan.[119]

The North American Marine Protected Areas Network (NAMPAN) is a trilateral initiative aimed primarily at conserving biodiversity in critical marine habitats and enabling knowledge exchange among experts from the United States, Canada and Mexico.[120] Initiated in November 1999 under the North American Free Trade Agreement's Commission for Environmental Cooperation, NAMPAN focuses its work in Baja California to Bering Sea Region and includes the territories of the three countries.[121] NAMPAN hopes to complement existing conservation efforts in the three countries and integrate their conservation initiatives through collaboration.[122] It also seeks to boost cooperation in information sharing, new technologies and management strategies in a bid to find solutions to the common challenges facing marine and coastal habitats in North America.[123] The network of MPAs exemplified in the NAMPAN initiative can facilitate the ecosystem approach[124] to MEP, which looks at different MPAs as part of a large interconnected ecosystem. Conservation efforts adopting this comprehensive approach may yield more effective outcomes.

2) Forging Partnerships

SCS states may consider another lesson from the Mediterranean Action Plan in terms of bringing together regional stakeholders, including non-state actors, to build a network of MPAs and strengthen its management effectiveness. The Mediterranean Regional Seas Programme conducts multiple projects, one of which is the Network of Managers of MPAs in the Mediterranean (MedPAN). MedPAN brings together 100 institutions and environmental NGOs that either have direct responsibility for managing MPAs or are involved in the development of MPAs in the Mediterranean Sea.[125] MedPAN's mission is to promote, through a partnership approach, the sustainability and operation of a network of MPAs in the Mediterranean, which are ecologically representative.[126] As a result, through joint training and knowledge sharing among MPA managers, MedPan has reinforced the management efficiency of existing MPAs and promoted the creation of new MPAs in the twelve countries of the southern and eastern Mediterranean area.[127]

The cross-border marine protection cooperation in the Americas relies heavily on donors' support. The WWF and the World Bank/Global Environmental Facility played important roles in supporting the Mesoamerican Barrier Reef Initiative and its related projects.[128] But overreliance on donors' support may pose a problem to the sustainability of efforts. Funding as well as boundary or political disputes form part of the multiple challenges that Mexico, Belize, Guatemala and Honduras faced in managing the Mesoamerican Barrier Reef Initiative.[129]

The Marine Conservation Corridor of the Eastern Tropical Pacific (ETP), which covers Ecuador, Colombia, Panamá and Costa Rica, is facing similar problems in securing sustainable funding alongside with issues pertaining to governance structures and contesting views on the concept of cooperation by some stakeholders from Ecuador.[130] Despite the challenges, the commitment and attention the UNESCO World Heritage Centre placed on the ETP have brought about successful conservation efforts in the area, which have resulted in a World Heritage designation for Malpelo Flora and Fauna Sanctuary.[131] In 2016, the managers of the seven marine sites[132] signed the Carta de Punta Suarez Agreement that aims to *"promote the exchange of scientific and technical information to improve the management of each site, seek joint funding to support regional projects that will support effective conservation, and organize meetings to define joint actions that will serve common objectives"*.[133]

Sustained commitments from donors can provide the needed push for collaborations to move ahead despite issues relating to interaction among states that may hinder effective communication and implementation. The countries bordering the SCS may want to learn from these experiences by first, solidifying their commitment for MEP in the form of joint declarations and agreements and then securing donors and important international organizations such as the UNESCO World Heritage to support these initiatives. Having strong external support appears critical especially when there are political and territorial disputes among involved countries.

The aforementioned lessons, however, may still be difficult to realize in the SCS due to existing barriers to multilateral cooperation, even in protecting the marine ecosystem. For one, sovereignty discourse remains strong; competing territorial claims and historical animosities pose strong barriers to intergovernmental cooperation on marine and fisheries issues.[134] A legally-binding regional framework on MEP, for instance, may be hard to achieve at the moment. It is because there could be domestic perceptions that cooperation implies some concessions on sovereignty claims and fears of domination by larger states in a cooperative framework.[135]

Another barrier is strategic distrust among littoral states. It restricts the cooperation necessary to deal with non-traditional security issues, such as MEP and sustainable fishing.[136] Provocative actions and statements only serve to add to distrust and frustrate cooperation. Escalating provocation and counter-provocation have resulted in increased strategic distrust.[137] Provocations emanate from rapid naval and coast guard buildups, construction of military facilities, and other related activities in and around the disputed waters. Diplomatic tensions typically arise from ramming and harassment of fishing boats, obstruction of survey ships, stand-offs, and collisions. MEP cooperation will be challenging under this volatile security environment.

Scientific collaboration, which is very robust in other regions, may face hurdles in the SCS. One lesson learnt from the outcomes of earlier MEP projects was the need to separate scientific and technical issues from political decision-making, nationalist rhetoric and sovereignty claims.[138] Essentially, geopolitics should not hinder scientific cooperation in the region for the protection of the marine environment in the SCS.

Possible Avenues for Strengthening Cooperation

Despite the recognition of the importance of coordination and cooperation, however, the necessary collective action between ASEAN and China has yet to be fully realized primarily due to aforesaid obstacles. Although past and existing measures have been initiated by littoral states to address marine environmental challenges, this chapter finds that these measures have been essentially fragmented and ineffective. In fact, at least three ASEAN-China frameworks espouse multilateral and regional cooperation on MEP, although they are not legally binding and do not have enforcement mechanisms. Firstly, there was an understanding reached in the Declaration on the Conduct of Parties in the South China Sea concerning the marine environment: *"Pending a comprehensive and durable settlement of the disputes, the Parties concerned may explore or undertake cooperative activities. These may include the following: a. marine environmental protection; b. marine scientific research ..."*[139] As ASEAN and China are to start talks on details of the COC, more balanced attention should be given to both maritime disputes and the marine ecosystem as the latter is no less important for national and human securities in the region.

Secondly, ASEAN member states and China can initiate new collaborative efforts based on their Declaration for the Decade of Coastal and Marine Environmental Protection in the South China Sea (2017–2027), which is one of the positive outcomes of the ASEAN-China Summit process. This joint declaration recognizes the importance of MEP to economic prosperity and human development of the peoples of ASEAN member states and China. Given the current environmental situation in the SCS, it encourages ASEAN and China to take collective action to save the marine ecosystem and biodiversity.[140]

Thirdly, marine environment is important for socio-economic development in ASEAN countries. As mentioned earlier, the protection of our oceans is one of the SDGs. Moreover, the *ASEAN Socio-Cultural Community Blueprint 2025* encourages member states to *"[p]romote cooperation for the protection, restoration and sustainable use of coastal and marine environment, respond and deal with the risk of pollution and threats to marine ecosystem and coastal environment, in particular in respect of ecologically sensitive areas"*.[141] These goals create stronger incentives for ASEAN countries to implement effective MEP jointly. It is imperative for SCS littoral states to operationalize the collective action approach recommended by existing ASEAN-China regional frameworks. The potential for SCS claimants to carry out and strengthen MEP cooperation should be further explored. The "depoliticisation" of MEP in the SCS may hold the key to building mutual trust and confidence among littoral states. Instead of further militarizing the troubled waters, ASEAN together with China may form a cooperative management framework in the SCS with MEP as one of its main pillars.

As the marine environment in the SCS has been quickly degrading, it has become more urgent for relevant states to separate geopolitics or sovereignty claims from the need for crucial civil maritime cooperation on NTS issues, primarily MEP. The urgency of accelerating marine conservation in the SCS can hardly be overstated.

NOTES

1. UN General Assembly, Resolution 71/312, "Our Ocean, Our Future: Call for Action", 6 July 2017, http://www.un.org/ga/search/view_doc. asp?symbol=A/RES/71/312&Lang=E.

2. Lauren Anderson, "An Ocean in Chains: Reviewing SDG 14 in Advance of the HLPF", Policy Brief, International Institute for Sustainable Development, 6 July 2017, http://sdg.iisd.org/commentary/policy-briefs/an-ocean-in-chains-reviewing-sdg-14-in-advance-of-the-hlpf/.

3. United Nations, "Registry of Voluntary Commitments", The Ocean Conference, undated, https://oceanconference.un.org/commitments/ (accessed 15 October 2017).

4. We used "South China Sea" as the key word in the headline and lead paragraph to search for news articles between 2009 and 2016 in Factiva, a database of global news reports. The result shows that there are 71,013 entries on the SCS in total. The search was conducted on 16 September 2017.

5. "Declaration for the Decade of Coastal and Marine Environmental Protection in the South China Sea (2017–2027)", Manila, Philippines, 13 November 2017.

6. United Nations, *Our Common Future – Brundtland Report* (Oxford: Oxford University Press, 1987), p. 9.

7. J. Jackson Ewing, "Environmental Security", in *An Introduction to Non-Traditional Security Studies: A Transnational Approach*, edited by Mely Caballero-Anthony (London: Sage, 2016), pp. 97–98.

8. Ove Hoegh-Guldberg et al., *Reviving the Ocean Economy: The Case for Action –2015* (Gland, Switzerland: WWF, 2015), p. 12.

9. Food and Agriculture Organization (FAO), *The State of World Fisheries and Aquaculture: Opportunities and Challenges* (Rome: FAO, 2014), p. 6.

10. Ibid.

11. United Nations, "Goal 14: Conserve and Sustainably Use the Oceans, Seas and Marine Resources", Sustainable Development Goals (New York: United Nations, undated), http://www.un.org/sustainabledevelopment/oceans/ (accessed 23 June 2019).

12. Ibid.

13. Abhit Singh, "A Looming Environmental Crisis in the South China Sea", *Asia Maritime Transparency Initiative*, 12 August 2016, https://amti.csis.org/looming-environmental-crisis-south-china-sea/.

14. Marie Antonette Juinio-Menez, "Biophysical and Genetic Connectivity Considerations in Marine Biodiversity Conservation and Management in the South China Sea", *Journal of International Wildlife Law and Policy* 18, no. 2 (2015): 111.

15. "South China Sea Countries Continue to Cooperate on Integrating Fisheries and Marine Ecosystem Management", *SEAFDEC News*, 1 November 2016, http://www.seafdec.org/south-china-sea-countries-cooperate-integrating-fisheries-marine-ecosystem-management/.

16. Akshat Rathi, "The Most Ignored Aspect of the South China Sea Brawl Might be the Key to Solving it", *Quartz*, 26 July 2016, https://qz.com/741989/the-most-ignored-aspect-of-the-south-china-sea-brawl-might-be-the-key-to-solving-it/.

17. Ibid.

18. Si Tuan Vo, John C. Pernetta, and Christopher J. Paterson, "Status and Trends in Coastal Habitats of the South China Sea", *Ocean and Coastal Management* 85, Part B (2013): 156.

19. UN Environmental Programme (UNEP), "Land-Based Pollution in the South China Sea", UNEP/GEF/SCS Technical Publication No. 10 (Bangkok, Thailand: UNEP, 2007), https://www.unepscs.org/google/South-China-Sea-Technical-Publication-Land-Based-Pollution-South-China-Sea.pdf.

20. Ibid.

21. According to the data from the World Bank DataBank, the population of ASEAN and China was 1.83 billion and the world's total was about 7.44 billion in 2016. See World Bank, "2.1 World Development Indicators: Population Dynamics", World Development Indicators, New York, undated, http://wdi.worldbank.org/table/2.1 (accessed 23 June 2019).

22. Andrew Jacobs, "China's Appetite Pushes Fisheries to the Brink", *New York Times*, 30 April 2017, https://www.nytimes.com/2017/04/30/world/asia/chinas-appetite-pushes-fisheries-to-the-brink.html.

23. "Battle to Save Dwindling Fish Stocks in S-E Asia", *Straits Times*, 31 August 2017, http://www.straitstimes.com/asia/se-asia/battle-to-save-dwindling-fish-stocks-in-s-e-asia.

24. Vo, Pernetta, and Paterson, "Status and Trends", p. 157.

25. Li Jing, "China Produces about a Third of Plastic Waste Polluting the World's Oceans, Says Report", *South China Morning Post*, 14 February 2015, http://www.scmp.com/article/1711744/china-produces-about-third-plastic-waste-polluting-worlds-oceans-says-report.

26. Graeme Wearden, "More Plastic than Fish in the Sea by 2050, says Ellen MacArthur", *The Guardian*, 19 January 2016, https://www.theguardian.com/business/2016/jan/19/more-plastic-than-fish-in-the-sea-by-2050-warns-ellen-macarthur.

27. Jose G.B. Derraik, "The Pollution of the Marine Environment by Plastic Debris: A Review", *Marine Pollution Bulletin* 44, no. 9 (2002): 844–47; Susan Smillie, "From Sea to Plate: How Plastic Got into Our Fish", *The Guardian*, 14 February 2017, https://www.theguardian.com/lifeandstyle/2017/feb/14/sea-to-plate-plastic-got-into-fish.

28. Gabriel Blanco et al., "Drivers, Trends and Mitigation", in *Climate Change 2014: Mitigation of Climate Change. Contribution of Working Group III to the Fifth Assessment Report of the Intergovernmental Panel on Climate Change*, edited by O. Edenhofer et al. (Cambridge, UK: Cambridge University Press, 2014), pp. 351–412.

29. Cai Rongshuo et al., "Response and Adaptation to Climate Change in the South China Sea and Coral Sea", in *Climate Change Adaptation in Pacific Countries: Fostering Resilience and Improving the Quality of Life*, edited by Walter Leal Filho (Basel, Switzerland: Springer International Publishing AG, 2017): 163–76.

30. Ibid.

31. Chlorophyll-a is a specific form of pigments used in oxygenic photosynthesis. Its concentrations are often measured to indicate marine productivity.

32. Cai et al., "Response and Adaptation", pp. 163–76.

33. Louise Maureen Simeon, "Sustainable Mangrove Management Pushed amid Climate Change", *Philippine Star*, 3 September 2017, http://www.philstar.com/agriculture/2017/09/03/1735155/sustainable-mangrove-mngmt-pushed-amid-climate-change.

34. Beth A. Polidoro et al., "The Loss of Species: Mangrove Extinction Risk and Geographic Areas of Global Concern", *PLoS ONE* 5, no. 4 (2010): e10095, https://doi.org/10.1371/journal.pone.0010095; Mark Spalding, Mami Kainuma, and Lorna Collins, *World Atlas of Mangroves* (London, UK: Earthscan, 2010); UNEP, *National Reports on Mangroves in South China Sea*, UNEP/GEF/THE SOUTH CHINA SEA Technical Publication No. 14 (Bangkok, Thailand: UNEP, 2008); Vo, Pernetta, and Paterson, "Status and Trends", pp. 153–63.

35. UNEP, *Strategic Action Programme for the South China Sea*, UNEP/GEF/THE SOUTH CHINA SEA Technical Publication No. 16 (Bangkok, Thailand: UNEP, 2008).

36. Jashimuddin Karim and Ansarul Karim, "Effect of Salinity on the Growth of Some Mangrove Plants in Bangladesh", in *Towards the Rational Use of High Salinity Tolerant Plants. Vol 1: Deliberations about High Salinity Tolerant Plants and Ecosystems,* edited by Helmut Lieth and A. Al Masoom (The Netherlands: Kluwer Academic Publishers, 1993), pp. 187–92, https://link.springer.com/chapter/10.1007/978-94-011-1858-3_20.

37. Angus C. Jackson and Jason MacIlvenny, "Coastal Squeeze on Rocky Shores in Northern Scotland and Some Possible Ecological Impacts", *Journal of Experimental Marine Biology and Ecology* 400, no. 1–2 (2011): 314–21.

38. Ibid.

39. Mario D.P. Godoy and Luiz D. De Lacerda, "Mangroves Response to Climate Change: A Review of Recent Findings on Mangrove Extension and Distribution", *Annals of the Brazilian Academy of Sciences* 87, no. 2 (2015): 651–67, http://www.scielo.br/pdf/aabc/v87n2/0001-3765-aabc-201520150055.pdf.

40. Peter Saenger, *Mangrove Ecology, Silviculture and Conservation* (Dordrecht, the Netherlands: Springer, 2002); Spalding, Kainuma, and Collins, *World Atlas of Mangroves.*

41. Raymond D. Ward et al., "Impacts of Climate Change on Mangrove Ecosystems: A Region by Region Overview", *Ecosystem Health and Sustainability* 2, no. 4 (2016): 1–25, http://onlinelibrary.wiley.com/doi/10.1002/ehs2.1211/full.

42. University of York, "Further, Faster, Higher: Wildlife Responds Increasingly Rapidly to Climate Change", News Release, 18 August 2011, https://www.york.ac.uk/news-and-events/news/2011/research/wildlife-responds/.

43. The Office of the Oceanographer of the Navy, *Arctic Environmental Assessment and Outlook Report*, August 2011, https://www.hsdl.org/?view&did=685137.

44. William W.L. Cheung et al., "Large-scale Redistribution of Maximum Fisheries Catch Potential in the Global Ocean under Climate Change", *Global Change Biology* 16, no. 1 (2010): 24–35.

45. William W.L. Cheung et al., "Shrinking of Fishes Exacerbates Impacts of Global Ocean Changes on Marine Ecosystems", *Nature Climate Change* 3 (2013): 254–58, http://www.nature.com/nclimate/journal/v3/n3/full/nclimate1691.html?foxtrotcallback=true.

46. UNEP, *Seagrass in the South China Sea*, UNEP/GEF/THE SOUTH CHINA SEA Technical Publication No. 3 (Bangkok, Thailand: UNEP, 2004), http://iwlearn.net/resolveuid/6abc857925542c108f72e2f1e9147b97.

47. Biodiversity Information Sharing Service (ASEAN Clearing House Mechanism), "Seagrass", undated, http://chm.aseanbiodiversity.org/index.php?option=com_content&view=article&id=169&Itemid=169.

48. UNEP, *Reversing Environmental Degradation Trends in the South China Sea and Gulf of Thailand*, Report of the Seventh Meeting of the Regional Working Group for the Seagrass (Bangkok, Thailand: UNEP, 2006).

49. Ibid.

50. UNEP, *Seagrass in the South China Sea*.

51. China-SNAP, *The Second National Chinese Assessment Report on Climate Change Chinese* Government (in Chinese, with English abstract) (Beijing: Science Press, 2011), pp. 245–56; Ove Hoegh-Guldberg et al., *The Coral Triangle and Climate Change: Ecosystems, People and Societies at Risk* (Brisbane, Australia: World Wide Fund for Nature (WWF) Australia, 2009), p. 276, cited in Cai (2017).

52. UNEP, *Strategic Action Programme for the South China Sea*.

53. Thomas M. DeCarlo et al., "Mass Coral Mortality under Local Amplification of 2°C Ocean Warming", *Science Reports* 7, no. 44586 (2017), doi: 10.1038/srep44586.

54. Hoegh-Guldberg et al., "The Ocean", in *Climate Change 2014: Impacts, Adaptation, and Vulnerability. Part B: Regional Aspects, Contribution of Working Group II to the Fifth Assessment Report of the Intergovernmental Panel on Climate Change*, edited by Vicente R. Barros et al. (Cambridge, UK: Cambridge University Press, 2014), pp. 1655–731.

55. Carles Pelejero et al., "Preindustrial to Modern Interdecadal Variability in Coral Reef Ph", *Science* 309, no. 5744 (2005): 2204–7.

56. The ASEAN Secretariat, *ASEAN 2025: Forging Ahead Together* (Jakarta: ASEAN Secretariat, 2015), http://www.asean.org/storage/2015/12/ASEAN-2025-Forging-Ahead-Together-final.pdf.

57. Permanent Court of Arbitration, "The South China Sea Arbitration Award of 12 July 2016", PCA Case No. 2013-19, 2016, https://pca-cpa.org/wp-content/uploads/sites/175/2016/07/PH-CN-20160712-Award.pdf.

58. United Nations Educational, Scientific and Cultural Organization (UNESCO), "Facts and Figures on Marine Biodiversity", Paris, undated, http://www.unesco.org/new/en/natural-sciences/ioc-oceans/focus-areas/rio-20-ocean/blueprint-for-the-future-we-want/marine-biodiversity/facts-and-figures-on-marine-biodiversity/ (accessed 17 July 2019).

59. International Union for Conservation of Nature (IUCN), "What is a Protected Area?" undated, https://www.iucn.org/theme/protected-areas/about (accessed 17 July 2019).

60. Elizabeth R. Selig and John F. Bruno, "A Global Analysis of the Effectiveness of Marine Protected Areas in Preventing Coral Loss", *PLoS One* 5 (2010): e9278, https://dx.doi.org/10.1371%2Fjournal.pone.0009278.

61. Gary W. Allison, Jane Lubchenco, and Mark H. Carr, "Marine Reserves are Necessary but Not Sufficient for Marine Conservation", *Ecological Application* 8, no. sp1 (1998): 79–92, https://doi.org/10.1890/1051-0761(1998)8[S79:MRANBN]2.0.CO;2.

62. Edgardo D. Gomez, "Marine Scientific Research in the South China Sea and Environmental Security", *Ocean Develoment & International Law* 32, no. 2 (2001): 205–11, https://doi.org/10.1080/00908320151100343.

63. *ASEAN Declaration on Heritage Parks*, Yangon, Myanmar, 18 December 2003, https://asean.org/?static_post=asean-declaration-on-heritage-parks.

64. Vu Hai Dang, *Marine Protected Areas Network in the South China Sea: Charting a Course for Future Cooperation* (Leiden: Koninklijke Brill NV, 2014).

65. Proper management of MPAs requires implementing adequate MPA management plans, putting in place robust monitoring and reporting frameworks, ensuring solid compliance and enforcement mechanisms, mobilizing sufficient finance to enable sustainable management, and embedding MPAs in an effective and balanced policy mix so as to address multiple pressures from various stakeholders. See Organisation for Economic Co-operation and Development (OECD), *Marine Protected Areas: Economics, Management and Effective Policy Mixes* (Paris: OECD Publishing, 2017), https://www.oecd.org/env/marine-protected-areas-9789264276208-en.htm.

66. Biodiversity Information Sharing Service, "Protected Area Gap Analysis in the ASEAN Region", 2010, http://chm.aseanbiodiversity.org/index.php?option=com_content&view=article&id=145&Itemid=231.

67. Tuan Si Vo, "Development of a Coral Reef Management Strategy within the Framework of the UNEP/GEF South China Sea Project", *Galaxea, Journal of Coral Reef Studies* 15, Special Issue (2013): 11, https://doi.org/10.3755/galaxea.15.9.

68. Ibid.

69. Ibid.

70. Gregg Yan, "Philippines Declares Largest Marine Protected Areas", *Amazon of the Ocean*, 8 November 2016, http://thecoraltriangle.com/stories/philippines-declares-largest-marine-protected-area.

71. Nguyen Chu Hoi and Vu Hai Dang, "Building a Regional Network and Management Regime of Marine Protected Areas in the South China Sea for Sustainable Development", *Journal of International Wildlife Law & Policy* 18, no. 2 (2015): 133–36, https://doi.org/10.1080/13880292.2015.1044797.

72. Ibid.

73. Even though China is the largest littoral state, the Philippines has more MPAs than China. This is because the Philippine archipelago consists of 7,107 islands, with a total coastline of 36,289 km, one of the longest in the world. China's mainland coastline measures approximately 18,000 km. See World Bank, *Philippines Environment Monitor 2005: Coastal and Marine Resource Management* (English) (Washington, D.C.: World Bank, 2005); Wanfei Qui et al., "Challenges in Developing China's Marine Protected Area System", *Marine Policy* 33, no. 4 (2009): 599–605.

74. "Eleven Provinces Designate Red Line", *People's Daily*, 9 January 2017, http://society.people.com.cn/n1/2017/0109/c1008-29006930.html.

75. Yuzhou Li and David Fluharty, "Marine Protected Area Networks in China: Challenges and Prospects", *Marine Policy* 85 (2017): 9, https://doi.org/10.1016/j.marpol.2017.08.001.

76. Ibid.

77. UNEP and the World Conservation Monitoring Centre, as compiled by the World Resources Institute, "Marine Protected Areas", 2014, https://data.worldbank.org/indicator/ER.MRN.PTMR.ZS?end=2014&locations=BN-KH-ID-MY-PH-TH-VN-CN&start=2014&view=bar.

78. Li and Fluharty, "Marine Protected Area", p. 9.

79. "China National Biodiversity Conservation Strategy and Action Plan (2011–2030)", 2011, https://www.cbd.int/doc/world/cn/cn-nbsap-v2-en.pdf.

80. Li and Fluharty, "Marine Protected Area", p. 9.

81. Ibid.

82. Qui et al., "Challenges in Developing China's Marine Protected Area System", p. 601.

83. Li and Fluharty, "Marine Protected Area", p. 10.

84. Nguyen and Vu, "Building a Regional Network", p. 135.

85. Pham Thi Gam, *Coastal and Island Governance in Vietnam*, UN Ocean and Law of the Sea and Nippon Foundation, 2013, http://www.un.org/depts/los/nippon/unnff_programme_home/fellows_pages/fellows_papers/Pham_1314_VietNam.pdf.

86. Li and Fluharty, "Marine Protected Area", pp. 9–10.

87. Ibid.

88. Gloria Estenzo Ramos, "Protecting Our Protected Areas", *Inquirer.net*, 31 January 2016, http://cebudailynews.inquirer.net/84169/protecting-protected-areas.

89. Senate of the Philippines, "Expanded National Integrated Protected Areas System (NIPAS) Act", 23 May 2017, https://www.senate.gov.ph/lis/bill_res.aspx?congress=17&q=SBN-1444.

90. National Economic and Development Authority, "LEDAC Approves Legislative Agenda for the 17th Congress", 30 August 2017, http://www.neda.gov.ph/2017/08/30/ledac-approves-legislative-agenda-for-17th-congress/.

91. Ramos, "Protecting Our Protected Areas".

92. Jonathan Mayuga, "DENR Official Backs Bill Expanding Nipas Coverage", *Business Mirror*, 9 September 2016, https://businessmirror.com.ph/denr-official-backs-bill-expanding-nipas-coverage/; Yan, "Philippines Declares Largest Marine Protected Areas"; and Dean Rawlins, "The Marine Protected Area Network of Batangas Province, Philippines: An Outcome-Based Evaluation of Effectiveness and Performance", 2008, https://www.apu.ac.jp/rcaps/uploads/fckeditor/publications/journal/RJAPS_V25_Dean.pdf.

93. Ibid.

94. Marc Hockings et al., *Evaluating the Management Effectiveness of Thailand's Marine and Coastal Protected Area* (Gland, Switzerland: International Union for Conservation of Nature, 2012), https://www.mangrovesforthefuture.org/assets/Repository/Documents/Management-Effectiveness-MFF-IUCN-2012.pdf.

95. Khairunnisa Ahmad Kamil et al., "An Assessment of Marine Protected Areas as a Marine Management Strategy in Southeast Asia: A Literature Review", *Ocean and Coastal Management* 145 (2017): 72–81, https://doi-org.ezlibproxy1.ntu.edu.sg/10.1016/j.ocecoaman.2017.05.008.

96. Ibid.

97. Ibid.

98. Rawlins, "The Marine Protected Area".

99. Ibid.

100. Yan, "Philippines Declares Largest Marine Protected Areas".

101. Ibid.

102. Nicolas Leong, "Catch-22 in the South China Sea: Why Preserving Fish Stocks is Key to a Resolution", *Global Risks Insights*, 10 December 2017, https://globalriskinsights.com/2017/12/south-china-sea-environment-fishery/.

103. A.C. Alcala, *Proceedings of Conference on the Philippines-Vietnam Joint Oceanographic and Marine Scientific Research Expedition in the South China Sea* (Dumaguete City: Oceanfriends Foundation Inc., 2008).

104. Nguyen and Vu, "Building a Regional Network".

105. Ibid.

106. Ibid.

107. Ibid.

108. Ibid.

109. Vaudine Engalnd, "Why are South China Sea Tensions Rising?" *BBC News*, 10 September 2017, http://www.bbc.com/news/world-asia-pacific-11152948.

110. Vo Si Tuan and John Pernetta, "The UNEP/GEF South China Sea Project: Lessons Learnt in Regional Cooperation", *Ocean and Coastal Management* 53, no. 9 (2010): 589–96.

111. Ibid.

112. Ibid.

113. MedPAN et al., *The 2016 Status of Marine Protected Areas in the Mediterranean* (Athens: MedPAN and UNEP-MAP-SPA/RAC, 2016), http://d2ouvy59p0dg6k.cloudfront.net/downloads/medpan_forum_mpa_2016___brochure_a4_en_web_1_.pdf.

114. Ibid.

115. Ibid.

116. Ibid.

117. Ibid.

118. Philip A. Kramer and Patricia Richards Kramer, *Ecoregional Conservation Planning for the Mesoamerican Caribbean Reef* (Washington, D.C.: WWF, 2002), https://www.researchgate.net/profile/Philip_Kramer/publication/242549382_Ecoregional_Conservation_Planning_for_the_Mesoamerican_Caribbean_Reef/links/5553ba6b08ae980ca6085ac4/Ecoregional-Conservation-Planning-for-the-Mesoamerican-Caribbean-Reef.pdf.

119. Rosario Alvarez and Karen Wong, *Mesoamerican Reef: Building the Future after Tulum 1997* (Guatemala, C.A.: Mesoamerican Reef Fund (MAR Fund), 2015), http://www.marfund.org/wp-content/uploads/2015/08/Building-the-Future-after-Tulum-1997.pdf.

120. North American Marine Protected Areas Network, "What is the North American Marine Protected Areas Network?" undated, http://www2.cec.org/nampan/ (accessed 17 July 2019).

121. Ibid.

122. Ibid.

123. Ibid.

124. The Convention on Biological Diversity defines ecosystem approach as a strategy for the integrated management of land, water and living resources that promotes conservation and sustainable use in an equitable way. See Convention on Biological Diversity (CBD) Secretariat, "Decision V/6 Ecosystem Approach. Document UNEP/CBD/COP/5/6", Nairobi, Kenya, 2000, https://www.cbd.int/decision/cop/?id=7148.

125. Corine Brunois and Magali Mabari, "Report: MedPan Network Regional Training Workshop – Towards More Effective Communication of Mediterranean Marine Protected Areas", Tunisia, 25–27 April 2017, https://drive.google.com/file/d/0Bw8D-TFFFccxSVhIaUIxM3ZETU0/view.

126. Ibid.

127. Ibid.

128. Alvarez and Wong, *Mesoamerican Reef.*

129. Ibid.

130. Robert Bensted-Smith and Hugh Kirkman, *Comparison of Approaches to Management of Large Marine Areas* (Cambridge, UK: Publ. Fauna & Flora International, and Washington, D.C.: Conservation International, 2010).

131. UNESCO, "Seven Marine Sites Sign Historic Agreement", 19 October 2016, http://whc.unesco.org/en/news/1575/.

132. The seven marine sites included in the marine corridor are Galapagos Islands, Coiba National Park, Cocos Island National Park, Malpelo Fauna and Flora Sanctuary, Area de Conservación Guanacaste, Archipiélago de Revillagigedo, and Islands and Protected Areas of the Gulf of California.

133. UNESCO, "Seven Marine Sites".

134. Li Jing, "The South China Sea Feud is Taking a Serious Toll on Fish and Reefs", *South China Morning Post*, 10 June 2016, http://www.businessinsider.com/south-china-sea-dispute-harming-fish-and-reefs-2016-6/?IR=T.

135. Sam Bateman, "Building Cooperation for Managing the South China Sea Without Strategic Trust", *Asia and the Pacific Policy Studies* 4, no. 2 (2017): 254.

136. Ibid.

137. Ibid.

138. Ibid.

139. "Declaration on the Conduct of Parties in the South China Sea", Phnom Penh, Cambodia, 4 November 2002.

140. "Declaration for the Decade".

141. The ASEAN Secretariat, *ASEAN 2025*, p. 110.

REFERENCES

Alcala, A.C. 2008. *Proceedings of Conference on the Philippines-Vietnam Joint Oceanographic and Marine Scientific Research Expedition in the South China Sea*. Dumaguete City: Oceanfriends Foundation Inc.

Allison, Gary W., Jane Lubchenco, and Mark H. Carr. 1998. "Marine Reserves are Necessary but Not Sufficient for Marine Conservation". *Ecological Application* 8: 79–92. https://doi.org/10.1890/1051-0761(1998)8[S79:MRANBN]2.0.CO;2.

Alvarez, Rosario and Karen Wong. 2015. *Mesoamerican Reef: Building the Future after Tulum 1997*. Guatemala, C.A.: Mesoamerican Reef Fund (MAR Fund). http://www.marfund.org/wp-content/uploads/2015/08/Building-the-Future-after-Tulum-1997.pdf.

Anderson, Lauren. 2017. "An Ocean in Chains: Reviewing SDG 14 in Advance of the HLPF". Policy Brief. International Institute for Sustainable Development, 6 July 2017. http://sdg.iisd.org/commentary/policy-briefs/an-ocean-in-chains-reviewing-sdg-14-in-advance-of-the-hlpf/.

ASEAN Declaration on Heritage Parks. Yangon, Myanmar, 18 December 2003.

ASEAN Secretariat. 2015. "ASEAN 2025: Forging Ahead Together". Jakarta: ASEAN Secretariat. http://www.asean.org/storage/2015/12/ASEAN-2025-Forging-Ahead-Together-final.pdf.

Bateman, Sam. 2017. "Building Cooperation for Managing the South China Sea Without Strategic Trust". *Asia and the Pacific Policy Studies* 4, no. 2: 251–59.

"Battle to Save Dwindling Fish Stocks in S-E Asia". *Straits Times*, 31 August 2017. http://www.straitstimes.com/asia/se-asia/battle-to-save-dwindling-fish-stocks-in-s-e-asia.

Bensted-Smith, Robert and Hugh Kirkman. 2010. *Comparison of Approaches to Management of Large Marine Areas*. Cambridge, UK: Publ. Fauna & Flora International, and Washington, D.C.: Conservation International.

Biodiversity Information Sharing Service (ASEAN Clearing House Mechanism). Undated. "Seagrass". http://chm.aseanbiodiversity.org/index.php?option=com_content&view=article&id=169&Itemid=169.

————. 2010. "Protected Area Gap Analysis in the ASEAN Region". http://chm.aseanbiodiversity.org/index.php?option=com_content&view=article&id=145&Itemid=231.

Blanco G., R. Gerlagh, S. Suh, J. Barrett, H. C. de Coninck, C. F. Diaz Morejon, R. Mathur, N. Nakicenovic, A. Ofosu Ahenkora, J. Pan, H. Pathak, J. Rice, R. Richels, S. J. Smith, D. I. Stern, F. L. Toth, and P. Zhou. 2014. "Drivers, Trends and Mitigation". In *Climate Change 2014: Mitigation of Climate Change. Contribution of Working Group III to the Fifth Assessment Report of the Intergovernmental Panel on Climate Change*, edited by O. Edenhofer, R. Pichs-Madruga, Y. Sokona, E. Farahani, S. Kadner, K. Seyboth, A. Adler, I. Baum, S. Brunner, P. Eickemeier, B. Kriemann, J. Savolainen, S. Schlomer,

C. von Stechow, T. Zwichel, and J.C. Minx. Cambridge, UK: Cambridge University Press, pp. 351–412.

Brunois, Corine and Magali Mabari. 2017. "Report: MedPan Network Regional Training Workshop – Towards More Effective Communication of Mediterranean Marine Protected Areas". Tunisia, 25–27 April 2017. https://drive.google.com/file/d/0Bw8D-TFFFccxSVhIaUIxM3ZETU0/view.

Cai Rongshuo, Haixia Guo, Di Fu, Xiuhua Yan, and Hongjian Tan. 2017. "Response and Adaptation to Climate Change in the South China Sea and Coral Sea". In *Climate Change Adaptation in Pacific Countries: Fostering Resilience and Improving the Quality of Life*, edited by Walter Leal Filho. Basel, Switzerland: Springer International Publishing AG, pp. 163–76.

Carew-Reid, Jeremy. 2007. "Rapid Assessment of the Extent and Impact of Sea Level Rise in Viet Nam". Climate Change Discussion Paper 1. Brisbane, Australia: International Centre for Environmental Management. http://www.icem.com.au/documents/climatechange/icem_slr/ICEM_SLR_final_report.pdf.

Chan, Francis. 2017. "Indonesia Blows Up and Sinks Another 81 Fishing Boats for Poaching". *Straits Times*, 2 April 2017. http://www.straitstimes.com/asia/se-asia/indonesia-blows-up-and-sinks-another-81-fishing-boats-for-poaching.

Cheung, William W.L., Jorge L. Sarmiento, John Dunne, Thomas L. Frölicher, Vicky W.Y. Lam, M.L. Deng Palomares, Reg Watson, and Daniel Pauly. 2013. "Shrinking of Fishes Exacerbates Impacts of Global Ocean Changes on Marine Ecosystems". *Nature Climate Change* 3: 254–58. http://www.nature.com/nclimate/journal/v3/n3/full/nclimate1691.html?foxtrotcallback=true.

Cheung, William W., R. Watson, and D. Pauly. 2013. "Signature of Ocean Warming in Global Fisheries Catch". *Nature* 497: 365–68.

Cheung, William W.L., Vicky W.Y. Lam, Jorge L. Sarmiento, Kelly Kearney, Reg Watson, Dirk Zeller, and Daniel Pauly. 2010. "Large-scale Redistribution of Maximum Fisheries Catch Potential in the Global Ocean under Climate Change". *Global Change Biology* 16, no. 1: 24–35.

"China National Biodiversity Conservation Strategy and Action Plan (2011–2030)", 2011. https://www.cbd.int/doc/world/cn/cn-nbsap-v2-en.pdf.

"China's Gross Oceanic Product Exceeds $1 Trillion". *Xinhua*, 17 March 2017. http://www.chinadaily.com.cn/business/2017-03/17/content_28589909.htm.

China-SNAP. 2011. *The Second National Chinese Assessment Report on Climate Change Chinese Government* (in Chinese, with English abstract). Beijing: Science Press, pp. 245–56.

"China Trade Depends More on Peace in South China Sea Shipping Lanes". *China Daily*, 7 August 2017. http://usa.chinadaily.com.cn/epaper/2017-08/07/content_30359481.htm.

Chuang, J. 2016. "The United States as Global Sheriff: Using Unilateral Sanctions to Combat Human Trafficking". *Michigan Journal of International Law* 37, no. 4: 611–59.

Convention on Biological Diversity (CBD) Secretariat. 2000. "Decision V/6 Ecosystem Approach. Document UNEP/CBD/COP/5/6". Nairobi, Kenya. https://www.cbd.int/decision/cop/?id=7148.

DeCarlo, Thomas M., Anne L. Cohen, George T.F. Wong, Kristen A. Davis, Pat Lohmann, and Keryea Soong. 2017. "Mass Coral Mortality under Local Amplification of 2°C Ocean Warming". *Science Reports* 7, no. 44586. Doi: 10.1038/srep44586.

"Declaration for the Decade of Coastal and Marine Environmental Protection in the South China Sea (2017–2027)". Manila, Philippines, 13 November 2017.

"Declaration on the Conduct of Parties in the South China Sea". Phnom Penh, Cambodia, 4 November 2002.

Derraik, Jose G.B. 2002. "The Pollution of the Marine Environment by Plastic Debris: A Review". *Marine Pollution Bulletin* 44, no. 9: 844–47.

"Eleven Provinces Designate Red Line". *People's Daily*, 9 January 2017. http://society.people.com.cn/n1/2017/0109/c1008-29006930.html.

Engalnd, Vaudine. 2017. "Why are South China Sea Tensions Rising?" *BBC News*, 10 September 2017. http://www.bbc.com/news/world-asia-pacific-11152948.

Ewing, J. Jackson. 2016. "Environmental Security". In *An Introduction to Non-Traditional Security Studies: A Transnational Approach*, edited by Mely Caballero-Anthony. London: Sage, pp. 95–113.

Filho, Walter Leal, ed. 2017. *Climate Change Adaptation in Pacific Countries: Fostering Resilience and Improving the Quality of Life*. Basel, Switzerland: Springer International Publishing AG.

Food and Agriculture Organization (FAO). 2014. "Fishery and Aquaculture Country Profiles: The Republic of the Philippines; and the Republic of Indonesia". Country Profile Fact Sheets. Rome. http://www.fao.org/fishery/facp/PHL/en and http://www.fao.org/fishery/facp/IDN/en.

———. 2014. *The State of World Fisheries and Aquaculture: Opportunities and Challenges*. Rome: FAO.

Giri, C., E. Ochieng, L.L. Tieszen, Z. Zhu, A. Singh, T. Loveland, J. Masek, and N. Duke. 2011. "Status and Distribution of Mangrove Forests of the World Using Earth Observation Satellite Data". *Global Ecology and Biogeography* 20, no. 1: 154–59.

Godoy, Mario D.P. and Luiz D. De Lacerda. 2015. "Mangroves Response to Climate Change: A Review of Recent Findings on Mangrove Extension and Distribution". *Annals of the Brazilian Academy of Sciences* 87, no. 2: 651–67. http://www.scielo.br/pdf/aabc/v87n2/0001-3765-aabc-201520150055.pdf.

Gomez, Edgardo D. 2001. "Marine Scientific Research in the South China Sea and Environmental Security". *Ocean Development & International Law* 32, no. 2: 205–11. https://doi.org/10.1080/00908320151100343.

Hockings, Marc, Peter Shadie, Geoff Vincent, and Songtam Suksawang. 2012. *Evaluating the Management Effectiveness of Thailand's Marine and Coastal Protected Area*. Gland, Switzerland: International Union for Conservation of Nature. https://www.mangrovesforthefuture.org/assets/Repository/Documents/Management-Effectiveness-MFF-IUCN-2012.pdf.

Hoegh-Guldberg, Ove, Hans Hoegh-Guldberg, Charlie Veron, Alison Green, Ed Gomez, Melanie King, Janice Lough, Ambariyanto, Lara Hansen, Josh Cinner, Geoff Dews, C. Mark Eakin, Tyler Christensen, Garry Russ, Heidi Schuttenberg, Michael Abbey, Francis Areki, Rosemary A. Kosaka, Eileen L. Peña, Alexander Tewfik, and Jamie Oliver. 2009. *The Coral Triangle and Climate Change: Ecosystems, People and Societies at Risk*. Brisbane, Australia: World Wide Fund for Nature (WWF) Australia.

Hoegh-Guldberg, O., R. Cai, E.S. Poloczanska, P.G. Brewer, S. Sundby, K. Hilmi, V.J. Fabry, and S. Jung. 2014. "The Ocean". In *Climate Change 2014: Impacts, Adaptation, and Vulnerability. Part B: Regional Aspects, Contribution of Working Group II to the Fifth Assessment Report of the Intergovernmental Panel on Climate Change*, edited by V.R. Barros, C.B. Field, D.J. Dokken, M.D. Mastrandrea, K.J. Mach, T.E. Bilir, M. Chatterjee, K.L. Ebi, Y.O. Estrada, R.C. Genova, B. Girma, E.S. Kissel, A.N. Levy, S. MacCracken, P.R. Mastrandrea, and L.L. White. Cambridge, UK: Cambridge University Press, pp. 1655–731.

Hoegh-Guldberg, Ove, et al. 2015. *Reviving the Ocean Economy: The Case for Action—2015*. Gland, Switzerland: WWF.

International Union for Conservation of Nature (IUCN). Undated. "What is a Protected Area?" https://www.iucn.org/theme/protected-areas/about (accessed 17 July 2019).

Jackson, Angus C. and Jason MacIlvenny. 2011. "Coastal Squeeze on Rocky Shores in Northern Scotland and Some Possible Ecological Impacts". *Journal of Experimental Marine Biology and Ecology* 400, no. 1–2: 314–21.

Jacobs, Andrew. 2017. "China's Appetite Pushes Fisheries to the Brink". *New York Times*, 30 April 2017. https://www.nytimes.com/2017/04/30/world/asia/chinas-appetite-pushes-fisheries-to-the-brink.html.

Juinio-Menez, Marie Antonette. 2015. "Biophysical and Genetic Connectivity Considerations in Marine Biodiversity Conservation and Management in the South China Sea". *Journal of International Wildlife Law and Policy* 18, no. 2: 110–19.

Kamil, Khairunnisa Ahmad, Atakelty Hailu, Abbie Rogers, and Ram Pandit. 2017. "An Assessment of Marine Protected Areas as a Marine Management Strategy in Southeast Asia: A Literature Review". *Ocean and Coastal*

Management 145: 72–81. https://doi-org.ezlibproxy1.ntu.edu.sg/10.1016/j. ocecoaman.2017.05.008.

Karim, Jashimuddin and Ansarul Karim. 1993. "Effect of Salinity on the Growth of Some Mangrove Plants in Bangladesh". In *Towards the Rational Use of High Salinity Tolerant Plants, Vol. 1: Deliberations about High Salinity Tolerant Plants and Ecosystems*, edited by Helmut Lieth and A. Al Masoom. The Netherlands: Kluwer Academic Publishers, pp. 187–92. https://link.springer. com/chapter/10.1007/978-94-011-1858-3_20.

Kramer, Philip A. and Patricia Richards Kramer. 2002. *Ecoregional Conservation Planning for the Mesoamerican Caribbean Reef*. Washington, D.C.: WWF. https:// www.researchgate.net/profile/Philip_Kramer/publication/242549382_ Ecoregional_Conservation_Planning_for_the_Mesoamerican_Caribbean_Reef/ links/5553ba6b08ae980ca6085ac4/Ecoregional-Conservation-Planning-for-the-Mesoamerican-Caribbean-Reef.pdf.

Leong, Nicolas. 2017. "Catch-22 in the South China Sea: Why Preserving Fish Stocks is Key to a Resolution". *Global Risks Insights*, 10 December 2017. https:// globalriskinsights.com/2017/12/south-china-sea-environment-fishery/.

Li, Jing. 2015. "China Produces about a Third of Plastic Waste Polluting the World's Oceans, Says Report". *South China Morning Post*, 14 February 2015. http://www.scmp.com/article/1711744/china-produces-about-third-plastic-waste-polluting-worlds-oceans-says-report.

―――. 2016. "The South China Sea Feud is Taking a Serious Toll on Fish and Reefs". *South China Morning Post*, 10 June 2016. http://www.businessinsider. com/south-china-sea-dispute-harming-fish-and-reefs-2016-6/?IR=T.

Li, Yuzhou and David Fluharty. 2017. "Marine Protected Area Networks in China: Challenges and Prospects". *Marine Policy* 85: 8–16. https://doi. org/10.1016/j.marpol.2017.08.001.

Mayuga, Jonathan. 2016. "DENR Official Backs Bill Expanding Nipas Coverage". *Business Mirror*, 9 September 2016. https://businessmirror.com.ph/denr-official-backs-bill-expanding-nipas-coverage/.

MedPAN et al. 2016. *The 2016 Status of Marine Protected Areas in the Mediterranean*. Athens: MedPAN and UNEP-MAP-SPA/RAC. http://d2ouvy59p0dg6k. cloudfront.net/downloads/medpan_forum_mpa_2016___brochure_a4_en_ web_1_.pdf.

Nadhira, Rodzi. 2017. "Malaysia Turns up the Heat, Sets Foreign Boats Ablaze for Illegal Fishing". *Straits Times*, 30 August 2017. http://www.straitstimes. com/asia/se-asia/malaysia-turns-up-the-heat-sets-foreign-boats-ablaze-for-illegal-fishing.

National Economic and Development Authority. 2017. "LEDAC Approves Legislative Agenda for the 17th Congress", 30 August 2017. http://www.neda. gov.ph/2017/08/30/ledac-approves-legislative-agenda-for-17th-congress/.

Nguyen, Chu Hoi and Vu Hai Dang. 2015. "Building a Regional Network and Management Regime of Marine Protected Areas in the South China Sea for Sustainable Development". *Journal of International Wildlife Law & Policy* 18, no. 2: 128–38. https://doi.org/10.1080/13880292.2015.1044797.

North American Marine Protected Areas Network. Undated. "What is the North American Marine Protected Areas Network?" http://www2.cec.org/nampan/ (accessed 17 July 2019).

Oceanographer of the Navy, The Office of the. 2011. *Arctic Environmental Assessment and Outlook Report*. https://www.hsdl.org/?view&did=685137.

O'Loughlin, Toni. 2009. "WWF Warns Vast Coral Reef in Southeast Asia May Disappear by End of the Century". *Guardian*, 13 May 2009. https://www.theguardian.com/environment/2009/may/13/coral-reef-asia-disappearing/.

Organisation for Economic Co-operation and Development (OECD). 2017. *Marine Protected Areas: Economics, Management and Effective Policy Mixes*. Paris: OECD Publishing. https://www.oecd.org/env/marine-protected-areas-9789264276208-en.htm.

Pelejero, Carles, Eva Calvo, Malcolm T. McCulloch, John F. Marshall, Michael K. Gagan, Janice M. Lough, and Bradley N. Opdyke. 2005. "Preindustrial to Modern Interdecadal Variability in Coral Reef Ph". *Science* 309, no. 5744: 2204–7.

Permanent Court of Arbitration. 2016. "The South China Sea Arbitration Award of 12 July 2016". PCA Case No. 2013–19. https://pca-cpa.org/wp-content/uploads/sites/175/2016/07/PH-CN-20160712-Award.pdf.

Pham, Thi Gam. 2013. *Coastal and Island Governance in Vietnam*. UN Ocean and Law of the Sea and Nippon Foundation. http://www.un.org/depts/los/nippon/unnff_programme_home/fellows_pages/fellows_papers/Pham_1314_VietNam.pdf.

Polidoro, Beth A., Kent E. Carpenter, Lorna Collins, Norman C. Duke, Aaron M. Ellison, Joanna C. Ellison, Elizabeth J. Farnsworth, Edwino S. Fernando, Kandasamy Kathiresan, Nico E. Koedam, Suzanne R. Livingstone, Toyohiko Miyagi, Gregg E. Moore, Vien Ngoc Nam, Jin Eong Ong, Jurgenne H. Primavera, Severino G. Salmo III, Jonnell C. Sanciangco, Sukristijono Sukardjo, Yamin Wang, and Jean Wan Hong Yong. 2010. "The Loss of Species: Mangrove Extinction Risk and Geographic Areas of Global Concern". *PLoS ONE* 5, no. 4: e10095. https://doi.org/10.1371/journal.pone.0010095.

Poling, Gregory B. and Conor Cronin. 2017. *Illegal, Unreported, and Unregulated Fishing as a National Security Threat*. Washington, D.C.: Center for Strategic and International Studies (CSIS).

Qui, Wanfei, Bin Wang, Peter J.S. Jones, and Jan Axmacher. 2009. "Challenges in Developing China's Marine Protected Area System". *Marine Policy* 33, no. 4: 599–605.

Ramos, Gloria Estenzo. 2016. "Protecting Our Protected Areas". *Inquirer.net*, 31 January 2016. http://cebudailynews.inquirer.net/84169/protecting-protected-areas.

Rathi, Akshat. 2016. "The Most Ignored Aspect of the South China Sea Brawl Might be the Key to Solving it". *Quartz*, 26 July 2016. https://qz.com/741989/the-most-ignored-aspect-of-the-south-china-sea-brawl-might-be-the-key-to-solving-it/.

Rawlins, Dean. 2008. "The Marine Protected Area Network of Batangas Province, Philippines: An Outcome-Based Evaluation of Effectiveness and Performance". https://www.apu.ac.jp/rcaps/uploads/fckeditor/publications/journal/RJAPS_V25_Dean.pdf.

Saenger, Peter. 2002. *Mangrove Ecology, Silviculture and Conservation*. Dordrecht, the Netherlands: Springer.

Sarkar, Md. Sujahangir Kabir, Rawshan Ara Begum, Joy Jacqueline Pereira, Abdul Hamid Jaafar, and Mohd Yusof Saari. 2014. "Impacts of and Adaptations to Sea Level Rise in Malaysia". *Asian Journal of Water, Environment and Pollution* 11, no. 2: 29–36.

Selig, Elizabeth R. and John F. Bruno. 2010. "A Global Analysis of the Effectiveness of Marine Protected Areas in Preventing Coral Loss". *PLoS One* 5: e9278. https://dx.doi.org/10.1371%2Fjournal.pone.0009278.

Senate of the Philippines. 2017. "Expanded National Integrated Protected Areas System (NIPAS) Act", 23 May 2017. https://www.senate.gov.ph/lis/bill_res.aspx?congress=17&q=SBN-1444.

Simeon, Louise Maureen. 2017. "Sustainable Mangrove Management Pushed amid Climate Change". *Philippine Star*, 3 September 2017. http://www.philstar.com/agriculture/2017/09/03/1735155/sustainable-mangrove-mngmt-pushed-amid-climate-change.

Singh, Abhit. 2016. "A Looming Environmental Crisis in the South China Sea". *Asia Maritime Transparency Initiative*, 12 August 2016. https://amti.csis.org/looming-environmental-crisis-south-china-sea/.

Smillie, Susan. 2017. "From Sea to Plate: How Plastic Got into Our Fish". *The Guardian*, 14 February 2017. https://www.theguardian.com/lifeandstyle/2017/feb/14/sea-to-plate-plastic-got-into-fish.

"South China Sea Countries Continue to Cooperate on Integrating Fisheries and Marine Ecosystem Management". *SEAFDEC News*, 1 November 2016. http://www.seafdec.org/south-china-sea-countries-cooperate-integrating-fisheries-marine-ecosystem-management/.

Spalding, Mark, Mami Kainuma, and Lorna Collins. 2010. *World Atlas of Mangroves*. London, UK: Earthscan.

Sulehan, Junaenah, Rahamah Abu Bakar Noor, Abd Hair Awang, Mohd Yusof b. Abdullah, and Puay Liu Ong. 2013. "Development at the Margins: Livelihood and Sustainability of Communities at Malaysia-Indonesia Borders". *Sociology & Space* 51, no. 3: 547–61.

The Pew Charitable Trusts. 2013. "Warming Oceans are Reshaping Fisheries: Scientists Detect Global Shift in Species". http://www.pewtrusts.org/~/media/assets/2013/05/15/osdwarmingoceansweb.pdf.

United Nations. Undated. "Goal 14: Conserve and Sustainably Use the Oceans, Seas and Marine Resources". Sustainable Development Goals. New York: United Nations. http://www.un.org/sustainabledevelopment/oceans/ (accessed 23 July 2019).

————. Undated. "Registry of Voluntary Commitments". The Ocean Conference. https://oceanconference.un.org/commitments/ (accessed 15 October 2017).

————. 1987. *Our Common Future – Brundtland Report*. Oxford: Oxford University Press.

United Nations Educational, Scientific and Cultural Organization (UNESCO). Undated. "Facts and Figures on Marine Biodiversity". Paris. http://www.unesco.org/new/en/natural-sciences/ioc-oceans/focus-areas/rio-20-ocean/blueprint-for-the-future-we-want/marine-biodiversity/facts-and-figures-on-marine-biodiversity/ (accessed 17 July 2019).

————. 2016. "Seven Marine Sites Sign Historic Agreement". News and Events, 19 October 2016. http://whc.unesco.org/en/news/1575/.

UN Environmental Programme (UNEP). 2004. *Seagrass in the South China Sea*. UNEP/GEF/THE SOUTH CHINA SEA Technical Publication No. 3. Bangkok, Thailand: UNEP. http://iwlearn.net/resolveuid/6abc857925542c108f72e2f1e9147b97.

————. 2006. *Reversing Environmental Degradation Trends in the South China Sea and Gulf of Thailand*. Report of the Seventh Meeting of the Regional Working Group for the Seagrass. Bangkok, Thailand: UNEP.

————. 2007. *Land-Based Pollution in the South China Sea*. UNEP/GEF/SCS Technical Publication No. 10. Bangkok, Thailand: UNEP.

————. 2008. *National Reports on Mangroves in South China Sea*. UNEP/GEF/THE SOUTH CHINA SEA Technical Publication No. 14. Bangkok, Thailand: UNEP.

————. 2008. *Strategic Action Programme for the South China Sea*. UNEP/GEF/THE SOUTH CHINA SEA Technical Publication No. 16. Bangkok, Thailand: UNEP.

UNEP and the World Conservation Monitoring Centre, as compiled by the World Resources Institute. 2014. "Marine Protected Areas". https://data.worldbank.org/indicator/ER.MRN.PTMR.ZS?end=2014&locations=BN-KH-ID-MY-PH-TH-VN-CN&start=2014&view=bar.

UN General Assembly. 2017. "Our Ocean, Our Future: Call for Action". Resolution 71/312, 6 July 2017. http://www.un.org/ga/search/view_doc.asp?symbol=A/RES/71/312&Lang=E.

University of York. 2011. "Further, Faster, Higher: Wildlife Responds Increasingly Rapidly to Climate Change". News Release, 18 August 2011. https://www.york.ac.uk/news-and-events/news/2011/research/wildlife-responds/.

Vo, Si Tuan. 2013. "Development of a Coral Reef Management Strategy within the Framework of the UNEP/GEF South China Sea Project". *Galaxea, Journal of Coral Reef Studies* 15, Special Issue: 9–15. https://doi.org/10.3755/galaxea.15.9.

Vo, Si Tuan and John C. Pernetta. 2010. "The UNEP/GEF South China Sea Project: Lessons Learnt in Regional Cooperation". *Ocean and Coastal Management* 53, no. 9: 589–96.

Vo, Si Tuan, John C. Pernetta, and Christopher J. Paterson. 2013. "Status and Trends in Coastal Habitats of the South China Sea". *Ocean and Coastal Management* 85, Part B: 153–63.

Vu, Hai Dang. 2014. *Marine Protected Areas Network in the South China Sea: Charting a Course for Future Cooperation.* Leiden: Koninklijke Brill NV.

Ward, Raymond D., Daniel A. Friess, Richard H. Day, and Richard A. MacKenzie. 2016. "Impacts of Climate Change on Mangrove Ecosystems: A Region by Region Overview". *Ecosystem Health and Sustainability* 2, no. 4: 1–25. http://onlinelibrary.wiley.com/doi/10.1002/ehs2.1211/full.

Wearden, Graeme. 2016. "More Plastic than Fish in the Sea by 2050, says Ellen MacArthur". *The Guardian*, 19 January 2016. https://www.theguardian.com/business/2016/jan/19/more-plastic-than-fish-in-the-sea-by-2050-warns-ellen-macarthur.

World Bank. Undated. "2.1 World Development Indicators: Population Dynamics". World Development Indicators, New York. http://wdi.worldbank.org/table/2.1 (accessed 23 June 2019).

———. 2005. *Philippines Environment Monitor 2005: Coastal and Marine Resource Management (English).* Washington, D.C.: World Bank.

Wu, Zhai, Ye Xu, Minggang Cai, Sha-Yen Cheng, Huorong Chen, Dongren Huang, Kai Chen, Yan Lin, Tianyao Li, Mengyang Liu, Hengxiang Deng, Minjie Ni, and Hongwei Ke. 2017. "Metals in the Fishes from Yongshu Island, Southern South China Sea: Human Health Risk Assessment". *Journal of Toxicology*: 1–17. https://doi.org/10.1155/2017/2458293.

Yan, Gregg. 2016. "Philippines Declares Largest Marine Protected Areas". *Amazon of the Ocean*, 8 November 2016. http://thecoraltriangle.com/stories/philippines-declares-largest-marine-protected-area.

Zhang, Hongzhou. 2016. "China's Fishing Industry: Current Status, Government Policies and Future Prospects". In *Becoming a Great "Maritime Power": A Chinese Dream*, edited by Michael McDevitt. Arlington, VA: CNA. https://www.cna.org/news/events/china-and-maritime-power.

5

HUMANITARIAN ASSISTANCE AND DISASTER RESPONSE

Christopher Chen, Yen Ne Foo and Margareth Sembiring

5.1 Simultaneous Disasters in Southeast Asia: Is Risk Outpacing Resilience?

Since Southeast Asian leaders signed the ASEAN Agreement on Disaster Management and Emergency Response (AADMER) in 2005, the region has prioritized developing national and regional disaster management capabilities to respond to disasters. However, the recent back-to-back disasters that occurred between July and August 2018 tested the response capacities of national governments and the humanitarian community. Parts of Myanmar, Vietnam, Laos, Cambodia and the Philippines battled floods of varying severity induced by seasonal monsoon rains, tropical storms and a dam collapse on a tributary of the Mekong River. Meanwhile, Indonesia's Lombok Island, West Nusa Tenggara was hit by multiple earthquakes and aftershocks between 29 July and 19 August. The ASEAN Coordinating Centre for Humanitarian Assistance on disaster management (AHA Centre) reported that at the peak of these disasters, over 588,000 people were displaced and more than 5.2 million people in Southeast Asia were affected.[1] Against the backdrop of recent disasters generating simultaneous responses, this chapter makes key observations on Southeast Asia's ability to meet the immediate needs of disaster-affected communities while building greater disaster resilience for the future. It assesses the (i) institutionalization of disaster management in ASEAN; (ii) localization of disaster response; and (iii) opportunities for financial risk management for building disaster-resilient communities.

5.2 ASEAN in the Eye of the Storm—Institutionalization of Disaster Management in ASEAN

In assessing current and future disaster management capabilities, this chapter focuses on the floods in Laos and Cambodia after the collapse of a saddle dam of the Xe Pian-Xe Nam Noy hydropower project, floods in Myanmar caused by heavy monsoon rainfall and a breached dam in the Bago region, and the earthquakes and aftershocks in Lombok, West Nusa Tenggara, Indonesia. It identifies the evolution of a regional mechanism to respond to disasters grounded in the legally-binding AADMER. This agreement was ratified by all ASEAN member states and came into force in 2009 and represented ASEAN's regional commitment to respond to disasters. Its objectives are to provide effective disaster management mechanisms and to have ASEAN member states "jointly respond to disaster emergencies" through regional cooperation.[2] AADMER's most significant contribution has been to institutionalize disaster management within and between ASEAN member states. This framework provides a solid basis to further strengthen regional disaster response architecture as can be seen in the recent disasters in Indonesia, Laos and Myanmar.

Simultaneous Disasters

Heavy rainfall from the Southwest Monsoon since 4 June 2018 brought floods and landslides to 9 out of 14 regions in Myanmar. According to the AHA Centre, as of 6 August 2018, there were 17 recorded deaths and more than 150,000 people affected by the floods in Myanmar. It reported that although the Government of Myanmar issued flood warnings, their effectiveness was hindered by the lack of electricity and low mobile phone penetration in rural areas. The floods led to the closure of schools and damage to homes and crops, disrupting the country's rice supply. As part of the Government of Myanmar's disaster relief efforts, the country's Department of Disaster Management, Ministry of Social Welfare, Relief and Resettlement provided affected communities with rice, seeds and building materials to facilitate early recovery. Separately, the Swar irrigation dam in the Bago region was breached on 29 August 2018. Media outlets reported that the resulting floods from the breach inundated two villages in the nearby town of Swar and two villagers. More than 50,000 people were evacuated and a bridge on a major highway linking Yangon, Mandalay and Naypyitaw was damaged by surging flood waters.

A month or so later, on 23 July 2018, a saddle dam that was part of the Xe Pian-Xe Nam Noy hydropower project in Laos collapsed and let out five billion cubic litres of water into the Attapeu region. It washed away entire downstream villages, led to the evacuation of more than 1,000 families, and destroyed critical infrastructure including roads. It was reported that early warnings to villages in Attapeu were issued only three to four hours before the dam burst. Tides from the dam also washed into neighbouring Cambodia and an estimated 25,000 people in the northern Cambodian province of Stung Treng were evacuated. SK Engineering & Construction, a South Korean firm that was part of the joint venture to build the dam called the collapse an "accident" and stated that they had warned Laotian authorities about the possibility of a breach. The collapse of the dam coincided with rainfall brought by tropical storm Son-Tinh in July 2018 which flooded 349 villages in 41 districts of 10 provinces in Laos. The AHA Centre reported that 42.36 sq. km, of which 32.53 sq. km is agricultural land, was inundated. Within the flooded area, 302 buildings and 31.5 km of road length were submerged.

A series of moderate and strong earthquakes hit Lombok Island, West Nusa Tenggara (NTB), Indonesia between 29 July 2018 and 19 August 2018. Following the first magnitude of a 6.4 earthquake on 29 July, the NTB Governor declared an emergency response period that lasted until 11 August. This was subsequently extended to 25 August. The Government of Indonesia and the country's National Disaster Management Authority (BNPB) officially declined international assistance on the basis that national capacity and resources were sufficient to support emergency response and recovery led by the Provincial government. At the end of the emergency period, BNPB reported that the total number of fatalities were 561 and that over 430,000 people were displaced. It also put the value of loss and damage at IDR7.7 trillion.

Regional Response

At the regional level, the AHA Centre mobilized to respond to the floods in Laos, Myanmar and the earthquakes in Indonesia, in support of the National Disaster Management Organisations (NDMOs) and relevant government ministries of ASEAN member states. This was the first time the AHA Centre had responded to multiple disasters simultaneously. Various ASEAN-led disaster management mechanisms were activated during the response, including the In-Country Liaison Teams to facilitate coordination through the web-based Emergency Operations Centre and the Emergency Response and Assessment Team (ERAT) to support local procurement and reception of incoming ASEAN relief materials from the Disaster Emergency Logistic Stockpile of ASEAN (DELSA). In Lombok, the AHA Centre seconded staff to the Indonesian BNPB's Data and Information Centre to support dissemination of official information to international stakeholders.[3] Through its periodic Situation Updates, the AHA Centre also provided timely information and recommendations to humanitarian partners on operational needs in disaster-affected areas.

The AHA Centre's seamless integration into national disaster management operations, especially in countries where national governments have refrained from seeking international assistance, reveals its comparative advantage. Unlike a conventional humanitarian agency, the AHA Centre operates as an auxiliary to national governments; its mandate is to support national-led operations. Its contribution to disaster zones around Southeast Asia is indicative of strong working relationships within ASEAN through national disaster management actors not only at the strategic and policy levels but also at practical and operational levels. This is attributable to AADMER's focus on building a knowledge and skills base for disaster management at the regional and national levels. Many of the AHA Centre-led capacity development programmes such as the ASEAN-ERAT training, the AHA Centre Executive (ACE) Programme and the ASEAN Standards and Certification for Experts on Disaster Management (ASCEND) are intended not only to enhance its own preparedness and response capacity but also to create a network of disaster responders who abide by the "One ASEAN One Response" philosophy.

Further, AADMER pays particular attention to operationalizing joint responses by practising, assessing and reviewing ASEAN disaster management mechanisms and their interoperability with national and other international mechanisms through joint trainings, exercises and simulations. One example is the participation of ASEAN member states in the ASEAN Disaster Emergency Response Simulation Exercise (ARDEX), designed to test and validate the ASEAN Standard Operating Procedure for Regional Standby Arrangements and Coordination of Joint Disaster Relief and Emergency Response Operations. Another is the bi-annual ASEAN Regional Forum Disaster Relief Exercise (DiREx) which focuses on inter-agency and civil-military coordination. The AHA Centre has also attributed its ability to activate multiple responses to preparedness exercises like the ARDEX.[4]

Notwithstanding ASEAN's success at establishing and activating regional systems for disaster response, there are challenges to realizing AADMER's vision of institutionalizing disaster management in the region. AADMER envisions the AHA Centre as central to all stages of the disaster management cycle in the region. More than just building response capacity, the current AADMER Work Programme (2016–20) focuses on building disaster-resilient communities in ASEAN in response to future disasters. It places greater emphasis on areas such as enhancing risk assessments and improving risk awareness, building disaster-resilient infrastructure and services, establishing regional risk financing and insurance frameworks and developing capacity for post-disaster recovery. But, the AHA Centre is primarily a disaster responder; its strengths are in providing a platform for information sharing between ASEAN member states and their partners, response capacity building and coordinating interventions on the ground during an emergency. Recent engagements with representatives of the AHA Centre inform the authors that in responding to the multiple disasters in 2018, the AHA Centre's material and personnel resources have been stretched.

Expanding the AHA Centre's role beyond response to include post-disaster recovery programmes would require substantial investment in material and personnel resources. At the moment, ASEAN member states make a mandatory contribution of US$90,000 each to the AHA Centre budget. ASEAN member states also make voluntary contributions in funds and in kind. For instance, Indonesia provides the office space for the AHA Centre office and Malaysia contributes storage facilities for DELSA. But, 92 per cent of the total costs for AHA Centre programmes and operations in 2017 was funded by ASEAN Dialogue Partners.[5] ASEAN is aware of the need to secure the financial future of the AHA Centre. The ASEAN Vision 2025 on Disaster Management which charts the strategic direction for disaster management in the region identifies finance and resource mobilization as a key challenge to the implementation of AADMER.[6] As it is unlikely that ASEAN member states would substantively increase the level of mandatory contributions in the near term to the AHA Centre, ASEAN needs to explore other innovative financial sourcing strategies. This includes building partnerships with the private sector and tapping onto capital markets. The potential for leveraging funds from the capital markets is discussed in the section below.

Secondly, the effectiveness of regional disaster management mechanisms depends substantially on national capabilities. The response to the recent spate of disasters in the region shows that the institutionalization of disaster management and response capabilities among ASEAN member states is uneven. In Laos, the inadequacy of early warning systems was exposed when flood survivors said that they received no warning or instructions for evacuations before the collapse of the dam. Despite being aware of the risk, it was reported that the only warning from Vientiane came in the form of "a message on a piece of paper with a map telling residents to be careful, not to evacuate".[7] In Lombok, relief efforts in the aftermath of a 7.0 magnitude earthquake was said to be hampered by the lack of heavy lifting equipment, with rescuers being forced to dig by hand. This also hindered the removal of debris from damaged roads.[8]

AADMER places the biggest onus for institutionalizing the agreement on ASEAN member states. NDMOs who are represented on the ASEAN Committee of Disaster Management (ACDM) drive the implementation of AADMER and the prioritization of the items on the AADMER Work Programme at the regional level and are the national focal points for the implementation of AADMER at the national level. But, monitoring national progress in implementation is challenging. The gap between regional and national disaster management capacity suggests that AADMER is largely seen and implemented as a regional project, with more limited impact on national disaster risk management frameworks. There is room for NDMOs to consider how it can align national disaster management goals with regional ones and better leverage regional resources for national capacity building in technical and operational aspects of disaster management. Doing so would position national disaster management stakeholders for a more localized approach to disaster management.

5.3   Localization: Moving from Rhetoric to Practice

This brings us to the next point—the localization of disaster management in ASEAN. The localization agenda was one of the key discourses that came out of the World Humanitarian Summit (WHS) in 2016. The WHS pushed for sustained investment in local capacities, and the continued reinforcement of national and local systems. In the recent ASEAN Strategic Policy Dialogue on Disaster Management, it was heartening to note that participants and practitioners alike recognized the importance of a Community-Based Disaster Risk Management (CBDRM) approach, as well as a whole of society approach in disaster risk reduction.[9] While countries and humanitarian organizations in the region are starting to embrace this concept, much more needs to be done at a faster pace. Investing in community resilience and the capacities of first responders should be a priority.

As mentioned before, in the recent dam disaster in Laos, villagers in the Attapeu province received no warning before the hydropower dam collapsed. A spokesperson for the Mekong River Commission (MRC) indicated that "[r]obust emergency preparedness plan[s] [should] include specification of roles and responsibilities of all parties when dam failure is considered imminent, as well as communication flow charts and contact lists for households at risk".[10] The recurrent nature of disasters in the Southeast Asian region creates "opportunities to anticipate threats and proactively mitigate harmful impacts".[11] Indeed, as the Laos example highlights, it is important to involve the people who are potentially affected by disasters in emergency preparedness planning. These people have the most to lose, but many of them are still not actively involved in "official" disaster risk reduction initiatives.

Women should also be actively involved in emergency preparedness and response. Women have skills and expertise that can be tapped on in times of disasters, and should not be left out of the conversation. For example, the YAKKUM Emergency Unit runs programmes to help women protect their communities from disasters in Central Java and Yogyakarta.[12] It provides disaster training to women, teaching them first aid skills and evacuation procedures. Through this process, it seeks to raise awareness among the local community about the importance of robust preparedness measures and response mechanisms. Acknowledging the fact that Indonesian women are "often forgotten when a community draws up plans to deal with disasters"[13], YAKKUM hopes that women will be more involved in national disaster risk reduction strategies. Such initiatives help to empower women as agents of change and central actors in their communities, and should be scaled up and adopted in other Southeast Asian countries.

Finally, a localization agenda should be about the matching of capacities. As the WHS reiterates, it is not about replacing current national and local systems, but about reinforcing them.[14] International and regional humanitarian actors should adopt a people-centred, localized approach, and leverage on the comparative advantages of all actors. The International Federation of Red Cross and Red Crescent Societies, for example, works through its National Societies. Apart from having a continued presence in the countries, National Societies are staffed by individuals who possess local knowledge, who are aware of the social, cultural and political nuances of the specific countries they operate in. In the event of a disaster, the National Societies, along with other grassroots organizations, will be the first responders on the ground. Consequently, the emphasis should be on ensuring that these local actors are well equipped to deal with any disasters. Instead of comparing and critiquing local and international actors, the complementarity of both should be explored.[15]

5.4 Institutionalization and Localization of Climate Change Adaptation Initiatives

It is important to build on the Sendai Framework for Disaster Risk Reduction 2015–2030, specifically regarding climate change issues. With the recent onset of floods in the region, much more needs to be done to integrate climate change adaptation initiatives into disaster risk reduction strategies.

Given the frequent occurrence of climate-induced disasters in Southeast Asia, the region has been making efforts to mitigate and adapt to the changing climate in the last decade. Climate change has indeed been given a space in relevant policies and regulations at the national level despite varying scope and priority areas across states. Measuring the degree of resilience that is resulted from climate adaptation initiatives is not an easy undertaking. There is no standardized format to making such measurement. This is evidenced in the formulation of at least three different approaches namely vulnerability indicators, climate adaptation indicators and resilience indicators. The indicators may also adopt different conceptual frameworks by either monitoring and measuring the *process*, or focusing on the *outcome*. The former keeps track on the development of climate change plans at the national or local levels,[16] while the latter concerns more about the effectiveness of such policies[17] and the concrete advancement towards set objectives.[18] Regardless of different emphases and approaches, most countries in Southeast Asia have identified flooding as a common major risk that they face due to the changing climate.

Based on the *process* approach, Vietnam, Thailand, Lao PDR and Cambodia have increased their resilience through the enactment of climate-relevant policies in recent years as follows. Short of a dedicated climate change adaptation policy, Vietnam has promulgated a number of climate change-related policies including Central Party Committee's Resolution 24/NQ/TW (2013) on Responding to Climate Change, National Climate Change Strategy 2011, National Action Plan on Climate Change 2012–2020, National Green Growth Strategy 2012, and National Action Plan on Green Growth 2014. Thailand has drafted a dedicated National Adaptation Plan 2015–2023 in complement of the National Strategy on Climate Change 2008–2012 and the Climate Change Master Plan 2012–2050. Similarly, Lao PDR has developed its National Adaptation Programme of Action (NAPA) and Strategy in Climate Change whereas Cambodia has come up with NAPA, National Climate Change Strategic Plan (2014–2023) and the National Policy on Green Growth Development and National Strategic Plan on Green Growth Development 2013–2030. In addition to national policies, Vietnam, Thailand, Lao PDR and Cambodia are part of the MRC's Climate Change Adaptation Initiative (CCAI). Within the subregional grouping, these countries have consolidated their climate vision and are working on collective climate adaptation projects. According to the *process* approach, therefore, the subregion is attempting to become climate resilient through these efforts.

While a *process-based* framework may suggest that Vietnam, Thailand, Lao PDR, and Cambodia have made progress in building climate resilience through their domestic policies and subregional efforts, an *outcome-based* framework shows that the scale of recent flooding in Vietnam, Thailand, Laos PDR and Cambodia may prove insufficient in withstanding current and future climate challenges.

Considering the series of large-scale flooding in different parts of Vietnam, Thailand, Lao PDR and Cambodia that affected thousands of people, damaged houses, farms and the environment between July and August 2018, it is timely to ask whether process indicators are sufficient to conclude that existing initiatives are adequate to meet current and future climate challenges. One of the most striking observations is in the apparent mismatch between the pilot sites for MRC CCAI's climate adaptation projects and the areas impacted by the floods in Vietnam, Thailand, Lao PDR and Cambodia. There is an urgent need, therefore, to go beyond existing measures and expands climate adaptation efforts to cover more areas within the affected countries to shore up their disaster preparedness.

5.5   Financial Risk Management

The recent influx of disasters in the region has also drawn attention to the financial aspect of disaster risk management strategies. While the saving of lives during the onset of a disaster is an immediate priority, there is also a need to ensure that mechanisms are in place to help restore the livelihoods of the affected people. The United Nations Economic and Social Commission for Asia and the Pacific (UNESCAP) recently forecasted that disasters and natural catastrophes in the Asia-Pacific region could result in US$160 billion in assets lost annually by the year 2030.[19] The consequences are potentially worsened given that only 8 per cent of the region's losses are currently insured. Moreover, insurance penetration in emerging markets is still very low (less than 10 per cent) compared to that of developed countries.[20] This section examines some of the factors behind the low insurance penetration in the Southeast Asian region, and the importance of incorporating financial risk management into disaster risk reduction strategies.

The protection gap—the difference between insured losses and economic losses, or simply uninsured losses[21]—is widening in the region. In countries with inadequate disaster preparedness and mitigation plans, and where resilience is already low, this can mean that the cost of disasters on livelihoods are magnified. The earthquake of magnitude 7.0 which hit Lombok, Indonesia on 5 August damaged tens of thousands of homes and displaced several hundred thousand people.[22] As of 13 August, the estimated economic toll of the earthquake, which considers damages to infrastructure and loss of productivity, has hit five trillion rupiah (S$471 million).[23] Evidently, this will place considerable financial strain on individuals and the government, as they have to bear the full brunt of this cost.

Low insurance penetration in developing countries can be attributed to a few factors. Affordability and lack of knowledge are probably two of the main reasons for a lack of insurance coverage at the individual level. Lower-income households, particularly those residing in rural areas, often cannot afford to pay for the insurance premiums. There is also a significant knowledge gap. A farmer residing in the Mekong region is more than likely to not have any experience with insurance, and thus will not understand its role in protecting them from the financial impact of disasters.[24] In such instances, personal experience with a disaster would be the main driver of insurance adoption; by then it would have been too late. Moreover, many communities expect their governments to render post-disaster assistance, particularly in the form of monetary aid.[25] This reduces the demand for private insurance.

Financial risk transfer and insurance should be part of a country's holistic disaster risk management strategy. In fact, at the regional level, steps have already been taken to implement risk pooling. In May 2018, Finance Ministers from Cambodia, Japan, Lao PDR, Myanmar and Singapore agreed to establish the Southeast Asia Disaster Risk Insurance Facility (SEADRIF).[26] A Memorandum of Understanding was signed recently and it is scheduled to be officially established by mid-2019.[27] Primarily a regional facility to provide "advisory services at the national level to build and implement comprehensive disaster risk finance strategies",[28] it also incorporates a regional catastrophe risk pool, which is slated to provide "participating countries in Southeast Asia affected by natural disasters with immediate rapid response financing".[29] As the first of its kind in Asia, it will aim to strengthen the resilience of its members against disasters. Sovereign risk pools in the Caribbean, Africa and the Pacific have shown their efficacy in helping transfer excess risk to the reinsurance and capital markets, thus mitigating some of the financial burdens brought about by disasters.[30] Lao PDR and Myanmar are expected to be the first beneficiaries of the catastrophe risk insurance pool. With both countries devastated by floods in recent times, it provides a great impetus to push for the operationalization of the SEADRIF initiative.

Another proposed solution is the use of parametric insurance. Traditional insurance usually requires the insured party to file a claim, before the company sends someone to assess the value of the insured's loss.[31] This is a lengthy process which slows down the release of a claim payment.[32] The nature of the disaster and the damage it inflicts can also hinder the claim process. In a flood, for example, it will be difficult to place a dollar sum on property and livestock that have been swept away. In contrast, parametric insurance operates on a model of predicted loss that the insured will occur in a disaster. Once a set of pre-determined threshold parameters are met such as an earthquake of a certain magnitude, or a certain amount of rainfall, then the insurance product provides an automatic payout to the insured parties.[33] Both the parameters and the sum of the payout are based on quantitative data provided by recognized third party entities.[34] The National Catastrophe Data Analytics Exchange (NatCatDax) project in Singapore, for example, uses satellites and drones to collect building images and extrapolate them to calculate potential economic exposure and losses. This data is then used to inform stakeholders and policymakers from both the public and the insurance sectors to create sustainable, robust solutions to address the disaster protection gap. Through the use of satellite images and sensors, post-disaster insurance claims can be processed more efficiently. Payouts can be disbursed quickly without the need to send loss surveyors to the sites. Moreover, it removes the need for the buyer of the insurance coverage to document the losses, which speeds up the payment claims process.[35]

Southeast Asian countries have taken steps to address the issue of financial risk accrued during disasters. However, as the past few months have demonstrated, disaster risk is quickly outpacing resilience. There is an urgency to accelerate initiatives such as SEADRIF in the region. Coordinated efforts need to be undertaken by the different stakeholders and sectors. Partnerships between national governments, the insurance industry, international organizations, and grassroots leaders are essential for the successful implementation of disaster risk insurance schemes.[36] Governments can provide tiered subsidies to people from all income brackets, thus incentivizing enrolment in disaster insurance schemes. They can also provide oversight over the insurance industry to ensure fair and equitable products.[37] The insurance sector should strive to offer innovative insurance solutions to consumers, while making it a point to share risk data and information with policymakers.[38] International organizations, or in ASEAN's case, regional organizations, can help to facilitate regional risk pooling mechanisms and programmes. Finally, grassroots leaders should be involved in the process as well. They can act as intermediaries between their communities and the bigger stakeholders, namely the government and insurance companies. Outreach activities can help to raise awareness among individuals at the rural level.

While insurance is definitely not the be-all and end-all of disaster risk management—one can never put a price on a human life—it certainly plays an important role in ensuring the mitigation of natural catastrophe risk. The funds from insurance payouts can help survivors rebuild their homes and work towards restoring their pre-disaster livelihoods. At the national level, payments from regional risk pools can ease some of the financial burden of governments. As mentioned earlier, the economic toll of the Lombok earthquake so far is hovering around the three trillion rupiah mark. In such an instance, parametric insurance schemes with fast payout structures would definitely have provided the Indonesian government with some form of financial protection and respite.

5.6 Conclusion

In the face of multiple catastrophes and burgeoning risk in the region, the need for robust disaster management and risk reduction mechanisms becomes even more apparent. ASEAN has made much progress in terms of institutionalizing disaster management in the region. However, the recent spate of disasters have stretched regional and national capacities to the limit, and in the process, exposed some of the fragilities and limitations of the current humanitarian system in the region.

While institutional policies and frameworks at the regional level tend to get a lot of attention, it is important that policymakers do not neglect capacity at the national and grassroots levels. There is still much room for NDMOs to leverage regional resources for national capacity building. Local organizations could also benefit from more support—in the form of resources, media coverage and training—as they strive to develop more robust policies and systems. Climate change adaptation initiatives also need to be better incorporated into disaster preparedness efforts.

The huge economic losses stemming from the multiple disasters also necessitate a drastic re-evaluation of the way financial risk is managed in the region. Engagement with the private sector, particularly with insurers and reinsurers, should be a policy imperative. The private sector can help national governments implement disaster risk financing tools and build up financial resilience. Post-disaster rebuilding efforts are very costly. Coupled with the fact that insurance markets are still very much under-developed in many developing countries in the Southeast Asian region, affected communities are placed under considerable financial strain. Insurance allows countries to transfer some of the financial risk to the capital market and the private sector, thereby lifting some of the burden off governments and affected populations.

The region cannot afford to let disaster management mechanisms and standards lapse, lest disaster risk will outpace resilience in the region. States in the region have already demonstrated their commitment to reinforcing regional and national disaster management capacities. However, they are still in the process of finding ways to integrate local capacity into the regional disaster management architecture. They have also begun to explore options to mitigate the financial risks that accompany disasters. The challenge now is for them to strengthen and implement these mechanisms before the next inevitable series of disasters hit the region.

NOTES

1. AHA Centre, "Weekly Disaster Update 13–19 August 2018", 2018, https://reliefweb.int/sites/reliefweb.int/files/resources/D-Week-33_13-19-Aug-2018-rev.pdf.
2. See Article 2 of AADMER, http://agreement.asean.org/media/download/20140119170000.pdf.
3. AHA Centre, "Situation Update No. 5 M6.4 Lombok Earthquake (29 July 2018) & M7.0 Lombok Earthquake (5 August 2018), Indonesia", 13 August 2018, https://ahacentre.org/wp-content/uploads/2018/08/AHA-Situation_Update_no_5_M-7.0-Lombok-Earthquake-final.pdf.
4. Maizura Ismail, "Southeast Asia: Hit by Multiple Disasters", *The Asean Post*, 10 August 2018, https://theaseanpost.com/article/southeast-asia-hit-multiple-disasters.
5. AHA Centre, *Annual Report 2017*, 2017, https://ahacentre.org/wp-content/uploads/2018/06/AHA-Centre-Annual-report-2017.pdf.
6. ASEAN Secretariat, "ASEAN Vision 2025 on Disaster Management", 2016, http://www.asean.org/storage/2012/05/fa-220416_DM2025_email.pdf.
7. Pichayada Promchertchoo, "Bodies, Mud and Destruction: Rescuer Describes Bleak Aftermath of Laos Dam Collapse", *Channel News Asia*, 1 August 2018, https://www.channelnewsasia.com/news/asia/laos-dam-collapse-sanamxai-destruction-aftermath-attapeu-10578460.

8. Kate Lamb and Luke Harding, "Indonesia Earthquake: Lack of Equipment Hampers Rescue Efforts", *The Guardian*, 6 August 2018, https://www.theguardian.com/world/2018/aug/06/indonesia-earthquake-lack-of-equipment-hampers-rescue-efforts.

9. ASEAN, "ASEAN: Stronger Collaboration and Innovative Approaches Needed to Enhance Disaster Management Capabilities", *ASEAN Secretariat News*, 19 August 2018, http://asean.org/asean-stronger-collaboration-innovative-approaches-needed-enhance-disaster-management-capabilities/.

10. Kelli Rogers, "Laos Dam Disaster Reignites Calls for Stronger Safety Systems", Devex, 30 July 2018, https://www.devex.com/news/laos-dam-disaster-reignites-calls-for-stronger-safety-systems-93198.

11. Larissa Fast and Kate Sutton, "Protection in Local Response to Disasters: Challenges and Insights from the Pacific Region", HPG Working Paper, October 2018, https://www.odi.org/sites/odi.org.uk/files/resource-documents/12450.pdf.

12. Michael Taylor, "With Warning Drums and River Clean-ups, Indonesian Women Head Off Disasters", *Reuters*, 30 April 2018, https://www.reuters.com/article/us-indonesia-disaster-women/with-warning-drums-and-river-clean-ups-indonesian-women-head-off-disasters-idUSKBN1I1036.

13. Ibid.

14. Agenda for Humanity, "World Humanitarian Summit: Commitments to Action", World Humanitarian Summit, Istanbul, 23–24 May 2016, https://www.agendaforhumanity.org/sites/default/files/resources/2017/Jul/WHS_Commitment_to_Action_8September2016.pdf.

15. Fast and Sutton, "Protection in Local Response to Disasters".

16. Mike Harley and Jelle van Minnen, "Development of Adaptation Indicators", ETC/ACC Technical Paper 2009/6, European Topic Centre on Air and Climate Change, December 2009, https://www.eionet.europa.eu/etcs/etc-cca/products/etc-cca-reports/etcacc_tp_2009_6_etcacc_tp_2009_6_adapt_ind-1.

17. Mike Harley, Lisa Horrocks, and Nikki Hodgson, "Climate Change Vulnerability and Adaptation Indicators", ETC/ACC Technical Paper 2008/9, European Topic Centre on Air and Climate Change, December 2008, https://www.eionet.europa.eu/etcs/etc-cca/products/etc-cca-reports/etcacc_tp_2008_9_ccvuln_adapt_indicators-1.

18. Natural England, "Climate Change Adaptation Indicators for the Natural Environment", Natural England Commissioned Report NECR038, 13 July 2010, http://publications.naturalengland.org.uk/publication/45007.

19. Sukhbold Sukhee, "Opening Statement at Innovative Financing for Disaster Risk Reduction in Asia-Pacific", Speech delivered at Innovative Financing for Disaster Risk Reduction in Asia-Pacific in United Nations Headquarters, New York, 24 April 2018, https://www.unescap.org/speeches/opening-statement-innovative-financing-disaster-risk-reduction-asia-pacific.

20. Shaun Crawford, Luca Russignan, and Nilabh Kumar, "Global Insurance Trends Analysis 2018", Earnest and Young, June 2018, https://www.ey.com/Publication/vwLUAssets/ey-global-insurance-trends-analysis-2018/$File/ey-global-insurance-trends-analysis-2018.pdf.

21. Thomas Holzheu and Ginger Turner, "The Natural Catastrophe Protection Gap: Measurement, Root Causes and Ways of Addressing Underinsurance for Extreme Events", *The Geneva Papers on Risk and Insurance* 43, no. 1 (2018): 2.

22. "Indonesian Earthquake Swarm Kills 12 People", *Associated Press*, 21 August 2018, https://www.news.com.au/world/asia/indonesian-earthquake-swarm-kills-12-people/news-story/31455f05fe609e4b6bf1e8611d1371f3.

23. "Lombok Quake Death Toll Rises to 436 as Economic Losses, Damage Hit $470 Million", *Straits Times*, 13 August 2018, https://www.straitstimes.com/asia/se-asia/lombok-death-toll-rises-to-436-as-economic-losses-damage-hits-472m.

24. *Clyde and Co.* (blog), "How Parametric Insurance Can Help After Natural Catastrophes", 22 November 2016, https://www.clydeco.com/blog/insurance-hub/article/how-parametric-insurance-can-help-after-natural-catastrophes.

25. Thomas Holzheu and Ginger Turner, "The Natural Catastrophe Protection Gap: Measurement, Root Causes and Ways of Addressing Underinsurance for Extreme Events", *The Geneva Papers on Risk and Insurance* 43, no. 1 (2018): 5.

26. "Joint Statement of the Finance Ministers' Meeting on the Establishment of the Southeast Asia Disaster Risk Insurance Facility", Manila, the Philippines, 4 May 2018, https://www.mof.gov.sg/aseanfinance2018/newsroom/press-releases/joint-statement-of-the-finance-ministers-meeting-on-the-establishment-of-the-southeast-asia-disaster-risk-insurance-facility-(seadrif).

27. World Bank, "ASEAN Asia First Regional Climate Disaster Risk Financing Facility", 18 December 2018, http://www.worldbank.org/en/news/feature/2018/12/18/asean3-countries-establish-asias-first-regional-climate-and-disaster-risk-financing-facility.

28. "Joint Statement of the Finance Ministers' Meeting".

29. World Bank, "Southeast Asian Countries Reach Milestone Agreement to Strengthen Resilience", 5 May 2017, http://www.worldbank.org/en/events/2017/05/05/southeast-asian-countries-reach-milestone-agreement.

30. World Bank, "What Makes Catastrophe Risk Pools Work: Lessons for Policymakers", 14 November 2017, http://www.worldbank.org/en/news/feature/2017/11/14/what-makes-catastrophe-risk-pools-work.

31. Nigel Brook, "Legal Perspective: Increasing Awareness of Parametric Insurance", Commercial Risk, 19 December 2016, https://www.commercialriskonline.com/legal-perspective-increasing-awareness-of-parametric-insurance/.

32. Ibid.

33. *Clyde and Co.* (blog), "Parametrics: Closing the Protection Gap", 14 September 2016, https://www.clydeco.com/blog/insurance-hub/article/parametrics-closing-the-protection-gap.

34. Ibid.

35. Brook, "Legal Perspective".

36. United Nations Development Programme, "Financing Solutions for Sustainable Development: Disaster Risk Insurance", undated, http://www.undp.org/content/sdfinance/en/home/solutions/disaster-risk-insurance.html.

37. Ibid.

38. Ibid.

REFERENCES

Agenda for Humanity. 2016. "World Humanitarian Summit: Commitments to Action". World Humanitarian Summit, Istanbul, 23–24 May 2016. https://www.agendaforhumanity.org/sites/default/files/resources/2017/Jul/WHS_Commitment_to_Action_8September2016.pdf.

AHA Centre. 2017. *Annual Report 2017*. https://ahacentre.org/wp-content/uploads/2018/06/AHA-Centre-Annual-report-2017.pdf.

———. 2018. "Situation Update No. 5 M6.4 Lombok Earthquake (29 July 2018) & M7.0 Lombok Earthquake (5 August 2018), Indonesia", 13 August 2018. https://ahacentre.org/wp-content/uploads/2018/08/AHA-Situation_Update_no_5_M-7.0-Lombok-Earthquake-final.pdf.

———. 2018. "Weekly Disaster Update 13–19 August 2018". https://reliefweb.int/sites/reliefweb.int/files/resources/D-Week-33_13-19-Aug-2018-rev.pdf.

ASEAN. 2018. "ASEAN: Stronger Collaboration and Innovative Approaches Needed to Enhance Disaster Management Capabilities". *ASEAN Secretariat News*, 19 August 2018. http://asean.org/asean-stronger-collaboration-innovative-approaches-needed-enhance-disaster-management-capabilities/.

ASEAN Secretariat. 2016. "ASEAN Vision 2025 on Disaster Management". http://www.asean.org/storage/2012/05/fa-220416_DM2025_email.pdf.

Brook, Nigel. 2016. "Legal Perspective: Increasing Awareness of Parametric Insurance". Commercial Risk, 19 December 2016. https://www.commercialriskonline.com/legal-perspective-increasing-awareness-of-parametric-insurance/.

Clyde and Co. (blog). 2016. "How Parametric Insurance Can Help After Natural Catastrophes", 22 November 2016. https://www.clydeco.com/blog/insurance-hub/article/how-parametric-insurance-can-help-after-natural-catastrophes.

————. 2016. "Parametrics: Closing the Protection Gap", 14 September 2016. https://www.clydeco.com/blog/insurance-hub/article/parametrics-closing-the-protection-gap.

Crawford, Shaun, Luca Russignan, and Nilabh Kumar. 2018. "Global Insurance Trends Analysis 2018". Earnest and Young. https://www.ey.com/Publication/vwLUAssets/ey-global-insurance-trends-analysis-2018/$File/ey-global-insurance-trends-analysis-2018.pdf.

Fast, Larissa and Kate Sutton. 2018. "Protection in Local Response to Disasters: Challenges and Insights from the Pacific Region". HPG Working Paper. https://www.odi.org/sites/odi.org.uk/files/resource-documents/12450.pdf.

Harley, Mike and Jelle van Minnen. 2009. "Development of Adaptation Indicators". ETC/ACC Technical Paper 2009/6. European Topic Centre on Air and Climate Change. https://www.eionet.europa.eu/etcs/etc-cca/products/etc-cca-reports/etcacc_tp_2009_6_etcacc_tp_2009_6_adapt_ind-1.

Harley, Mike, Lisa Horrocks, and Nikki Hodgson. 2008. "Climate Change Vulnerability and Adaptation Indicators". ETC/ACC Technical Paper 2008/9. European Topic Centre on Air and Climate Change. https://www.eionet.europa.eu/etcs/etc-cca/products/etc-cca-reports/etcacc_tp_2008_9_ccvuln_adapt_indicators-1.

Holzheu, Thomas and Ginger Turner. 2018. "The Natural Catastrophe Protection Gap: Measurement, Root Causes and Ways of Addressing Underinsurance for Extreme Events". *The Geneva Papers on Risk and Insurance* 43, no. 1.

"Indonesian Earthquake Swarm Kills 12 People". *Associated Press*, 21 August 2018. https://www.news.com.au/world/asia/indonesian-earthquake-swarm-kills-12-people/news-story/31455f05fe609e4b6bf1e8611d1371f3.

Ismail, Maizura. 2018. "Southeast Asia: Hit by Multiple Disasters". *The Asean Post*, 10 August 2018. https://theaseanpost.com/article/southeast-asia-hit-multiple-disasters.

"Joint Statement of the Finance Ministers' Meeting on the Establishment of the Southeast Asia Disaster Risk Insurance Facility". Manila, the Philippines, 4 May 2018. https://www.mof.gov.sg/aseanfinance2018/newsroom/press-releases/joint-statement-of-the-finance-ministers-meeting-on-the-establishment-of-the-southeast-asia-disaster-risk-insurance-facility-(seadrif).

Lamb, Kate and Luke Harding. 2018. "Indonesia Earthquake: Lack of Equipment Hampers Rescue Efforts". *The Guardian*, 6 August 2018. https://www.theguardian.com/world/2018/aug/06/indonesia-earthquake-lack-of-equipment-hampers-rescue-efforts.

"Lombok Quake Death Toll Rises to 436 as Economic Losses, Damage Hit $470 Million". *Straits Times*, 13 August 2018. https://www.straitstimes.com/asia/se-asia/lombok-death-toll-rises-to-436-as-economic-losses-damage-hits-472m.

Natural England. 2010. "Climate Change Adaptation Indicators for the Natural Environment". Natural England Commissioned Report NECR038, 13 July 2010. http://publications.naturalengland.org.uk/publication/45007.

Promchertchoo, Pichayada. 2018. "Bodies, Mud and Destruction: Rescuer Describes Bleak Aftermath of Laos Dam Collapse". *Channel News Asia*, 1 August 2018. https://www.channelnewsasia.com/news/asia/laos-dam-collapse-sanamxai-destruction-aftermath-attapeu-10578460.

Rogers, Kelli. 2018. "Laos Dam Disaster Reignites Calls for Stronger Safety Systems". Devex, 30 July 2018. https://www.devex.com/news/laos-dam-disaster-reignites-calls-for-stronger-safety-systems-93198.

Sukhee, Sukhbold. 2018. "Opening Statement at Innovative Financing for Disaster Risk Reduction in Asia-Pacific". Speech delivered at Innovative Financing for Disaster Risk Reduction in Asia-Pacific in United Nations Headquarters, New York, 24 April 2018. https://www.unescap.org/speeches/opening-statement-innovative-financing-disaster-risk-reduction-asia-pacific.

Taylor, Michael. 2018. "With Warning Drums and River Clean-ups, Indonesian Women Head Off Disasters". *Reuters*, 30 April 2018. https://www.reuters.com/article/us-indonesia-disaster-women/with-warning-drums-and-river-clean-ups-indonesian-women-head-off-disasters-idUSKBN1I1036.

United Nations Development Programme. Undated. "Financing Solutions for Sustainable Development: Disaster Risk Insurance". http://www.undp.org/content/sdfinance/en/home/solutions/disaster-risk-insurance.html.

World Bank. 2017. "Southeast Asian Countries Reach Milestone Agreement to Strengthen Resilience", 5 May 2017. http://www.worldbank.org/en/events/2017/05/05/southeast-asian-countries-reach-milestone-agreement.

———. 2017. "What Makes Catastrophe Risk Pools Work: Lessons for Policymakers", 14 November 2017. http://www.worldbank.org/en/news/feature/2017/11/14/what-makes-catastrophe-risk-pools-work.

———. 2018. "ASEAN Asia First Regional Climate Disaster Risk Financing Facility", 18 December 2018. http://www.worldbank.org/en/news/feature/2018/12/18/asean3-countries-establish-asias-first-regional-climate-and-disaster-risk-financing-facility.

6

ADVANCING A REGIONAL PATHWAY TO ENHANCE NUCLEAR ENERGY GOVERNANCE IN SOUTHEAST ASIA

Julius Cesar I. Trajano

6.1   Introduction

Most of the new nuclear projects are now taking place in Asia. The growth of the nuclear power industry, since the Fukushima nuclear accident, has been pivoting from Europe towards Asia, with China leading the growth of nuclear power. In 2018, nearly two-thirds or 37 of nuclear reactors being constructed globally were located in Asia, across nine countries, 20 of which were in China.[1] China currently accounts for more than half of the world's new nuclear power investment. In 2018, only the United States and France operated more nuclear power plants (NPPs) than China. China's nuclear power production may exceed that of the United States, which has led the world in nuclear power generation for over half a century, sometime before 2030.[2] In South Korea, two new reactors are being completed, after President Moon Jae-in had initially ordered halting the construction in 2017, but later changed it as a result of a government-convened citizens' jury that voted 59.5 per cent in favour of completing the units.[3] In Japan, after the 2011 Fukushima nuclear accident, 9 out of its 54 operable nuclear reactors have been restarted while 18 reactors are being considered to be re-opened within the next twenty years.[4]

Meanwhile, several Southeast Asian states are studying the option to include nuclear energy in their future and long-term power generation sources to boost their energy security and reduce their greenhouse gas emissions from fossil fuels. The *Pre-Feasibility Study on Nuclear Power in Southeast Asia* (2018) by the ASEAN Centre for Energy foresees that nuclear power will be added to Southeast Asia's energy mix between 2030 and 2035. The study identifies five ASEAN member states—Indonesia, Malaysia, Vietnam, Thailand and the Philippines—as frontrunners in the race to establish civilian nuclear energy programmes in the region. They have achieved some milestones in this field with their advanced legal and regulatory frameworks, nuclear energy infrastructures and the required human resources and organization in place.

While Vietnam cancelled its first NPP project in 2016, Indonesia, Thailand, and the Philippines are in the process of building up their human resource capacity and amending legal and regulatory frameworks. The development of small modular nuclear reactors (land-based and floating) as an emerging nuclear technology is closely being monitored by several countries in the region such as the Philippines and Indonesia. Myanmar, Laos and Cambodia have also recently signed nuclear cooperation deals with countries like China and Russia for financial, technological and training assistance.

Although there is no operable NPP in the region currently, radio-active sources are widely used for civilian applications in medical, industrial, agricultural, and scientific research fields. Without stringent oversight on the use and handling of radioactive materials, there are potential risks of these being accidentally leaked, stolen and used for malicious purposes, or released indiscriminately by non-state actors/terrorists through "dirty bombs". While nuclear security is often understood to be about securing NPPs and nuclear weapons, it is also very much about the security of radioactive materials. As defined by the International Atomic Energy Agency (IAEA), nuclear security is *"the prevention and detection of, and response to, theft, sabotage, unauthorized access, illegal transfer or other malicious acts involving nuclear material, other radioactive substances or their associated facilities"*.[5]

ASEAN member states have a collective interest in ensuring that future NPPs or small modular reactors (SMRs) constructed in this region, and the utilization of radioactive materials, are safe and secure. A nuclear disaster, due to weak nuclear energy governance, would have transboundary impact on ASEAN member states. Establishing an effective and sustainable nuclear energy infrastructure is crucial for the protection of states, people, society and the environment.

In this regard, this chapter discusses the opportunities and challenges associated with nuclear energy plans of Southeast Asian states and the utilization of radioactive materials in the region. There is a need to examine the current gaps in nuclear governance in the region and how Southeast Asia, through the ASEAN Network of Regulatory Bodies on Atomic Energy (ASEANTOM), deepens cooperation on civilian nuclear energy, including radiological security, and on nuclear emergency preparedness and response. This chapter examines key nuclear governance challenges, national approaches, best practices and regional cooperation on civilian nuclear energy and radiological security in Southeast Asia.

6.2   Nuclear Energy Plans in Southeast Asia

The International Energy Agency (IEA) estimated that Southeast Asia's energy demand would grow 60 per cent by 2040.[6] In view of growing domestic energy needs, some Southeast Asian states are also exploring the option of nuclear energy for power generation. By 2040, 4GW of nuclear power will be generated in the region.[7]

Vietnam used to be the lead driver of nuclear power development in ASEAN from 2009 when it decided to build its first NPP until November 2016 when its government decided to scrap its plan primarily due to the soaring cost of the project. The cost of two proposed NPPs

FIGURE 6.1
Forecasted Electricity Generation Capacity in Gigawatt (GW) by Energy Source in Southeast Asia, 2040

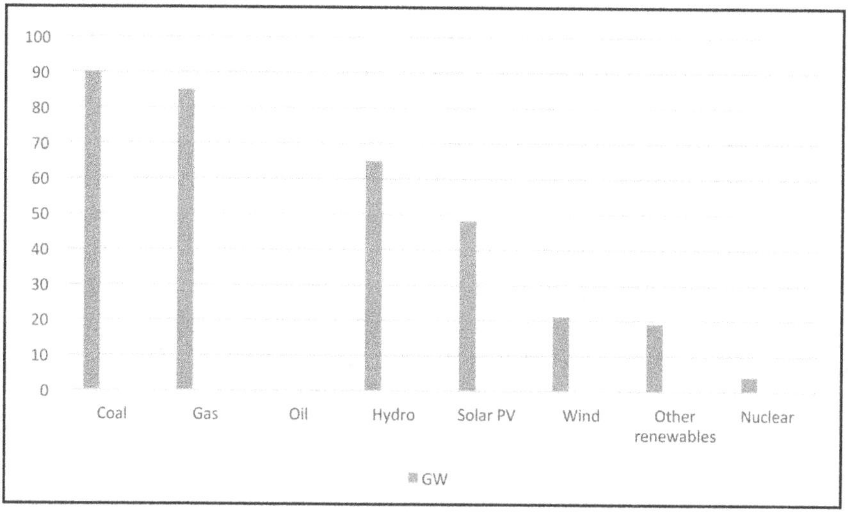

Source: IEA (2017).

in central Ninh Thuan province, slated to be the first NPPs to be commissioned in Southeast Asia, doubled since they were first tabled in 2009 to an estimated $18 billion.

As Vietnam discarded its Ninh Thuan NPP project, the Philippines was mulling the opening of the mothballed Bataan Nuclear Power Plant (BNPP). The first 620 MWe unit of the Bataan plant was completed in 1984 but was never operated due to concerns over its safety and proximity to active faults and a dormant volcano. The Philippines' Department of Energy has been pushing for nuclear power as a long-term energy option for the country. In 2018, it submitted a national policy proposal on nuclear energy to the Office of the President. As of writing, the proposal is currently being studied.[8] The Philippines has been trying to diversify its energy sources. Almost half (48 per cent) of the country's installed electrical capacity was generated using imported fossil fuels, particularly coal, in 2016.[9] Hence, the possible inclusion of nuclear power in the current energy mix is consistent with the national policy towards a technology-neutral energy sector.[10] Furthermore, domestic demand for electricity is expected to grow by an average of 5 per cent a year until 2030.[11] To meet rising demand, the Philippines is weighing all alternative sources, with emphasis not just on meeting capacity requirements but also on sustainability and climate change mitigation obligations.

Although Thailand has not committed to a nuclear power programme, it issued a power development plan in 2015 that envisages a 1-gigawatt NPP running by 2035, and a second one the following year. In 2016, Thailand's parliament enacted the new Nuclear Energy Act which contains regulations for the management of nuclear-related activities and radioactive materials, seen as a first step in a long process to build the country's first NPP.[12]

The Philippines and Indonesia are carefully monitoring the development of SMRs as a potential NPP technology in the future. It can be useful for the off-grid areas of the archipelagic islands of the two countries. Russia offered in April 2018 technical assistance to the Philippines in studying the potential of SMRs and floating NPPs.[13] Russia is currently a major developer of SMR technology. Indonesia is receiving assistance from the IAEA in terms of research on small experimental power reactor technology.[14] However, public acceptance has yet to be addressed by the two countries, on the use of nuclear power whether by conventional or small nuclear reactors.

If successfully commercialized, ASEAN member states may find floating small reactors more acceptable and less controversial than building land-based NPPs. The IAEA considers small reactors as a good option to electrify "remote regions with less developed infrastructures".[15] Floating NPPs may help energize Southeast Asia's far-flung regions and islands and feed into the region's decentralized power grid system. In terms of desirable features, floating NPPs may be more affordable than conventional NPPs with cheaper construction cost, higher safety levels, less radioactive waste, and reduced opportunity for nuclear weapons proliferation.

6.3 Key Issues and Challenges

1. From Potential Deployment of Floating Reactors

There are key challenges to the possible deployment of floating NPPs in the region. There is a need to adopt a dedicated international legal framework for this new technology that adheres to nuclear safety and security conventions. Currently, the Convention on Nuclear Safety is only limited to land-based NPPs. Countries that will utilize floating NPPs also have to come up with a broader regulatory framework that governs oversight of this technology. Another challenge is that national regulatory bodies need to have competent staff who can undertake independent reviews of the adherence of floating NPPs to nuclear safety and security within their jurisdictions. There is also a complex issue of whose national regulatory frameworks will be applied to floating reactors located in disputed waters of the South China Sea. It must be noted that China may add a "nuclear element" to the South China Sea disputes as it plans to construct up to twenty floating NPPs to provide electricity and desalinated water to its artificial islands and military outposts.[16]

In addition, any radioactive leaks or accidents at floating reactors may have severe environmental impact on the South China Sea affecting the safety, public health and sources of livelihood of coastal communities. It remains to be seen how floating NPPs in the South China Sea can withstand the risks from natural hazards such as tsunamis, earthquakes and typhoons that may trigger transboundary nuclear accidents.[17] With Southeast Asia's persistent maritime security issues such as piracy, territorial disputes, smuggling and hijacking,[18] the security of these floating reactors could be undermined if states are not prepared to address such perennial maritime security issues of the region.

2. Nuclear Power Plants near Southeast Asia

While there are no operable nuclear plants currently in Southeast Asia, a nuclear disaster in China may still affect the region in light of Chinese NPPs located near Vietnam and possible future deployment of offshore reactors in the South China Sea. The cancellation of Vietnam's first NPP project should not stall regional efforts to build joint nuclear emergency preparedness and response in ASEAN. Vietnam and the rest of Southeast Asia should stay vigilant and be prepared for a nuclear incident near the region's borders. Three Chinese nuclear stations are located near the Vietnamese border and one of them, Yangjiang NPP in Guangdong province, has recorded an operational blunder and subsequent cover-up attempt by operators in 2015.[19]

Meanwhile, Bangladesh began construction of its first NPP started in 2017 with Russian collaboration and completion slated for 2024. It must be noted that this first NPP is just 500 km away from Myanmar.[20] Any potential accident or nuclear security breach could cause radioactive leaks that might have transboundary non-traditional security consequences on the environment, public health, and food safety in Myanmar and other Southeast Asian countries.

If a nuclear accident, as catasthropic as the Fukushima accident, occurred in the region or South China Sea, the public health and environmental implications would cross national borders primarily due to massive radioactive plumes as radioactive material can be carried by wind and rain far away from the source, contaminating water and soil. Atmospheric and ocean plumes may affect farmlands, rich fishing grounds, wildlife and public health in the region. As seen after the Chernobyl nuclear accident, the transboundary radioactive plumes from a nuclear meltdown may have severe consequences, such as higher cancer risk and contamination of food and water sources, irrespective of national boundaries in the region. Being located thousands of kilometres away from a nuclear accident is not a guarantee that a particular country will be safe from radioactive plume.[21] In a scientific study made by researchers of the Centre of Excellence for Climate System Science of the Australian Research Council on Fukushima's radioactive plume, radioactive particles in the ocean plume take considerably longer to travel the same distance so it may also be hard to forecast the exact time they will reach a particular destination. Also, there would be uncertainties as to the total amount of radioactive particles released and the likely concentrations that would be observed. Atmospheric and ocean plumes get diluted as it travels away from the source. In the Fukushima plume case, circular wave current and giant whirlpools—some tens of kilometres wide—and other currents in the open ocean continue this dilution process and direct the radioactive particles to different areas along the US west coast.[22] A maximum concentration of radiation may still hit a specific area, endangering the ecosystem there.[23]

Depending on the extent of an accident, the food supply chain can be disrupted as sources of food can be contaminated by either airborne radiation or radioactive water from affected power plants. Locations of sources of different food commodities would determine the extent of susceptibility to a nuclear accident. For instance, transboundary radioactive plumes from any accident near Vietnam-China border may contaminate agricultural farmlands not just in Vietnam but also in its rice-producing neighbours in mainland Southeast Asia like Thailand and Cambodia. It must be noted that Vietnam and Thailand are the world's top rice exporters. Contamination of farmlands can significantly disrupt the region's and global food supply chain. An accident in the South China Sea can also contaminate rich fishing grounds in the region, undermining the regional supply of seafood and fish.

3. Nuclear Security Challenges

Case Studies on Status of Radioactive Materials

Nuclear security matters in Southeast Asia: Recent cases of missing radioactive materials in Southeast Asia in 2018 vividly highlight the significance of enhancing nuclear security in the region. In Malaysia, a radioactive device was reportedly lost in August 2018 while being transported by two employees of an industrial company that owned the missing device.[24] In the Philippines, an industrial equipment containing radioactive materials was stolen from the facility of a construction firm, also in August 2018.[25] There were concerns that the unknown amount of radioactive materials contained in the missing devices could potentially emit harmful radiation if handled improperly or be used as a weapon, otherwise known as "dirty bomb".

According to Malaysia's Atomic Energy Licensing Board, over 16 cases involving trespassing, loss or theft of radioactive materials from the 1990s to 2017 had occurred due to failure of radiological security systems, mainly during transportation.[26] In the Philippines, 15 licensed users of radioactive materials were found to be violating radiological safety and security regulations in 2018.[27]

Radioactive sources are widely used for non-power applications especially in medicine, industry, agricultural research and educational research. For instance, three research reactors in Indonesia, Vietnam's sole research reactor, 17 hospitals in Thailand and seven hospitals in the Philippines possess radioactive sources.[28] With a total of 423 current licensees in the Philippines, around 40 per cent of the licensees use radioactive materials in industrial applications, 30 per cent apply radioactive materials for diagnosing or treating diseases, while the rest are involved in commercial sales and services.[29] In Malaysia, 1,365 licenses for using radioactive materials for various applications were issued by the regulatory board in 2017.[30] Considering the increased flow of nuclear and radioactive materials in Southeast Asia, not to mention the security challenges the region is facing, it is crucial for the region to have a strong nuclear security.

According to the latest Global Incidents and Trafficking Database prepared by the James Martin Center for Non-proliferation Studies (CNS), from 2013 to 2017, there were four reported cases in Southeast Asia involving illicit trafficking and theft of radioactive materials.[31] Hence, a key point to note is that the security of radiological materials is an important component of nuclear security. Potential utilization of nuclear energy programmes to new countries, together with an increase in the number of nuclear sites, quantities of nuclear material, number of transport movements and number of people involved may all lead to increased security challenges.[32]

Selected ASEAN member states have initiated various measures to foster radiological security.

1. In Indonesia, the CSCA/BATAN introduced the concept and terms of nuclear security culture to all stakeholders by conducting self-assessment on nuclear security culture in a local radioactive source facility in 2018. CSCA also developed a nuclear security practical pocketbook in 2019. The pocketbook identifies the roles of individual/managers to enhance nuclear security culture at nuclear facilities. Two national universities also developed curriculum on nuclear security culture for their MSc programme in nuclear security in 2017/18. Meanwhile, three International Nuclear Security Education Network (INSEN) member-universities in the country collaborated in establishing a research centre on nuclear security issues in 2019. Indonesia widely shared its experience in conducting self-assessment of nuclear security culture at its three research reactors, through a report submitted to IAEA.[33]

2. In Malaysia, authorities held the following: the National Workshop on Nuclear Security Culture and Self-Assessment in October 2017; Train the Trainers Workshop on Nuclear Security Culture and Self-Assessment in November 2017; and Seminar for Senior Managers on Nuclear Security Culture and National Workshop on Nuclear Security Culture in March 2017. Malaysia also shared its experience in conducting self-assessment of nuclear security

culture at a local hospital in Kuala Lumpur, through a report submitted to the IAEA. Subsequently, an IAEA's expert mission to support and review nuclear security culture self-assessment visited Malaysia in March 2018.[34]

3. In Vietnam, the regulatory body conducted a project on "Nuclear security foundation and self-assessment methodology" in 2016. Under this project, self-assessment questionnaires were distributed to nuclear and radiation facilities.[35]

4. In the Philippines, the regulatory body incorporated nuclear security culture in all security trainings for licensees/users of radioactive sources. Licensees violating the law and regulations are given sanctions in accordance with the government's regulatory enforcement policy. In 2018, the regulatory body also conducted specialized courses, benefitting 100 trainees, in environmental monitoring, reactor engineering and emergency preparedness and response in cooperation with the Japan Atomic Energy Agency (JAEA).[36]

5. In Thailand, there have been continuous trainings and stakeholder communications on security culture for licensees. Regulations and guidelines on the promotion of a security culture were revised under the new Nuclear Energy for Peace Act.[37]

This listing of empirical cases (plans and activities) provides indications as to how selected ASEAN states attempt to deeply institutionalize radiological security. Without policy frameworks and interventions from the State, it would be challenging for licensees and users of radioactive and nuclear materials to develop their safety and security plans concerning radiological materials, in view of three main security challenges in the region.

Firstly, the region is home to a number of active terrorist groups. The presence of ISIS-inspired terrorist groups in the region should compel ASEAN member states to broaden the threat horizon and improve their nuclear security capability, including security culture. There is a rising fear that ISIS-inspired militants are pursuing radioactive materials to make "dirty bombs" for its attacks in the region i.e., nuclear terrorism, with reported missing or unaccounted radioactive materials.[38] Terrorists and criminals may try to exploit any vulnerability in the global nuclear security system, and any country may become a transit point or target of attack. Southeast Asia has very long land and sea borders, but weak border security capabilities. Weak border security may also facilitate the illicit transfer of nuclear and radiological materials.

Secondly, not all Southeast Asian states are parties to important global nuclear conventions, including nuclear security treaties (see Table 6.1). In Southeast Asia, physical protection of nuclear facilities, a critical element of nuclear security, is not being enhanced given the absence of NPPs in the region. Consequently, not all ASEAN member states have signed or ratified the Convention on the Physical Protection of Nuclear Materials (CPPNM) and its Amendment. However, many hospitals, research reactors, laboratories and factories that utilize radioactive sources also require utmost physical protection. They are easier to be sabotaged compared to highly secured NPPs and research reactor spent fuel can be used in making radiological "dirty bombs". Given that the risks to the physical protection of nuclear facilities and materials such as stealing of radioactive materials and nuclear terrorism have regional consequences, it is important for all ASEAN member states to collectively adhere to the CPPNM Amendment.[39]

It is essential for countries with nuclear activities and radioactive sources for non-power applications to ratify all treaties and to contribute to the enhancement of treaty regimes.[40] With the ratification of these treaties, nuclear security policies can be enhanced given that nuclear trade and research networks have been broadened substantially in Southeast Asia in recent years. Without a more robust regulatory and legal frameworks at the national level, the region will be vulnerable to illicit trafficking of nuclear materials and technologies.[41]

And thirdly, one evident gap in nuclear security governance in Southeast Asia is weak nuclear security culture, accentuating the significance of human factors, such as attitudes, awareness and behaviours. Harnessing nuclear energy and utilization of radioactive material for non-power applications are not just about the technological aspects. Human failures due to complacency and the lack of critical thinking are significant factors in most reported incidents, including cases of loss and theft. Hence, the development and deepening of the security culture of individuals, organizations and institutions that handle radioactive material must be pursued.

For instance, the incident in August 2018 was not the first time that a radioactive device has gone missing in Malaysia as there were no less than twenty cases recorded involving radioactive and nuclear materials which have "gone missing" over recent years.[42] In Thailand,

TABLE 6.1
Participation of ASEAN Member States in Key Global Nuclear Agreements

	Safeguards Additional Protocol	Convention on Physical Protection (CPP) 2016 CPPNM Amendment	Convention on Physical Protection (CPP) 1980 CPPNM only	Nuclear Terrorism Convention (ICSANT)	Comprehensive Nuclear Test-Ban Treaty (CTBT)	Convention on Nuclear Safety (CNS)	Joint Convention on Spent Fuel and Radiological Waste	Convention Early Notification of a Nuclear Accident	Nuclear Assistance Convention
Brunei					✓				
Cambodia	✓		✓	signed	✓	✓		✓	
Indonesia	✓	✓	✓	✓	✓	✓	✓	✓	✓
Laos	signed		✓		✓			✓	✓
Malaysia	signed		✓	signed	✓			✓	✓
Myanmar	signed	✓	✓		✓	✓		✓	
Philippines	✓		✓	signed	✓	signed	signed	✓	✓
Singapore	✓	✓	✓	✓	✓	✓		✓	✓
Thailand	✓	✓	✓	signed	✓	✓	✓	✓	✓
Vietnam	✓	✓	✓	✓	✓	✓	✓	✓	✓

Sources: IAEA, 29 November 2018; CTBO, 25 September 2018; UN Treaty Collection, "International Convention for the Suppression of Acts of Nuclear Terrorism", 3 December 2018.

in an assessment study on the security of radioactive sources in the country's hospitals, hospital staff handling radioactive sources were found to have incomplete understanding of nuclear and radiological security laws and policies. Meanwhile in Vietnam, a former head of the nuclear regulatory body, Dr Vuong Huu Tan claimed that Vietnamese national culture may create limitations in the development of a safety culture and a security culture as well. He argued that personal emotions trump "rules in working" in the country. He said that *as an agricultural country, most people working in the industrial zones come from rural areas with habits and practices of agricultural production that limit the formation of industrial working style and sense for compliance with labor rules*.[43]

4. Capacity-building Issues in Regulatory Bodies

One crucial and common challenge that needs to be addressed is the enhancement of the capacity of nuclear energy regulatory bodies in ASEAN member states. Concerning regulatory independence, with the exception of Indonesian and Singaporean regulatory bodies, most of nuclear regulatory agencies are regarded as semi-independent or having no independence. The basic explanation is that most of these agencies are connected to other agencies that encourage the utilization of radioactive material and nuclear energy. In fact, some of them are even users of radioactive material. Hence, the promotional and regulatory activities within the same regulatory body could be raised as a regulatory independence issue. One reason why regulatory independence is not being institutionalized is that in most Southeast Asian states close inter-agency cooperation, involving all concerned ministries and regulatory bodies, is considered as far more significant at this time than having an independent regulator as they cautiously study the use of nuclear energy in the future.[44] Independent monitoring and inspections are a powerful tool for raising standards of security culture and safety culture and instilling professional discipline among licensees.

But beyond the issue of independence is the lack of human resource capacity undermining the institutionalization of a safety culture and a security culture even in regulatory bodies. In the absence of national policies on the future of nuclear energy, not many universities have established a specific programme on nuclear sciences and nuclear engineering.[45] In Vietnam, for instance, the regulatory body and other nuclear research agencies lack the necessary skilled human resources including experts on organizational culture with a specialization in nuclear technology and operation, human and organizational factors, and safety culture assessment.[46] An IAEA peer-review mission in 2014 also saw no indication of a systematic approach for institutionalization of a safety culture and a security culture (i.e., checklists, reports, inspections, action plans, outreach activities, etc.) by the Vietnamese regulatory body.[47]

Across Southeast Asia, key challenges to nuclear safety and security include the lack of funding support to implement capacity-building projects, varying degrees of knowledge and expertise among ASEAN member states, lack of well-trained staff and infrastructure, and weak commitment from policymakers down to the technical staff.[48] All of which may have an impact on how nuclear safety-security culture is cultivated in Southeast Asia. Some Southeast Asian countries, such as Malaysia, the Philippines, Vietnam, Indonesia, and Thailand, have more advanced technical expertise and their regulatory bodies can still organize workshops on safety-security cultures for their licensees, despite limited human resources. However, there are also a few states in the region, such as Myanmar, Laos and Cambodia, that have less organized regulatory body infrastructure and capacity. This capacity gap in the region can be filled in by regional cooperation and capacity-building assistance among Southeast Asian states.

6.4   Nuclear Energy Cooperation and Governance in ASEAN

ASEAN member states have been forging regional cooperation on civilian nuclear energy to address shared challenges to nuclear safety and security. In this regard, ASEANTOM has been driving regional cooperation on civilian nuclear capacity-building among ASEAN member states. ASEANTOM has made significant progress since its inaugural meeting in 2013. Through cooperation between ASEAN regulatory agencies, ASEANTOM has been addressing key challenges to nuclear safety and security such as lack of funding support to implement capacity-building projects, varying degrees of knowledge and expertise among ASEAN member states, lack of well-trained staff and infrastructure, and weak commitment from policymakers down to the technical staff on safety-security cultures. All of which may have an impact on how nuclear safety-security culture is cultivated in Southeast Asia. Hence, ASEANTOM conducts, throughout the region, expert missions/exchange programmes, workshops, and technical cooperation projects with international organizations to address such challenges.[49] For instance, ASEANTOM also organizes annually the "Regional Workshop on Capacity-Building and Strengthening the Nuclear and Radiation Safety and Security Network in the ASEAN Region", which includes 130 participants, lecturers, and speakers from ASEAN member states, South Korea, Japan and Taiwan.[50]

Furthermore, global and regional institutions provide technical and funding assistance to ASEANTOM. For instance, ASEANTOM and the IAEA co-organize workshops, training courses, expert missions, and meetings under the *Technical Cooperation Project on Supporting Regional Nuclear Emergency Preparedness and Response in the Member States of ASEAN Region*. ASEANTOM and the European Union (EU) jointly manage a capacity-building project entitled *Enhancing Emergency Preparedness and Response in ASEAN: Technical Support for Decision Making*. These regional projects are aimed at enhancing the quality and coherence of decision-making within ASEAN following a radiological or nuclear emergency. Through ASEANTOM's regional projects and initiatives, with the generous assistance from the IAEA and the EU, it is hoped that a collective nuclear safety-security culture among ASEAN member states will begin taking root in the region.[51]

Nuclear security is another regional agenda set by ASEANTOM in view of the need to increase awareness among state and non-state actors on the importance of nuclear security governance in Southeast Asia. Given the regional challenges for nuclear security, it is crucial to enhance cooperation on nuclear energy governance in Southeast Asia. While not all ASEAN member states have acceded to or ratified major nuclear security international conventions, regional cooperation can help member states strengthen nuclear security governance in Southeast Asia. ASEANTOM has been conducting regional workshops and training courses to boost capacity building in the region, which is extremely vital to strengthen nuclear security. For instance, highlighting the importance of collectively adhering to CPPNM and its Amendments, ASEANTOM held a "Regional Workshop on Sensitization on the Amendment of CPPNM" in 2016.[52] In order to boost the national capabilities of ASEAN member states to investigate illicit use and trafficking of radioactive materials which are widely used in industries, research laboratories, hospitals, and research reactors, ASEANTOM has been hosting the "Regional Workshop on Introduction to Nuclear Forensics and Biological Dosimetry" since 2016. The workshop is expected to facilitate discussions on the regional work plan on nuclear forensics and establish common knowledge among ASEAN member states about nuclear forensics and biological dosimetry.[53]

ASEANTOM also collaborates with international organizations in organizing activities under the regional nuclear security agenda. IAEA and ASEANTOM, for instance, jointly conduct the "IAEA Regional Workshop on Strategy to Establish Inventory for the Security of Radioactive Sources", "IAEA Regional Workshop on Security Management and Security Plan on Radioactive Materials and Associated Facilities", and the "IAEA Regional Training Course on Nuclear Security Culture".[54]

It must be noted that ASEANTOM's cooperation with international organizations such as the IAEA and the European Commission on achieving its nuclear governance agenda on security, safety and emergence preparedness and response in Southeast Asia can serve two purposes. Firstly, ASEAN collectively does not have first-hand experience and high-end expertise on nuclear energy governance, with special emphasis on regulatory framework on NPPs. Hence, the transfer of knowledge from much capable international organizations such as the IAEA to ASEANTOM through workshops and technical meetings would greatly benefit the region and boost the national capacities of nuclear energy regulatory agencies. Secondly, ASEANTOM members do not have the financial resources to implement most of the activities mentioned above that are all aimed at enhancing nuclear energy governance in the region. The financial resources being spent by international organizations for these activities and projects such as the "Enhancing Emergency Preparedness and Response in ASEAN: Technical Support for Decision Making" by the European Commission can definitely help ASEANTOM members realize the nuclear governance agenda for the region. As mentioned earlier, there are significant capacity-building challenges among ASEAN member states. ASEANTOM plans to conduct expert missions/exchange programmes, technical workshops and technical cooperation with international organizations to address such challenges.[55]

Initiatives among neigbouring states are also conducted to address their aforementioned common challenges. These bilateral and trilateral initiatives complement the regional activities organized by the ASEANTOM. Cambodia and Laos do not have enough well-trained staff and regulatory infrastructure, especially for the regulation of radioactive materials. Their neighbour, Thailand, which has more robust nuclear expertise, has reached out to them for capacity building on the regulation of nuclear activities and monitoring of radiation in the environment. Thailand's initiatives include the "2017 Lao PDR-Thailand Technical Cooperation Workshop on Strengthening Capacity-Building on Radiation Safety and Radioactive Measurement and Monitoring in the Environment" and the "2018 Thai-Cambodia Technical Cooperation Workshop on Capacity Building on Radiation Safety and Radioactivity Measurement and Monitoring in the Environment". These workshops entailed on-site training and expert missions by the Office of Atoms for Peace, Thailand's regulatory body, to help Laos and Cambodia establish their own regulatory infrastructure.[56]

Under the ASEANTOM Framework, Malaysia and Thailand since 2015 have been co-hosting annual nuclear security border exercises, including table-top and field exercises in their shared borders and have been involving nuclear regulatory bodies, customs, police, and emergency response teams. All ASEAN member states are invited to participate in these exercises that test their capability to jointly detect, respond to and interdict illicit trafficking of radioactive materials.[57]

In August 2018, as a regional Nuclear Security Support Centre (NSSC), Malaysia hosted a Trilateral Exercise jointly with Indonesia and the Philippines, given that they share maritime borders with persistent common security threats. The table-top exercise and workshop on cooperation to manage and respond to security threats within their shared maritime borders was supported by the IAEA in collaboration with the Global Initiative to Combat Nuclear Terrorism. The table top exercise helped participants strengthen their capacity to detect and respond to nuclear security events in coastal and maritime areas. The workshop looked at mechanisms to create national preparedness strategies, models for regional and international coordination, and cooperation during the detection and response to a nuclear security event.[58]

6.5 Lack of COEs and Training Support Centres

Apart from regional bodies such as the ASEANTOM, centres of excellence (COEs) and training support centres play a key role for global nuclear security and safety architecture. As demonstrated in Japan, South Korea and China, COEs can provide the much needed human resource practical training and promoting nuclear security culture and safety culture. Southeast Asian states should emulate this good practice and increase the number of COEs in the region dedicated to nuclear safety and security. In the context of security culture, however, only a few Southeast Asian countries such as Indonesia, Thailand and Malaysia have established nuclear security support centres of excellence that can provide holistic education and training for radiation workers, researchers, hospital staff and industrial workers. Indonesia appears to have the most significant progress in the region in terms of promoting a nuclear security culture. Leading the promotion of a security culture is BATAN's Centre for Security Culture and Assessment which was established in 2014. The self-assessment pilot project of the Centre has yielded significant and tangible results for BATAN. It offered not only an assessment of the status of security culture at three research reactors, but also a learning experience for management and the workforce of BATAN to identify gaps and improve their security culture.[59] But one significant gap is the need to expand security culture self-assessment training to hospitals, industrial facilities, and other stakeholders that utilize radioactive material, apart from the government's research reactors.

Complementing the work of CSCA is the Indonesia-Centre of Excellence on Nuclear Security and Emergency Preparedness (I-CONSEP), serving as the nuclear security support and training centre to facilitate the development of human resources and the provision of support services for nuclear security and emergency preparedness. One of its priority areas is the development of a nuclear safety culture and a security culture through its training, awareness and educational activities for frontline officers, emergency responders, security officials and border officers.[60] With the establishment of these two specialized centres, Indonesia recognizes the importance of sustainable efforts to achieve an effective nuclear safety and security regime, with safety-security cultures as essential elements.

Meanwhile, support and training centres in the Philippines, Malaysia, Thailand and Vietnam offer training courses, workshops and seminars for licensees and relevant government bodies on nuclear safety and security but these are currently focused on building capacity at the more technical level. Limited workshops on safety-security cultures are overshadowed by technical training work they conduct. Surely, these technical-oriented training activities enhance the domestic technical expertise in nuclear safety and security. However, to make the domestic expertise on nuclear energy more comprehensive, it is important to complement technical training workshops with enhanced training and educational activities promoting a security culture and a safety culture.

Another significant gap is the lack of nuclear training COEs in other Southeast Asian countries. It would be more difficult to inculcate safety-security cultures without even a training institution, such as a nuclear security support centre/COE. These countries should therefore consider setting up their national COEs that are mainly dedicated to fostering a safety culture and a security culture. Furthermore, a potential network of COEs in Southeast Asia can complement the work of ASEANTOM in terms of sharing good practices, resources, expertise and information. It would definitely help deepen cooperation on safety-security cultures in Southeast Asia and institutionalize collaboration with the COEs of Northeast Asia. COEs and nuclear training centres signify a bright future for nuclear security and safety education in East Asia, a region that will definitely need significant capacity building in the coming decades.

6.6 Conclusion

Current gaps in nuclear security governance in Southeast Asia include inadequate funding support to implement capacity-building projects and broad differences in nuclear expertise and infrastructure among ASEAN member states. Significant efforts are therefore necessary to increase capacity in the least developed ASEAN member states. Moreover, several ASEAN member states have yet to ratify and incorporate global nuclear security agreements into their national legal frameworks.

The growing regional cooperation on civilian nuclear energy among ASEAN member states can help plug these gaps in nuclear safety and security governance. The ASEANTOM has been conducting regular exchanges of best practices, capacity-building efforts, and assistance to member states to implement key international agreements.

Apart from regional bodies such as the ASEANTOM, nuclear security COEs and training and support centres can potentially play a key role in establishing a regional nuclear security architecture. In Northeast

Asia, COEs can develop the human resources and technical support services needed for a sustainable nuclear security regime. Southeast Asian states may emulate this good practice by establishing their national COEs. So far, only a few ASEAN member states have established their nuclear security training centres. A collaborative network of COEs in Southeast Asia can complement the work of ASEANTOM in terms of sharing good practices, resources, expertise and information. Promoting a nuclear security culture, together with a nuclear safety culture, is likewise becoming more relevant in Southeast Asia in view of long-term plans by several Southeast Asian states to build NPPs and recent incidents of missing radioactive sources in the region.

With the ever-present transboundary risks of radiological emergencies and stolen radioactive materials, improving the rate at which security policies are fully implemented and understood by all stakeholders could dramatically narrow the gaps in nuclear energy governance in the region.

NOTES

1. World Nuclear Association, *World Nuclear Performance Report 2018: Asia Edition* (London: World Nuclear Association, 2018).
2. Mark Hibbs, *The Future of Nuclear Power in China* (Washington, D.C.: Carnegie Endowment for International Peace, 2018).
3. World Nuclear Association, *World Nuclear Performance Report 2018: Asia Edition*.
4. Tatsujiro Suzuki, "Nuclear Energy Governance in Japan: Lessons Learnt from the Fukushima Accident", Presentation, RSIS Roundtable on Nuclear Energy Development in Southeast Asia: Emerging Challenges and Opportunities, Singapore, 11 December 2018.
5. IAEA (International Atomic Energy Agency), *Nuclear Security Culture: Implementing Guide* (Vienna: IAEA, 2008).
6. IEA (International Energy Agency), *Southeast Asia Energy Outlook 2017* (Paris: IEA, 2017).
7. Ibid.
8. M. Velasco, "Cusi Pitches for Nuclear at ASEAN", *Manila Bulletin*, 3 November 2018.
9. Kristine Bersamina, "Can Nuclear Power Solve Energy Gap in the Philippines? Scientist Explains", *Philippine Star*, 22 May 2018, https://www.philstar.com/headlines/2018/05/22/1817362/can-nuclear-power-solve-energy-gap-philippines-scientist-explains#dezD4EVJ3q1qMYeI.99.

10. Victor Saulon, "DoE in Discussions for CEZA Nuclear Power Plant Study", *Business World*, 6 June 2018.

11. Aberon Voltaire Palana, "DOE Sees Potential of Nuclear Energy", *Manila Times*, 30 August 2016.

12. ASEAN Center for Energy, *Pre-Feasibility Study on the Establishment of Nuclear Power Plant in Southeast Asia* (Jakarta: ASEAN Center for Energy, 2018).

13. Bersamina, "Can Nuclear Power Solve Energy Gap in the Philippines?"

14. Statement by His Excellency Ambassador Dr Darmansjah Djumala, Ambassador Extraordinary and Plenipotentiary/Permanent Representative of the Republic of Indonesia Head of Delegation of the Republic of Indonesia at the 62nd General Conference of the International Atomic Energy Agency, Vienna, Austria, 17–21 September 2018, https://www.iaea.org/sites/default/files/18/09/gc62-indonesia-statement.pdf.

15. IAEA, "Small Modular Reactors", undated, https://www.iaea.org/topics/small-modular-reactors (accessed 17 December 2018).

16. Viet Phuong Nguyen, "China's Risky Plan for Floating Nuclear Power Plants in the South China Sea", *The Diplomat*, 10 May 2018.

17. For further information about tsunami and earthquake hazards in the South China Sea, see Adam Switzer and Shireen Federico, "Tsunami Hazard in South China Sea is Likely Greater Than Previously Thought", *EOS News*, 19 October 2016, https://earthobservatory.sg/news/tsunami-hazard-south-china-sea-likely-greater-previously-thought.

18. Francesca Giovannini, "A New Pathway to Enhance the Nuclear Security Regime", *International Journal of Nuclear Security* 2, no. 3 (2016).

19. Eric Ng, "China's Nuclear Error and Cover-up Unlikely to Hurt Reactor Exports, Industry Competitiveness", *South China Morning Post*, 14 August 2016.

20. Yutthana Tumnoi, "ASEANTOM & Its Activities to Enhance RN Governance in the Region", Presentation, RSIS Roundtable on Nuclear Energy Development in Southeast Asia: Emerging Challenges and Opportunities, Singapore, 11 December 2018.

21. Twenty-eight years after the Chernobyl nuclear disaster, some areas in Germany, such as in Saxony, are still being affected by radiation in the form of radioactive animals and soil. It must be noted that Saxony lies some 1,100 km from Chernobyl while wind and rain carried the radioactivity across western Europe. Soil contamination was even detected in some areas in France. See Justin Huggler, "Radioactive Wild Boar Roaming the Forests of Germany", *The Telegraph*, 1 September 2014.

22. Vincent Rossi et al., "Multi-decal Projections of Surface and Interior Pathways of the Fukushima Cesium-137 Radioactive Plume", *Deep Sea Research Part I: Oceanographic Research Papers* 82 (2013): 37–46.

23. David Gutierrez, "Massive Radiation Plume from Fukushima Heading Toward American West Coast According to a Scientific Report", *Global Research*, 11 September 2014, http://www.globalresearch.ca/massive-radiation-plume-from-fukushimaheading-toward-american-west-coast-according-to-a-scientific-report/5401006.
24. Mely Caballero-Anthony and Julius Cesar Trajano, "Missing Iridium: Enhancing Regional Nuclear Security", *RSIS Commentary*, 29 August 2018, https://www.rsis.edu.sg/rsis-publication/nts/co18142-missing-iridium-enhancing-regional-nuclear-security/#.XBcJV2gza70.
25. Dhel Nazario, "Scientific Equipment Containing Radioactive Materials Reported Lost", *Manila Bulletin*, 18 September 2018.
26. Atomic Energy Licensing Board (AELB), *Annual Report 2017* (Kuala Lumpur: AELB, 2018).
27. Philippine Nuclear Research Institute (PNRI), *2018 Annual Report* (Quezon City: PNRI, 2019).
28. National Progress Report: Thailand, Nuclear Security Summit, March 2016; National Progress Report: Philippines, Nuclear Security Summit, March 2016; National Progress Report: Vietnam, Nuclear Security Summit, March 2016; National Progress Report: Indonesia, Nuclear Security Summit, March 2016, http://www.nss2016.org/2016-progress-reports/.
29. PNRI, *2018 Annual Report*.
30. AELB, *Annual Report 2017*.
31. Shea Cotton, Sam Meyer, and Anne Pellegrino, *CNS Global Incidents and Trafficking Database, 2017 Annual Report*, Nuclear Threat Initiative and James Martin Center for Nonproliferation Studies, 2018.
32. John Carlson, "Strengthening Nuclear Security – Practical Steps for Asia Pacific Countries", *APLN Policy Brief No. 22*, October 2016, http://www.nti.org/media/documents/PB_22_Carlson_NS_practical_steps.pdf?_=1477080304.
33. Forum for Nuclear Cooperation in Asia, "Summary of Country Reports: 8th Workshop on Nuclear Security and Safeguards Project of Forum for Nuclear Cooperation in Asia (FNCA)", Tokyo, Japan, 12 September 2018, https://www.fnca.mext.go.jp/nss/2018-01.pdf.
34. Ibid.
35. Ibid.
36. Ibid.; PNRI, *2018 Annual Report*.
37. Ibid.
38. *New Straits Times*, "IS Supporters in Malaysia May Build Bombs with Radioactive Materials", *Today*, 2 January 2018, https://www.todayonline.com/world/supporters-malaysia-may-build-bombs-radioactive-materials.
39. CSCAP Nuclear Energy Experts Group Meeting, Singapore, 27 February 2017.
40. Carlson, "Strengthening Nuclear Security".

41. CSCAP NEEG Meeting Key Findings, Singapore, 22–23 January 2018, https://csis-prod.s3.amazonaws.com/s3fs-public/event/180122_keyfindings.pdf?NKYhZib2KcGSZ25S2suHCGB0xPMCK8T8.

42. *New Straits Times*, "IS Supporters in Malaysia".

43. Vuong Huu Tan, "Safety Culture in Vietnam", Presentation, Technical Meeting on Topical Issues in the Development of Nuclear Power Infrastructure, Vienna, Austria, 3–6 February 2015, https://www-legacy.iaea.org/NuclearPower/Downloadable/Meetings/2014/2015-02-03-02-06/D4_S10_Vietnam_Vuong.pdf.

44. Mely Caballero-Anthony and Julius Cesar Trajano, "Enhancing Nuclear Energy Cooperation in ASEAN: Regional Norms and Challenges", in *Learning from Fukushima: Nuclear Power in East Asia*, edited by Peter Van Ness and Mel Gurtov (Canberra: ANU Press, 2017), pp. 187–218.

45. ASEAN Center for Energy, *Pre-Feasibility Study on the Establishment of Nuclear Power Plant in Southeast Asia*.

46. Hong Anh Duong, "First Steps of VARANS Towards a Strong Safety Culture", Presentation, IAEA TM Technical Meeting on Integration of Safety Culture into Regulatory Practices and the Regulatory Decision Making Process, Vienna, Austria, 6–8 October 2014.

47. IAEA, *Integrated Regulatory Review Service (IRRS) Follow-Up Report to Vietnam*, Hanoi, Vietnam, September 29 to October 9, 2014, https://www.iaea.org/sites/default/files/documents/review-missions/irrs_follow-up_viet_nam.pdf.

48. Phiphat Phruksarojanakun, "National and Regional Effort on Fostering Nuclear Safety and Security", Presentation, SIEW RSIS Roundtable on Nuclear Safety and Security Culture in East Asia, Singapore, 27 October 2017.

49. RSIS' Centre for Non-Traditional Security Studies (NTS Centre), *Nuclear Safety and Security Culture: Powering Nuclear Governance in East Asia, 27 October 2017, Event Report* (Singapore: RSIS' Centre for NTS Studies, 2018).

50. Ibid.

51. Ibid.

52. CSCAP Nuclear Energy Experts Group Meeting, Singapore, 19–20 September 2016.

53. Ibid.

54. Ibid.

55. Yuthiana Tumnoi, "ASEAN Network of Regulatory Bodies on Atomic Energy (ASEANTOM) and its Activity", Presentation, CSCAP Nuclear Energy Experts Group Meeting, Singapore, 27 February 2017.

56. Tumnoi, "ASEANTOM & Its Activities".

57. Ibid.

58. Statement by H.E. Ganeson Sivagurunathan, Head of Delegation of Malaysia to the 62nd Regular Session of the General Conference of the International

Atomic Energy Agency, Vienna, Austria, 18 September 2018; Catherine Friedly, "IAEA Holds Table Top Exercise to Strengthen Detection and Response Capabilities in Maritime Nuclear Security Events", *IAEA Newscentre*, 3 October 2018.

59. Anhar R. Antariksawan, "Nuclear Security Culture and BATAN's Assessment: BATAN's Experience", *International Journal of Nuclear Security* 2, no. 2 (2016).

60. Hendriyanto Haditjahyono, "Capacity Building Development in Nuclear Security", Presentation, International Forum on the Peaceful Use of Nuclear Energy, Nuclear Non-Proliferation, and Nuclear Security, Tokyo, Japan, 29 November 2016, https://www.jaea.go.jp/04/iscn/activity/2016-11-29/2016-11-29-09.pdf.

REFERENCES

Antariksawan, Anhar R. 2016. "Nuclear Security Culture and BATAN's Assessment: BATAN's Experience". *International Journal of Nuclear Security* 2, no. 2.

ASEAN Center for Energy. 2018. *Pre-Feasibility Study on the Establishment of Nuclear Power Plant in Southeast Asia*. Jakarta: ASEAN Center for Energy.

Atomic Energy Licensing Board (AELB). 2018. *Annual Report 2017*. Kuala Lumpur: AELB.

Bersamina, Kristine. 2018. "Can Nuclear Power Solve Energy Gap in the Philippines? Scientist Explains". *Philippine Star*, 22 May 2018. https://www.philstar.com/headlines/2018/05/22/1817362/can-nuclear-power-solve-energy-gap-philippines-scientist-explains#dezD4EVJ3q1qMYeI.99.

Caballero-Anthony, Mely and Julius Cesar Trajano. 2017. "Enhancing Nuclear Energy Cooperation in ASEAN: Regional Norms and Challenges". In *Learning from Fukushima: Nuclear Power in East Asia*, edited by Peter Van Ness and Mel Gurtov. Canberra: ANU Press, pp. 187–218.

———. 2018. "Missing Iridium: Enhancing Regional Nuclear Security". *RSIS Commentary*, 29 August 2018. https://www.rsis.edu.sg/rsis-publication/nts/co18142-missing-iridium-enhancing-regional-nuclear-security/#.XBcJV2gza70.

Carlson, John. 2016. "Strengthening Nuclear Security – Practical Steps for Asia Pacific Countries". *APLN Policy Brief No. 22*. http://www.nti.org/media/documents/PB_22_Carlson_NS_practical_steps.pdf?_=1477080304.

Comprehensive Nuclear-Test-Ban Treaty Organization (CTBTO). 2018. "Status of Signature and Ratification", 25 September 2018. https://www.ctbto.org/the-treaty/status-of-signature-and-ratification/.

Cotton, Shea, Sam Meyer, and Anne Pellegrino. 2018. *CNS Global Incidents and Trafficking Database, 2017 Annual Report*. Nuclear Threat Initiative and James Martin Center for Nonproliferation Studies.

CSCAP NEEG Meeting. Key Findings, Singapore, 22–23 January 2018. https://
csis-prod.s3.amazonaws.com/s3fs-public/event/180122_keyfindings.
pdf?NKYhZib2KcGSZ25S2suHCGB0xPMCK8T8.

———. Singapore, 19–20 September 2016.

———, 27–28 February 2017.

Duong, Hong Anh. 2014. "First Steps of VARANS Towards a Strong Safety Culture". Presentation, IAEA TM Technical Meeting on Integration of Safety Culture into Regulatory Practices and the Regulatory Decision Making Process, Vienna, Austria, 6–8 October 2014.

Forum for Nuclear Cooperation in Asia. 2018. "Summary of Country Reports: 8th Workshop on Nuclear Security and Safeguards Project of Forum for Nuclear Cooperation in Asia (FNCA)". Tokyo, Japan, 12 September 2018. https://www.fnca.mext.go.jp/nss/2018-01.pdf.

Friedly, Catherine. 2018. "IAEA Holds Table Top Exercise to Strengthen Detection and Response Capabilities in Maritime Nuclear Security Events". *IAEA Newscentre*, 3 October 2018.

Giovannini, Francesca. 2016. "A New Pathway to Enhance the Nuclear Security Regime". *International Journal of Nuclear Security* 2, no. 3.

Gutierrez, David. 2014. "Massive Radiation Plume from Fukushima Heading Toward American West Coast According to a Scientific Report". *Global Research*, 11 September 2014. http://www.globalresearch.ca/massive-radiation-plume-from-fukushimaheading-toward-american-west-coast-according-to-a-scientific-report/5401006.

Haditjahyono, Hendriyanto. 2016. "Capacity Building Development in Nuclear Security". Presentation, International Forum on the Peaceful Use of Nuclear Energy, Nuclear Non-Proliferation, and Nuclear Security, Tokyo, Japan, 29 November 2016. https://www.jaea.go.jp/04/iscn/activity/2016-11-29/2016-11-29-09.pdf.

Hibbs, Mark. 2018. *The Future of Nuclear Power in China*. Washington, D.C.: Carnegie Endowment for International Peace.

Huggler, Justin. 2014. "Radioactive Wild Boar Roaming the Forests of Germany". *The Telegraph*, 1 September 2014.

International Atomic Energy Agency (IAEA). Undated. "Small Modular Reactors". https://www.iaea.org/topics/small-modular-reactors (accessed 17 December 2018).

———. 2008. *Nuclear Security Culture: Implementing Guide*. Vienna: IAEA.

———. 2014. *Integrated Regulatory Review Service (IRRS) Follow-Up Report to Vietnam, Hanoi, Vietnam, September 29 to October 9, 2014*. https://www.iaea.org/sites/default/files/documents/review-missions/irrs_follow-up_viet_nam.pdf.

———. 2018. "Factsheets: Country List", 29 November 2018. https://www.iaea.org/resources/legal/country-factsheets.

International Energy Agency (IEA). 2017. *Southeast Asia Energy Outlook 2017*. Paris: IEA.

National Progress Report: Indonesia. Nuclear Security Summit, March 2016.

National Progress Report: Philippines. Nuclear Security Summit, March 2016.

National Progress Report: Thailand. Nuclear Security Summit, March 2016.

National Progress Report: Vietnam. Nuclear Security Summit, March 2016.

Nazario, Dhel. 2018. "Scientific Equipment Containing Radioactive Materials Reported Lost". *Manila Bulletin*, 18 September 2018.

New Straits Times. 2018. "IS Supporters in Malaysia May Build Bombs with Radioactive Materials". *Today*, 2 January 2018. https://www.todayonline.com/world/supporters-malaysia-may-build-bombs-radioactive-materials.

Ng, Eric. 2016. "China's Nuclear Error and Cover-up Unlikely to Hurt Reactor Exports, Industry Competitiveness". *South China Morning Post*, 14 August 2016.

Nguyen, Viet Phuong. 2018. "China's Risky Plan for Floating Nuclear Power Plants in the South China Sea". *The Diplomat*, 10 May 2018.

Palana, Aberon Voltaire. 2016. "DOE Sees Potential of Nuclear Energy". *Manila Times*, 30 August 2016.

Philippine Nuclear Research Institute (PNRI). 2019. *2018 Annual Report*. Quezon City: PNRI.

Phruksarojanakun, Phiphat. 2017. "National and Regional Effort on Fostering Nuclear Safety and Security". Presentation, SIEW RSIS Roundtable on Nuclear Safety and Security Culture in East Asia, Singapore, 27 October 2017.

Rossi, Vincent, Erik Van Sebille, Alexander Sen Gupta, Véronique Garçon, and Matthew H. England. 2013. "Multi-decal Projections of Surface and Interior Pathways of the Fukushima Cesium-137 Radioactive Plume". *Deep Sea Research Part I: Oceanographic Research Papers* 82: 37–46.

RSIS' Centre for Non-Traditional Security Studies (NTS Centre). 2018. *Nuclear Safety and Security Culture: Powering Nuclear Governance in East Asia, 27 October 2017, Event Report*. Singapore: RSIS' Centre for NTS Studies.

Saulon, Victor. 2018. "DoE in discussions for CEZA Nuclear Power Plant Study". *Business World*, 6 June 2018.

Statement by H.E. Ganeson Sivagurunathan, Head of Delegation of Malaysia to the 62nd Regular Session of the General Conference of the International Atomic Energy Agency, Vienna, Austria, 18 September 2018.

Statement by His Excellency Ambassador Dr Darmansjah Djumala, Ambassador Extraordinary and Plenipotentiary/Permanent Representative of the Republic of Indonesia Head of Delegation of the Republic of Indonesia at the 62nd General Conference of the International Atomic Energy Agency, Vienna, Austria, 17–21 September 2018. https://www.iaea.org/sites/default/files/18/09/gc62-indonesia-statement.pdf.

Suzuki, Tatsujiro. 2018. "Nuclear Energy Governance in Japan: Lessons Learnt from the Fukushima Accident". Presentation, RSIS Roundtable on

Nuclear Energy Development in Southeast Asia: Emerging Challenges and Opportunities, Singapore, 11 December 2018.

Switzer, Adam and Shireen Federico. 2016. "Tsunami Hazard in South China Sea is Likely Greater Than Previously Thought". *EOS News*, 19 October 2016. https://earthobservatory.sg/news/tsunami-hazard-south-china-sea-likely-greater-previously-thought.

Tumnoi, Yutthana. 2017. "ASEAN Network of Regulatory Bodies on Atomic Energy (ASEANTOM) and its Activity". Presentation, CSCAP Nuclear Energy Experts Group Meeting, Singapore, 27 February 2017.

———. 2018. "ASEANTOM & Its Activities to Enhance RN Governance in the Region". Presentation, RSIS Roundtable on Nuclear Energy Development in Southeast Asia: Emerging Challenges and Opportunities, Singapore, 11 December 2018.

UN Treaty Collection. 2018. "International Convention for the Suppression of Acts of Nuclear Terrorism", 3 December 2018. https://treaties.un.org/pages/ViewDetailsIII.aspx?src=TREATY&mtdsg_no=XVIII-15&chapter=18&Temp=mtdsg3&clang=_en.

Velasco, M. 2018. "Cusi Pitches for Nuclear at ASEAN". *Manila Bulletin*, 3 November 2018.

Vuong, Huu Tan. 2015. "Safety Culture in Vietnam". Presentation, Technical Meeting on Topical Issues in the Development of Nuclear Power Infrastructure, Vienna, Austria, 3–6 February 2015. https://www-legacy.iaea.org/NuclearPower/Downloadable/Meetings/2014/2015-02-03-02-06/D4_S10_Vietnam_Vuong.pdf.

World Nuclear Association. 2018. *World Nuclear Performance Report 2018: Asia Edition*. London: World Nuclear Association.

7

TRAFFICKING IN PERSONS

Julius Cesar I. Trajano and Yen Ne Foo

7.1 Combatting Human Trafficking in East Asia: Mind the Gaps

Across the world, human trafficking is being committed every hour of the day and is viewed as one of the largest criminal enterprises. Human trafficking, dubbed as modern-day slavery, is an enduring global problem with approximately 40 million men, women and children trapped in horrendous trafficking situations such as forced labour, sexual exploitation and forced marriage.[1] This extremely high figure is a wake-up call to the global community which has committed to eradicating modern slavery and human trafficking by the year 2030 (Sustainable Development Goals (SDGs) Targets 5.2, 8.7, and 16.2).[2] According to some estimates, human trafficking has become one of the most lucrative organized crimes, with illicit profits exceeding US$150 billion every year.[3]

Human trafficking remains an endemic security problem in East Asia, threatening states and societies, as discussed and analysed in this chapter. Two-thirds or 25 million of global trafficking victims were identified to be in the region.[4]

TABLE 7.1
Estimated Annual Profits Generated From Trafficking

Region	Annual Profits per Region in (US$ billion)
Asia-Pacific	51.8
European Union	46.9
Central and Southeastern Europe and CIS	18
Africa	13.1
Latin America and the Carribean	12
Middle East	8
GLOBAL PROFIT	150

Source: ILO (2014).

FIGURE 7.1
Number of Victims of Modern Slavery by Region

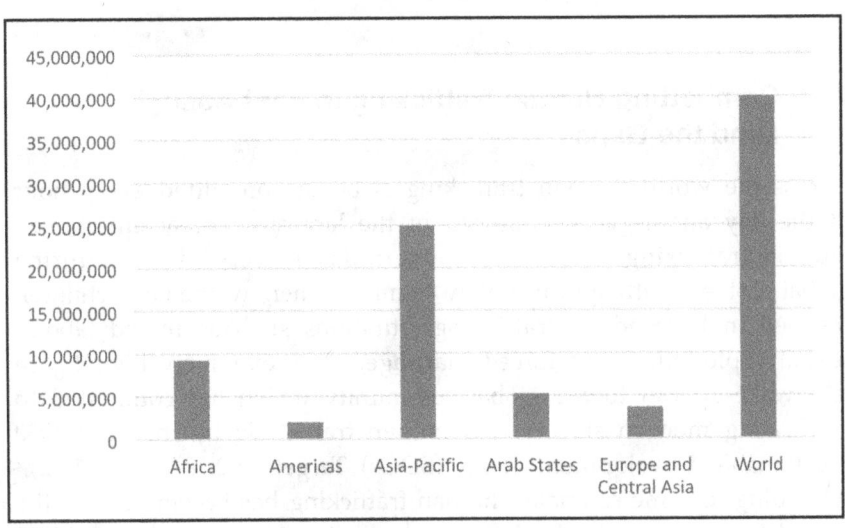

Source: ILO (2017).

To provide an overview of the extent of human trafficking in East Asia, this chapter briefly reviews trends and patterns of trafficking in the region. It then primarily analyses three fundamental issues that impede the eradication of human trafficking in East Asia. Firstly, the key issue of weak implementation of relevant anti-trafficking frameworks at the national level remains. Secondly, the longstanding problems of corruption and the failure of the state to prosecute complicit officials still exacerbate human trafficking in most states of East Asia. Thirdly, the lack of appropriate protection and assistance mechanisms for victims heightens the vulnerabilities that can push people into trafficking or being victimized again. Lastly, human trafficking as a crime is often "hidden" from the one-size-fits-all global anti-trafficking legal regime that is adopted by national governments in East Asia.

Current Trends and Patterns

1) Intra-regional trafficking is the major pattern reported in East Asia.

The great majority—more than 85 per cent—of the victims rescued in East Asia and the Pacific were trafficked from within the region in 2016.[5] About 6 per cent of the victims were trafficked from South Asia, specifically from Bangladesh and India.[6] Another 5 per cent of victims belonged to stateless ethnic minorities such as the Rohingya in Myanmar.[7]

Thailand has been detecting foreign victims from neighbouring countries such as Cambodia, Laos and Myanmar, in addition to victims of domestic trafficking. Malaysia has been a main destination of trafficking victims from Indonesia, the Philippines and Vietnam.[8] China has been repatriating trafficked Cambodians, Indonesians, Mongolians and Vietnamese. Taiwan has been rescuing and repatriating Indonesians, Filipinos and other nationalities from Southeast Asia. In Japan, most of the identified victims are from Southeast Asia, although domestic trafficking is also reported there.[9]

2) Majority of trafficking victims are women and girls. Trafficking for sexual exploitation is the most frequently detected form.

According to UN Office on Drugs and Crimes' (UNODC) *Global Report on Trafficking in Persons Report 2016*, 51 per cent of trafficking victims in the Asia Pacific were women.[10]

FIGURE 7.2
Victims of Trafficking by Gender and Age in Asia-Pacific

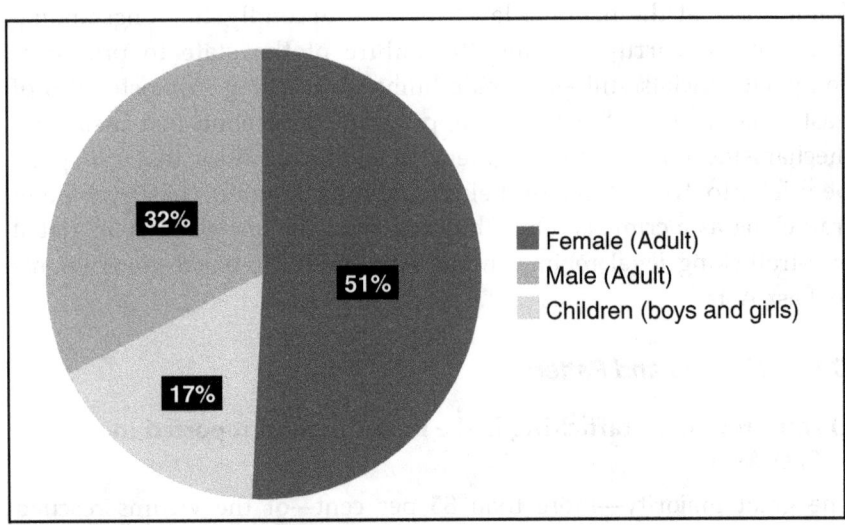

Source: UNODC (2017).

As a consequence of frequent trafficking of minor girls, children comprised nearly a third of the victims detected in East Asia. More than 60 per cent of the 7,800 victims rescued between 2012 and 2014 in the region were trafficked for sexual exploitation.[11] For instance, women and children from the Philippines' impoverished indigenous communities are the most vulnerable to sex trafficking. They are also susceptible to domestic servitude that enslaves domestic helpers without compensation in private residences and other forms of forced labour such as debt-bondage, commercial sexual exploitation, forced confinement in factories and plantations, and illegal recruitment.[12] Trafficked women and children from Thailand, Myanmar, Laos, and Cambodia are forced to work in Thailand's vast commercial sex industry.[13]

3) Trafficking for online sexual exploitation of children is now an alarming trend.

In recent years, child trafficking for sexual exploitation has been exacerbated by the proliferation of new technologies, including the online live-streaming of sexual abuse of children. Child trafficking is being committed with great frequency as various estimates indicate that tens of thousands of children in the Philippines alone are subjected to online sexual abuse while Thailand and Cambodia have been tagged as major source countries of child sexual abuse images.[14] The Philippines has been tagged as the "global epicentre of the live stream sexual abuse trade".[15] In fact, makers of online child sexual abuse materials in the Philippines generate up to US$1 billion of annual revenue.[16] Globally, this industry earns between US$3 billion and US$20 billion annually.[17]

4) Forced labour is the second most prominent form of trafficking.

The International Organization for Migration (IOM) reported that forced labour is prevalent within Southeast Asia and among labour migrants destined for other regions.[18] Labour migrants might end up as victims of forced labour and sex trafficking. Their migration is mostly facilitated by brokers and recruiters, some are not legally registered. Migrants might be charged with exorbitant recruitment fees along with plane tickets, loan interest and boarding expenses. But excessive fees and debts incurred by migrant workers to obtain employment abroad made them vulnerable to sexual exploitation, forced labour and exploitative conditions. Their dire working situations might compel them to find alternate options, such as wading into the sex industry. Others are simply duped into entering the sex industry from the beginning and are forced to perform acts they never agreed to.[19] In 2015, IOM helped 1,564 victims of trafficking in Southeast Asia, 85 per cent of whom were men trafficked for forced labour.[20] Meanwhile, UNODC claimed that about 32 per cent of the reported trafficking victims in East Asia were subjected to forced labour. One of the prominent forms of trafficking is forced labour in the fishing industry particularly in Indonesia and Thailand.[21]

5) Armed conflicts and climate change-induced disasters are increasingly exacerbating human trafficking.

According to the IOM, the impact of climate change is seldom regarded as a contributing factor to human trafficking in global, regional, and national-level policy frameworks.[22] However, with the increasing evidence that environmental and climate changes drive sudden migration, more studies are needed to clearly understand the direct implications for human trafficking.[23] For instance, in 2013, Typhoon Haiyan hit Philippine provinces that were already suffering from extreme poverty and prevalent trafficking. Out of 112 randomly selected villages in two Haiyan-devastated regions, 39 per cent reported an increase in the number of children involved in forced labour.[24]

Persons who are fleeing armed conflicts and humanitarian emergencies are highly vulnerable to trafficking in their desperate attempt to seek safety and protection. For instance, displaced Rohingyas are at great risk of human trafficking in Myanmar-Bangladesh border. In fact, more than 5,000 Rohingyas trafficked or smuggled in different parts of Bangladesh were rescued and transported by police back to the camp areas.[25]

Gaps in Enforcing Anti-trafficking Legal Frameworks

The fight against human trafficking is not a straightforward process. In East Asia, there are big wins in this battle such as the passage of strong national anti-trafficking laws in accordance with the Palermo Protocol, also known as the Protocol to Prevent, Suppress and Punish Trafficking in Persons Especially Women and Children, supplementing the United Nations Convention against Transnational Organized Crime (UNCTOC). In 2017, six ASEAN member states ratified the ASEAN Convention Against Trafficking in Persons, Especially Women and Children (ACTIP). However, it is also important to note that the ratification of the Palermo Protocol and ACTIP coupled with the enactment of national legislative framework are only the first steps in building an effective anti-trafficking regime at the national level. Other important measures include effective law enforcement, prosecution, eradication of official complicity, and robust assistance for trafficked victims.[26] Nevertheless, there are still significant gaps at the national level.

1) Weak law enforcement capacity of states

The "3P" paradigm (prosecution, protection, and prevention) serves as the fundamental global framework for combatting human trafficking, as reflected in the Palermo Protocol. State parties to the Protocol have an obligation to adopt legislative frameworks and other measures as may be necessary to criminalize human trafficking activities and to provide for the physical, psychological and social recovery of victims of trafficking.[27] At the regional level in Southeast Asia, the legally binding ACTIP adopts the international anti-trafficking framework based on the "3Ps" notion.[28]

The lack of convergence between (i) the global/regional norms on combatting trafficking and (ii) national law enforcement/criminal justice system is very evident in the region. The limitations of the anti-trafficking law enforcement approach in the region are most apparent when perpetrators cannot be held accountable and trafficking remains endemic.[29] While there is enough national legislation, the main problem is the limited capability of law enforcers, labour inspectors, and other officials tasked to handle trafficking cases. This limited capability entails inadequate criminal justice response, law enforcers' lack of understanding of relevant anti-trafficking laws, enforcement agencies' limited funding and resources, skewed implementation of relevant laws, and lack of coordination among agencies. Consequently, as claimed by the UNODC, there is an overall stagnation in the number of convictions in East Asia, despite the enactment of anti-trafficking laws.[30] Several examples of these challenges from East Asian states are provided in this section.

The ineffectiveness of the law enforcement approach is primarily due to lack of law enforcement understanding of the multifaceted human trafficking issue. While the Palermo Protocol, ACTIP and even most of the current national laws are specific enough in explaining trafficking and the necessary "3P" responses that need to be done, law enforcers, labour inspectors and first responders are still baffled by the questions: *"What does human trafficking really entail?; How do we identify a trafficking victim?; and What are the needs of the victims?"*[31] As explained in various human trafficking reports, the legislation and unswerving enforcement of comprehensive legal frameworks serve as cornerstones to a multifaceted anti-trafficking regime.[32] A comprehensive anti-trafficking law vividly defines the crime consistent with international law—identifying the acts, means, and ends of trafficking. It provides framework for all domestic anti-trafficking efforts. In order to boost prosecution and law enforcement, a strong anti-trafficking law includes: (1) the criminalization of all types of human trafficking; (2) accurate definition of human trafficking that enumerates the acts, means, and ends, in order to differentiate it from related crimes; (3) mandated penalties of imprisonment that must be equivalent with those for other heinous crimes; and (4) a mandate delineating roles and responsibilities for relevant government agencies, including inter-ministerial coordination of anti-trafficking policies.[33]

Without comprehensive legal frameworks and consistent law enforcement, no government can prosecute traffickers, eliminate human trafficking, and provide the needs of victims. Traffickers would simply take advantage of legal gaps and the inability of authorities to strictly implement anti-trafficking policies.[34]

For instance, the respective anti-human trafficking laws of Myanmar, Cambodia, Thailand and Laos criminalize sex and labour trafficking, and the penalties for human trafficking stipulated in these laws are sufficiently stringent.[35] However, an estimated 451,000 migrants are smuggled into Thailand annually from Myanmar, 55,000 from Cambodia and 44,000 from Laos.[36] According to the UNODC, between 4 and 23 per cent of these irregular migrants could be considered as trafficking victims.[37] Identifying whether a case is one of human trafficking or migrant smuggling can be very difficult for a number of reasons. While consent of victims is present in smuggling, sometimes trafficking and smuggling overlap. Some trafficked persons might at the beginning consent to be smuggled into a country illegally, but find themselves deceived, coerced or forced into an exploitative situation later in their journey.[38] Insufficient resourcing of law enforcement has been identified as a challenge to anti-trafficking regime in these countries. Their law enforcement agencies often lack personnel and equipment to conduct proactive, intelligence-driven investigations in remote areas while inter-agency coordination mechanisms remain weak. Furthermore, the number of female law enforcers is often inadequate to provide specialized assistance to female victims.[39]

Improper identification of victims also dents enforcement of relevant domestic laws. This has primarily affected child victims of trafficking. For example, due to the Thai government's complicated implementing guidelines for the identification and treatment of trafficking victims, children are erroneously treated by law enforcers as illegal migrants rather than as victims of human trafficking. This restricts their right to protection and assistance.[40]

Malaysia's anti-trafficking law was twice amended (in 2010 and 2015) to expand its coverage by prohibiting all forms of trafficking, imposing stricter penalties, and enhancing the rights of trafficking victims.[41] However, two crucial factors limit the execution of their duties, namely, the lack of manpower and expertise, and inadequate facilities and equipment. Law enforcement bodies of Malaysia have insufficient number of officers as well as labour inspectors who can detect and investigate trafficking indicators.[42] The lack of proper equipment for surveillance and monitoring has prevented Malaysia's maritime enforcement bodies to prevent trafficking activities at sea.[43]

The Philippines' anti-trafficking legal framework is regarded to be the most comprehensive in the East Asian region and has a Tier 1 status accorded by the US State Department.[44] However, the difficulties faced by the government in combating the proliferation of online sexual exploitation of children pose a challenge to the effective enforcement of its anti-trafficking law. In handling cases of trafficking for online sexual exploitation, police and prosecutors reported challenges, including difficulty in obtaining search warrants and arresting perpetrators mainly due to insufficient personnel, inadequate resources for operations logistics and computer evidence analysis, and the need for training on presenting digital evidence in court.[45]

Meanwhile, in Japan, due to the absence of a comprehensive anti-trafficking law, existing criminal and immigration statutes are applied in trafficking cases.[46] Consequently, authorities detain, charge, and in some cases deport victims, rather than send them to shelters for trafficked victims.[47] In the case of China, there is no anti-trafficking law that fully meets the international standards, according to the *Trafficking in Persons Report 2018*.[48] Instead, its criminal code criminalizes some forms of sex and labour trafficking. The government handles most cases with indicators of forced labour merely as administrative issues and seldom initiates prosecutions of such cases.[49]

2) The symbiotic relationship between corruption and trafficking

Another shared problem that exacerbates human trafficking in East Asian states is the unpunished complicity of officials, criminal justice actors and law enforcers in human trafficking. The UNODC has identified corruption and lack of accountability as factors underpinning human trafficking in Southeast Asian countries.[50] As a framework on trafficking-corruption nexus, the UNODC, Anti-Slavery International and Transparency International have specifically identified a number of mechanisms wherein corruption in the public sector facilitates trafficking:[51]

- recruitment, transportation and exploitation of victims with the help of corrupt public officials;
- undermined or delayed investigation, prosecution and adjudication of trafficking cases due to corrupt criminal justice officials;
- scarce information and data collection on, as well as reporting of, human trafficking-related corruption;
- obstruction of social and protective services for victims by corrupt public officials; and
- insufficient responses to underlying causes of trafficking.

The aforementioned trafficking-corruption nexus mechanisms are vividly seen in East Asia. In some countries, law enforcers ignore evidence of exploitation or even actively participate in human trafficking. Some government officials in China and Myanmar, for instance, are often involved in state-sponsored forced labour for infrastructure projects and in state facilities.[52]

Traffickers bribe border and immigration officials to permit illegal entry of trafficking victims or smuggled migrants who are susceptible to trafficking and may later face exploitation.[53] In the borders of Malaysia and Thailand, the discovery of huge mass graves of suspected victims of trafficking and smuggling in 2015 generated reports that law enforcers and military officers facilitated migrant smuggling and trafficking crimes.[54] But in an *unprecedented effort by Thai authorities to hold perpetrators of human trafficking accountable*[56] in 2017, a Thai local court convicted 62 trafficking perpetrators, including 11 government officials and a Thai army general, in the largest-ever human trafficking trial in the region.[57] However, Thailand has yet to prosecute and convict the rest of corrupt government officials involved in trafficking.[58] In 2017, the government launched investigations of 26 officials (10 in 2016), but initiated prosecution of 7, and convicted 12 officials complicit in trafficking crimes.[59] In the Philippines, there are ongoing cases of police and immigration officers actively facilitating illegal recruitment and sex trafficking involving online sexual exploitation of minors.[60]

In order to cut the corruption-trafficking nexus, states must aggressively prosecute and seek conviction of corrupt officials involved in human trafficking. However, in most countries in the region that have endemic human trafficking problems, there seem to be no serious state efforts to consistently investigate, prosecute and convict complicit law enforcers.[61] In addition, military and police officials reportedly facilitating recruitment of child soldiers, sex trafficking, and trafficking of people for forced labour in state-led projects, such as in Myanmar, have never been prosecuted and convicted in civilian courts.[62]

It is therefore vital that governments investigate and prosecute vigorously official complicity, in order to deter officials from conniving with criminal syndicates. Complicit government officials should face criminal accountability, prosecution and stern verdicts to strengthen the enforcement of anti-trafficking laws. Credible prosecution of complicit officials is an essential element of a sustainable anti-trafficking regime, given that organized trafficking requires systemic corruption. Countries are therefore recommended to adopt strategies that jointly combat corruption and human trafficking.[63]

3) Limited support services and protection for victims

While prevention and prosecution, through effective law enforcement, are crucial in combatting human trafficking, the protection aspect is also an indispensable element of any anti-trafficking regime. As seen in several East Asian countries, the criminal law enforcement-led approach to counter-trafficking[64] does not often include what the Palermo Protocol prescribes on the protection of victims, especially women and children.[65]

Criminal law enforcement alone cannot sufficiently address the protection needs of trafficking victims whose profiles do not fit in with the normative expectations of criminal justice gatekeepers and welfare officials. Trafficked persons who do not meet the normative expectations of what victims look like, how they act, or what they need, may be denied legitimate victim status. The "ideal" trafficked victims for law enforcers are those who are willing to cooperate and participate in the criminal justice process. However, trafficked persons who do not trust the authorities or service providers and refuse to cooperate due to their trauma may not be given protection and assistance.[66] Hence, a victim-centred and trauma-informed approach is crucial in establishing trust between the victims and law enforcers.[67] Such an approach seeks to understand the vast impact of trauma on victims and craft special response measures in addressing their peculiar needs.[68] Survivors of human trafficking have often suffered complex trauma substantial enough to cause long-term psychological and physical effects. To appropriately support survivors, a trauma-informed approach should be incorporated with the criminal justice process and victim protection.[69]

Apart from being a law enforcement issue, human trafficking is also a public health problem. The implications of human trafficking on public health are vividly evident. Victims of human trafficking often suffer unsanitary and unsafe work environments, poor living conditions, malnutrition, exposure to sexually transmitted and other communicable diseases (including HIV/AIDS) and limited access to any health care services.[70] For instance, among trafficking survivors in Southeast Asia in 2016, 22 per cent sustained severe physical injuries and reported symptoms of depression.[71]

However, regional governments have made slow progress on the protection of trafficking victims.[72] Trafficking victims still struggle to receive protection and health care. For instance, in Cambodia, Thailand and Vietnam, survivors of human trafficking desperately need better access to comprehensive health services, especially related to mental health. More than 60 per cent of the victims from the three countries reported symptoms of depression and 40 per cent were diagnosed with post-traumatic stress disorder.[73]

Unconditional support for child victims needs to be tailored to their special needs. According to UNICEF, several countries in Southeast Asia have just partly established or are in the process of developing special support services to child victims.[74]

In the Philippines, despite the government's serious and sustained efforts to prosecute perpetrators and dismantle online sex trafficking syndicates, specialized shelter and mental health services are not given strong state support and are inadequate to address the specific needs of child victims of online sexual exploitation.[75] Minor victims are not always guided and accompanied by child psychologists and/or a guardian throughout the criminal justice process.[76]

The lack of sustainable rehabilitation and reintegration programmes for returning irregular migrants, including rescued trafficking victims, also exacerbates human trafficking in the region. Without stronger efforts on the sustainability of their return, there would be a greater risk that returnees may once again be victimized by traffickers or smugglers.[77] In many documented cases in Cambodia, Laos and Myanmar, illegal recruiters prey upon returning and deported migrants from Thailand, due to the absence of sustainable full-time employment and livelihood assistance.[78] Similarly, in the southern Philippines, internally displaced persons are subjected to forced labour and sex trafficking in major Philippine cities.[79] They become more susceptible to be victimized again as they are not aware of or do not have sufficient access to reintegration and livelihood programmes in their communities.[80]

Moving Forward

This section demonstrates that robust legal frameworks, while absolutely important, are not sufficient to eradicate and prevent human trafficking in East Asia. Significant gaps at the national level have effectively hindered the eradication of trafficking in the region. Firstly, the lack of effective law enforcement efforts, as a primarily tool to implement states' robust legal frameworks, remain a challenge. Inadequate institutional resources, funding and training for frontline officers and law enforcers impede the investigation of human trafficking cases. These issues must be addressed head-on by governments.

Secondly, corruption and trafficking are deeply intertwined in the region. The failure of governments to run after and prosecute complicit officials and law enforcers exacerbates the corruption-trafficking nexus in the region. In this regard, undertaking robust efforts to jail complicit officials involved in trafficking is crucial to deterring trafficking crimes from taking place, especially in the region's porous state borders.

Thirdly, the lack of protection and social services for the victims also undermines the fight against trafficking. In many East Asian states, the lack of provision for victim protection reflects broader capacity questions, akin to the challenge to effective enforcement of anti-trafficking regime. The protection needs of victims of trafficking are oftentimes secondary concerns to other priorities such as the criminalization approach and prosecution. Government agencies, while assuming primary responsibility, should enhance their cooperation with the civil society and humanitarian organizations that assist and provide support services for victims of trafficking in order to promote a victim-centred, trauma-informed approach to counter trafficking.

Given the abovementioned common challenges among regional states, the opportunities provided by regional cooperation remain underutilized and trafficking syndicates take advantage of the limitations of national anti-trafficking regimes and agencies to move beyond national borders. It is important therefore for ASEAN member states to work together to fully utilize the ACTIP, which provides a framework for member states to enter into direct law enforcement cooperation on human trafficking cases and common standards for the protection of victims.[81] If multiple actors (state and non-state) in ASEAN and the broader East Asian region pool together their expertise, resources, and capacity, preventing trafficking and prosecuting perpetrators can be comprehensively implemented in parallel with protection initiatives that address the vulnerabilities of trafficking victims.

7.2   Human Trafficking: In the Shadows of the Law

Building on the findings of Section 7.1 of this chapter, Section 7.2 examines the nature of international legal frameworks that address human trafficking and their effectiveness. It scrutinizes the way international legal frameworks have influenced the form and substance of regional and domestic anti-trafficking legislation and their application in the East Asia context. This section argues that human trafficking as a crime is often "hidden" from the one-size-fits-all anti-trafficking legal regime that is adopted by national governments. It also argues that drawing the crime of human trafficking out of the shadows is made difficult by (i) the ambiguous definition of human trafficking in persons in international law; and (ii) the disjuncture between human trafficking contexts in East Asia and what international anti-trafficking legal regimes seek to address.

Human Trafficking and the Law

1) The UNCTOC and the Trafficking Protocol

Combating human trafficking was thrust into the "global agenda of high politics" in the last quarter of the twentieth century with the adoption of the UNCTOC, and the Palermo Protocol in 2000.[82] The most significant contribution of the UNCTOC and the Palermo Protocol is turning human trafficking into a crime that can be detected and prosecuted, institutionalizing the discourse of "trafficking-as-transnational crime".[83] The Palermo Protocol breaks the offence of human trafficking into three components—action, means and purpose.[84] The exploitative purposes include prostitution of others or other forms of sexual exploitation, forced labour or services, slavery or practices similar to slavery, servitude or the removal of organs.[85] The State's obligation is to criminalize, investigate and punish offenders for human trafficking. Because the Palermo Protocol must be read with the UNCTOC, governments are also obliged to criminalize the laundering of the proceeds of human trafficking, establish a long period for statute of limitations for human trafficking offenses, trace, freeze and confiscate proceeds of human trafficking, provide mutual legal assistance and information sharing with other countries, and protect victims and witnesses throughout the prosecution of offenders.[86]

The UNCTOC and the Palermo Protocol are statist in construct.[87] They require states to "legislatively arm themselves to confront" human trafficking as a serious crime and frame States' commitments in terms of border protection.[88] For instance, Article 11 of the Palermo Protocol obliges states to strengthen "border controls" to prevent and detect human trafficking through immigration laws. Each State Party is expected to pass domestic laws to ensure travellers are in possession of travel documents required for entry into the receiving state and sanction those who fail to comply with this requirement.[89] Article 12 states that these documents cannot be easily misused, falsified, unlawfully altered, duplicated or issued.[90]

As reported in Section 7.1 of this chapter, protection issues surface when the statist and criminal justice approach is used to address human trafficking. Trafficked persons enter a country using a variety of formal and informal migration networks. Their legal status can be ephemeral, tweaked by circumstances or changed by sudden shifts in national policies. In that sense, labels such as "legal", "illegal", "regular", "irregular" and "undocumented" do not always fit neatly into the modality of the Palermo Protocol. With border controls as a starting point to tackling human trafficking, trafficked persons are often cast as unwanted "Others" within international law. They are *"to be dealt with first and foremost as illegal immigrants who have to be 'rescued' and returned home, to where they belong or, better still, immobilised before they arrive".*[91]

Provisions within the Palermo Protocol which deal with the protection of trafficked persons have been described as "weak", "vague"[92] and a "disappointment".[93] Article 6 of the Palermo Protocol provides that States' victim protection duties are applicable "in appropriate cases" and only "to the extent possible under its domestic law".[94] The protection afforded to the trafficked person is left solely to the discretion of the states. An example of this cursory nature of states' duty to protect trafficked persons is found in Article 7 of the Palermo Protocol which requires that the privilege of remaining in the receiving country ought to be weighed inter alia against "humanitarian and compassionate factors". If it is determined that the trafficked person should not remain in the receiving country, repatriation is reduced to a government-to-government arrangement. States of origin are obliged to facilitate and accept, without undue and unreasonable delay trafficked nationals or those with the right to permanent residence.[95] There is no requirement that the repatriation be voluntary or is consented to by the trafficked person, only that it is preferably voluntary.[96]

2) The TVPA and the US State Department Trafficking in Persons Report

The Trafficking Victims Protection Act of 2000 (TVPA) is a legal regime that operates independently of the UNCTOC and the Palermo Protocol. It is a United States domestic law but is considered as part of the international anti-trafficking regime here because of the global reach of its sanctions regime and how it shapes states' anti-trafficking behaviour. As Catherine Renshaw observes, the *"US approach and the UN approach to the issue of trafficking in persons have been conflated, both in perception and in the way that anti-trafficking measures are undertaken by UN agencies and NGOs"* over time.[97] Under the TVPA, the US government can withhold non-humanitarian, non-trade related foreign assistance to any government not making efforts to comply with the TVPA's "minimum standards for eliminating trafficking".[98] The US State Department conducts an annual assessment on a country's efforts to comply with the TVPA minimum standards and publishes an annual report known as the *Trafficking in Persons Report* (TIP Report). Countries are assessed based on the "3 Ps" framework and are ranked on four tiers in the TIP Report.

There are *"multiple instances in which the open threat of a negative grade in the TIP Report provided the impetus for major reform initiatives, including the criminalisation of trafficking"*.[99] Government discourses on new anti-trafficking laws and policies are often framed in terms of a response to the TIP Report rankings.[100] For example, Cambodia was placed on the Tier 2 Watch list of the TIP Report in 2006 and 2007 and was at risk of an automatic downgrade to Tier 3 and sanctions under the TVPA. Under pressure, it passed the Law on Suppression of Human Trafficking and Commercial Sexual Exploitation which criminalizes all forms of human trafficking and was upgraded to Tier 2 on the TIP Report in 2008.[101]

Despite the TIP Report's "power of shame", many are critical about the way it is used to impose the United States' domestic priorities and interests on other countries.[102] The TVPA was motivated by the desire to abolish trafficking of women and children into the sex industry in the United States.[103] This domestic preference is transferred to other states through the TIP Report's sanctions regime. In the 2004 TIP Report, the US government said it would take a *"firm stand against proposals to legalise prostitution because prostitution directly contributes to the modern day slave trade"*.[104] It added that the United States would deny funds to foreign NGOs that support legal prostitution and prohibit US funds for programmes that promote, support or advocate for the legalization or practice of prostitution and for organizations that do not work toward abolishing prostitution.[105] One example of the impact of US domestic preference on the laws of other countries is Cambodia's Suppression of Human Trafficking and Sexual Exploitation 2007, drafted with the help of the United States and adopted under the threat of economic and other sanctions.[106] The law's expressed objective is to "suppress the acts of human trafficking and sexual exploitation in order to protect the rights and dignity of human beings". It criminalizes activities seen as linked to human trafficking, including child and adult prostitution, pornography, indecency against minors, and the management of prostitution. Keo observes that although voluntary prostitution was not specifically targeted, the law created conditions that made lawful prostitution virtually impossible.[107]

3) Regional Anti-Trafficking Frameworks in Asia

In the decade after the introduction of the Palermo Protocol and the TVPA, there was a sharp increase in the number of treaty and non-treaty instruments relating directly and indirectly to countering human trafficking adopted by states.[108] In Asia, a regime of legal frameworks to criminalize human trafficking developed alongside international ones.

The extent to which regional and bilateral anti-trafficking frameworks and processes in Asia are consistent with the UNCTOC and Trafficking Protocol varies. Some, like the ACTIP, are substantially similar to the UNCTOC and the Palermo Protocol. ACTIP's main purpose is to institutionalize coordinated enforcement and collaborative action to prevent human trafficking and to protect trafficked persons. ACTIP adopts the Palermo Protocol's definition of human trafficking as well as the general prevention and victim protection measures.[109] It also adopts the UNCTOC's provisions on criminalization of human trafficking, laundering of proceeds of human trafficking, corruption, obstruction of justice, and jurisdiction in their entirety. The ACTIP is the culmination of various non-binding instruments in the region since the 1990s that deals with human trafficking.[110] Because the ACTIP is legally binding, it compels even ASEAN member states which did not ratify the UNCTOC or the Palermo Protocol to develop anti-trafficking legislation that are consistent with international law.

At the subregional level, countries within the Greater Mekong Subregion (GMS) have combined through the Coordinated Mekong Ministerial Initiative against Trafficking (COMMIT), a multilateral Memorandum of Understanding (MOU) to enhance cooperation between governments and other stakeholders to close all avenues of exploitation.[111] COMMIT adopts the Palermo Protocol's definition of human trafficking. As a process, COMMIT promotes compliance with the UNCTOC and the Palermo Protocol;[112] it facilitates GMS states with the formulation and strengthening of National Plans of Action and bilateral partnerships to reduce vulnerabilities to human trafficking, strengthen victim identification guidelines and mechanisms, a migration policy that combats human trafficking, and labour laws and regulating recruitment practices.

A by-product of COMMIT is the number of bilateral agreements that emerged in the GMS aimed at facilitating cooperation between states. Cambodia entered into a number of MOUs with countries in GMS[113] that adopted the definition of human trafficking used in the Palermo Protocol but restricted their application to women and children. Meanwhile, Vietnam entered into the Memorandum of Understanding on Bilateral Cooperation for Eliminating Trafficking in Persons, Especially Women and Children and Assisting Victims of Trafficking with Thailand in 2008. The agreement made no mention of the Palermo Protocol but used its definition of human trafficking. Recognizing the role of poverty, Myanmar and Thailand signed a MOU in 2008 to take preventative measures such as provision of educational and vocational training as well as improvement of social services and income generation to prevent human trafficking.[114] In 2005, Lao People's Democratic Republic and Thailand entered into a MOU with similar terms to address human trafficking as a transnational crime in accordance with the Palermo Protocol.[115]

Human Trafficking in East Asia—Hidden from the Law

The above survey is not intended to provide an exhaustive list of regional anti-trafficking frameworks but to highlight a dense regional regime that has embraced the UNCTOC, the Palermo Protocol and the TVPA's sanctions regime. It is the norm for regional anti-trafficking frameworks and processes in Asia to view human trafficking through the lens of transnational crime and migration control. National anti-trafficking laws draw heavily on the text of the UNCTOC and the Palermo Protocol. Anne Gallagher is correct to point out that only a transnational crime framework would have led to an international legal instrument with *"detailed obligations for tackling corruption, exchanging evidence across national borders and seizing of assets of offenders"* and so enthusiastically seized by governments within so short a time.[116]

But, as pointed out in Section 7.1, even a comprehensive legal framework has failed to yield the conviction rates, one measure of successful law enforcement. So much of human trafficking operate in the shadows of the law. Jo Goodey writes that accurate data on human trafficking "does not exist" because the crime is under-reported, under-detected and therefore under-prosecuted.[117] Laczko, too, points to its "clandestine" nature, adding that under-reporting occurs because victims are usually reluctant to report to authorities for fear of intimidation and reprisals.[118] For this, Jessie Brunner calls human trafficking a "hidden crime" where statistics reflect only those who have been identified as victims or perpetrators.[119] Though neither Brunner nor Laczko were speaking specifically about Asia, their observations raise pertinent points about the way international anti-trafficking instruments are applied to local trafficking contexts.

The next part highlights the challenges of applying international anti-trafficking legal regimes in East Asia. Two aspects are explored: (a) the ambiguities in the legal definition of human trafficking; and (b) the disjuncture between what international law defines as human trafficking and how it is practised in East Asia.

1) The Ambiguities in Definitions

The great promise of the UNCTOC and the Palermo Protocol is the standardization of what human trafficking means for all states.

A common definition of human trafficking is critical to consistent enforcement of anti-trafficking laws and promoting transnational cooperation. However, different iterations of the Palermo Protocol (or parts of it) have materialized when regional and national frameworks model anti-trafficking laws on it.[120] In ASEAN, for example, where ACTIP adopts Article 3 of the Palermo Protocol without modification, each of its member states still has different definitions of human trafficking within its national laws that diverges from Article 3 to different degrees.[121] Article 3 of the Protocol was the result of negotiations between states with different legal traditions and interests. Their compromises led to an Article 3 that is *challenging for national legislatures to meaningfully formulate in legislation and difficult for law enforcement to prove in court*.[122]

The law constructs human trafficking as a crime based on three elements (act-means-purpose) and views human trafficking independently of the social dynamics linked to it such as forced migration, labour issues and human rights. In reality, human trafficking is a fluid process and people in the region are driven by varied circumstances to move—development, modernization, poverty.[123] The law is insensitive to these nuances and their enforcers are compelled to compartmentalize trafficking-related activities into Article 3's act-means-purpose mold. However, as an operational definition for a crime that needs to be detected and prevented, the parameters of Article 3 are blurry. Key terms within Article 3 such as "exploitation", "sexual exploitation", "forced labour", "slavery", "practices similar to slavery" and "servitude" are undefined. Substantive understandings of these terms vary between jurisdictions. The lines that make them prohibitive can also shift because of culture and national contexts. In some countries, low wages, poor working conditions and deception are elements of forced labour or trafficking. In others, they may be labour law violations. The demarcation of human trafficking from other forms of exploitation is further complicated by what Chuang calls the "exploitation creep" where trafficking is discursively conflated with forced labour and slavery.[124] For Chuang, "recasting all forced labour as trafficking and all trafficking as slavery, exploitation creep re-labels abuses as more extreme than is legally accurate".[125] This increases support for their eradication but produces laws that lack legal and operational nuance.

Further, there is lack of agreement on what exploitative practices other than those specified in Article 3 should be identified as an element of human trafficking. Production of pornography, child sex tourism, commercial surrogacy and sale of children for purposes of adoption rife in East Asia, for instance, would fulfil Article 3's act-means-purpose criteria. Clarity is needed on whether these practices should be treated as a crime on its own or as part of the process of human trafficking. To expand the definition of human trafficking is to widen the potential pool of victims and perpetrators. But, it could also weaken the underlying legal prohibition and *"undermine broader goals related to international cooperation and standardisation of concepts that requires shared understanding of the nature of the problem to be addressed"*.[126]

The danger in definitional ambiguities surfaces when frontline law enforcement agencies who do not have sufficient knowledge or substantive understanding of human trafficking are left to interrogate the scope and the limitations of Article 3. Studies show that frontline law enforcement officers do not always understand the nature of human trafficking or have the ability to define human trafficking,[127] may focus only on certain types of human trafficking due to the lack of experience, and may conflate human trafficking with undocumented migration and prostitution.[128] In a study of fourteen countries, UNODC found that anti-trafficking practitioners were generally unclear on the distinction between key terms like slavery, practices similar to slavery and forced labour.[129]

The corollary to this is the failure of the criminal justice system to consistently and correctly identify instances of human trafficking, prosecute perpetrators and most importantly, identify victims who need assistance, support and protection.[130] A process for predictable and systematic identification of trafficked persons is imperative because under existing international anti-trafficking legal frameworks and many national ones, only individuals who have been identified as "victims" or trafficked persons are accorded with certain rights. Other frameworks such as those dealing with human rights, humanitarian assistance, refugees and labour laws, which offer alternative protection mechanisms, have generally been underutilized.[131] Trafficked persons who are misidentified as irregular migrants are routinely arrested, detained, charged, prosecuted and deported for offences such as entering illegally, working illegally, possession of false documents, and non-possession of documents. In this sense, misidentification is tantamount to criminalization of trafficked persons.

2) Differing Contexts: Local Human Trafficking Trends and International Legal Regimes

The anti-trafficking legal framework assumes that human trafficking involves the movement of people across national borders.[132] However, border control measures in anti-trafficking legal frameworks can be counterproductive in Asia; borders in the region are not only porous but also situated in "frontier areas" where people have historically crossed for trade and employment without restriction.[133] In many places, people have continued to navigate informal border crossings and anti-trafficking regulations are blind to the complexity of the region's histories.[134] In the Sino-Vietnamese border, for example, there has been a long history of undocumented Sino-Vietnamese ethnic marriages. Viewed through the transnational crime lens, Chinese authorities have investigated Vietnamese women living with Chinese men as cases of human trafficking and repatriated them for "illegal entry, illegal residence, and illegal cohabitation". However, it was common for women who were "sent back in the morning to come back in the evening".[135] Similarly, the border that separates Malaysia's Sarawak from Indonesia's Kalimantan on the Borneo Island are crossed daily through remote forest tracks known as *"jalan tikus"* [illegal routes] by people seeking employment, conducting trade and looking for access to social services, mostly without valid documentation.[136]

Furthermore, the international anti-trafficking legal regime presupposes that human trafficking is committed by transnational criminal groups.[137] Governments that model their anti-trafficking laws on international frameworks design laws to target the criminal elements of organized crime. This is at odds with what occurs on the ground in Asia. Studying the Southeast Asian landscape, Renshaw says that there is little evidence to show that human trafficking is practised as a systematic, patterned and organized form of crime.[138] Instead, people on the move in the region are often linked to exploitative situations by intimate social networks of friends and relatives. A study by Human Rights Watch into forced labour in Thailand's fishing industry found that local brokers were a mainstay in the labour recruitment process but they were "typically flexible and lack central coordination" common in organized criminal groups.[139] The main path to Thai fishing boats were recommendations from friends, relatives or acquaintances about employment opportunities, who provide information on specific companies, advice of ports, and contact details for a broker or boatswain looking to hire.[140] In Vidyamali Samarasinghe's work on sex trafficking in Cambodia, she notes that recruitment into the trade is done by those one would call "ordinary people"—friends, boyfriends and family members.[141]

A blind spot in the legal justice system exists when there is mismatch between what is regarded as human trafficking internationally and how and why it actually happens in domestic contexts. Human trafficking in Asia is often made possible because individual access to resources is restricted by imperfections in the labour and financial markets. The studies above show that traffickers who are familiar with local systems, power networks and social structures are able to mask TIP with the appearance of routine transactions in an imperfect market and navigate around anti-trafficking laws. This partly explains low prosecution and conviction rates for human trafficking cases and points to the need for locally-relevant governance frameworks and partnerships that engage stakeholders outside the criminal justice system. They include the academia, private sector, trade unions, media, healthcare providers, financial institutions, industrial standard boards and associations.

Conclusion: Challenges Ahead

The legacy of the UNCTOC and the Palermo Protocol is the regional and national anti-trafficking legal frameworks that are based on them. As the discussion in this section shows, this is inadequate for tackling human trafficking in East Asia. The design of the UNCTOC and the Palermo Protocol is the result of negotiations and compromises of their time. They view human trafficking predominantly through the lens of transnational crime, nebulously define the boundaries of human trafficking, and are generally insensitive to regional and national human trafficking practices. This leaves much of human trafficking in East Asia hidden in the shadows of the law. If the law is to be the bedrock of counter-trafficking measures in the region, human trafficking terminologies and definitions must be clearly defined, understood by law enforcers and responsive to the region's human trafficking context and emerging trends. The challenge for regional and national governments now is to bridge the gap between what the law aspires to achieve and law enforcement realities on the ground.

NOTES

1. ILO and Walk Free Foundation, *Global Estimates of Modern Slavery: Forced Labour and Forced Marriage* (Geneva: ILO and Walk Free Foundation, 2017), http://www.ilo.org/wcmsp5/groups/public/---dgreports/---dcomm/documents/publication/wcms_575479.pdf.
2. UNICEF USA, "The Sustainable Development Goals that Aim to End Human Trafficking", 29 January 2016, https://www.unicefusa.org/stories/sustainable-development-goals-aim-end-human-trafficking/29864.
3. David Luna, "Ending Human Trafficking: Building a Better World and Partnerships for Sustainable Security and Human Dignity", Opening Statement at OECD-APEC Roundtable on Combating Corruption Related to Human Trafficking, Cebu, the Philippines, 25 August 2017, https://www.oecd.org/gov/risk/HumanTraffickingStatement-D.M.Luna-27August2015.pdf.
4. Walk Free Foundation, *Global Slavery Index 2016* (Australia: The Minderoo Foundation Pty Ltd., 2016), https://www.globalslaveryindex.org/region/asia-pacific/.
5. UNODC, *Global Report on Trafficking in Persons 2016* (New York: UNODC, 2016).
6. Ibid.
7. Ibid.; Human Rights Council, *Situation of Human Rights of Rohingya Muslims and Other Minorities in Myanmar: Report of the United Nations High Commissioner for Human Rights*, 28 June 2016.
8. UNODC, *Global Report*.
9. Ibid.
10. Ibid.
11. Ibid.
12. US State Department, *Trafficking in Persons Report 2018* (Washington, D.C.: US State Department, 2018).
13. Ibid.
14. Deanna Davy, *Regional Overview: Sexual Exploitation of Children in Southeast Asia* (Bangkok: ECPAT International, 2017).
15. Andy Brown, "Safe from Harm: Tackling Online Child Sexual Abuse in the Philippines", PREDA Foundation, 4 July 2017, http://www.preda.org/world/safe-from-harm-tackling-online-child-sexual-abuse-in-the-philippines/.

16. Davy, *Regional Overview*; Terre des Hommes, *Becoming Sweetie: A Novel Approach to the Global Rise of Webcam Child Sex Tourism*, 2013, http://www.terredeshommes.org/wp-content/uploads/2013/11/Webcam-child-sex-tourism-terre-des-hommes-NL-nov-2013.pdf.

17. Davy, *Regional Overview*.

18. International Organization for Migration (IOM), *IOM Strategy in Asia and the Pacific 2017-2020* (Bangkok: IOM, 2017).

19. US State Department, *Trafficking in Persons Report 2018*; The China Post, "How Migrant Workers Become Human Trafficking Victims in Taiwan", *Asia One*, 2 August 2016, http://www.asiaone.com/asia/how-migrant-workers-become-human-trafficking-victims-taiwan.

20. IOM, *IOM Strategy*.

21. David Murphy, "Hidden Chains: Rights Abuses and Forced Labor in Thailand's Fishing Industry", *Human Rights Watch*, 23 January 2018, https://www.hrw.org/report/2018/01/23/hidden-chains/rights-abuses-and-forced-labor-thailands-fishing-industry; UNODC, *Global Report*.

22. IOM, *The Climate Change-Human Trafficking Nexus* (Bangkok: IOM, 2016).

23. Ibid.

24. Netsanet Tesfay, *Impact of Livelihood Recovery Initiatives on Reducing Vulnerability to Human Trafficking and Illegal Recruitment: Lessons from Typhoon Haiyan* (Geneva: IOM and ILO, 2015).

25. Jack Board, "Displaced Rohingyas at Great Risk of Human Trafficking in Overwhelmed Camps", *Channel News Asia*, 28 September 2017, https://www.channelnewsasia.com/news/asiapacific/displaced-rohingyas-at-great-risk-of-human-trafficking-in-9258108.

26. Song Jiyoung, "Australia and the Anti-Trafficking Regime in Southeast Asia", Lowy Institute, 15 November 2016, https://www.lowyinstitute.org/sites/default/files/documents/Song%2C%20Australia%20and%20the%20anti-trafficking%20regime%20in%20Southeast%20Asia%2C%20WP1%5B1%5D.pdf.

27. Liberty Asia, *Legal Gap Analysis of Thailand's Anti-Trafficking Legislation*, June 2017, http://un-act.org/publication/view/legal-analysis-human-trafficking-thailand/.

28. ASEAN Convention Against Trafficking in Persons, Especially Women and Children, Kuala Lumpur, Malaysia, November 2015, http://www.asean.org/wp-content/uploads/2015/12/ACTIP.pdf.

29. Maggy Lee, *Trafficking and Global Crime Control* (London: Sage Publications Ltd., 2011).

30. UNODC, *Global Report*.

31. RSIS' Centre for Non-Traditional Security Studies (NTS Centre), *Consultative Roundtable on the Humanitarian Dimension and Protection Aspect of Trafficking*

in Persons, 26-27 June 2014, Event Report (Singapore: RSIS' Centre for NTS Studies, 2014).

32. UNODC, *Trafficking in Persons from Cambodia, Lao PDR and Myanmar to Thailand* (Bangkok: UNODC, 2017); US State Department, *Trafficking in Persons Report 2018.*

33. US State Department, *Trafficking in Persons Report 2018.*

34. UNODC, *Trafficking in Persons from Cambodia, Lao PDR and Myanmar to Thailand.*

35. Ibid.

36. Ibid.

37. Ibid.

38. Ibid.

39. US State Department, *Trafficking in Persons Report 2018*; UNODC, *Trafficking in Persons from Cambodia, Lao PDR and Myanmar to Thailand.*

40. Allen & Overy and Liberty Asia, *Policy Overview: Gaps in the Implementation of Child Trafficking Laws in Thailand and Recommendations for Reform,* 2017, https://static1.squarespace.com/static/53038dd2e4b0f8636b5fa8c3/t/59f497 ea64265f811b2d94a6/1509201926457/Policy+Overview.pdf.

41. Suhana Saad and Ali Salman, "Government Policy and the Challenge of Eradicating Human Trafficking in Malaysia", *Malaysian Journal of Society and Space* 10, no. 6 (2014): 66–74; Steven Sim, "Enforce Immediately Anti-Trafficking Law Amendments", *Malaysiakini,* 15 August 2016, https://www.malaysiakini.com/letters/352304.

42. US State Department, *Trafficking in Persons Report 2018.*

43. Zuraini Ab Hamid, Noor Shuhadawati Mohamad Amin and Norjihan Ab Aziz, "The Challenges Faced by the Enforcement Bodies in Malaysia", *Proceedings of INTCESS 2017 4th International Conference on Education and Social Sciences,* Istanbul, Turkey, 6–8 February 2017, http://www.ocerint.org/intcess17_epublication/papers/292.pdf.

44. US State Department, *Trafficking in Persons Report 2018*; Andrea Varella, "Live Streaming of Child Sexual Abuse: Background, Legislative Frameworks and the Experience of the Philippines, Online Child Sexual Exploitation: An Analysis of Emerging and Selected Issues", *ECPAT International Journal* 12 (2017).

45. US State Department, *Trafficking in Persons Report 2018.*

46. Ibid.

47. Ibid.; Justin Stafford, "Japan's Battle Against Human Trafficking: A Victim-Oriented Solution", *The George Washington International Law Review* 50, no. 1 (2017): 181–207.

48. US State Department, *Trafficking in Persons Report 2018.*

49. Ibid.

50. UNODC, *Trafficking in Persons from Cambodia, Lao PDR and Myanmar to Thailand.*

51. UNODC, Anti-Slavery International, and Transparency International, *The Role of Corruption in Trafficking in Persons* (Vienna: UNODC, 2011), p. 27, https://www.unodc.org/documents/human-trafficking/2011/Issue_Paper_-_The_Role_of_Corruption_in_Trafficking_in_Persons.pdf.

52. Ibid.

53. Devy Ernis and Aditya Budiman, "Pusaka Benjina Admits Bribing Govt Officials", *Tempo*, 6 April 2015, https://en.tempo.co/read/news/2015/04/06/056655625/Pusaka-Benjina-Admits-Bribing-Govt-Officials.

54. Kocha Olarn and James Griffiths, "Thai Court Convicts Dozens in Large Human-Trafficking Trial", *CNN*, 19 July 2017, https://edition.cnn.com/2017/07/19/asia/thai-human-trafficking-trial/index.html.

55. Ibid.

56. Tan Hui Yee, "Thai Army General Gets 27 Years Jail for Human Trafficking", *Straits Times*, 19 July 2017, http://www.straitstimes.com/asia/se-asia/verdict-due-in-major-thai-human-trafficking-trial.

57. Patchanee Malikhao and Fiona Servaes, "Human Trafficking in Thailand: A Culture of Corruption", in *Culture and Communication in Thailand. Communication, Culture and Change in Asia*, Vol. 3 (Singapore: Springer, 2017).

58. US State Department, *Trafficking in Persons Report 2018*.

59. Boy Ryan B. Zabal, "Immigration Officers, Recruiters Nabbed for Human Trafficking", *Rappler*, 20 January 2017, https://www.rappler.com/nation/158999-immigration-officers-recruiters-nabbed-human-trafficking.

60. Ibid.

61. Fortify Rights, "Myanmar, Thailand, Malaysia: End Human Trafficking, Protect Survivors", *Press Release*, 1 July 2016, http://www.fortifyrights.org/publication-20160701.html.

62. OECD, *Trafficking in Persons and Corruption: Breaking the Chain* (Paris: OECD Publishing, 2016).

63. Lee, *Trafficking and Global Crime Control*; RSIS' Centre for Non-Traditional Security Studies (NTS Centre), *Consultative Roundtable on the Humanitarian Dimension and Protection Aspect of Trafficking in Persons, 26-27 June 2014, Event Report* (Singapore: RSIS' Centre for NTS Studies, 2014).

64. Protocol to Prevent, Suppress and Punish Trafficking in Persons Especially Women and Children, supplementing the United Nations Convention against Transnational Organized Crime, 15 November 2000, http://www.ohchr.org/EN/ProfessionalInterest/Pages/ProtocolTraffickingInPersons.aspx.

65. Lee, *Trafficking and Global Crime Control*.

66. UNODC, *Trafficking in Persons from Cambodia, Lao PDR and Myanmar to Thailand*; US State Department, *Trafficking in Persons Report 2018*.

67. Ibid.

68. Ibid.

69. Margeaux Gray, "Why Human Trafficking is a Public Health Problem", *CNN*, 25 July 2016, https://edition.cnn.com/2016/07/11/opinions/human-trafficking-health-margeaux-gray/index.html.

70. Cathy Zimmerman and Ligia Kiss, "Human Trafficking and Exploitation: A Global Health Concern", *PLoS Medicine* 14, no. 11 (2017).

71. Song, "Australia and the Anti-Trafficking Regime in Southeast Asia".

72. Mike Ives, "Mental Health of Trafficking Victims Overlooked", *SciDevNet*, 11 March 2015, https://www.scidev.net/global/vulnerability/news/mental-health-trafficking-victims.html.

73. UNICEF, *Child Protection in the Digital Age: National Responses to Online Child Sexual Abuse and Exploitation in ASEAN Member States* (Bangkok: UNICEF EAPRO, 2016).

74. US State Department, *Trafficking in Persons Report 2018*.

75. UNICEF, *Child Protection*.

76. IOM, *The Causes and Consequences of Re-trafficking: Evidence from the IOM Human Trafficking Database* (Geneva: IOM, 2010).

77. UNODC, *Trafficking in Persons from Cambodia, Lao PDR and Myanmar to Thailand*.

78. US State Department, *Trafficking in Persons Report 2018*.

79. Anders Lisborg, "Rethinking Reintegration: What do Returning Victims Really Want? Evidence from Thailand and the Philippines", *SIREN Report*, 28 August 2009, https://childhub.org/en/system/tdf/library/attachments/siren_09_tra_reintegration_1009.pdf?file=1&type=node&id=18987.

80. ASEAN Convention Against Trafficking in Persons, Especially Women and Children.

81. Diana Wong, "The Rumour of Trafficking", in *Illicit Flows and Criminal Things – States, Borders, and the Other Side of Globalisation*, edited by William van Schendel and Itty Abraham (Indiana: Indiana University Press, 2005), p. 69.

82. Anne Gallagher, *The International Law of Human Trafficking* (Cambridge: Cambridge University Press, 2010), pp. 1–11.

83. Article 3 of the Palermo Protocol.

84. Ibid.

85. Articles 6, 11, 12, 13, 14, 18, 26 and 27 of the United Nations Convention against Transnational Organized Crime.

86. See for example, Capous Moushoula Desyllas, "A Critique of the Global Trafficking Discourse and US Policy", *Journal of Sociology and Social Welfare* 34, no. 4 (2007): 57–79; Wong, "The Rumour of Trafficking"; Maggy Lee, "Human Trafficking and Border Control in the Global South", in *The Borders of Punishment: Migration, Citizenship and Social Exclusion*, edited by Katja Franko Aas and Mary Bosworth (Oxford: Oxford University Press, 2013).

87. United Nations Global Initiative to Fight Human Trafficking, "023 Workshop: The Effectiveness of Legal Frameworks and Anti-Trafficking Legislation", *Background Paper*, Austria Center Vienna, the Vienna Forum to fight Human Trafficking, 13–15 February 2015.

88. Articles 11(2) and 11(3) of the Palermo Protocol.

89. Articles 12(a) and 12(b) of the Palermo Protocol.

90. Lee, *Trafficking and Global Crime Control*, p. 80.

91. Laura Gomez-Mera, "The Global Governance of Trafficking in Persons: Toward a Transnational Regime Complex", *Journal of Human Trafficking* 3, no. 4 (2017): 307.

92. Gallagher, *The International Law of Human Trafficking*.

93. Article 6(1) of the Palermo Protocol.

94. Article 8(2) of the Palermo Protocol.

95. Ibid.

96. Catherine Renshaw, "Human Trafficking in Southeast Asia: Uncovering the Dynamics of State Commitment and Compliance", *Michigan Journal of International Law* 37, no. 4 (2016): 626.

97. Victims of Trafficking and Violence Protection Act of 2000, Public Law No. 106-386 (2000).

98. Gallagher, *The International Law of Human Trafficking*, p. 485.

99. Renshaw, "Human Trafficking in Southeast Asia", pp. 637–38.

100. Chenda Keo et al., "Human Trafficking and Moral Panic in Cambodia", *The Annals* 653, no. 1 (2014): 207.

101. Janie Chuang, "The United States as Global Sheriff: Using Unilateral Sanctions to Combat Human Trafficking", *Michigan Journal of International Law* 37, no. 4 (2016): 611–59.

102. Janie Chuang, "Rescuing Trafficking from Ideological Capture: Prostitution Reform and Anti-Trafficking Law and Policy", *University of Pennsylvania Law Review* 158 (2010): 1678.

103. US State Department, "Trafficking in Persons Report", 14 June 2004, https://www.state.gov/j/tip/rls/tiprpt/2004/34021.htm.

104. Ibid.

105. Larissa Sandy, "International Politics, Anti-Trafficking Measure and Sex Work in Cambodia", in *Labour Migration and Human Trafficking in Southeast Asia: Critical Perspectives*, edited by Willem van Schendel, Lenore Lyons, and Michele Ford (New York: Routledge, 2012), p. 41.

106. Chenda Keo, *Hard Life for a Legal Work: The 2008 Anti-Trafficking Law and Sex Work* (Phnom Penh: Cambodian Alliance for Combatting HIV/AIDS, 2009).

107. Paulette Lloyd and Beth A. Simmons, "Framing for a New Transnational Legal Order: The Case of Human Trafficking", *Public Law and Legal Theory Research Paper Series*, Research Paper No. 16–43 (2015).

108. Article 2 of the ACTIP.

109. For example, in 1997, ASEAN adopted the Declaration on Transnational Crime and established the AMMTC to facilitate cooperation for fighting transnational crime. In 2004, ASEAN adopted the ASEAN Declaration against Trafficking in Persons Particularly in Women and Children and the Treaty on Mutual Legal Assistance in Criminal Matters. The latter provided the basis for cooperation in criminal investigations and prosecutions among member states.

110. Countries in the Greater Mekong Subregion are Cambodia, China, Laos, Myanmar, Vietnam and Thailand.

111. Susan Kneebone and Julie Debeljak, *Transnational Crime and Human Rights: Responses to Human Trafficking in the Greater Mekong Subregion* (New York: Routledge, 2012), pp. 209–11.

112. Memorandum of Understanding between Cambodia and Thailand on Bilateral Cooperation in Eliminating Trafficking in Children and Women and Assisting Victims of Trafficking (2003); Agreement between the Royal Government of Cambodia and the Socialist Republic of Vietnam and Bilateral Cooperation for Eliminating Trafficking in Women and Children and Assisting Victims of Trafficking (2005).

113. Memorandum of Understanding between the Government of the Kingdom of Thailand and the Government of the Union of Myanmar on Cooperation to Combat Trafficking in Persons, Especially Women and Children (2009).

114. Memorandum of Understanding between the Government of Lao People's and the Government of the Kingdom of Thailand on Labour Cooperation (2002).

115. Gallagher, *The International Law of Human Trafficking*, p. 4.

116. Jo Goodey, "Human Trafficking: Sketchy Data and Policy Responses", *Criminology and Criminal Justice* 8, no. 4 (2008): 424–25.

117. Frank Laczko, "Enhancing Data Collection and Research on Trafficking in Persons", in *Measuring Human Trafficking*, edited by Ernesto U. Savona and Sonia Stefanizzi (New York: Springer, 2007), p. 40. See also Dang Nguyen Anh, "Cross-Border Migration and Sexuality in Vietnam: Reality and Policy Responses", in *Living on the Edges: Cross-Border Mobility and Sexual Exploitation in the Greater Southeast Asia Sub-Region*, edited by Thomas E. Blair (Bangkok: Southeast Asian Consortium on Gender, Sexuality and Health, 2006).

118. Jessie Brunner, *Inaccurate Numbers, Inadequate Policies: Enhancing Data to Evaluate the Prevalence of Human Trafficking in ASEAN* (Hawaii: East West Center, 2015).

119. Michael Dottridge, "Trafficked and Exploited: The Urgent Need for Coherence in International Law", in *Revisiting the Law and Governance of Trafficking, Forced Labor and Modern Slavery*, edited by Prabha Kotiswaran (Cambridge: Cambridge University, 2017), pp. 59–82.

120. ASEAN, *Regional Review on Laws, Policies and Practices within ASEAN relating to the Identification, Management and Treatment of Victims of Trafficking, especially Women and Children* (Jakarta: ASEAN Secretariat, 2016), pp. 17–28.

121. See Tom Obokata, "The Value of International Law in Combatting Transnational Organised Crime in the Asia Pacific", *Asian Journal of International Law* 7, no. 1 (2017): 39–60; Inter-Agency Coordination Group Against Trafficking in Persons, *The International Legal Frameworks Concerning Trafficking in Persons*, Vienna, October 2012, https://www. unodc.org/documents/human-trafficking/ICAT/ICAT_Policy_Paper_1_The_ International_Legal_Instruments.pdf.

122. Gergana Danailova-Trainor and Frank Laczko, "Trafficking in Persons and Development: Towards Greater Policy Coherence", *International Migration* 48, no. 4 (2010): 65.

123. Janie Chuang, "Exploitation Creep and the Unmaking of Human Trafficking Law", *The Journal of International Law* 108, no. 4 (2014): 611.

124. Ibid.

125. Gallagher, *The International Law of Human Trafficking*, p. 51.

126. Susan Mapp et al., "Local Law Enforcement Officers' Knowledge of Human Trafficking: Ability to Define, Identify and Assist", *Journal of Human Trafficking* 2, no. 4 (2016): 329–42.

127. See for example Amy Ferrell and Rebecca Pfeffer, "Policing Human Trafficking: Cultural Blinders and Organisational Barriers", *The Annals of the American Academy of Political and Social Science* 653, no. 1 (2014): 46–64; Amy Farrell, Jack McDevitt, and Stephanie Fahy, *Understanding and Improving Law Enforcement Responses to Human Trafficking: Final Report* (Boston: Northeastern University Institute on Race and Justice, 2008); Amy Farrell, Colleen Owens, and Jack McDevitt, "New Laws but Few Cases: Understanding the Challenges to the Investigation and Prosecution of Human Trafficking Cases", *Crime, Law and Social Change* 61, no. 2 (2013): 139–68.

128. UNODC, *The Concept of 'Exploitation' in the Trafficking in Persons Protocol*, 2015, p. 110, https://www.unodc.org/documents/congress/background-information/Human_Trafficking/UNODC_2015_Issue_Paper_Exploitation. pdf.

129. See for example Anne Gallagher and Paul Holmes, "Developing an Effective Criminal Justice Response to Human Trafficking: Lessons from the Front Line", *International Criminal Justice Review* 18, no. 3 (2008): 36.

130. Inter-Agency Coordination Group Against Trafficking in Persons, *The International Legal Frameworks*.

131. See UNCTOC Article 3(2)

132. Renshaw, "Human Trafficking in Southeast Asia", p. 631.

133. Caroline Grillot, "The Fringes of Conjugality: On Fantasies, Tactics and

Representations of Sino-Vietnamese Encounters in Borderlands" (Doctoral dissertation, Vrije Universiteit Amsterdam, 2006).

134. Elena Barabantseva, "When Borders Lie Within: Ethnic Marriages and Illegality on the Sino-Vietnamese Border", *International Political Sociology* 9 (2015): 363.

135. Junaenah Sulehan et al., "Development at the Margins: Livelihood and Sustainability of Communities at Malaysia-Indonesia Borders", *Sociology & Space* 51, no. 3 (2013): 549; Peter Sibon, "State Losing Control Over Border Crossing", *Borneo Post Online*, 13 March 2015, http://www.theborneopost.com/2015/03/13/state-losing-control-over-border-crossing/.

136. See UN General Assembly Resolution 55/25 of 15 November 2000, https://www.unodc.org/documents/middleeastandnorthafrica/organised-crime/UNITED_NATIONS_CONVENTION_AGAINST_TRANSNATIONAL_ORGANIZED_CRIME_AND_THE_PROTOCOLS_THERETO.pdf.

137. Renshaw, "Human Trafficking in Southeast Asia", p. 628.

138. Murphy, "Hidden Chains", p. 30.

139. Ibid.

140. Vidyamali Samarasinghe, *Female Sex Trafficking in Asia: The Resilience of Patriarchy in a Changing World* (New York: Routledge, 2008), p. 95.

REFERENCES

Allen & Overy and Liberty Asia. 2017. *Policy Overview: Gaps in the Implementation of Child Trafficking Laws in Thailand and Recommendations for Reform*. https://static1.squarespace.com/static/53038dd2e4b0f8636b5fa8c3/t/59f497ea64265f811b2d94a6/1509201926457/Policy+Overview.pdf.

ASEAN. 2016. *Regional Review on Laws, Policies and Practices within ASEAN Relating to the Identification, Management and Treatment of Victims of Trafficking, Especially Women and Children*. Jakarta: ASEAN Secretariat.

ASEAN Convention Against Trafficking in Persons, Especially Women and Children. Kuala Lumpur, Malaysia, November 2015. http://www.asean.org/wp-content/uploads/2015/12/ACTIP.pdf.

Barabantseva, Elena. 2015. "When Borders Lie Within: Ethnic Marriages and Illegality on the Sino-Vietnamese Border". *International Political Sociology* 9: 363.

Board, Jack. 2017. "Displaced Rohingyas at Great Risk of Human Trafficking in Overwhelmed Camps". *Channel News Asia*, 28 September 2017. https://www.channelnewsasia.com/news/asiapacific/displaced-rohingyas-at-great-risk-of-human-trafficking-in-9258108.

Brown, Andy. 2017. "Safe from Harm: Tackling Online Child Sexual Abuse in the Philippines". PREDA Foundation, 4 July 2017. http://www.preda.org/world/safe-from-harm-tackling-online-child-sexual-abuse-in-the-philippines/.

Brunner, Jessie. 2015. *Inaccurate Numbers, Inadequate Policies: Enhancing Data to Evaluate the Prevalence of Human Trafficking in ASEAN*. Hawaii: East West Center.

Chuang, Janie. 2010. "Rescuing Trafficking from Ideological Capture: Prostitution Reform and Anti-Trafficking Law and Policy". *University of Pennsylvania Law Review* 158: 1678.

———. 2014. "Exploitation Creep and the Unmaking of Human Trafficking Law". *The Journal of International Law* 108, no. 4: 611.

———. 2016. "The United States as Global Sheriff: Using Unilateral Sanctions to Combat Human Trafficking". *Michigan Journal of International Law* 37, no. 4: 611–59.

Danailova-Trainor, Gergana and Frank Laczko. 2010. "Trafficking in Persons and Development: Towards Greater Policy Coherence". *International Migration* 48, no. 4: 65.

Dang, Nguyen Anh. 2006. "Cross-Border Migration and Sexuality in Vietnam: Reality and Policy Responses". In *Living on the Edges: Cross-Border Mobility and Sexual Exploitation in the Greater Southeast Asia Sub-Region*, edited by Thomas E. Blair. Bangkok: Southeast Asian Consortium on Gender, Sexuality and Health.

Davy, Deanna. 2017. *Regional Overview: Sexual Exploitation of Children in Southeast Asia*. Bangkok: ECPAT International.

Desyllas, Capous Moushoula. 2007. "A Critique of the Global Trafficking Discourse and US Policy". *Journal of Sociology and Social Welfare* 34, no. 4: 57–79.

Dottridge, Michael. 2017. "Trafficked and Exploited: The Urgent Need for Coherence in International Law". In *Revisiting the Law and Governance of Trafficking, Forced Labor and Modern Slavery*, edited by Prabha Kotiswaran. Cambridge: Cambridge University, pp. 59–82.

Ernis, Devy and Aditya Budiman. 2015. "Pusaka Benjina Admits Bribing Govt Officials". *Tempo*, 6 April 2015. https://en.tempo.co/read/news/2015/04/06/056655625/Pusaka-Benjina-Admits-Bribing-Govt-Officials.

Farrell, Amy, Colleen Owens, and Jack McDevitt. 2013. "New Laws but Few Cases: Understanding the Challenges to the Investigation and Prosecution of Human Trafficking Cases". *Crime, Law and Social Change* 61, no. 2: 139–68.

Farrell, Amy, Jack McDevitt, and Stephanie Fahy. 2008. *Understanding and Improving Law Enforcement Responses to Human Trafficking: Final Report*. Boston: Northeastern University Institute on Race and Justice.

Farrell, Amy and Rebecca Pfeffer. 2014. "Policing Human Trafficking: Cultural Blinders and Organisational Barriers". *The Annals of the American Academy of Political and Social Science* 653, no. 1: 46–64.

Fortify Rights. 2016. "Myanmar, Thailand, Malaysia: End Human Trafficking, Protect Survivors". *Press Release*, 1 July 2016. http://www.fortifyrights.org/publication-20160701.html.

Gallagher, Anne. 2010. *The International Law of Human Trafficking*. Cambridge: Cambridge University Press.

Gallagher, Anne and Paul Holmes. 2008. "Developing an Effective Criminal Justice Response to Human Trafficking: Lessons from the Front Line". *International Criminal Justice Review* 18, no. 3.

Gomez-Mera, Laura. 2017. "The Global Governance of Trafficking in Persons: Toward a Transnational Regime Complex". *Journal of Human Trafficking* 3, no. 4.

Goodey, Jo. 2008. "Human Trafficking: Sketchy Data and Policy Responses". *Criminology and Criminal Justice* 8, no. 4: 424–25.

Gray, Margeaux. 2016. "Why Human Trafficking is a Public Health Problem". *CNN*, 25 July 2016. https://edition.cnn.com/2016/07/11/opinions/human-trafficking-health-margeaux-gray/index.html.

Grillot, Caroline. 2006. "The Fringes of Conjugality: On Fantasies, Tactics and Representations of Sino-Vietnamese Encounters in Borderlands". Doctoral dissertation, Vrije Universiteit Amsterdam.

Hamid, Zuraini Ab, Noor Shuhadawati Mohamad Amin, and Norjihan Ab Aziz. 2017. "The Challenges Faced by the Enforcement Bodies in Malaysia". *Proceedings of INTCESS 2017 4th International Conference on Education and Social Sciences*, Istanbul, Turkey, 6–8 February 2017. http://www.ocerint.org/intcess17_epublication/papers/292.pdf.

Hockings, Marc, Peter Shadie, Geoff Vincent, and Songtam Suksawang. 2012. *Evaluating the Management Effectiveness of Thailand's Marine and Coastal Protected Area*. Gland, Switzerland: International Union for Conservation of Nature.

Human Rights Council. 2016. *Situation of Human Rights of Rohingya Muslims and Other Minorities in Myanmar: Report of the United Nations High Commissioner for Human Rights*, 28 June 2016.

Inter-Agency Coordination Group Against Trafficking in Persons. 2012. *The International Legal Frameworks Concerning Trafficking in Persons*. Vienna. https://www.unodc.org/documents/human-trafficking/ICAT/ICAT_Policy_Paper_1_The_International_Legal_Instruments.pdf.

International Labor Organization (ILO). 2014. *Profits and Poverty: The Economic of Forced Labour*. Geneva: ILO.

International Labor Organization (ILO) and Walk Free Foundation. 2017. *Global Estimates of Modern Slavery: Forced Labour and Forced Marriage*. Geneva: ILO and Walk Free Foundation. http://www.ilo.org/wcmsp5/groups/public/---dgreports/---dcomm/documents/publication/wcms_575479.pdf.

International Organization for Migration (IOM). 2010. *The Causes and Consequences of Re-trafficking: Evidence from the IOM Human Trafficking Database*. Geneva: IOM.

———. 2016. *The Climate Change-Human Trafficking Nexus*. Bangkok: IOM.

————. 2017. *IOM Strategy in Asia and the Pacific 2017-2020*. Bangkok: IOM.

Ives, Mike. 2015. "Mental Health of Trafficking Victims Overlooked". *SciDevNet*, 11 March 2015. https://www.scidev.net/global/vulnerability/news/mental-health-trafficking-victims.html.

Keo, Chenda. 2009. *Hard Life for a Legal Work: The 2008 Anti-Trafficking Law and Sex Work*. Phnom Penh: Cambodian Alliance for Combatting HIV/AIDS.

Keo, Chenda, Thierry Bouhours, Roderic Broadhurst, and Brigitte Bouhours. 2014. "Human Trafficking and Moral Panic in Cambodia". *The Annals* 653, no. 1.

Kneebone, Susan and Julie Debeljak. 2012. *Transnational Crime and Human Rights: Responses to Human Trafficking in the Greater Mekong Subregion*. New York: Routledge.

Laczko Frank. 2007. "Enhancing Data Collection and Research on Trafficking in Persons". In *Measuring Human Trafficking*, edited by Ernesto U. Savona and Sonia Stefanizzi. New York: Springer.

Lee, Maggy. 2011. *Trafficking and Global Crime Control*. London: Sage Publications Ltd.

————. 2013. "Human Trafficking and Border Control in the Global South". In *The Borders of Punishment: Migration, Citizenship and Social Exclusion*, edited by Katja Franko Aas and Mary Bosworth. Oxford: Oxford University Press.

Liberty Asia. 2017. *Legal Gap Analysis of Thailand's Anti-Trafficking Legislation*. http://un-act.org/publication/view/legal-analysis-human-trafficking-thailand/.

Lisborg, Anders. 2009. "Rethinking Reintegration: What do Returning Victims Really Want? Evidence from Thailand and the Philippines". *SIREN Report*, 28 August 2009. https://childhub.org/en/system/tdf/library/attachments/siren_09_tra_reintegration_1009.pdf?file=1&type=node&id=18987.

Lloyd, Paulette and Beth A. Simmons. 2015. "Framing for a New Transnational Legal Order: The Case of Human Trafficking". *Public Law and Legal Theory Research Paper Series*. Research Paper No. 16–43.

Luna, David. 2017. "Ending Human Trafficking: Building a Better World and Partnerships for Sustainable Security and Human Dignity". Opening Statement at OECD-APEC Roundtable on Combating Corruption Related to Human Trafficking. Cebu, the Philippines, 25 August 2017. https://www.oecd.org/gov/risk/HumanTraffickingStatement-D.M.Luna-27August2015.pdf.

Malikhao, Patchanee and Fiona Servaes. 2017. "Human Trafficking in Thailand: A Culture of Corruption". In *Culture and Communication in Thailand. Communication, Culture and Change in Asia*, Vol 3. Singapore: Springer.

Mapp, Susan, Emily Hornung, Madeleine D'Almeida, and Jessica Juhnke. 2016. "Local Law Enforcement Officers' Knowledge of Human Trafficking:

Ability to Define, Identify and Assist". *Journal of Human Trafficking* 2, no. 4: 329–42.

Murphy, David. 2018. "Hidden Chains: Rights Abuses and Forced Labor in Thailand's Fishing Industry". *Human Rights Watch*, 23 January 2018. https:// www.hrw.org/report/2018/01/23/hidden-chains/rights-abuses-and-forced-labor-thailands-fishing-industry.

Obokata, Tom. 2017. "The Value of International Law in Combatting Transnational Organised Crime in the Asia Pacific". *Asian Journal of International Law* 7, no. 1: 39–60.

Olarn, Kocha and James Griffiths. 2017. "Thai Court Convicts Dozens in Large Human-Trafficking Trial". *CNN*, 19 July 2017. https://edition.cnn. com/2017/07/19/asia/thai-human-trafficking-trial/index.html.

Organisation for Economic Co-operation and Development (OECD). 2016. *Trafficking in Persons and Corruption: Breaking the Chain*. Paris: OECD Publishing.

Protocol to Prevent, Suppress and Punish Trafficking in Persons Especially Women and Children, Supplementing the United Nations Convention Against Transnational Organized Crime, 15 November 2000. http://www. ohchr.org/EN/ProfessionalInterest/Pages/ProtocolTraffickingInPersons. aspx.

Renshaw, Catherine. 2006. "Human Trafficking in Southeast Asia: Uncovering the Dynamics of State Commitment and Compliance". *Michigan Journal of International Law* 37, no. 4: 611–59.

RSIS' Centre for Non-Traditional Security Studies (NTS Centre). 2014. *Consultative Roundtable on the Humanitarian Dimension and Protection Aspect of Trafficking in Persons, 26–27 June 2014, Event Report*. Singapore: RSIS' Centre for NTS Studies.

Saad, Suhana and Ali Salman. 2014. "Government Policy and the Challenge of Eradicating Human Trafficking in Malaysia". *Malaysian Journal of Society and Space* 10, no. 6: 66–74.

Samarasinghe, Vidyamali. 2008. *Female Sex Trafficking in Asia: The Resilience of Patriarchy in a Changing World*. New York: Routledge.

Sandy, Larissa. 2012. "International Politics, Anti-Trafficking Measure and Sex Work in Cambodia". In *Labour Migration and Human Trafficking in Southeast Asia: Critical Perspectives*, edited by Willem van Schendel, Lyons Lenore, and Michele Ford. New York: Routledge.

Sibon, Peter. 2015. "State Losing Control Over Border Crossing". *Borneo Post Online*, 13 March 2015. http://www.theborneopost.com/2015/03/13/state-losing-control-over-border-crossing/.

Sim, Steven. 2016. "Enforce Immediately Anti-Trafficking Law Amendments". *Malaysiakini*, 15 August 2016. https://www.malaysiakini.com/letters/352304.

Song, Jiyoung. 2016. "Australia and the Anti-Trafficking Regime in Southeast Asia". Lowy Institute, 15 November 2016. https://www.lowyinstitute.org/sites/default/files/documents/Song%2C%20Australia%20and%20the%20anti-trafficking%20regime%20in%20Southeast%20Asia%2C%20WP1%5B1%5D.pdf.

Stafford, Justin. 2017. "Japan's Battle Against Human Trafficking: A Victim-Oriented Solution". *The George Washington International Law Review* 50, no. 1: 181–207.

Sulehan, Junaenah, Noor Rahamah Abu Bakar, Abd Hair Awang, Mohd Yusof Abullah, and Ong Puay Liu. 2013. "Development at the Margins: Livelihood and Sustainability of Communities at Malaysia-Indonesia Borders". *Sociology & Space* 51, no. 3: 547–62.

Tan Hui Yee. 2017. "Thai Army General Gets 27 Years Jail for Human Trafficking". *Straits Times*, 19 July 2017. http://www.straitstimes.com/asia/se-asia/verdict-due-in-major-thai-human-trafficking-trial.

Terre des Hommes. 2013. *Becoming Sweetie: A Novel Approach to the Global Rise of Webcam Child Sex Tourism*. http://www.terredeshommes.org/wp-content/uploads/2013/11/Webcam-child-sex-tourism-terre-des-hommes-NL-nov-2013.pdf.

Tesfay, Netsanet. 2015. *Impact of Livelihood Recovery Initiatives on Reducing Vulnerability to Human Trafficking and Illegal Recruitment: Lessons from Typhoon Haiyan*. Geneva: IOM and ILO.

The China Post. 2016. "How Migrant Workers Become Human Trafficking Victims in Taiwan". *Asia One*, 2 August 2016. http://www.asiaone.com/asia/how-migrant-workers-become-human-trafficking-victims-taiwan.

UN General Assembly Resolution 55/25 of 15 November 2000. https://www.unodc.org/documents/middleeastandnorthafrica/organised-crime/UNITED_NATIONS_CONVENTION_AGAINST_TRANSNATIONAL_ORGANIZED_CRIME_AND_THE_PROTOCOLS_THERETO.pdf.

United Nations Global Initiative to Fight Human Trafficking. 2015. "023 Workshop: The Effectiveness of Legal Frameworks and Anti-Trafficking Legislation". *Background Paper*. Austria Center Vienna, the Vienna Forum to Fight Human Trafficking, 13–15 February 2015.

UNICEF. 2016. *Child Protection in the Digital Age: National Responses to Online Child Sexual Abuse and Exploitation in ASEAN Member States*. Bangkok: UNICEF EAPRO.

UNICEF USA. 2016. "The Sustainable Development Goals that Aim to End Human Trafficking", 29 January 2016. https://www.unicefusa.org/stories/sustainable-development-goals-aim-end-human-trafficking/29864.

United Nations Office on Drugs and Crime (UNODC). 2015. *The Concept of 'Exploitation' in the Trafficking in Persons Protocol*. https://www.unodc.org/documents/congress/background-information/Human_Trafficking/UNODC_2015_Issue_Paper_Exploitation.pdf.

————. 2016. *Global Report on Trafficking in Persons 2016*. New York: UNODC.

————. 2017. *Trafficking in Persons from Cambodia, Lao PDR and Myanmar to Thailand*. Bangkok: UNODC.

UNODC, Anti-Slavery International, and Transparency International. 2011. *The Role of Corruption in Trafficking in Persons*. Vienna: UNODC. http://www.unodc.org/documents/human-trafficking/2011/Issue_Paper_-_The_Role_of_Corruption_in_Trafficking_in_Persons.pdf.

US State Department. 2004. "Trafficking in Persons Report", 14 June 2004. https://www.state.gov/j/tip/rls/tiprpt/2004/34021.htm.

————. 2017. *Trafficking in Persons Report 2017*. Washington, D.C.: US State Department.

————. 2018. *Trafficking in Persons Report 2018*. Washington, D.C.: US State Department.

Varella, Andrea. 2017. "Live Streaming of Child Sexual Abuse: Background, Legislative Frameworks and the Experience of the Philippines, Online Child Sexual Exploitation: An Analysis of Emerging and Selected Issues". *ECPAT International Journal* 12.

Walk Free Foundation. 2016. *Global Slavery Index 2016*. Australia: The Minderoo Foundation Pty Ltd. https://www.globalslaveryindex.org/region/asia-pacific/.

Wong, Diana. 2005. "The Rumour of Trafficking". In *Illicit Flows and Criminal Things – States, Borders, and the Other Side of Globalisation*, edited by William van Schendel and Itty Abraham. Indiana: Indiana University Press.

World Bank. Undated. "2.1 World Development Indicators: Population Dynamics". World Development Indicators. http://wdi.worldbank.org/table/2.1 (accessed 3 June 2019).

Zabal, Boy Ryan B. 2017. "Immigration Officers, Recruiters Nabbed for Human Trafficking". *Rappler*, 20 January 2017. https://www.rappler.com/nation/158999-immigration-officers-recruiters-nabbed-human-trafficking.

Zimmerman, Cathy and Ligia Kiss. 2017. "Human Trafficking and Exploitation: A Global Health Concern". *PLoS Medicine* 14, no. 11.

8

DISPLACED POPULATIONS AND REGIONAL GOVERNANCE IN SOUTHEAST ASIA

Alistair D.B. Cook

8.1 Introduction

Over the past decade, the global security environment has undergone significant shifts. There is a noticeable downturn in political will to solve pressing issues collectively. There is a rise in state-centred politics that focuses on the notion of "taking back control"—whether domestically from political rivals or externally from multilateral or supranational organizations—that resonates worldwide.[1] It is therefore unsurprising that macroeconomic slowdown and geopolitical tensions dominate news headlines—a battle between sustaining globalism and an emerging nationalism. While this division is surmountable, the utilization of new technologies and social media as platforms to convey political messages to a greater number of people make it more pronounced. Many established, new or emerging democracies have not yet dealt with the political fragmentation and polarization they now face, which makes consolidated and effective governance difficult. These domestic political and economic challenges have made global and regional efforts to govern transnational and non-traditional security issues more difficult. This has led to disproportionately negative effects on marginalized communities both within and across borders.

In South and Southeast Asia, displacement has three major causes—disaster, development and conflict. Disaster impacts have remained localized areas of vulnerability within countries for short periods of time in general. The impacts of development on the displacement of people are harder to monitor with the main driver being rapid urbanization and large-scale infrastructure projects. Finally, but most significantly, conflict as a driver tends to lead to more protracted displacement both within countries and across international borders. Across Southeast Asia, the Internal Displacement Monitoring Centre identifies the new displacements in 2018 as an estimated 365,000 disaster displaced and 3,000 conflict displaced in Indonesia; 3,800,000 disaster displaced and 188,000 conflict displaced in the Philippines; 82,000 disaster displaced in Malaysia; 315,000 disaster displaced and 57,000 conflict displaced in Myanmar; 50,000 disaster displaced in Thailand; and 633,000 disaster displaced in Vietnam.[2]

From this broad overview of 2018, Southeast Asia as a region remains significantly impacted by disaster displacement over the short term. The numbers of newly displaced by conflict remain relatively low in Southeast Asia in 2018. More broadly, the world also saw numbers of civilian casualties in conflict plateau in 2018. However, there were three notable global developments that have implications and reflections in Southeast Asia. The first is that conflict actors are proliferating—there was a 23 per cent increase in the numbers of distinct, named actors from 2017 to 2018. This comes with an important caveat that even with this substantial increase, new conflict actors remained only 7 per cent of total organized violence events in 2018. This underlines that while there are more actors emerging, the longer standing conflict actors remain dominant. A second development was that state actors remain the most violent actors accounting for the most direct number of civilian deaths in conflict. The third global development is that close-proximity violence against civilians is increasing, while remote targeting of civilians decreased.[3] These trends all point to significant implications and reflections for the internal conflicts in Southeast Asia. While 2018 saw a decline in conflict displacement, within the context of Southeast Asia the largest movement of people across an international border remained under previous years with the vast majority of Rohingya fleeing Myanmar into neighbouring Bangladesh who were consolidated into the world's largest refugee camp in Cox's Bazar in the Southeast of the country.

The Rohingya are a stateless Muslim minority in Rakhine State with the vast majority of whom fled their homes after the outbreak of violence on 25 August 2017. The overwhelming majority of those who fled Myanmar into Bangladesh are women and children, with more than 40 per cent under the age of twelve. Understood from both geostrategic and human security perspectives, the Rohingya crisis falls firmly under the non-traditional security umbrella. The aim of this chapter therefore is to articulate these framings and the governance mechanisms they activate to respond to this crisis as the most significant and expectedly long-running example of displacement in Southeast Asia. With the history of low-intensity conflict running many decades on the one hand, and the emergence of governance mechanisms to oversee short term disaster displaced populations on the other, there are notable overlaps as governments in the region seek to find common ground to address the Rohingya crisis. This attempt has significant implications for humanitarian work in the region with wider implications over the direction of the humanitarian system in the coming years as countries seek to fulfil the United Nations Secretary-General's Report—An Agenda for Humanity. This includes a commitment to the localization of humanitarian assistance and the experience of Southeast Asia in this regard will likely influence key global debates on the humanitarian reform agenda.

Since the late 2000s, the frame of the irregular Rohingya migrants from Myanmar travelling through the Bay of Bengal by boat to reach the shores of Thailand, Malaysia or Indonesia is an existential threat to the security and stability of the recipient states. The fear is that the incoming irregular migrants might either be radicalized posing a terrorism threat or they may upset the ethnic or religious balance within recipient states. Since the mass exodus in late 2017, the narrative has largely shifted towards a human security lens for many ASEAN member states and its regional mechanisms. While the terror threat remains a frame, the humanitarian dynamic of the displaced population is more dominant in regional discourse. Further, this chapter will assess the prospects and challenges for national, regional and international governance mechanisms to resolve the fundamental political issue at hand—the voluntary repatriation of Rohingya to Rakhine State and their future in Myanmar—and the capacity of regional mechanisms activated to govern the displacement response. This will offer key insights into the state of regional governance and its interaction with the global humanitarian system.

8.2   The Makings of Southeast Asia's Displacement Crisis

Southeast Asia is home to heterogenous populations of different ethnicities and religions making up nation states. The post-colonial character of the countries and their different types of government have long set the stage for the dominant regional norms of consensus-building decision-making and non-interference in the domestic affairs of another ASEAN member state to ensure national and regional stability since its founding in 1967. More recent efforts to move the regional grouping beyond these core norms have had periods of relative success both collectively as a grouping and bilaterally, particularly captured in the realm of non-traditional security and humanitarian assistance and disaster relief in particular.

Across the region, the triple drivers of displacement—disaster, development and conflict—have had different response capacities with disaster displacement generating the most significant levels of cooperation over the short term to provide relief to affected populations. Development displacement remains largely out of the picture as a policy frame in regional discussions. Conflict displacement has had much more variations and context-specific cooperation. Indonesia, Malaysia, Philippines and Thailand have either offered sanctuary to populations displaced by conflict in neighbouring countries or been the source of internal conflict generating displacement for fellow ASEAN member states. While presently only the Philippines is a signatory to the UN Refugee Convention, all have offered some form of sanctuary to displaced persons.

Within the broader Asia and Pacific, the top four hosting countries are Bangladesh, Malaysia, Thailand and Indonesia. Bangladesh hosts 907,199 refugees and asylum-seekers, the vast majority of which are Rohingya from Myanmar. Malaysia has around 160,000 refugees and asylum-seekers registered with the UN High Commissioner for Refugees (UNHCR) Office in Kuala Lumpur of which around 140,000 of these originated from Myanmar. This number comprises an estimated 75,000 Rohingya, 30,000 Chins, 10,000 Myanmar Muslims, 4,000 Rakhines, and Arakanese and other ethnicities. There are also 22,000 refugees and asylum seekers from elsewhere including Pakistan, Yemen, Somalia, Syria, Sri Lanka, Afghanistan, Iraq and Palestine. Thailand is host to 95,644 refugees and asylum-seekers, most of whom are ethnic minorities from Myanmar, mainly Karen and Karenni, who live in nine camps in four provinces along the Thai-Myanmar border. Most of these have been fleeing conflict in Myanmar for nearly thirty years. Indonesia hosts an estimated 14,067 refugees and asylum-seekers. Some 72 per cent of these originate from Afghanistan, Somalia and Myanmar.[4] Presently by far the largest single group of displaced persons are Rohingya from Myanmar with the vast majority found in Bangladesh and smaller numbers found in Indonesia, Malaysia and Thailand.

Given the importance of context-specificity, this chapter will focus on the Rohingya from Myanmar and their implications for regional governance mechanisms. It is therefore important to understand the drivers behind the waves of exodus of Rohingya from Myanmar. In June 2012, riots broke out in Rakhine State, Myanmar, in response to the gang rape and murder of a Buddhist woman and the subsequent killing of ten Muslims, who were not Rohingya, following a public call for retribution. Violence escalated and relations between Buddhists and Muslims hit a new low. In October 2012, riots and organized violence broke out again, displacing more people. These two periods of violence disproportionately affected Muslims, with an estimated 140,000 people displaced. These riots caught international attention and prompted diplomatic activity in response to the plight of the Muslim community across the Muslim world.

While there is a clear role for the international community its influence remains limited, and any significant political change is still seen as most likely coming from within the country itself.[5] Indeed, this extends firmly into the humanitarian aid and relief field.

With Bangladeshi policy framed in traditional security terms, the focus is on the security of the host state with the perception that the forced migrants are an existential threat. This framing translates into hostility towards the forced migrants and in turn threatens them with forced repatriation, closed camps, and non-recognition of their status. Thus, the human security dilemma of the Rohingya affects the bilateral relations between Myanmar and recipient states.[6] Similar concerns over refugees are reflected throughout the region like in Malaysia, Thailand and Indonesia with the overwhelming majority of states being non-signatory to the UN Refugee Convention and the continuation to focus on refugees as destabilizing and a threat to national security. These concerns are replicated across South Asia as well where waves of Rohingya fled beginning in the 1960s.[7]

As a result of the deteriorating situation in Rakhine State and an increasingly hostile social environment more widely in Myanmar for Muslims, people fled by boat. From 2012 through the first half of 2015, an estimated 100,000 people risked their lives in hazardous journeys by boat to neighbouring countries, notably Thailand, Malaysia and Indonesia.[8] These migrants were not welcomed on arrival but instead faced "forced pushbacks" until a temporary ad hoc agreement was reached that allowed them to stay, pending a determination of their status, for a period of up to a year.[9] This initial reaction by Southeast Asian governments to the flow of migrants through the Bay of Bengal and Andaman Sea reflected the dominant perceptions of migrants as posing a threat to state security and stability. The reaction also highlighted their reliance on bilateral or mini-lateral attempts to address the situation, rather than system-wide responses that engage all important stakeholders.

The policies initiated by governments in the region were in many ways strikingly similar to those put into effect in the late 1970s in response to the so-called Indochinese exodus. Yet, it is important to note that, in the earlier case, the regional actors ultimately achieved a compromise solution to the Indochinese refugee situation, in the form of the Comprehensive Plan of Action. Revisiting the circumstances under which this solution was attained could provide valuable lessons regarding how states and communities in the region might work together, in conjunction with major international actors, to develop a humane and sustainable solution to the root causes of irregular migration that dominated the news.

In Indonesia, Acehnese fishermen abided by Adat, a local customary law which calls for kindness to those in difficult situations, and rescued many irregular migrants who were in distress at sea. The fishermen conveyed the migrants to Aceh, and provided them with essentials such as shelter, food, water and a place to wash—all this in breach of the position held by the Indonesian government in Jakarta, which initially had refused to allow the irregular migrants entry.[10] The humanitarianism demonstrated by the Acehnese fishermen caused Jakarta to rethink its policies towards the irregular migrants in this particular instance and to revisit its policies towards refugees in general. This episode illustrates the power of communities in drawing on their own experiences and, in turn, influencing national policies. In Malaysia, there is a history of humanitarian exceptionalism towards the Rohingya, where the government have offered ad hoc sanctuary to those arriving on its shores.[11] These examples underscore the fact that even though some states may not be signatories to the Refugee Convention, local norms exist that essentially promote what it stands for in an ad hoc manner. These local customary norms and laws should be identified, as in the case of the Acehnese fishermen, and used to demonstrate the consistency between local communities and international conventions.

8.3   The 2017 Exodus and Regional Implications

In August 2017, the Arakan Rohingya Salvation Army (ARSA) claimed responsibility for attacks on thirty police posts and an army base in Maungdaw, Buthidaung and Rathedaung townships in Northwestern Rakhine. The attacks came the day after the Advisory Commission on Rakhine State delivered its report. In the first month after the attacks an estimated 6,700 Rohingya deaths were reported according to Medicins Sans Frontiers. The Myanmar security services reportedly opened fire on fleeing civilians and planted landmines in border thoroughfares used to flee Rakhine State. The violence targeted at the Rohingya population led to the exodus of over 670,000 people from Myanmar to Bangladesh.

Local communities in Teknaf and Ukhia subdistricts were still reeling from the impact of Cyclone Mora that hit the district in May when the first arrivals of Rohingya refugees appeared at the end of August 2017. The UNHCR declared the situation as a "Level 3 Emergency". "Level 3 emergencies" were "major sudden onset humanitarian crises triggered by natural disasters or conflict which require system-wide mobilisation". Such categorizations have since gone by the wayside and replaced with a more nebulous call for an augmented international response, which largely reflects the perceived negative light this level placed on national governments and became a hindrance to humanitarian access. Many of the arrivals were women and unaccompanied children who were physically injured and deeply traumatized having lost their homes and family members. Prior to this influx, Bangladesh was already hosting 303,070 Rohingya or what the Government of Bangladesh refers to as "forcibly displaced Myanmar Nationals" in unofficial settlements in the upazilas of Teknaf and Ukhia in Cox's Bazar. In addition, there are 34,000 Rohingya officially recognized as refugees living in two camps managed by UNHCR in Nayapara and Kutupalong respectively. The Rohingya population occupies a sprawling complex of shelters built with bamboo and plastic sheets on 4,800 acres of reserve forestland in Cox's Bazar allocated by the Government of Bangladesh. Many living within the camps are still in need of urgent life-saving assistance.

Refugee arrivals from Myanmar have slowed but have not stopped by the end of 2018 as the majority of the Rohingya population is now in exile. The governments of Bangladesh and Myanmar signed a Memorandum of Understanding (MOU) on 23 November 2017 for the "safe, voluntary and dignified" repatriation of displaced Rohingya population to Myanmar. The deal was reached without the involvement of the international community and its operationalization is unclear. In February 2017, Bangladesh handed a list of 8,032 "eligible returnees" to the Burmese government for repatriation but it was reported that Myanmar was willing to accept less than 400 Rohingya on the list. This bilateral MOU contrasted with the earlier Rohingya repatriation in 1992, which briefly involved the UNHCR alongside Bangladesh and Myanmar. Continued pressure by China—as an intermediary—as well as ASEAN countries ensured that the matter was contained as a bilateral government-to-government issue, without Western involvement before UNHCR technically oversaw and organized the repatriation.[12]

The relationship between Bangladesh and the UNHCR ended abruptly on 22 December 1992, as there were reports of coerced repatriation, which is in contravention of the Refugee Convention and was a direct threat to the personal and political security of the Rohingya. The withdrawal of the UNHCR from the repatriation programme was a significant blow to Bangladesh's international image. The criticism also focused on UNHCR for reporting authoritatively that the situation in Myanmar had improved including the cessation of forced labour.[13] Critics argued that the UNHCR's access to the return population was impinged by the accompaniment of military officials, which prevented an independent evaluation of the situation.[14] Indeed, the 1992 Repatriation offers several lessons for regional governance efforts on the most recent repatriation plan for the Rohingya.

The debate over the UNHCR's role in the repatriation exercise placed the agency between Bangladesh and Myanmar on the one hand, and the humanitarian community on the other. The UNHCR sought to balance its interactions to leverage its position but ultimately came up short of the expectations of the humanitarian community. When considering the role of ASEAN in the repatriation efforts there will also be constraints as it remains a consensus decision-making process and while the perception on non-intervention has shifted towards a "surge capacity" model where fellow member states augment national capacity in humanitarian assistance and disaster relief scenarios, it remains at the invitation and under the auspices of the individual government. Criticism of the UNHCR involvement in the Rohingya repatriation focused on the shape of the emerging regional norms, which are seen as reducing commitments to human security in favour of more traditional state security. The UNHCR had carried out a survey in the refugee camps to determine whether the Rohingya were willing to repatriate. However, there were serious flaws in the collection of this data that threatened Rohingya personal and political security, which undermined the repatriation exercise.[15] A subsequent survey was carried out by Medecins-Sans-Frontiers (MSF)–Holland, which concluded that refugees did want to return, but only when the situation had improved in Myanmar. The reason the refugees had agreed to return home in the first instance was through ignorance of the voluntary nature of the repatriation.[16] The most recent efforts could rather be characterized as state-based human security concerns where the government has captured and mimicked the humanitarian space taking national policy past the signposts of humanitarian affairs whilst defining the parameters under which it will apply and to what extent.

While the UNHCR had received formal agreement from the Myanmar military government that international norms would be upheld, their implementation was another matter.[17] It is at this level that criticism of the UNHCR was made and the agency's inability to transfer the norms in the MOU into an acceptable programme and practice. This experience shaped the way UNHCR perceives its involvement and at what cost, in the current discussion around the Rohingya bilateral repatriation with UN engagement, which was due to start in earnest in early 2018 to no avail. While an MOU was signed between the UN and Myanmar in mid-2018, no significant number of people have returned to Rakhine under it. More recent projections from the field are sceptical about the potential safe and dignified repatriation back to Rakhine under earlier arrangements or through regional governance mechanisms anytime soon.

8.4   ASEAN's Emerging Role as Regional Humanitarian Actor

Since its birth over fifty years ago, ASEAN has become central to regional diplomacy. More recently, humanitarian assistance and emergency response in ASEAN has highlighted a successful avenue for the regional grouping to build trust between different civilian and military actors and provide primarily state-based relief to affected populations. ASEAN has moved towards a networked regional grouping that demonstrates a greater potential to push through simple tit-for-tat negotiations. The shift towards a network approach sees ASEAN member states working together to aid local communities. Through this approach fellow ASEAN member states provide surge capacity to national government agencies to provide its affected population with relief items.

However, this networked approach is rather limited to disaster relief and, more recently, provision of relief items to those displaced by conflict in Myanmar's Rakhine State and Marawi in the Southern Philippines. It was in the aftermath of the Indian Ocean Tsunami and Earthquake in 2004 that countries in Southeast Asia developed the legally binding Association of Southeast Asian Nations Agreement on Disaster Management and Emergency Response (AADMER). ASEAN member states signed the AADMER in 2008 and it came into force a year later. The Agreement paved the way for the establishment in Jakarta, Indonesia, of the ASEAN Coordinating Centre for Humanitarian Assistance on disaster management (AHA Centre) in 2011. The AHA Centre is the agreement's operational hub to facilitate and support disaster affected states and facilitate real-time information sharing with relevant United Nations and international organisations in promoting regional collaboration.[18] The AHA Centre is governed by the ASEAN Committee on Disaster Management (ACDM), which made up of the National Disaster Management Organisations (NDMOs) of member states.

At the 28th ASEAN Summit in Vientiane, Lao PDR in 2016, the Leaders signed the Declaration on One ASEAN One Response: ASEAN

Responding to Disaster as One in the Region and Outside the Region. The Declaration affirms the principle to harness the individual and collective strengths of different sectors and stakeholders in ASEAN to respond to disasters inside and outside the region. The Declaration confirms the AADMER as the central disaster response mechanism in Southeast Asia.[19] It therefore recognized the networked approach adopted by ASEAN member states to facilitate a more effective state-led humanitarian system in Southeast Asia. Indeed, the ASEAN Vision 2025 on disaster management calls for a networked approach to be developed with more focus on the multi-stakeholder environment.[20] However, such an approach is no small feat, given the changing and diverse nature of the communities of actors, which often times have competing mandates, if we are to move towards a more people-centred approach and more malleable model of regional disaster response architecture in Southeast Asia by 2025. As the recent involvement of the AHA Centre in a new disaster setting in Marawi, the Philippines and Rakhine, Myanmar in 2017 demonstrates, there is political confidence being built in the AHA Centre as the point institution for humanitarian assistance within the region. It places the AHA Centre well to further develop its role as the lynchpin of the regional relief managed by the state, as a global leader in disaster response, and to share its expertise with other regional organizations. Not only has ASEAN committed to becoming a global leader in disaster management by 2025 but also is making significant progress toward doing so. This has demonstrated that line ministries and sectoral practitioners are able to negotiate solid agreements and get to work implementing them. As one practitioner put it, "we're a 'can-do' sector. We're engineers. We see a problem and go fix it." It still requires the invitation of the affected member state but it is building a culture of trust and cooperation working through NDMOs. ASEAN member states effectively remain both the provider and client with the AHA Centre illustrating a restricted mandate for the regional governance mechanism.

This regional mandate emerged more forcefully in the aftermath of the 2008 Cyclone Nargis. During the emergency period, the Myanmar military was slow to respond to the humanitarian disaster in the coastal Irrawaddy Division, south of Yangon. The international community sought to assist in the disaster with relief supplies and aid workers, but it was initially rejected by the Myanmar military. The rejection of international assistance was greeted with disbelief by the international community. This rejection and frustration over the slow and poor response led to some countries contemplating unilateral aid drops and the invocation of the Responsibility to Protect (R2P).[21] While the R2P principles focus on crimes of mass atrocity, the French Foreign Minister Bernard Kouchner argued that the R2P principle should apply in times of natural disaster when the host government is unresponsive to the needs of its people—an argument now known as R2P-Plus.[22] In 2008, the Myanmar military saw the possibility of intervention from Western states under humanitarian auspices to protect a particular community as a direct security threat to the state so there remains suspicion of humanitarian organizations in Myanmar.

However, the regional mandate can be traced back to the late Dr Surin Pitsuwan who advocated "flexible engagement" first as Thai Foreign Minister (1997–2001) back in 1998, which was rejected by the regional grouping to a more open and frank discussion of domestic issues which have implications on other members and the group's destiny. Yet by the time he became ASEAN Secretary-General in 2008, member states launched the ASEAN Community which saw a more comprehensive and networked approach to regional security issues, particularly in the realm of non-traditional security. It is most notably seen through the AADMER, which laid the legally-binding framework for the establishment of the AHA Centre in 2011. The AHA Centre not only facilitates assistance from member states to the affected but through its Emergency Response and Assessment Team and AHA Certificate of Excellence nurtured a sense of "we" primarily among government agencies. It is now less about other states helping the affected state but activating a more comprehensive sectoral response to both natural and human-induced disasters with the decision by the affected state. With a similar sense of solidarity, the ASEAN Defense Ministers Meeting has agreed to the Militaries Ready Group on Humanitarian Assistance and Disaster Relief to further civil-military cooperation[23] showing the diverse line ministries involved in relief activities. However, the role of humanitarian champion within regional governance in a position of influence remains unfilled by someone who can rally support for humanitarian response that bridges the regional and global levels. What has emerged is a more state-led and focused regional response which chimes in tune with national priorities.

8.5 Conclusion

Globally there are three main drivers for displacement—disasters, development and conflict. Within Southeast Asia regional governance has focused on disasters but there are recent attempts to extend this governance framework to conflict displacement. While conflict displacement is not new to the region, finding sustainable regional solutions and developing regional mechanisms to facilitate provisions and protections for the displaced have had varied levels of success. When considering the most significant displacement in the region for many years, the Rohingya example provides a challenge to regional mechanisms established primarily for disasters to be adapted to conflict settings. While on the face of it, displaced populations whatever the driver require similar responses, the reality is quite different. AADMER provides an avenue through which ASEAN member states can provide relief through the disaster management focal point, the Myanmar Ministry of Social Welfare. Indeed if we look at the normative and rhetorical development that has taken place within a regional context including the establishment of the ASEAN Troika in 1999,[24] the enactment of the ASEAN Charter in 2008, the formation of the Tripartite Core Group in the aftermath of Cyclone Nargis[25] as well as the endorsement of the ASEAN Human Rights Declaration in 2012,[26] there is perhaps cause for cautious optimism. Taken together, these developments are evidence that it might indeed be possible to forge regional agreements that are comprehensive in nature and that recognize the multi-stakeholder environment (i.e., that include civil society groups, local governments as well as the more traditional actors such as national governments, international organizations, and others). It may be possible to draw on the experiences of these regional mechanisms to identify ways and means that ASEAN has facilitated processes to forge solutions to non-traditional security issues such as humanitarian concerns at the regional level. However, the absence of a regional humanitarian champion within ASEAN and the present dominance of a state-led approach to the regional humanitarian mechanism offer pause for thought and the need to moderate expectations. While state-led humanitarianism lends itself to disasters, the same cannot be said for conflict given that states themselves are parties directly involved in conflicts making it impossible at present for regional governance to offer anything more than short-term relief to those displaced at best.

While there is currently little appetite for a durable long-term solution to the displaced Rohingya, the fourteen-year period between the beginning of the Indochinese exodus in 1975 and the second Geneva conference on Indochinese refugees in 1989—the last time the region comprehensively dealt with a significant population of concern—highlights the protracted nature of negotiations and offers a humbling reminder that the path to sustainable political solutions is long and context-specific. It is therefore also important for an interim arrangement, like that agreed at the first Geneva conference on Indochinese refugees, to ensure that the principles of humanitarianism and civilian protection are upheld for the displaced population in the immediate term. Southeast Asia experiences all three major drivers of displacement—disaster, development and conflict—but conflict remains the one driver that will continue to challenge regional governance for some time to come.

NOTES

1. World Economic Forum, *The Global Risks Report 2019*, 4th ed. (Geneva: World Economic Forum, 2019), p. 6.
2. Internal Displacement Monitoring Centre (IDMC), *Global Report on Displacement [GRID] 2018* (Geneva: Internal Displacement Monitoring Centre, 2019), http://www.internal-displacement.org/global-report/grid2018/.
3. Roudabeh Kishi and Melissa Pavlik, *ACLED 2018 – The Year in Review* (London: Armed Conflict Location & Event Data Project, 2019), https://www.acleddata.com/wp-content/uploads/2019/01/ACLED-2018-The-Year-in-Review_Final_Pub.pdf.
4. United Nations High Comissioner for Refugees (UNHCR), Refugee Population Overview, 2019, http://popstats.unhcr.org/en/overview.
5. Andrew Selth, "Even Paranoids Have Enemies: Cyclone Nargis and Myanmar's Fears of Invasion", *Contemporary Southeast Asia* 30, no. 3 (2008): 379.
6. Syeda Naushin Parnini, Mohammad Redzuan Othman, and Amer Saifude Ghazali, "The Rohingya Refugee Crisis and Bangladesh-Myanmar Relations", *Asian and Pacific Migration Journal* 22, no. 1 (2013): 287.
7. Nausheen H. Anwar, "Negotiating New Conjunctures of Citizenship: Experiences of 'Illegality' in Burmese-Rohingya and Bangladeshi Migrant Enclaves in Karachi", *Citizenship Studies* 17, nos. 3–4 (2013): 414.
8. Oliver Holmes, "Rohingya in Burma: Claim that One in Ten have Fled on Boats", *The Guardian*, 9 June 2015, http://www.theguardian.com/world/2015/jun/09/ten-percent-of-rohingya-in-burma-have-fled-on-boats.

9. Reuters, "Indonesia and Malaysia Agree to Offer 7,000 Migrants Temporary Shelter", *The Guardian*, 20 May 2015, http://www.theguardian.com/world/2015/may/20/hundreds-more-migrants-rescued-off-indonesia-as-pope-calls-for-help.

10. Kate Lamb, "'We Helped Out of Solidarity': Indonesian Fishermen Come to Aid of Boat Migrants", *The Guardian*, 18 May 2015, http://www.theguardian.com/world/2015/may/18/solidarity-indonesian-fishermen-boat-migrants-aceh.

11. Alistair D.B. Cook and Liliane Fan, "Malaysia – A State of Sanctuary", in *Minorities Matter: Malaysian Politics and People Volume III*, edited by Sophie Lemiere (Petaling Jaya: Gerak Budaya, 2019), pp. 89–103.

12. Martin Smith, "The Muslim Rohingya of Burma", Delivered at Conference of Burma Centrum Nederland, 11 December 1995.

13. Michael N. Barnett and Martha Finnemore, *Rules for the World: International Organisations in Global Politics* (Ithaca: Cornell University Press, 2004), p. 12.

14. Barnett and Finnemore, *Rules for the World*, p. 16.

15. The UNHCR carried out their first survey but as the Bangladeshi authorities had control over who they could interview, they had an unrepresentative sample of people in transit camps—people who had already decided to repatriate—so the overwhelming result that those surveyed wanted to repatriate. A second survey was held in non-transit camps. This survey found that in one camp only 27 per cent wanted to return. However, the UNHCR conducted a second round of interviews a few days later and discovered that nearly 97 per cent wanted to return. The exact cause for the significant change of result was unknown. The UNHCR cited a "delayed band-wagoning effect" and the NGO community "suspecting coercion" (Barnett and Finnemore 2004, p. 112).

16. Barnett and Finnemore, *Rules for the World*, p. 113.

17. Alistair D.B. Cook, "Human Insecurity and Displacement along Myanmar's Borders", in *Irregular Migration and Human Security in East Asia*, edited by Jiyoung Song and Alistair D.B. Cook (Abingdon: Routledge, 2015), pp. 68–83.

18. Association of Southeast Asian Nations (ASEAN), Agreement on the Establishment of the ASEAN Coordinating Center for Humanitarian Assistance on Disaster Management, 17 November 2011.

19. ASEAN, Declaration on One ASEAN One Response: ASEAN Responding to Disaster as One in the Region and Outside the Region, Vientiane, Lao PDR, 6 September 2016.

20. Ibid.

21. Selth, "Even Paranoids Have Enemies", pp. 389–91.

22. Mely Caballero-Anthony and Belinda Chng, "Cyclones and Humanitarian Crises: Pushing the Limits of R2P in Southeast Asia", *Global Responsibility to Protect* 1, no. 2 (2009): 135.

23. ASEAN, "Terms of Reference ASEAN Militaries Ready Group on Humanitarian Assistance and Disaster Relief (AMRG on HADR)", 22 April 2016, http://mod.gov.la/10thADMM/assets/4.7.1-tor-on-amrg-as-of-20160422.pdf (accessed 31 January 2019).

24. Donald E. Weatherbee, *International Relations in Southeast Asia: The Struggle for Autonomy* (Lanham, MD: Rowman and Littlefield, 2005), p. 122.

25. ASEAN, "Myanmar: First Press Release of Tripartite Core Group", 24 June 2008, http://reliefweb.int/report/myanmar/myanmar-1st-press-release-tripartite-core-group (accessed 1 February 2019).

26. ASEAN, "ASEAN Human Rights Declaration", 18 November 2012, http://aichr.org/?dl_name=ASEAN-Human-Rights-Declaration.pdf (accessed 1 February 2019).

REFERENCES

Abrar, Chowdhury R. 1995. "Repatriation of Rohingya Refugees". Regional Consultation on Refugee and Migratory Movements, Colombo, Sri Lanka.

Anwar, Nausheen H. 2013. "Negotiating New Conjunctures of Citizenship: Experiences of 'Illegality' in Burmese-Rohingya and Bangladeshi Migrant Enclaves in Karachi". *Citizenship Studies* 17, nos. 3–4: 414–28.

Association of Southeast Asian Nations (ASEAN). 2008. "The ASEAN Charter". www.asean.org/storage/images/ASEAN_RTK.../ASEAN_Charter.pdf (accessed 1 February 2019).

———. 2008. "Myanmar: First Press Release of Tripartite Core Group", 24 June 2008. http://reliefweb.int/report/myanmar/myanmar-1st-press-release-tripartite-core-group (accessed 1 February 2019).

———. 2011. Agreement on the Establishment of the ASEAN Coordinating Center for Humanitarian Assistance on Disaster Management, 17 November 2011.

———. 2012. "ASEAN Human Rights Declaration", 18 November 2012. http://aichr.org/?dl_name=ASEAN-Human-Rights-Declaration.pdf (accessed 1 February 2019).

———. 2016. Declaration on One ASEAN One Response: ASEAN Responding to Disaster as One in the Region and Outside the Region. Vientiane, Lao PDR, 6 September 2016.

———. 2016. "Terms of Reference ASEAN Militaries Ready Group on Humanitarian Assistance and Disaster Relief (AMRG on HADR)", 22 April 2016. http://mod.gov.la/10thADMM/assets/4.7.1-tor-on-amrg-as-of-20160422.pdf (accessed 31 January 2019).

Barnett, Michael N. and Martha Finnemore. 2004. *Rules for the World: International Organisations in Global Politics*. Ithaca: Cornell University Press.

Caballero-Anthony, Mely and Belinda Chng. 2009. "Cyclones and Humanitarian Crises: Pushing the Limits of R2P in Southeast Asia". *Global Responsibility to Protect* 1, no. 2: 135–55.

Cook, Alistair D.B. 2010. "Positions of Responsibility: A Comparison of ASEAN and EU Approaches Towards Myanmar". *International Politics* 47, nos. 3–4: 433–49. https://doi.org/10.1057/ip.2010.7.

———. 2015. "Human Insecurity and Displacement along Myanmar's Borders". In *Irregular Migration and Human Security in East Asia*, edited by Jiyoung Song and Alistair D.B. Cook. Abingdon: Routledge.

———. 2016. "Civilian Protection, Resilience and Insecurity in Myanmar". In *Civilian Protection in the Twenty-First Century: Governance and Responsibility in a Fragmented World*, edited by Cecilia Jacob and Alistair D.B. Cook. New Delhi: Oxford University Press.

———. 2016. "The Global and Regional Dynamics of Humanitarian Aid in Rakhine State". In *Islam and the State in Myanmar: Muslim-Buddhist Relations and the Politics of Belonging*, edited by Melissa Crouch. New Delhi: Oxford University Press.

Cook, Alistair D.B. and Liliane Fan. 2019. "Malaysia – A State of Sanctuary". In *Minorities Matter: Malaysian Politics and People Volume III*, edited by Sophie Lemiere. Petaling Jaya: Gerak Budaya, pp. 89–103.

Holmes, Oliver. 2015. "Rohingya in Burma: Claim that One in Ten have Fled on Boats". *The Guardian*, 9 June 2015. http://www.theguardian.com/world/2015/jun/09/ten-percent-of-rohingya-in-burma-have-fled-on-boats.

Internal Displacement Monitoring Centre (IDMC). 2019. *Global Report on Displacement [GRID] 2018*. Geneva: IDMC. http://www.internal-displacement.org/global-report/grid2018/.

Jones, Lee. 2008. "ASEAN's Albatros: ASEAN's Burma Policy, from Constructive Engagement to Critical Disengagement". *Asian Security* 4, no. 3: 271–93.

Kishi, Roudabeh and Melissa Pavlik. 2019. *ACLED 2018 – The Year in Review*. London: Armed Conflict Location & Event Data Project. https://www.acleddata.com/wp-content/uploads/2019/01/ACLED-2018-The-Year-in-Review_Final_Pub.pdf.

Lamb, Kate. 2015. "'We Helped Out of Solidarity': Indonesian Fishermen Come to Aid of Boat Migrants". *The Guardian*, 18 May 2015. http://www.theguardian.com/world/2015/may/18/solidarity-indonesian-fishermen-boat-migrants-aceh.

Parnini, Syeda Naushin, Mohammad Redzuan Othman, and Amer Saifude Ghazali. 2013. "The Rohingya Refugee Crisis and Bangladesh-Myanmar Relations". *Asian and Pacific Migration Journal* 22, no. 1: 133–46.

Pedersen, Morten B. 2012. "Rethinking International Assistance to Myanmar in a Time of Transition". In *Myanmar's Transition: Openings, Obstacles and*

Opportunities, edited by Nick Cheesman, Monique Skidmore and Trevor Wilson. Singapore: Institute of Southeast Asian Studies.

Reuters. 2015. "Indonesia and Malaysia Agree to Offer 7,000 Migrants Temporary Shelter". *The Guardian*, 20 May 2015. http://www.theguardian.com/world/2015/may/20/hundreds-more-migrants-rescued-off-indonesia-as-pope-calls-for-help.

Selth, Andrew. 2008. "Even Paranoids Have Enemies: Cyclone Nargis and Myanmar's Fears of Invasion". *Contemporary Southeast Asia* 30, no. 3: 379–402.

Smith, Martin. 1995. "The Muslim Rohingya of Burma". Delivered at Conference of Burma Centrum Nederland, 11 December 1995.

United Nations High Comissioner for Refugees (UNHCR). 2019. Refugee Population Overview. http://popstats.unhcr.org/en/overview.

Weatherbee, Donald E. 2005. *International Relations in Southeast Asia: The Struggle for Autonomy*. Lanham, MD: Rowman and Littlefield.

World Economic Forum. 2019. *The Global Risks Report 2019, 4th Edition*. Geneva: World Economic Forum.

9

HEALTH SECURITY CHALLENGES IN ASIA: NEW AGENDAS FOR STRENGTHENING REGIONAL COOPERATION IN HEALTH SECURITY

Mely Caballero-Anthony

9.1 Introduction

Much has changed in Asia's security environment as new security challenges emerge. This change can be clearly seen in the health security arena where new patterns of communicable and non-communicable diseases are significantly shifting the regional and global health agendas. Emerging types of diseases pose serious challenges in the ability of national and regional health systems to address them and to promote a healthy regional community.

The goal of promoting health security is particularly critical to a region that faced one of the most serious health threats in modern times. In 2003, the outbreak of Severe Acute Respiratory Syndrome (SARS), an unknown highly pathogenic infectious influenza virus, caught the region by surprise. What started as an infectious disease outbreak in China's Guangdong province quickly evolved into a global health crisis which spread across the globe and reached as far as North America and Europe. Since then, much attention has focused on preventing the outbreak of highly pathological influenza pandemics and spread of similar virulent viruses like the avian influenza strains of H1-H5N1, and Middle East Respiratory Syndrome Coronavirus (MERS-CoV).

While regional and global efforts have been focused on dealing with novel trains of influenza pandemic, new concerns about climate related health risks are also gaining more attention globally. From the increase in numbers and greater geographical spread of water-borne diseases like severe diarrhoeal diseases, typhoid and cholera to vector-borne diseases like Zika and Lyme disease as a result of rapidly changing climate, worries about the capacity of national health systems to deal with these growing risks to human health. In 2016, Zika emerged as the most recent infectious disease to be declared by the World Health Organization (WHO) as a "public health emergency of international concern" (PHEIC). For developing countries, particularly those in the tropics, health concerns are further compounded by the steady rise of endemic communicable diseases like dengue and malaria that now have longer transmission season due to climate change. Added to these new trends in human health risks are also the changing patterns of infectious diseases like tuberculosis which are drug resistant, as well as the rising threat of antimicrobial resistance. These health concerns are further stacked against another growing trend, which is the rising prevalence of non-communicable diseases (NCD) like diabetes, cardiovascular diseases, cancer and strokes—all of which are putting greater pressures on the ability and capacity of regional and global health systems to cope with more complex health challenges.

Against this background, the aim of the chapter is to analyse the impact of new challenges to regional health security in Southeast Asia and the wider East Asian region. It examines the extent to which current regional frameworks and approaches are able to deal with the speed of change in the burden of diseases in a highly interconnected and integrated community. The chapter focuses largely on the efforts by the Association of Southeast Asian Nations (ASEAN) which have been regarded as the key driver in regional cooperation on health issues. Since the early 2000, ASEAN has come up with a number of important initiatives geared towards promoting greater cooperation in addressing a number of regional health threats, including pandemic influenza viruses like SARS and H5N1. But while regional approaches are no doubt critical in effectively dealing with transborder health issues, the effectiveness of these policies are influenced by the way health issues are framed in ASEAN's security agenda and the current state of regional cooperation in ASEAN. With these considerations, the chapter argues that the success of regional approaches to health security are largely dependent on efforts at the national level to build strong health systems and having the capacity and adequate resources to detect, prevent, and control the spread of infectious diseases. Strong national health systems continue to be the foundation of regional and global efforts to promote health and human security.

9.2   Overview of Health and Human Security in Asia

Health is an integral part of human security which is about the protection of human lives from "critical pervasive threats" including illness and disability.[1] Good health was one of the key focus out of the eight Millennium Development Goals (MDGs),[2] and the same goal of achieving health security broadly framed as good health and well-being featured again in the Sustainable Development Goals (SDGs), ranking 3rd in 17 global development goals.[3] Health and human security therefore are mutually constitutive concepts. In doing so, one must regard health issues as no longer just "medical" concerns but also a human security concern. Arguably, it is important to emphasize the highly interdependent relationship between health and human security if one were to manage the different but interconnected non-traditional security challenges facing East Asia and the wider global community today.[4]

Being able to appreciate the intricate linkages between health and human security also makes for a better understanding of the nature of global health threats facing the international community today. At the turn of the millennium, the WHO had warned about the emerging threats of influenza pandemics. Many of their studies have pointed to the drivers of global health threats which include, among others: the increasing growth of international travel, rapid urbanization, changing sexual habits, misuse of antibiotics, poor water and air quality and the resettlement of humans into natural areas containing lethal pathogens. All these drivers have facilitated the emergence and spread of infectious diseases and the changing patterns and determinants of health worldwide.

Burden of Diseases in Asia

In Asia, people suffer a disproportionate burden of communicable diseases compared to the rest of the world. Of the 14 million deaths that occur annually in the region, 40 per cent are due to communicable diseases, compared with the global average of 28 per cent.[5] HIV/AIDS, tuberculosis (TB) and malaria are major infectious diseases that threaten people's health and life in the region. In 2014, the Southeast Asia region of WHO accounted for 41 per cent of the global burden of TB, with 4 million new cases and 460,000 deaths due to diseases in the region.[6] Nearly 5 million people in the countries of the region have been living with HIV/AIDS in 2015, with India, Thailand, Myanmar, Indonesia and Nepal representing the high burden countries.[7]

Apart from the epidemics like HIV/AIDS, the impacts of health insecurity are further demonstrated by the outbreaks of a string of emerging infectious diseases like SARS, Middle East Respiratory Syndrome (MERS) and Zika virus disease since the early 2000s. At the height of the SARS outbreak in 2003, the WHO had reported that China and Southeast Asian countries were affected the most, with reported 7,760 cases out of the world's total of 8,096 cases.[8] In 2015, South Korea saw the biggest outbreak of MERS out of Saudi Arabia where the disease was first diagnosed in 2012. 186 infections were diagnosed in the country during the outbreak, with 36 deaths associated with the disease.[9] In 2016, Zika emerged as the most recent infectious disease that was declared by the WHO as a PHEIC. Southeast Asia was not spared, with cases reported in Singapore, Malaysia and Thailand. These health emergencies have once again shown how globalization and increased connectivity in travel and infrastructure that result from this rapidly changing trend have made it extremely difficult to contain infectious diseases within national border.

Regional Approaches to Health Security

While ASEAN has had a comprehensive approach to security, it is interesting to note that until the early 2000, health concerns have not featured strongly in the region's security concerns. It was not therefore surprising that the ASEAN states were caught totally unprepared to deal with the outbreak of SARS in 2003 since at that time, there were no regional frameworks dealing with pandemic outbreaks and pandemic preparedness.[10] At the height of the SARS outbreak in 2003, the WHO had reported that China and Southeast Asian countries were affected the most, with reported 7,760 cases out of the world's total of 8,096 cases.[11] The health crisis further caused an array of negative impacts on regional countries with economic disruption as the most direct and visible consequence. The SARS crisis resulted in a loss of an estimated US$30 billion in the GDP of East and Southeast Asian economies in 2003.[12] Vietnam's saw its economic growth slide of 1.1 per cent while Singapore's GDP growth was reduced by 0.5 to 1 per cent.[13] As many countries in the region are popular tourist destinations, tourism was among the most affected sectors in the crisis. Tourist data from Hong Kong indicated that inbound tourist figures fell by 70 to 80 per cent, while outbound tourists were down 20 per cent. In Singapore, tourist arrivals fell to 70 per cent of previous levels. The decline of tourist arrivals also affected other tourist-related sectors like air travel, hotel, and retailing.[14]

The region's experiences with SARS, followed by H5N1 commonly known as bird flu in 2005–6, and its more recent strain of H1N1 (swine flu) in 2009 had brought home the point that infectious diseases pose a clear and present danger to the security and well-being of societies and states. Indeed, during the height of these pandemic outbreaks, it was estimated that a full-scale influenza pandemic could cost the global economy around US$500 billion within a year.[15] There are also the more indirect economic impacts of new diseases. Recent outbreaks of mosquito-borne viruses like Zika are now known to cause microcephaly among babies and neurological disorders like Barre syndrome (GBS) that causes paralysis and long hospital stays. While the short-term economic costs of Zika are relatively low compared to SARS, the World Bank had estimated that Zika cost 0.06 per cent of the GDP in Latin America and the Caribbean which saw the biggest outbreak,[16] it is the longer term costs from hospitalization and medical care from microcephaly that pose greater concern particularly among the poorer communities in affected developing countries. More often, these communities live in high densely populated areas with poor sanitation and where the risks of zoonotic transmissions are the highest. Yet, it is also in these areas where health systems are weak.

Note, however, that economic security is not the only area severely affected by health crises. As the SARS experience has demonstrated, health crisis can create political instability and even affect relations among states. In Hong Kong, when mandatory quarantine for people who were suspected of being exposed to the SARS virus, the order was met with resistance and was criticized as violating the rights of people. Governments can also lose credibility. In China, the central government had to replace the Health Minister and the mayor of Beijing in April 2003 due to his mismanagement of the epidemics in the initial phase of the crisis. In 2009, Beijing put in place an array of measures to prevent the spread of the H1N1 influenza at home like border control, quarantine of foreign visitors and trade restrictions. This heavy-handed approach however strained China's relations with some American countries that were affected by H1N1 like Mexico and Canada.[17] One of the key lessons learnt during the SARS crisis was to maintain transparency in reporting disease outbreaks both within and outside one's border and manage public information to avoid panic, maintain order and more importantly, get the citizens to be part of the coordinated solution to contain and eradicate the spread of pandemics in the population. It is beyond the scope of this chapter to deal with the latter issues. Suffice it to say that it was the rising awareness and appreciation of the risks that new kinds of highly infectious diseases pose to state and people's security that compelled governments to develop regional processes and mechanisms for health security.

9.3   Evolving Mechanisms for Health Security in ASEAN

One would note that most of the current regional health security initiatives started off as responses to the SARS and avian influenza outbreaks during their course from 2003 to 2009, which explains the high number of frameworks addressing emerging and re-emerging infectious diseases with pandemic potential, including but not limited to SARS (2003), H5N1 (2005–6), H1N1 (2009), and H7N9 (2013).[18] Since 2005, a number of regional mechanisms have been established in ASEAN. These included the ASEAN Task Force/ (and later on) Working Group on Communicable Diseases and the ASEAN Working Group on Pandemic Preparedness and Response. These mechanisms have carried out important regional health initiatives pertaining to infectious disease monitoring and control, such as the ASEAN Plus Three Emerging Infectious Disease (EID) Programme, the ASEAN Partnership Laboratories, and the Field Epidemiology Training Network among others.

Since then, a variety of mechanisms and networks have emerged to address different aspects of health security from regional surveillance and risk communication to capacity building. These are summarized in Figure 9.1 and Table 9.1.

TABLE 9.1
Regional Health Frameworks and Areas of Cooperation

Regional Frameworks	Areas of Health Security Cooperation			
	Emerging Infectious Diseases with Pandemic Potential	Infectious Diseases: HIV/AIDS, Malaria and Tuberculosis	Non-communicable Diseases	Health Systems Strengthening
ASEAN-China	✓		✓	
ASEAN-Japan	✓		✓	✓
ASEAN-Korea	✓	✓	✓	✓
ASEAN Plus Three Health Cooperation Framework	✓	✓		
East Asia Summit	✓	✓		

Source: Author.

FIGURE 9.1
Regional Frameworks on Health Cooperation in ASEAN

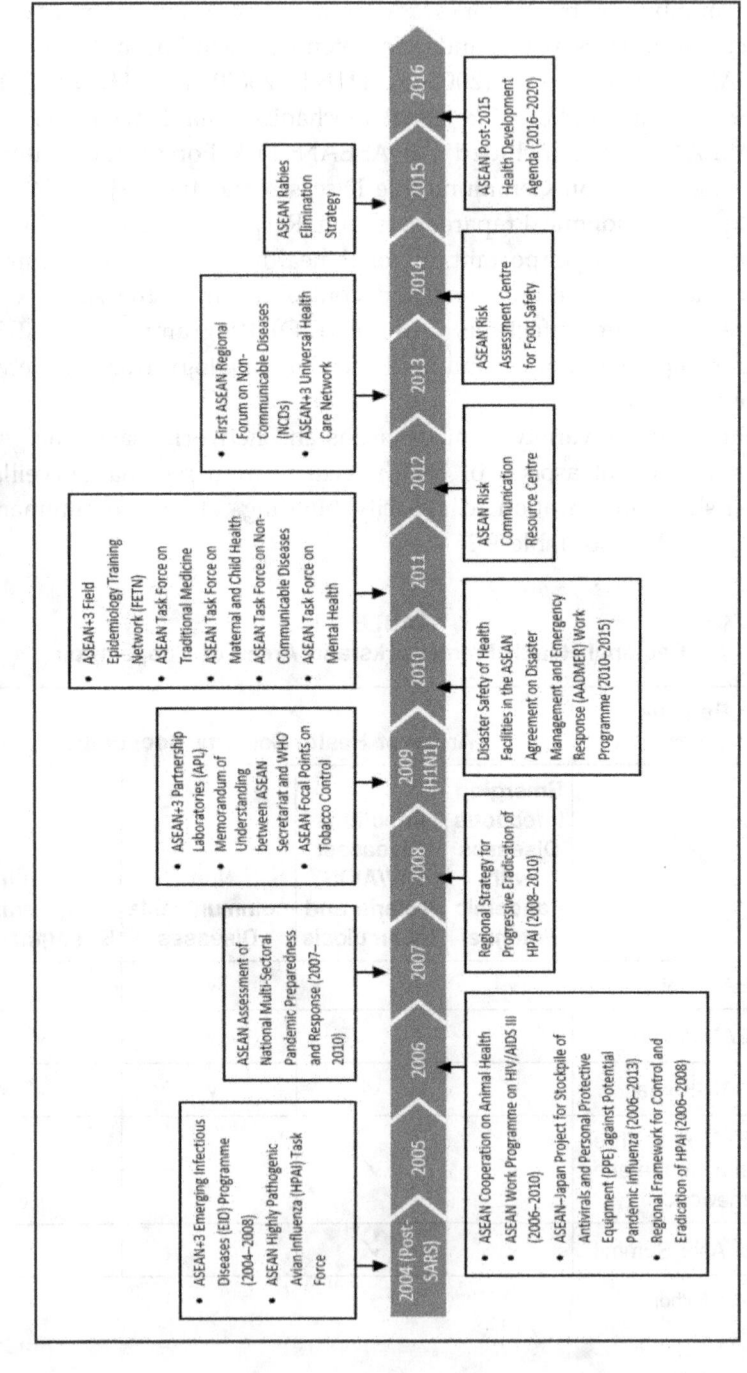

Source: ASEAN Secretariat.

9.4 Moving Beyond Pandemic Preparedness

In the last five years, the focus of ASEAN health cooperation has seen a visible shift from pandemic preparedness to broader approach to health security. As reflected in its post-2015 Health Development Agenda, more efforts are now being put to promote a more holistic approach to health security in Southeast Asia. The Agenda also incorporates the elements highlighted in the global SDG more broadly, and in particular SDG goal 3 which is on good health and well-being. ASEAN's regional health cooperation agenda thus sets out to list a number of health priorities, clustered into four areas namely: (1) promoting healthy lifestyle, including prevention and control of NCDs, (2) responding to all hazards and emerging threats, (3) strengthening health system and access to care, and (4) ensuring food safety which include access to safe food, safe drinking water and sanitation.[19]

With the changing patterns of infectious diseases and burden of diseases, the cluster approach certainly provides a more comprehensive agenda that would translate into actionable programmes and policies to address multiple threats to health security. Cluster 2 on responding to all hazards and emerging threats is timely given the possibilities of outbreaks of new types of viruses like Zika and re-emergence of highly pathogenic diseases like Ebola. Cluster 3 complements and provides critical support to cluster 2 as it aims to strengthen health systems to combat new health threats like Anti-Microbial Resistance (AMR) and improve means of implementation through the One Health Approach that engages other sectors beyond human health. Similarly, clusters 1 and 4 emphasize the seamless relationships between food security and nutrition, food safety and disaster health management and the importance of promoting healthy lifestyle. ASEAN's clustered approach to health development agenda for 2016–20 therefore fits well and contributes to the achievement of Sustainable Development Goals on ending hunger (SDG2), good health and well-being (SDG3) and related SDGs.

In sum, while the evolving regional health frameworks in ASEAN had started out with a strong global health security agenda which leaned more toward combatting pandemics, the more recent frameworks that have since been adopted move beyond the major focus on pandemic preparedness and response to dealing with non-communicable diseases and other types of health threats.

New Agenda in Health Security Cooperation in ASEAN

Non-Communicable Diseases (NCDs)

Of late, there has been a slight shift in WHO's global health agenda from traditional concerns in containing infectious diseases outbreaks towards addressing NCDs, especially those presenting chronic or lifelong care needs. This trend has been reflected by a 21 per cent increase in programme funding devoted to NCDs under the organization's 2014–15 biannual budget.[20] This is largely due to changing demographics of population growth and ageing that sees a shift in the diseases burden to NCDs. According to Garrett, the vast majority of the world's NCD patient population are seen by private health providers that are paid directly out-of-pocket by patients or in combination with the insurer or government financing.[21] However, as most nations age demographically, such out-of-pocket costs become existential threats to businesses, farms and the financial integrity of the family unit. Moreover, the costs of appropriate management of chronic NCDs are exponentially greater than those presented by infectious diseases, maternal health, and primary care issues, thereby posing a direct threat to health financing schemes in rich and poor countries alike. Yet, most NCDs continue to be left out from Universal Health Coverage (UHC) schemes today despite their rising numbers.[22]

A most recent study published by the Council on Foreign Relations in 2017 further indicates an increasing attention paid towards NCDs under the global health agenda, given the rise of cancers, diabetes, cardiovascular diseases and the likes. It argues that countries with the fastest increase in NCDs are the least prepared, most of which are poor and developing nations found in Asia such as Vietnam, Bangladesh, India, Pakistan, Indonesia, the Philippines and Myanmar.[23] With a relative lack of public health awareness on NCDs in these regions and most health services and medicines in poorer nations purchased out of pocket by patients rather than the government, late diagnoses and limited access to chronic care have become prevalent which lead to more working-age people becoming disabled or dying at a young age. External support continues to be skewed towards containing the spread of infectious diseases and addressing pandemics, as only 2 per cent of overall global health aid goes to addressing NCDs despite occupation of half of the entire global burden of disease. In contrast, HIV represented 4 per cent of the global burden of disease but received

29 per cent of global funds in 2014.[24] Furthermore, of the small amount donated, almost all has been devoted to prevention instead of treatment of NCDs. This is exemplified by WHO's global strategies for NCDs in the biennium 2018–19.[25]

The growing attention paid to NCDs, while being mindful of emerging threats, is indeed important given the rising prevalence of diabetes and obesity in the region. The notable emphasis on NCDs was seen during the 13th ASEAN Health Ministers Meeting (AHMM) held in September 2017, where ASEAN health ministers and heads of delegations reiterated the primary concern over the rising prevalence of NCDs in Southeast Asia, particularly obesity and diabetes, and the interventions and best practices to prevent risk factors and to promote health security through the delivery of relevant health services. Some ASEAN countries have been reported to put in a lot of effort in tackling NCDs. In Malaysia, for example, the National Strategic Plan for Non-Communicable Diseases (NSP-NCD) 2010–14 was developed in line with the WHO's "2008–2013 Action Plan for the Global Strategy for the Prevention and Control of NCDs". The NCD Prevention – 1Malaysia (NCDP-1M), which is the main programme under this strategy, undertook nation-wide NCD risk factor screening and intervention across three settings, i.e., community, workplace and schools, with the aim of achieving population-wide NCD risk factor screening to detect risk factors at their earliest stage, and used obesity as the main entry point for NCD risk factor intervention.[26] These projects were supported by a dedicated fund allocated by the Director General of Health in Malaysia and gradually increased in number that by 2012, the programme had an annual budget of RM4 million approved.[27]

While Singapore does not have a specific National Strategic Plan for NCDs, it has aimed to increase efforts in tackling diabetes. This is likely due to the fact that the country is experiencing one of the highest diabetes-related lower extremity amputations rates in the world, with three in four Singapore residents aged 65 and above affected by diabetes, high cholesterol or hypertension or a combination of the three.[28] A $15 million grant, for example, was added to the Health Promotion Board's Healthier Ingredients Development Scheme in 2018, on top of an existing $20 million grant introduced in July 2017, and the development of locally produced low-sugar foods and drinks will also get a financial boost to encourage people to eat more healthily. Similar to Malaysia, the critical role that volunteers play in Singapore's "war against diabetes" is underscored in Health Peers Programme, which looks to expand its outreach towards the western region of the country as part of the stepped-up measures to tackle diabetes at the community level.[29] Meanwhile, in Brunei the importance of the nation's health, including the impact of NCDs and calling for sustainable actions in adhering to healthier lifestyles in tackling NCDs has been repeatedly stressed by no other than the country's leader, Sultan Hassanal Bolkiah. The occupational health services (OHS) offered by the Brunei Darussalam's Ministry of Health provide screening and management of NCDs at various points of service (e.g. at entry points and periodic intervals of jobs), and complement other OHS activities such as workplace surveillance, workplace health advice and promotion, as well as workmen's compensation issues.[30] Such approach is in line with WHO recommendations of workplaces as healthy settings to promote health, including interventions for NCDs. It is also in accord with the WHO Global Plan of Action on Workers Health 2008–2017, which was adopted at the 60th World Health Assembly. In recent times, the government is becoming increasingly concerned with obesity, as cardiovascular diseases including heart diseases and stroke have become the leading causes of death in the country.

Furthermore, ASEAN has also recently been promoting the notion of "culture of prevention". Vongthep Arthakaivalvatee, former Deputy Secretary-General of ASEAN Socio-Cultural Community, noted the importance of fostering a "culture of prevention" and stressed the fundamental role of the region's health sector in building this norm to achieve health security for the peoples in the region. Consequently, the ASEAN Declaration on Culture of Prevention (CoP) for Peaceful, Inclusive, Resilient, Healthy and Harmonious Society was adopted by member states during the 31st ASEAN Summit held in Manila on 13 November 2017.[31] Additionally, the CoP approach was further emphasized at the 19th Meeting of the ASEAN Socio-Cultural Community on 21 March 2018, where the ministers discussed strategic issues on the development of preventive policies and programmes to address poverty, gender inequality, racial and religious discriminations, lack of access to education and employment opportunities, lack of access to a sustainable, safe and clean environment, as well as deprivation of physical and mental well-being—key issues deemed as obstacles to sustainable development.[32] It can therefore be said that ASEAN's post-2015 health agenda, particularly cluster 1, mirrors that of WHO's global health agenda sees an increasing emphasis on the threats of NCDs.

Although approaches to NCD prevention through education in proper diets to reduce obesity and control pollution are important, these are deemed insufficient to keep up with the demographic changes. As such, significantly more investment in a robust and cost-effective health system is crucial to enable poorer nations to respond to the staggering rise in premature deaths and disability from NCDs.

9.5 Filling in the Gaps

While ASEAN's health agenda is indeed comprehensive, there remains concerns about the capacity of individual countries to deal with emerging health threats. One is the rising incidence of climate-related health threats and the other is the rising threat of AMR.

1) Climate-related Health Threats

In a recent United Nations Framework Convention on Climate Change (UN FCCC) report entitled, *Human Health and Adaptation: Understanding Climate Impacts on Health and Opportunities for Action*, health and climate change experts highlighted how climate change can exacerbate health problems that already pose a major burden to vulnerable populations— children and elderly, pregnant women, the socially marginalized (to include poorest of the poor, indigenous groups, refugees), and those with existing health conditions like HIV.[33] According to the report, the socioeconomic costs of health problems for these vulnerable groups are considerable. The report further noted that heatwaves can severely impact working conditions increasing the risk of cardiovascular, respiratory and renal diseases. Moreover, human displacement caused by climate and weather-related disasters are expected to increase significantly, which in turn results in higher socioeconomic costs and affects mental and physical health. With the visible impacts of climate change already felt in the region, this would make for more compelling reasons for ASEAN countries to reassess current health frameworks and put more effort in boosting capacity of health systems in line with climate adaptation and mitigation strategies done in other sectors. In fact, the WHO in 2014 had already identified strengthening public health services as one critical component in the building blocks of climate-resilient health systems.

This agenda is particularly challenging for most countries in the region that are still struggling with healthcare delivery, access and affordability, especially for the poorer and more vulnerable segments of the population. With these realities, it is hard to tell whether existing health systems are in fact ready and robust enough to withstand potential health fallout of the changing climate. It is interesting to note the absence of climate change in ASEAN's 4-clustered health agenda. While concerning, this is not really surprising given that climate change work puts a lot of emphasis on adaptation and mitigation, and often require modelling of future projections and scenarios. In this regard, within the context of being "climate-ready/prepared", more attention should therefore be given to the national health systems of ASEAN. When it comes to adaptive capacity of the health sector, the WHO has noted that "strengthening a well-known and well-tested public health and health service interventions such as public education, disease surveillance, disaster preparedness, vector control, food hygiene and inspection, nutritional supplementation, vaccines, primary and mental health care, and training"[34] will enable protection from the impact of climate change on health.

Being able to measure the performance of national health systems would be a good starting point. The 2005 International Health Regulations (IHR) has specified thirteen core competencies.[35] In the 2017 World Health Statistics Report,[36] ASEAN members generally reported optimistic measures of their average IHR core competency and health emergency preparedness between 2010 and 2016, as follows: Malaysia (100), Indonesia, Singapore and Vietnam (99), Thailand (98), Brunei Darussalam (92), the Philippines (87), Myanmar (84), Lao DPR (75) and Cambodia (55). On paper, the scores suggest that their respective health systems are relatively strong. Despite the scores, however, other studies point out that health systems in more countries in the region are still struggling with healthcare delivery, access and affordability, especially for the poorer and more vulnerable groups. It is therefore hard to accurately tell whether existing health systems are ready and robust enough to withstand potential health impact of the changing climate.

2) The Fight Against Anti-Microbial Resistance (AMR)

The importance of having in place robust health system in ASEAN countries becomes even more critical in the global fight against AMR.

Given the complexity of the health threat and the interconnectedness between animal health, human health and agriculture, being able to achieve a more holistic, collaborative intersectoral approach requires strong foundation of a country and the region's public health systems.

Following the United Nation's General Assembly (UNGA) meeting on AMR in September 2016, where all UN members unanimously committed to addressing AMR, ASEAN developed the "ASEAN Regional Strategy on Antimicrobial Resistance Communication and Advocacy" in October that year and was subsequently adopted in September 2017 at the 39th ASEAN Ministerial Meeting on Agriculture and Forestry.[37] The regional strategy highlighted the lack of awareness within the region, across governments, animal health specialists, producers and traders, on AMR. It also noted that "there has been no systematic studies undertaken in the Southeast Asian Region to understand antimicrobial use or extent of antimicrobial resistance".[38] Based on a report by the UK government, though, the death toll in Asia could increase to 5 million annually by 2050, making up half of the global estimate of 10 million annually and a US$100 trillion "cost of inaction".[39]

Grounded in a participatory approach, it set forth a vision of "An ASEAN community promoting and practicing responsible and prudent use of antimicrobials. Prudent use of antimicrobials and good farming practices contribute to slowing antimicrobial resistance in ASEAN."[40] Components include technical ("To design and implement evidence-based communication and advocacy activities"), awareness and education ("To raise awareness by fostering knowledge exchange and understanding of AMR among key stakeholders"), networking collaboration ("To strengthen cooperation and collaboration among AMS in promoting prudent use of antimicrobials") and resource mobilization ("To ensure a sustainable and efficient approach to AMR education, communication and advocacy"), with primary responsibility given to members of the ASEAN Communication Group on Livestock (ACGL) and the ASEAN National Focal Points on Veterinary Products (ANFPVP).[41] Over a two-year period after being adopted by the ASEAN Sectoral Working Group on Livestock, the strategy sought to align with the 38th ASEAN Ministers on Agriculture and Forestry (AMAF)'s call to action on AMR, to be implemented by each ASEAN member state according to its current cultural and political norms, and with openness to technical assistance from international partners. A logical framework is also to be developed for monitoring and evaluation (M and E) purposes.

By November 2017, the "ASEAN Leaders' Declaration on AMR: Combating AMR through One Health Approach" was adopted in Manila.[42] This called for ASEAN member states to formulate and execute national plans aligned with the one health approach. This Declaration also recognized prior efforts apart from the Global Action, including (1) the "Asia Pacific Bi-Regional Commitment on the 'Communiqué of Tokyo Meeting of Health Ministers on AMR in Asia" that called for an "Asia-Pacific One Health Initiative on AMR" (April 2016) among its precedents and (2) the ASEAN post-2015 Health Development Agenda, endorsed at the 12th ASEAN Health Ministers Meeting.[43]

An important aspect of the November 2017 ASEAN Leaders' on AMR Declaration is the recognition "that the scale of the AMR situation extends beyond public health with socio-economic and environmental impacts which threatens global health security and the achievement of the Sustainable Development Goals (SDGs)", and its demand for "urgent, concerted, multisectoral and multidisciplinary collaboration at the national, regional and global levels". This led to specific recommendations, pertinent among which involve formulating and executing national plans in line with the One Health approach, that includes:[44]

- comprehensive multisectoral responsibility and governance;
- inclusive mechanisms to actively engage the participation of relevant stakeholders;
- defined objectives and goals that are aligned with the overarching Global Action Plan;
- activities and strategies will be sustainably financed by governments and other stakeholders; and,
- effective monitoring and evaluation mechanisms.

Among the means for achieving these include: awareness and advocacy (echoing the October 2016 ASEAN Regional Strategy on Antimicrobial Resistance Communication and Advocacy) and training and education programmes. Towards "(ensuring) equitable, timely and sustainable access to safe, efficacious, affordable and quality antimicrobials, environmental management of antibiotic residues and impacts", it also declared commitments to strengthening regulatory systems, pharmaceutical and food supply chain management, health financing mechanisms, and agricultural value chain management.

On the healthcare side, the regional strategy also echoes the global objective of greater antimicrobial stewardship. It seeks to "(implement) antimicrobial stewardship programs and infection prevention, control and treatment measures at all levels of healthcare and the community"[45] to reduce disease burden, and in a related manner, moving towards requiring prescriptions before being able to access antibiotics. On veterinary practice, the Declaration also discouraged use of antibiotics for growth promotion purposes, in the absence of risk analysis.

An overarching recommendation, regardless of sector, was to have greater capacity for integrated surveillance and monitoring of AMR, the consumption and use of antimicrobials and drug residues, and to promote research. Equally important was the need to strengthen regulatory capacity, and this hinges on research on AMR's impacts. The responsibility for this was placed on the AHMM, with support from the Senior Officials Meeting on Health Development (SOMHD), as well as related subsidiary bodies and sectors "to develop and monitor the implementation of the ASEAN strategic plan to combat AMR".[46]

To what extent has ASEAN complied? Since the adoption of the 2016 Regional Strategy on Antimicrobial Resistance: Communication and Advocacy and based on self-assessment reporting, none of ASEAN countries had completed the rather complex process of having in place a multisectoral national AMR action plan, with funding sources identified, implemented and with monitoring capacity. Although four countries were seen as being ahead, in particular, Cambodia, Malaysia, the Philippines and Singapore, with multisectoral AMR action plans that meet the requirements of the Global Action Plan objectives, the rest of the ASEAN members lag far behind.

Since 2018, no further comprehensive updates by the WHO were available, apart from the September 2017 update report.[47] The said report highlighted efforts by three countries in fighting AMR. Vietnam was cited for its commitment to stop the use of antibiotics in animal feeds by 2018, and to ban its use for livestock altogether by 2020. The Philippines also drew praises for its launch of its One Health-based National Action Plan in November 2015. Thailand has also developed its national strategic plan in end-2015, endorsed by the government in August 2016 after consultation with "several hundred stakeholders".

In brief, from available reports, it appears that progress on AMR preparedness in ASEAN is uneven with member countries reporting progress in different areas. Some ASEAN members have not gone beyond organizing meetings on AMR awareness.[48] In Myanmar, for instance, signs of plans being put into action include a document from the Ministry of Health's website likewise showing that a Strengths, Weaknesses, Opportunities, and Threats (SWOT) analysis has been conducted, which notes the challenge of insufficient public awareness, segment surveillance systems, and insufficient resources for implementation. The study also shows national studies being done to develop profiles of which antimicrobial agents are susceptible to AMR.[49] In brief, one can observe that regional response has been fragmented with ASEAN countries implementing it at their own pace and with the less developed countries lagging far behind. Clearly more work has to be done to get the region to work collectively in order to scale up preparedness in dealing with complex health risks. To a large extent, the pace at which the region is moving towards addressing the AMR challenge reflects either lack of prioritization at country-level, and/or that the complexity of the issue requires new modes of national and regional collaboration which are relatively new to ASEAN practices.

9.6 Conclusion

ASEAN has come a long way in developing its regional mechanisms to deal with health issues. Through its various regional health frameworks, ASEAN has been relatively successful in dealing with several cases of infectious diseases like H5N1 and SARS. Shifting from a largely security-focused approach to regional health governance to one that includes development and human security concerns of equity, protection and justice reflects ASEAN's recognition that regional health security is not only about preventing outbreaks and spread of infectious diseases but also about ensuring peoples' well-being and safety.

Moving forward, the immediate tasks to improve regional health governance is to be more proactive in mainstreaming climate change related issues in the agenda of health cooperation among ASEAN members. This requires greater efforts both at the national and regional levels to strengthen public health systems. This means that at the ASEAN level, there should be more time and resources invested in helping build the capacity of public health systems of ASEAN countries that are in need of support. One could argue, however, that the tasks of building capacity and improving health systems should not only be limited to states. Given stretched resources and the multiple demands on state action, ASEAN must be able to tap on the resources of non-state actors and the private sector in order to provide quality health care and inclusive access to health provision.

Moreover, the global health security agenda on prevention, detection and ability to respond further necessitates stronger health systems at the national level to address the gaps in regional pandemic preparedness and other health emergencies. Building on the existing frameworks of cooperation, this is now an opportune time for ASEAN to re-examine current regional modalities in information and data sharing arrangements with the aim of further improving disease surveillance and regional response. But in order to take these initiatives forward, sustained funding for building more capacity in scientific and technical expertise, laboratories and diagnostics, and training of more qualified healthcare workforce among others need to be addressed. All this means that more effort to advance targeted assistance in national capacity building must continue to further raise regional capacity to meet current and future regional health challenges.

NOTES

1. The Commission on Human Security defines human security as "[the protection of] the vital core of all human lives in ways that enhance human freedoms and human fulfilment". See Commission on Human Security, *Human Security Now: Protecting and Empowering People* (New York: Commission on Human Security, 2003), http://reliefweb.int/sites/reliefweb.int/files/resources/91BAEEDBA50C6907C1256D19006A9353-chs-security-may03.pdf.
2. United Nations, UN Millennium Development Goals, http://www.un.org/millenniumgoals/.
3. United Nations, Sustainable Development Goals, https://sustainabledevelopment.un.org/?menu=1300.
4. For more comprehensive discussion, see Mely Caballero-Anthony, "Non-Traditional Security and Infectious Diseases in ASEAN: Going Beyond the Rhetoric of Securitization to Deeper Institutionalisation", *The Pacific Review* 12, no. 4 (2008): 509–27.

5. Jai P. Narain and R. Bhatia, "The Challenge of Communicable Diseases in the WHO South-East Asia Region", *Bulletin of the World Health Organization* 88, no. 3 (2010): 162.

6. World Health Organization (WHO), *Tuberculosis Control in the South-East Asia Region: Annual Report 2016* (New Delhi: WHO, 2016), https://apps.who.int/iris/handle/10665/205286.

7. WHO, *Progress Report on HIV in the WHO South-East Asia Region 2016* (New Delhi: WHO, 2016), http://apps.searo.who.int/PDS_DOCS/B5282.pdf.

8. WHO, "Summary of Probable SARS Cases with Onset of Illness from 1 November 2002 to 31 July 2003", 31 December 2003, http://www.who.int/csr/sars/country/table2004_04_21/en/.

9. WHO, "Middle East Respiratory Syndrome Coronavirus (MERS-CoV) – Republic of Korea", 7 July 2015, http://www.who.int/csr/don/07-july-2015-mers-korea/en/.

10. For more analyses, see Mely Caballero-Anthony, "SARS in Asia: Crisis, Vulnerabilities and Regional Responses", *Asian Survey* 45, no. 3 (2005): 475–95.

11. "Summary of Probable SARS Cases".

12. Caballero-Anthony, "SARS in Asia", p. 482.

13. Ibid.; Melissa Curley and Nicholas Thomas, "Human Security and Public Health in Southeast Asia: The SARS Outbreak", *Australian Journal of International Affairs* 58, no. 1 (2004): 23.

14. Caballero-Anthony, "SARS in Asia".

15. David F. Bloom, Daniel Cadarette, and JP Sevilla, "Epidemics and Economics: New and Resurgent Infectious Diseases Can Have Far-reaching Economic Repercussions", *Finance & Development* 55, no. 2 (2018), https://www.imf.org/external/pubs/ft/fandd/2018/06/economic-risks-and-impacts-of-epidemics/bloom.htm.

16. World Bank Group, "The Short-Term Economic Costs of Zika in Latin America and the Caribbean", 18 February 2016, http://pubdocs.worldbank.org/en/410321455758564708/The-short-term-economic-costs-of-Zika-in-LCR-final-doc-autores-feb-18.pdf (accessed 1 February 2019).

17. Yanzong Huang, "Pursuing Health as Foreign Policy: The Case of China", *Indiana Journal of Global Legal Studies* 17, no. 1 (2010): 140–44.

18. This has also been noted by Fidler when he identified infectious diseases, HIV/AIDS, SARS, avian influenza and H1N1 as examples of health cooperation issues in APEC and ASEAN. See David Fidler, "Asia and Global Health Governance: Power, Principles and Practice", in *Asia's Role in Governing Global Health*, edited by Kelley Lee, Tikki Pang, and Yelling Tan (London: Routledge, 2013), p. 208.

19. ASEAN, "ASEAN Post-2015 Health Development Agenda", undated, http://asean.org/storage/2017/02/APHDA-In-a-Nutshell.pdf.

20. Yanzhong Huang, "How to Reform the Ailing World Health Organization", Council on Foreign Relations, 3 May 2016, https://www.cfr.org/expert-brief/how-reform-ailing-world-health-organization.

21. Oren Ahoobim, Daniel Altman, and Vicky Hausman, "The Universal Health Coverage Moment", in *The New Global Health Agenda: Universal Health Coverage*, edited by Oren Ahoobim, Daniel Altman, Laurie Garrett, Vicky Hausman, and Yanzhong Huang (New York: Council on Foreign Relations, 2012), p. 12.

22. Ibid.

23. Thomas J. Bollyky, "The Changing Demographics of Global Health", Council on Foreign Relations, 7 November 2017, https://www.cfr.org/article/changing-demographics-global-health.

24. Luke Nelson Allen, "Financing National Non-Communicable Disease Responses", *Global Health Action* 10, no. 1 (2017).

25. WHO, "Proposed Programme Budget 2018-2019", Seventieth World Health Assembly, 10 April 2017, p. 3, http://apps.who.int/gb/ebwha/pdf_files/WHA70/A70_7-en.pdf (accessed 4 October 2018).

26. F.I. Mustapha et al., "Addressing Non-Communicable Diseases in Malaysia: An Integrative Process of Systems and Community", *BMC Public Health* 14, Suppl 2: S4 (2014).

27. Ibid.

28. Felicia Choo, "Parliament: War Against Diabetes Gets Boost from $15m Grant for Low-Sugar Foods, More Leeway to use Medisave", *Straits Times*, 7 March 2018, http://www.straitstimes.com/politics/parliament-war-against-diabetes-gets-boost-from-15m-grant-for-low-sugar-foods-more-leeway.

29. Felicia Choo, "Community Scheme to Tackle Diabetes to be Expanded to Western Part of Singapore: Gan Kim Yong", *Straits Times*, 20 January 2018, http://www.straitstimes.com/singapore/community-scheme-to-tackle-diabetes-to-be-expanded-to-western-part-of-singapore-gan-kim.

30. P.K.P. Ismail and David Koh, "Role of Occupational Health in Managing Non-Communicable Diseases in Brunei Darussalam", *Global Health Action* 7, no. 1 (2014).

31. ASEAN, "ASEAN Renews Commitment for a Healthier ASEAN", 6 September 2017, https://asean.org/asean-renews-commitment-healthier-asean.

32. ASEAN, "ASEAN Ministers Discuss Ways to Instil a Culture of Prevention Among Citizens", 21 March 2018, http://asean.org/asean-ministers-discuss-ways-to-instil-a-culture-of-prevention-among-citizens/.

33. United Nations Framework Convention on Climate Change (UN FCCC), "Human Health and Adaptation: Understanding Climate Impacts on Health and Opportunities for Action", Synthesis Paper by the Secretariat for the Forty-Sixth Session of the Subsidiary Body for Scientific and Technological

Advice, Bonn, 8–18 May 2017, https://unfccc.int/resource/docs/2017/sbsta/eng/02.pdf.

34. WHO, "Protecting Health from Climate Change: 10 Actions for National and Local Policy-Makers", undated, http://www.who.int/globalchange/publications/10_actions_Policy_Makers_en.pdf (accessed 4 October 2018).

35. Thirteen core capacities defined by the WHO International Health Regulations (IHR) include: (1) National legislation, policy and financing; (2) Coordination and national focal point communications; (3) Surveillance; (4) Response; (5) Preparedness; (6) Risk communication; (7) Human resources; (8) Laboratory; (9) Points of entry; (10) Zoonotic events; (11) Food safety; (12) Chemical events; and (13) Radionuclear emergencies. Countries self-assess their implementation and report their scores.

36. World Health Organization, *World Health Statistics 2017: Monitoring Health for the Substainable Development Goals* (Geneva: World Health Organization, 2017), http://apps.who.int/iris/bitstream/handle/10665/255336/9789241565486-eng.pdf;jsessionid=4E24A6C5BE57F634CC1EA350BBCC8BCD?sequence=1.

37. ASEAN and FAO, "ASEAN Regional Strategy on Antimicrobial Resistance Communication and Advocacy", adopted at the 39th ASEAN Ministerial Meeting on Agriculture and Forestry, 28 September 2017, http://asean.org/storage/2012/05/15.-ASEAN-Regional-AMR-Communication-and-Strategy.pdf (accessed 24 May 2018).

38. Ibid.

39. Jim O'Neill, "Tackling Drug-Resistant Infections Globally: Final Report and Recommendations", *The Review on Antimicrobial Resistance*, May 2016, https://amr-review.org/sites/default/files/160525_Final%20paper_with%20cover.pdf (accessed 24 May 2018).

40. ASEAN and FAO, "ASEAN Regional Strategy".

41. Ibid.

42. "ASEAN Leaders' Declaration on Antimicrobial Resistance (AMR): Combating AMR through One Health Approach", adopted in Manila, the Philippines, 13 November 2017, http://asean.org/storage/2017/11/3.-ADOPTION_2017_ALD-on-AMR_Endorsed-13th-AHMM.pdf (accessed 24 May 2018).

43. Ibid.

44. Ibid.

45. Ibid.

46. Ibid.

47. Wellcome, *Sustaining Global Action on Antimicrobial Resistance* (Washington, D.C.: United Nations Foundation, 2017), https://wellcome.ac.uk/sites/default/files/sustaining-global-action-on-antimicrobial-resistance.pdf (accessed 23 May 2018).

48. FAO, "Cambodia is First to Organize a National High Level Tripartite Meeting on Multi-Sectoral Action Plan to Combat Antimicrobial Resistance

(AMR)", 22 December 2017, http://www.fao.org/cambodia/news/detail-events/en/c/1073997/ (accessed 24 May 2018).

49. Htay Htay Tin, "First National Multisectoral Steering Committee Meeting Combating AMR Myanmar", National Health Laboratory, Ministry of Health, Myanmar, 18 April 2018, https://tinyurl.com/y9qfuuto (accessed 24 May 2018).

REFERENCES

Ahoobim, Oren, Daniel Altman, Laurie Garrett, Vicky Hausman, and Yanzhong Huang. 2012. *The New Global Health Agenda: Universal Health Coverage*. New York: Council on Foreign Relations. http://apps.who.int/medicinedocs/documents/s19221en/s19221en.pdf.

Allen, Luke Nelson. 2017. "Financing National Non-Communicable Disease Responses". *Global Health Action* 10, no. 1.

Amaya, Ana B., Vincent Rollett, and Stephen Kingah. 2015. "What's in a Word? The Framing of Health at the Regional Level: ASEAN, EU, SADC and UNASUR". *Global Social Policy* 115, no. 3: 229–60.

ASEAN. Undated. "ASEAN Post-2015 Health Development Agenda". http://asean.org/storage/2017/02/APHDA-In-a-Nutshell.pdf.

———. 2009. *Community Blueprint*. Jakarta: ASEAN Secretariat.

———. 2016. *ASEAN Political-Security Blueprint 2025*. Jakarta: ASEAN Secretariat. https://www.asean.org/storage/2012/05/ASEAN-APSC-Blueprint-2025.pdf.

———. 2017. "ASEAN Renews Commitment for a Healthier ASEAN", 6 September 2017. https://asean.org/asean-renews-commitment-healthier-asean/.

———. 2018. "ASEAN Ministers Discuss Ways to Instil a Culture of Prevention among Citizens", 21 March 2018. http://asean.org/asean-ministers-discuss-ways-to-instil-a-culture-of-prevention-among-citizens/.

ASEAN and FAO. 2017. "ASEAN Regional Strategy on Antimicrobial Resistance Communication and Advocacy". Adopted at the 39th ASEAN Ministerial Meeting on Agriculture and Forestry, 28 September 2017. http://asean.org/storage/2012/05/15.-ASEAN-Regional-AMR-Communication-and-Strategy.pdf (accessed 24 May 2018).

"ASEAN Leaders' Declaration on Antimicrobial Resistance (AMR): Combating AMR through One Health Approach". Adopted in Manila, the Philippines, 13 November 2017. https://asean.org/wp-content/uploads/2017/11/3.-ADOPTION_2017_ALD-on-AMR_Endorsed-13th-AHMM.pdf (accessed 24 May 2018).

Bloom, David F., Daniel Cadarette, and JP Sevilla. 2018. "Epidemics and Economics: New and Resurgent Infectious Diseases Can Have Far-reaching

Economic Repercussions". *Finance & Development* 55, no. 2. https://www.imf.org/external/pubs/ft/fandd/2018/06/economic-risks-and-impacts-of-epidemics/bloom.htm.

Bollyky, Thomas J. and Amanda Shendruk. 2017. "The Changing Demographics of Global Health". Council on Foreign Relations, 7 November 2017. https://www.cfr.org/article/changing-demographics-global-health.

Caballero-Anthony, Mely. 2005. "SARS in Asia: Crisis, Vulnerabilities and Regional Responses". *Asian Survey* 45, no. 3: 475–95.

———. 2008. "Non-Traditional Security and Infectious Diseases in ASEAN: Going Beyond the Rhetoric of Securitization to Deeper Institutionalisation". *The Pacific Review* 12, no. 4: 509–27.

Center for Strategic & International Studies. 2016. "Global Security Forum 2016: The Global Health Security Agenda: Its First Years and the Way Forward", 1 December 2016. https://www.csis.org/analysis/global-security-forum-2016-global-health-security-agenda-its-first-years-and-way-forward.

Choo, Felicia. 2018. "Community Scheme to Tackle Diabetes to be Expanded to Western Part of Singapore: Gan Kim Yong". *Straits Times*, 20 January 2018. http://www.straitstimes.com/singapore/community-scheme-to-tackle-diabetes-to-be-expanded-to-western-part-of-singapore-gan-kim.

———. 2018. "Parliament: War Against Diabetes Gets Boost from $15m Grant for Low-sugar Foods, More Leeway to Use Medisave". *Straits Times*, 7 March 2018. http://www.straitstimes.com/politics/parliament-war-against-diabetes-gets-boost-from-15m-grant-for-low-sugar-foods-more-leeway.

Commission on Human Security. 2003. *Human Security Now: Protecting and Empowering People*. New York: Commission on Human Security. http://reliefweb.int/sites/reliefweb.int/files/resources/91BAEEDBA50C6907C1256D19006A9353-chs-security-may03.pdf.

Curley, Melissa and Nicholas Thomas. 2004. "Human Security and Public Health in Southeast Asia: The SARS Outbreak". *Australian Journal of International Affairs* 58, no. 1: 17–32.

Davies, Sara, Adam Kamradt-Scott, and Simon Rushton. 2015. *Disease Diplomacy: International Norms and Global Health Security*. Baltimore: Johns Hopkins University Press.

Emont, Jon. 2016. "A Country of a Quarter-billion People is Trying to Provide Health Care for All". *Washington Post*, 18 May 2016. https://www.washingtonpost.com/world/asia_pacific/a-country-of-a-quarter-billion-people-seeks-to-provide-free-health-care-for-all/2016/05/18/f36bf7b2-1b93-11e6-82c2-a7dcb313287d_story.html?utm_term=.12bc0437a462.

Fidler, David P. 2013. "Asia and Global Health Governance: Power, Principles and Practice". In *Asia's Role in Governing Global Health*, edited by Kelley Lee, Tikki Pang, and Yelling Tan. London: Routledge, pp. 198–214.

Finnemore, Martha and Kathryn Sikkink. 1998. "International Norm Dynamics and Political Change". *International Organization* 52, no. 4: 887–917.

Food and Agricultural Organization (FAO). 2017. "Cambodia is First to Organize a National High Level Tripartite Meeting on Multi-Sectoral Action Plan to Combat Antimicrobial Resistance (AMR)", 22 December 2017. http://www.fao.org/cambodia/news/detail-events/en/c/1073997/ (accessed 24 May 2018).

Fukuda-Parr, Sakiko and David Hulme. 2009. *International Norms Dynamics and 'the End of Poverty', Understanding the Millennium Development Goals (MDGs)*. Manchester: Brooks World Poverty Institute, The University of Manchester.

Garrett, Laurie. 2012. "Preface". In *The New Global Health Agenda: Universal Health Coverage*, edited by Oren Ahoobim, Daniel Altman, Laurie Garrett, Vicky Hausman, and Yanzhong Huang. New York: Council on Foreign Relations. http://apps.who.int/medicinedocs/documents/s19221en/s19221en.pdf.

Huang, Yanzong. 2010. "Pursuing Health as Foreign Policy: The Case of China". *Indiana Journal of Global Legal Studies* 17, no. 1: 140–44.

———. 2016. "How to Reform the Ailing World Health Organization". Council on Foreign Relations, 3 May 2016. https://www.cfr.org/expert-brief/how-reform-ailing-world-health-organization.

Ismail, P.K.P. and David Koh. 2014. "Role of Occupational Health in Managing Non-Communicable Diseases in Brunei Darussalam". *Global Health Action* 7, no. 1.

Labonte, Ronald and Michelle Gagnon. 2010. "Framing Health and Foreign Policy: Lessons for Global Health Diplomacy". *Globalisation and Health* 6, no. 14. https://globalizationandhealth.biomedcentral.com/articles/10.1186/1744-8603-6-14.

Lamy, Marie and Phua Kai Hong. 2012. "Regional Health Governance: A Comparative Perspective on EU and ASEAN". EU Centre Policy Brief No. 4. http://www.eucentre.sg/wp-content/uploads/2013/06/PB04.Issue4-Jun12.pdf.

McInnes, Colin and Kelley Lee. 2012. *Global Health and International Relations*. Cambridge, UK: Polity.

Ministry of Health, Agri-Food and Veterinary Authority of Singapore, The National Environment Agency, and Public Utilities Board. 2017. "National Strategic Action Plan on Antimicrobial Resistance (AMR)", 1 November 2017. https://www.moh.gov.sg/docs/librariesprovider5/resources-statistics/reports/sg-national-strategic-action-plan-on-amr.pdf (accessed 24 May 2018).

Ministry of Health and Ministry of Agriculture & Agro-Based Industry, Malaysia. 2017. *Malaysian Action Plan on Antimicrobial Resistance (MyAP-AMR) 2017–2021*. http://www.moh.gov.my/moh/resources/Penerbitan/Garis%20Panduan/Garis%20panduan%20Umum%20(Awam)/National_Action_Plan_-_FINAL_29_june.pdf (accessed 24 May 2018).

Mustapha, F., Omar Z., Mihat O., Md Noh K., Hassan N., Abu Bakar R., Abd Manan A., Ismail F., Jabbar N., Muhamad Y., Rahman LA, Majid FA, Shahrir S., Ahmad E., Davey T., and Allotey P. 2014. "Addressing Non-Communicable Diseases in Malaysia: An Integrative Process of Systems and Community". *BMC Public Health* 14, Suppl 2: S4.

Narain, Jai P. and R. Bhatia. 2010. "The Challenge of Communicable Diseases in the WHO South-East Asia Region". *Bulletin of the World Health Organization* 88, no. 3: 162.

O'Neill, Jim. 2016. "Tackling Drug-Resistant Infections Globally: Final Report and Recommendations". *The Review on Antimicrobial Resistance*. https://amr-review.org/sites/default/files/160525_Final%20paper_with%20cover.pdf.

Rushton, Simon. 2010. "Framing Aids: Securitization, Development-ization, Rights-ization". *Global Health Governance* 4, no. 1: 1–17.

Tin, Htay Htay. 2018. "First National Multisectoral Steering Committee Meeting Combating AMR Myanmar". National Health Laboratory, Ministry of Health, Myanmar, 18 April 2018. https://tinyurl.com/y9qfuuto (accessed 24 May 2018).

United Nations. Sustainable Development Goals. https://sustainabledevelopment.un.org/?menu=1300.

———. UN Millennium Development Goals. http://www.un.org/millenniumgoals/.

United Nations Framework Convention on Climate Change (UN FCCC). 2017. "Human Health and Adaptation: Understanding Climate Impacts on Health and Opportunities for Action". Synthesis Paper by the Secretariat for the Forty-Sixth Session of the Subsidiary Body for Scientific and Technological Advice, Bonn, 8–18 May 2017. https://unfccc.int/resource/docs/2017/sbsta/eng/02.pdf.

Wellcome. *Sustaining Global Action on Antimicrobial Resistance*. Washington, D.C.: United Nations Foundation, 2017. https://wellcome.ac.uk/sites/default/files/sustaining-global-action-on-antimicrobial-resistance.pdf (accessed 23 May 2018).

World Bank Group. 2016. "The Short-Term Economic Costs of Zika in Latin America and the Caribbean", 18 February 2016. http://pubdocs.worldbank.org/en/410321455758564708/The-short-term-economic-costs-of-Zika-in-LCR-final-doc-autores-feb-18.pdf (accessed 1 February 2019).

World Health Organization (WHO). Undated. "Protecting Health from Climate Change: 10 Actions for National and Local Policy-makers". http://www.who.int/globalchange/publications/10_actions_Policy_Makers_en.pdf (accessed 4 October 2018).

———. 2003. "Summary of Probable SARS Cases with Onset of Illness from 1 November 2002 to 31 July 2003", 31 December 2003. http://www.who.int/csr/sars/country/table2004_04_21/en/.

————. 2015. "Middle East Respiratory Syndrome Coronavirus (MERS-CoV) – Republic of Korea", 7 July 2015. http://www.who.int/csr/don/07-july-2015-mers-korea/en/.

————. 2016. *Progress Report on HIV in the WHO South-East Asia Region 2016.* New Delhi, India: WHO. http://apps.searo.who.int/PDS_DOCS/B5282.pdf.

————. 2016. *Tuberculosis Control in the South-East Asia Region: Annual Report 2016.* New Delhi, India: WHO. https://apps.who.int/iris/handle/10665/205286.

————. 2017. "Proposed Programme Budget 2018-2019". Seventieth World Health Assembly, 10 April 2017. http://apps.who.int/gb/ebwha/pdf_files/WHA70/A70_7-en.pdf (accessed 4 October 2018).

————. 2017. *World Health Statistics 2017: Monitoring Health for the Sustainable Development Goals.* Geneva: WHO. http://apps.who.int/iris/bitstream/handle/10665/255336/9789241565486-eng.pdf;jsessionid=4E24A6C5BE57F634CC1EA350BBCC8BCD?sequence=1.

WHO, FAO and OIE. Undated. "Global Database for AMRCSAT Country Self-Assessment Test". https://extranet.who.int/sree/Reports?op=vs&path=%2FWHO_HQ_Reports/G45/PROD/EXT/amrcsat_AnswersForPublic (accessed 24 May 2018).

ANNEXES

ASEAN Agreement on Disaster Management and Emergency Response Vientiane, 26 July 2005

The Parties to this Agreement,

REAFFIRMING their parties commitment to the aims and purposes of the Association of Southeast Asian Nations (ASEAN) as set forth in the Bangkok Declaration of 8 August 1967, in particular, to promote regional co-operation in Southeast Asia in the spirit of equality and partnership and thereby contribute towards peace, progress and prosperity in the region;

REAFFIRMING ALSO the objectives and principles of the Declaration of ASEAN Concord I of 24 February 1976, inter alia, declaring that within their capabilities Member Countries shall extend assistance for relief of Member Countries in distress, and the Declaration of ASEAN Concord II of 7 October 2003 where ASEAN shall, through the ASEAN Socio-Cultural Community, intensify co-operation in addressing problems associated with, inter alia, disaster management in the region to enable individual members to fully realise their development potentials to enhance the mutual ASEAN spirit;

REAFFIRMING ALSO the provisions of the Vientiane Action Programme 2004-2010 to pursue the comprehensive integration of ASEAN towards the realisation of an open, dynamic and resilient ASEAN Community by 2020 as envisioned in the Declaration of ASEAN Concord II through the action plans of the ASEAN Security Community (ASC), the ASEAN Socio-Cultural Community (ASCC) and the Recommendations of the High-Level Task Force on ASEAN Economic Integration;

RECALLING the Declaration on Action to Strengthen Emergency Relief, Rehabilitation, Reconstruction and Prevention in the Aftermath of the Earthquake and Tsunami Disaster of 26 December 2004, adopted at the Special ASEAN Leaders' Meeting on the Aftermath of Earthquake and Tsunami held in Jakarta on 6 January 2005;

RECALLING ALSO the ASEAN Declaration on Mutual Assistance on Natural Disasters of 26 June 1976, which calls on Member Countries to, inter alia, co-operate in the improvement of disaster management capacities, and in case of calamities, to extend assistance as may be needed upon the request from an affected Member Country;

RECALLING ALSO the ASEAN Agreement on Transboundary Haze Pollution of 10 June 2002, which provides the co-operative framework to prevent, monitor, mitigate and respond to trans-boundary haze pollution in the overall context of sustainable development;

RECALLING ALSO the ASEAN Agreement for the Facilitation of Search for Aircrafts in Distress and Rescue of Survivors of Aircraft Accidents of 14 April 1972 and the ASEAN Agreement for the Facilitation of Search of Ships in Distress and Rescue of Survivors of Ship Accidents of 15 May 1975, which call on ASEAN Member Countries to, inter alia, provide measures of assistance to aircrafts and ships in distress in their territories and to ensure entry and co-ordination of qualified personnel required for search and rescue operations;

RECALLING ALSO the Agreement on the ASEAN Food Security Reserve of 4 October 1979, which calls for effective and concerted effort to establish a food security reserve among ASEAN Member Countries to strengthen national and regional resilience and solidarity by, inter alia, establishing the ASEAN Emergency Rice Reserve for the purpose of meeting emergency requirements;

RECALLING ALSO United Nations General Assembly Resolution 59/279 of 19 January 2005 to strengthen emergency relief, rehabilitation, reconstruction and prevention in the aftermath of the Indian Ocean tsunami disaster; United Nations General Assembly Resolution 46/182 of 19 December 1991 to adopt an integrated approach for disaster management in all its aspects and to initiate a process towards a global culture of prevention; United Nations General Assembly Resolution 57/578 of 10 December 2002, which, inter alia, encourages the strengthening of co-operation among States at the regional and sub-regional levels in the field of disaster preparedness and response with particular respect to capacity-building at all levels;

RECALLING ALSO the Hyogo Declaration and the Hyogo Framework for Action set out by the World Conference on Disaster Reduction in January 2005, which, among others, stress the need to strengthen and when necessary develop co-ordinated regional approaches, and create or upgrade regional policies, operational mechanisms, plans and communication systems to prepare for and ensure rapid and effective disaster response in situations that exceed national coping capacities;

DETERMINED to give effect to the ASEAN Regional Programme on Disaster Management 2004 – 2010, which calls for the implementation of various project proposals and priority project proposals including the establishment of an ASEAN Response Action Plan;

CONCERNED by the increasing frequency and scale of disasters in the ASEAN region and their damaging impacts both short-term and long-term;

CONVINCED that an essential means to achieve such collective action is the conclusion and effective implementation of this Agreement;

Have agreed as follows:

PART I.
GENERAL PROVISIONS

Article 1
Use of Terms

For the purposes of this Agreement:

1. "Assisting Entity" means a State, international organisation, and any other entity or person that offers and/or renders assistance to a Receiving Party or a Requesting Party in the event of a disaster emergency.

2. "Competent Authorities" means one or more entities designated and authorised by each Party to act on its behalf in the implementation of this Agreement.

3. "Disaster" means a serious disruption of the functioning of a community or a society causing widespread human, material, economic or environmental losses.

4. "Disaster management" means the range of activities, prior to, during and after the disasters, designed to maintain control over disasters and to provide a framework for helping at-risk persons and/or communities to avoid, minimise or recover from the impact of the disasters.

5. "Disaster risk" means the probability of harmful consequences, or expected losses in terms of deaths, injuries, property, livelihoods, economic activity or damage to the environment resulting from interactions between natural or human-induced hazards and vulnerable conditions.

6. "Disaster risk reduction" means a conceptual framework of elements considered with the possibilities to minimise vulnerabilities and disaster risks throughout a society, to avoid through prevention or to limit through mitigation and preparedness the adverse impacts of hazards, within the broad context of sustainable development.

7. "Disaster emergency" means a situation where a Party declares that it is unable to cope with a disaster.

8. "National Focal Point" means an entity designated and authorised by each Party to receive and transmit information pursuant to the provisions of this Agreement.

9. "Hazard" means a potentially damaging physical event, phenomenon and/or human activity, which may cause the loss of life or injury, property damage, social and economic disruption or environmental degradation.

10. "Member State" means a Member Country of the Association of Southeast Asian Nations.

11. "Party" means a Member State that has consented to be bound by this Agreement and for which the Agreement is in force.

12. "Receiving Party" means a Party that accepts assistance offered by an Assisting Entity or Entities in the event of a disaster emergency.

13. "Requesting Party" means a Party that requests from another Party or Parties assistance in the event of a disaster emergency.

Article 2
Objective

The objective of this Agreement is to provide effective mechanisms to achieve substantial reduction of disaster losses in lives and in the social, economic and environmental assets of the Parties, and to jointly respond to disaster emergencies through concerted national efforts and intensified regional and international co-operation. This should be pursued in the overall context of sustainable development and in accordance with the provisions of this Agreement.

Article 3
Principles

The Parties shall be guided by the following principles in the implementation of this Agreement:

1.   The sovereignty, territorial integrity and national unity of the Parties shall be respected, in accordance with the Charter of the United Nations and the Treaty of Amity and Cooperation in Southeast Asia, in the implementation of this Agreement. In this context, each affected Party shall have the primary responsibility to respond to disasters occurring within its territory and external assistance or offers of assistance shall only be provided upon the request or with the consent of the affected Party.

2.   The Requesting or Receiving Party shall exercise the overall direction, control, co-ordination and supervision of the assistance within its territory.

3.   The Parties shall, in the spirit of solidarity and partnership and in accordance with their respective needs, capabilities and situations, strengthen co-operation and co-ordination to achieve the objectives of this Agreement.

4.   The Parties shall give priority to prevention and mitigation, and thus shall take precautionary measures to prevent, monitor and mitigate disasters.

5.   The Parties shall, to the extent possible, mainstream disaster risk reduction efforts into sustainable development policies, planning and programming at all levels.

6.   The Parties, in addressing disaster risks, shall involve, as appropriate, all stakeholders including local communities, non-governmental organisations and private enterprises, utilising, among others, community-based disaster preparedness and early response approaches.

Article 4
General Obligations

In pursuing the objective of this Agreement, the Parties shall:

a.   co-operate in developing and implementing measures to reduce disaster losses including identification of disaster risk, development of monitoring, assessment and early warning systems, standby arrangements for disaster relief and emergency response, exchange of information and technology, and the provision of mutual assistance;

b.   immediately respond to a disaster occurring within their territory. When the said disaster is likely to cause possible impacts on other Member States, respond promptly to a request for relevant information sought by a Member State or States that are or may be affected by such disasters, with a view to minimising the consequences;

c.   promptly respond to a request for assistance from an affected Party; and

d.   take legislative, administrative and other measures as necessary to implement their obligations under this Agreement.

PART II.
DISASTER RISK IDENTIFICATION, ASSESSMENT AND MONITORING

Article 5
Risk Identification and Monitoring

1.   Each Party shall take appropriate measures to identify disaster risks in its respective territories covering, among others, the following aspects:

  a. natural and human-induced hazards;

  b. risk assessment;

  c. monitoring of vulnerabilities; and

  d. disaster management capacities.

2.   The Parties shall assign risk levels to each identified hazard according to agreed criteria.

3.   Each Party shall ensure that its National Focal Point, at agreed regular intervals, communicates the above information to the ASEAN Co-ordinating Centre for Humanitarian Assistance on disaster management, hereinafter referred to as "the AHA Centre", established in accordance with Article 20 of this Agreement.

4.   The AHA Centre shall receive and consolidate data as analysed by and recommendations on risk level from the National Focal Points. On the basis of such information, the AHA Centre shall disseminate to each Party, through its National Focal Point, the analysed data and risk level arising from the identified hazards. The AHA Centre may also, where appropriate, conduct analysis on possible regional-level implications.

PART III.
DISASTER PREVENTION AND MITIGATION

Article 6
Prevention and Mitigation

1.   The Parties shall, jointly or individually, develop strategies to identify, prevent and reduce risks arising from hazards.

2.   Each Party shall undertake measures to reduce losses from disasters which include:

  a. developing and implementing legislative and other regulatory measures, as well as policies, plans, programmes and strategies;

  b. strengthening local and national disaster management capability and co-ordination;

  c. promoting public awareness and education and strengthening community participation; and

  d. promoting and utilising indigenous knowledge and practices.

3.   The Parties shall co-operate in developing and implementing regional disaster prevention and mitigation programmes to complement national-level efforts.

PART IV.
DISASTER PREPAREDNESS

Article 7
Disaster Early Warning

1.   The Parties shall, as appropriate, establish, maintain and periodically review national disaster early warning arrangements including:

a. regular disaster risk assessment;

b. early warning information systems;

c. communication network for timely delivery of information; and

d. public awareness and preparedness to act upon the early warning information.

2. The Parties shall co-operate, as appropriate, to monitor hazards which have trans-boundary effects, to exchange information and to provide early warning information through appropriate arrangements.

Article 8
Preparedness

1. The Parties shall, jointly or individually, develop strategies and contingency/response plans to reduce losses from disasters.

2. The Parties shall, as appropriate, prepare Standard Operating Procedures for regional co-operation and national action required under this Agreement including the following:

a. regional standby arrangements for disaster relief and emergency response;

b. utilisation of military and civilian personnel, transportation and communication equipment, facilities, goods and services and to facilitate their trans-boundary movement; and

c. co-ordination of joint disaster relief and emergency response operations.

3. The Parties shall, jointly or individually enhance their national capacities, as appropriate, inter alia, to:

a. facilitate mobilisation of national resources to support such regional standby arrangements for disaster relief and emergency response;

b. co-ordinate with the ASEAN Food Security Reserve Board to facilitate release of rice from the ASEAN Emergency Rice Reserve; and

c. conduct training and exercises to attain and maintain the relevance and applicability of such Standard Operating Procedures.

4. Each Party shall regularly inform the AHA Centre of its available resources for the regional standby arrangements for disaster relief and emergency response.

5. The AHA Centre shall facilitate the establishment, maintenance and periodical review of regional standby arrangements for disaster relief and emergency response.

6. The AHA Centre shall facilitate periodic review of regional standard operating procedures.

Article 9
ASEAN Standby Arrangements for Disaster Relief and Emergency Response

1. On a voluntary basis, each Party shall earmark assets and capacities, which may be available for the regional standby arrangements for disaster relief and emergency response, such as:

a. emergency response/search and rescue directory;

b. military and civilian assets;

c. emergency stockpiles of disaster relief items; and

d. disaster management expertise and technologies.

2.   Such earmarked assets and capacities shall be communicated to each Party as well as the AHA Centre and updated as necessary by the Party concerned.

3.   The AHA Centre shall consolidate, update and disseminate the data on such earmarked assets and capacities, and communicate with the Parties for their utilisation.

4.   To facilitate the utilisation of assets provided for in paragraph 1, each Party shall designate a network of pre-designated areas as entry points for supplies and expertise from Assisting Entities.

PART V.
EMERGENCY RESPONSE

Article 10
National Emergency Response

1.   Each Party shall ensure according to their national legislation that the necessary measures are taken to mobilise equipment, facilities, materials, human and financial resources required to respond to disasters.

2.   Each Party may forthwith inform other Parties and the AHA Centre of such measures.

Article 11
Joint Emergency Response through the
Provision of Assistance

1.   If a Party needs assistance in the event of a disaster emergency within its territory, it may request such assistance from any other Party, directly or through the AHA Centre, or, where appropriate, from other entities.

2.   Assistance can only be deployed at the request, and with the consent, of the Requesting Party, or, when offered by another Party or Parties, with the consent of the Receiving Party.

3.   The Requesting Party shall specify the scope and type of assistance required and, where practicable, provide the Assisting Entity with such information as may be necessary for that Party to determine the extent to which it is able to meet the request. In the event that it is not practicable for the Requesting Party to specify the scope and type of assistance required, the Requesting Party and Assisting Entity shall, in consultation, jointly assess and decide upon the scope and type of assistance required.

4.   Each Party to which a request for assistance is directed shall promptly decide and notify the Requesting Party, directly or through the AHA Centre, whether it is in a position to render the assistance requested, and of the scope and terms of such assistance.

5.   Each Party to which an offer of assistance is directed shall promptly decide and notify the Assisting Entity, directly or through the AHA Centre, whether it is in a position to accept the assistance offered, and of the scope and terms of such assistance.

6.   The Parties shall, within the limits of their capabilities, identify and notify the AHA Centre of military and civilian personnel, experts, equipment, facilities and materials which could be made available for the provision of assistance to other Parties in the event of a disaster emergency as well as the terms, especially financial, under which such assistance could be provided.

Article 12
Direction and Control of Assistance

Unless otherwise agreed:

1.   The Requesting or Receiving Party shall exercise the overall direction, control, co-ordination and supervision of the assistance within its territory. The Assisting Entity shall, where the assistance involves military personnel and related civilian officials, designate in consultation with the Requesting or Receiving Party, a person who shall be in charge of and retain immediate operational supervision over the personnel and the equipment provided by it. The designated person, referred to as the Head of the assistance operation, shall exercise such supervision in co-operation with the appropriate authorities of the Requesting or Receiving Party.

2.   The Requesting or Receiving Party shall provide, to the extent possible, local facilities and services for the proper and effective administration of the assistance. It shall also ensure the protection of personnel, equipment and materials brought into its territory by or on behalf of the Assisting Entity for such purposes. Such military personnel and related civilian officials are not to carry arms.

3.   The Assisting Entity and Receiving Party shall consult and co-ordinate with each other with regard to any claims, other than an act of gross negligence or contractual claims against each other, for damage, loss or destruction of the other's property or injury or death to personnel of both Parties arising out of the performance of their official duties.

4.   The relief goods and materials provided by the Assisting Entity should meet the quality and validity requirements of the Parties concerned for consumption and utilisation.

Article 13
Respect of National Laws and Regulations

1.   Members of the assistance operation shall refrain from any action or activity incompatible with the nature and purpose of this Agreement.

2.   Members of the assistance operation shall respect and abide by all national laws and regulations. The Head of the assistance operation shall take all appropriate measures to ensure observance of national laws and regulations. Receiving Party shall co-operate to ensure that members of the assistance operation observe national laws and regulations.

Article 14
Exemptions and Facilities in Respect of the Provision of Assistance

In accordance with its national laws and regulations, the Requesting or Receiving Party shall:

a.   accord the Assisting Entity exemptions from taxation, duties and other charges of a similar nature on the importation and use of equipment including vehicles and telecommunications, facilities and materials brought into the territory of the Requesting or Receiving Party for the purpose of the assistance;

b.   facilitate the entry into, stay in and departure from its territory of personnel and of equipment, facilities and materials involved or used in the assistance; and

c.   co-operate with the AHA Centre, where appropriate, to facilitate the processing of exemptions and facilities in respect of the provision of assistance.

Article 15
Identification

1.   Military personnel and related civilian officials involved in the assistance operation shall be permitted to wear uniforms with distinctive identification while performing official duties.

2.   For the purpose of entry into and departure from the territory of the Receiving Party, members of the assistance operation shall be required to have:

  a. an individual or collective movement order issued by or under the authority of the Head of the assistance operation or any appropriate authority of the Assisting Entity; and

  b. a personal identity card issued by the appropriate authorities of the Assisting Entity.

3.   Aircrafts and vessels used by the military personnel and related civilian officials of the Assisting Entity may use its registration and easily identifiable license plate without tax, licenses and/or any other permits. All authorised foreign military aircrafts will be treated as friendly aircrafts and will receive open radio frequencies and Identification Friend or Foe (IFF) by the Receiving Party authorities.

Article 16
Transit of Personnel, Equipment, Facilities and Materials in Respect of the Provision of Assistance

1.   Each Party shall, at the request of the Party concerned, seek to facilitate the transit through its territory of duly notified personnel, equipment, facilities and materials involved or used in the assistance to the Requesting or Receiving Party. The Party concerned shall exempt from taxation, duties and

other charges of a similar nature for such equipment, facilities and materials.

2.   AHA Centre, where possible and appropriate, shall facilitate the processing of transit of personnel, equipment, facilities and materials in respect of the provisions of assistance.

PART VI.
REHABILITATION

Article 17
Rehabilitation

For the purpose of the implementation of this Agreement, the Parties shall, jointly or individually, develop strategies and implement programmes for rehabilitation as a result of a disaster. The Parties shall promote, as appropriate, bilateral, regional and international co-operation for rehabilitation as a result of a disaster.

PART VII.
TECHNICAL CO-OPERATION AND
SCIENTIFIC RESEARCH

Article 18
Technical Co-operation

1.   In order to increase preparedness and to mitigate disasters, the Parties shall undertake technical co-operation, including the following:

    a. facilitate mobilisation of appropriate resources both within and outside the Parties;

b. promote the standardisation of the reporting format of data and information;

c. promote the exchange of relevant information, expertise, technology, techniques and know-how;

d. provide or make arrangements for relevant training, public awareness and education, in particular, relating to disaster prevention and mitigation;

e. develop and undertake training programmes for policy makers, disaster managers and disaster responders at local, national and regional levels; and

f. strengthen and enhance the technical capacity of the Parties to implement this Agreement.

2.   The AHA Centre shall facilitate activities for technical co-operation as identified in paragraph 1 above.

Article 19
Scientific and Technical Research

1.   The Parties shall individually or jointly, including in co-operation with appropriate international organisations, promote and, whenever possible, support scientific and technical research programmes related to the causes and consequences of disasters and the means, methods, techniques and equipment for disaster risk reduction. In this regard, the protection of the Intellectual Property Rights of the Parties concerned must be respected.

2.   The AHA Centre shall facilitate activities for scientific and technical research as identified in paragraph 1 above.

PART VIII.
ASEAN CO-ORDINATING CENTRE FOR HUMANITARIAN ASSISTANCE

Article 20
ASEAN Co-ordinating Centre for Humanitarian Assistance

1.   The ASEAN Co-ordinating Centre for Humanitarian Assistance on disaster management (AHA Centre) shall be established for the purpose of facilitating co-operation and co-ordination among the Parties, and with relevant United Nations and international organisations, in promoting regional collaboration.

2.   The AHA Centre shall work on the basis that the Party will act first to manage and respond to disasters. In the event that the Party requires assistance to cope with such a situation, in addition to direct request to any Assisting Entity, it may seek assistance from the AHA Centre to facilitate such request.

3.   The AHA Centre shall carry out the functions as set out in ANNEX and any other functions as directed by the Conference of the Parties.

PART IX.
INSTITUTIONAL ARRANGEMENTS

Article 21
Conference of the Parties

1.   A Conference of the Parties is hereby established. The first meeting of the Conference of the Parties shall be convened by the Secretariat not later than one year after the entry into

force of this Agreement. Thereafter, ordinary meetings of the Conference of the Parties shall continue to be held at least once every year, as far as possible, in conjunction with appropriate meetings of ASEAN.

2.   Extraordinary meetings shall be held at any other time upon the request of one Party provided that such request is supported by at least one other Party.

3.   The Conference of the Parties shall keep under continuous review and evaluation the implementation of this Agreement and to this end shall:

   a. take such action as is necessary to ensure the effective implementation of this Agreement;

   b. consider reports and other information which may be submitted by a Party directly or through the Secretariat;

   c. consider and adopt protocols in accordance with Article 25 of this Agreement;

   d. consider and adopt any amendment to this Agreement;

   e. adopt, review and amend as required any Annexes to this Agreement;

   f. establish subsidiary bodies as may be required for the implementation of this Agreement; and

   g. consider and undertake any additional action that may be required for the achievement of the objective of this Agreement.

Article 22
National Focal Point and Competent Authorities

1.   Each Party shall designate a National Focal Point and one or more Competent Authorities for the purpose of implementation of this Agreement.

2.   Each Party shall inform other Parties and the AHA Centre, of its National Focal Point and Competent Authorities, and of any subsequent changes in their designations.

3.   The AHA Centre shall regularly and expeditiously provide to the Parties and as necessary to relevant international organisations the information referred to in paragraph 2 above.

Article 23
The Secretariat

1.   The ASEAN Secretariat shall serve as the Secretariat to this Agreement.

2.   The functions of the Secretariat shall include the following:

a. arrange for and service meetings of the Conference of the Parties and of other bodies established by this Agreement;

b. transmit to the Parties notifications, reports and other information received in accordance with this Agreement;

c. consider inquiries by and information from the Parties, and consult with them on questions relating to this Agreement;

d. ensure the necessary co-ordination with other relevant international bodies and, in particular, to enter into administrative arrangements as may be required for the effective discharge of the Secretariat functions; and

e. perform such other functions as may be assigned to it by the Parties.

Article 24
Financial Arrangements

1.   A Fund is hereby established for the implementation of this Agreement.

2.   It shall be known as the ASEAN Disaster Management and Emergency Relief Fund.

3.   The Fund shall be administered by the ASEAN Secretariat under the guidance of the Conference of the Parties.

4.   The Parties shall, in accordance with the decisions of the Conference of the Parties, make voluntary contributions to the Fund.

5.   The Fund shall be open to contributions from other sources subject to the decision of or approval by the Parties.

6.   The Parties may, where necessary, mobilise additional resources required for the implementation of this Agreement from relevant international organisations, in particular, regional financial institutions and the international donor community.

PART X.
PROCEDURES

Article 25
Protocols

1.   The Parties shall co-operate in the formulation and adoption of protocols to this Agreement, prescribing agreed measures, procedures and standards for the implementation of this Agreement.

2.   The text of any proposed protocol shall be communicated to the Parties by the Secretariat at least sixty days before the opening of a Conference of the Parties.

3.   The Conference of the Parties may, at ordinary meetings, adopt protocols to this Agreement by consensus of all Parties to this Agreement.

4.   Any protocol to this Agreement adopted in accordance with the previous paragraph shall enter into force in conformity with the procedures as provided for in that protocol.

Article 26
Amendments to the Agreement

1.   Any Party may propose amendments to the Agreement.

2.   The text of any proposed amendment shall be communicated to the Parties by the Secretariat at least sixty days before the Conference of the Parties at which it is proposed for adoption. The Secretariat shall also communicate proposed amendments to the signatories to the Agreement.

3.   Amendments shall be adopted by consensus at an ordinary meeting of the Conference of the Parties.

4.   Amendments to this Agreement shall be subject to ratification, approval or acceptance by the Parties to this Agreement. The Depositary shall circulate the adopted amendment to all Parties for their ratification, approval or acceptance. The amendment shall enter into force on the thirtieth day after the deposit with the Depositary of the instruments of ratification, approval or acceptance of all Parties.

Article 27
Adoption and Amendment of Annexes

1.   Annexes to this Agreement shall form an integral part of the Agreement and, unless otherwise expressly provided, a reference to the Agreement constitutes at the same time a reference to the annexes thereto.

2.   Annexes shall be adopted by consensus at an ordinary meeting of the Conference of the Parties.

3.   Any Party may propose amendments to an Annex.

4.   Amendments to an Annex shall be adopted by consensus at an ordinary meeting of the Conference of the Parties.

5.   Annexes to this Agreement and amendments to the Annexes shall be subject to ratification, approval or acceptance. The Depositary shall circulate the adopted Annex or the adopted amendment to an Annex to all Parties for their ratification, approval or acceptance. The Annex or the amendment to an Annex shall enter into force on the thirtieth day after the deposit with the Depositary of the instruments of ratification, approval or acceptance of all Parties.

Article 28
Rules of Procedure and Financial Rules

The first Conference of the Parties shall by consensus adopt rules of procedure for itself and financial rules for the ASEAN Disaster Management and Emergency Relief Fund to determine, in particular, the financial participation of the Parties to this Agreement.

Article 29
Reports

The Parties shall transmit to the Secretariat reports on the measures taken for the implementation of this Agreement in such form and at such intervals as determined by the Conference of the Parties.

Article 30
Relationship with Other Instruments

The provisions of this Agreement shall in no way affect the rights and obligations of any Party with regard to any existing treaty, convention or instrument to which they are Parties.

Article 31
Settlement of Disputes

Any dispute between Parties as to the interpretation or application of, or compliance with, this Agreement or any protocol thereto, shall be settled amicably by consultation or negotiation.

PART XI.
FINAL CLAUSES

Article 32
Ratification, Acceptance, Approval and Accession

This Agreement shall be subject to ratification, acceptance, approval or accession by the Member States. Instruments of ratification, acceptance, approval or accession shall be deposited with the Depositary.

Article 33
Entry into Force

This Agreement shall enter into force on the sixtieth day after the deposit of the tenth instrument of ratification, acceptance, approval or accession.

Article 34
Reservations

Unless otherwise expressly provided by this Agreement no reservations may be made to the Agreement.

Article 35
Depositary

This Agreement shall be deposited with the Secretary-General of ASEAN, who shall promptly furnish each Member

State a certified copy thereof and certified copies of protocols, annexes and amendments.

Article 36
Authentic Text

This Agreement shall be drawn up in the English language and shall be the authentic text. IN WITNESS WHEREOF the undersigned, being duly authorised by their respective Governments have signed this Agreement.

DONE at Vientiane, Lao PDR, this Twenty-Sixth Day of July in the Year Two Thousand and Five, in a single copy in the English Language.

For Brunei Darussalam:

MOHAMED BOLKIAH
Minister of Foreign Affairs

For the Kingdom of Cambodia:

HOR NAMHONG
Deputy Prime Minister and Minister of
Foreign Affairs and International Cooperation

For the Republic of Indonesia:

DR. N. HASSAN WIRAJUDA
Minister for Foreign Affairs

For Lao People's Democratic Republic:

SOMSAVAT LENGSAVAD
Deputy Prime Minister and
Minister of Foreign Affairs

For Malaysia:

DATO' SERI SYED HAMID ALBAR
Minister of Foreign Affairs

For the Union of Myanmar:

NYAN WIN
Minister for Foreign Affairs

For the Republic of the Philippines:

ALBERTO G. ROMULO
Secretary of Foreign Affairs

For the Republic of Singapore:

GEORGE YONG-BOON YEO
Minister for Foreign Affairs

For the Kingdom of Thailand:

DR. KANTATHI SUPHAMONGKHON
Minister of Foreign Affairs

For the Socialist Republic of Viet Nam:

NGUYEN DY NIEN
Minister for Foreign Affairs

ANNEX

TERMS OF REFERENCE OF THE ASEAN CO-ORDINATING CENTRE FOR HUMANITARIAN ASSISTANCE (AHA CENTRE)

The ASEAN Co-ordinating Centre for Humanitarian Assistance on disaster management (AHA Centre) shall be established for the purpose of facilitating co-operation and co-ordination among the Parties, and with relevant United Nations and international organisations, in promoting regional collaboration. To this end, it shall perform the following functions:

(i) receive and consolidate data as analysed by and recommendations on risk level from the National Focal Points (Article 5.4);

(ii) on the basis of such information, disseminate to each Party, through its National Focal Point, the analysed data and risk level arising from the identified hazards (Article 5.4);

(iii) where appropriate, conduct analysis on possible regional-level implications (Article 5.4);

(iv) receive information regarding available resources for the regional standby arrangements for disaster relief and emergency response (Article 8.4);

(v) facilitate the establishment, maintenance and periodical review of regional standby arrangements for disaster relief and emergency response (Article 8.5);

(vi) facilitate periodic review of regional standard operating procedures (Article 8.6);

(vii) receive data on earmarked assets and capacities, which may be available for the regional standby arrangements for disaster relief and emergency response, as communicated by each Party, and their updates (Article 9.1);

(viii) consolidate, update and disseminate the data on such earmarked assets and capacities, and communicate with the Parties for their utilisation (Article 9.2);

(ix) receive information on measures taken by the Parties to mobilise equipment, facilities, materials, human and financial resources required to respond to disasters (Article 10.2);

(x) facilitate joint emergency response (Article 11);

(xi) where appropriate, facilitate the processing of exemptions and facilities in respect of the provision of assistance (Article 14.c);

(xii) where possible and appropriate, facilitate the processing of transit of personnel, equipment, facilities and materials in respect of the provisions of assistance (Article 16.2);

(xiii) facilitate activities for technical co-operation (Article 18.2);

(xiv) facilitate activities for scientific and technical research (Article 19.2);

(xv) receive from each Party information on designated National Focal Point and Competent Authorities and any subsequent changes in their designations (Article 22.2); and

(xvi) regularly and expeditiously provide to the Parties and, as necessary, to relevant international organisations, information referred to in paragraph (xv) above (Article 22.3).

ASEAN Convention Against Trafficking in Persons, Especially Women and Children

Member States of the Association of Southeast Asian Nations (hereinafter referred to as "ASEAN") - Brunei Darussalam, the Kingdom of Cambodia, the Republic of Indonesia, the Lao People's Democratic Republic, Malaysia, the Republic of the Union of Myanmar, the Republic of the Philippines, the Republic of Singapore, the Kingdom of Thailand, and the Socialist Republic of Viet Nam, hereinafter referred to individually as "the Party" and collectively as "the Parties";

RECOGNISING that trafficking in persons constitutes a violation of human rights and an offence to the dignity of human beings;

RECALLING the purpose and principles of the Charter of the United Nations, the Universal Declaration on Human Rights, the Charter of the Association of Southeast Asian Nations ("ASEAN Charter"), the ASEAN Human Rights Declaration, the United Nations Convention against Transnational Organized Crime, and where applicable, the Protocol to Prevent, Suppress and Punish Trafficking in Persons, Especially Women and Children, and other international agreements and resolutions of the United Nations on the eradication of trafficking in persons, in the promotion and protection of human rights, fundamental freedoms, fair treatment, rule of law and due process;

REAFFIRMING our commitment to the ASEAN Charter with a view to responding effectively, in accordance with the principle of comprehensive security, to all forms of transnational crimes and transboundary challenges;

REAFFIRMING also our commitment to the ASEAN Declaration Against Trafficking in Persons Particularly Women and Children adopted in 2004; the Criminal Justice Responses to Trafficking in Persons: Ending Impunity for Traffickers and Securing Justice for Victims in 2007 ("ASEAN Practitioner Guidelines"); the ASEAN Leaders' Joint Statement in Enhancing Cooperation against Trafficking in Persons in South East Asia in 2011; and ASEAN's efforts in promoting human rights, including the ASEAN Human Rights Declaration adopted in 2012;

REAFFIRMING further our commitment to a stronger and more effective regional and international cooperation against trafficking in persons where the offence is transnational in nature, including but not limited to crimes committed by organised criminal groups;

RECOGNISING that cooperation is imperative to the successful investigation, prosecution and elimination of safe havens for the perpetrators and accomplices of trafficking in persons and for the effective protection of, and assistance to, victims of trafficking;

RECOGNISING that trafficking in persons is caused by a combination of factors, including government corruption, poverty, economic instability, inefficient legal systems, organised crimes, and the demand that fosters all forms of exploitation of persons, especially women and children, that leads to trafficking, which must be effectively addressed;

REALISING that all ASEAN Member States, regardless of whether they are countries of origin, transit or destination, have a shared responsibility and a common goal to prevent trafficking in persons, prosecute and punish offenders of trafficking in persons and to protect and assist victims of trafficking in persons;

TAKING INTO consideration the proximity and connecting borders of ASEAN Member States and in the spirit of regionalism;

REALISING the need to establish a regional instrument that deals especially with trafficking in persons as a legal framework for regional action in preventing and combating trafficking in persons, including the protection of, and assistance to, victims of trafficking in persons;

RECOGNISING the importance of having in place a regional instrument against trafficking in persons that is legally binding and that would assist ASEAN Member States, as countries of origin, transit or destination, to deal with their diverse national challenges, priorities and strategies in the fight against trafficking in persons;

Have agreed as follows:

Chapter I
General Provisions

Article 1
Objectives

1. The objectives of this regional legal instrument are to effectively:

   a. Prevent and combat trafficking in persons, especially against women and children, and to ensure just and effective punishment of traffickers;

b. Protect and assist victims of trafficking in persons, with full respect for their human rights; and

c. Promote cooperation among the Parties in order to meet these objectives.

2.   The Parties agree that the measures set forth in this Convention must be construed and applied in a manner that is consistent with internationally and regionally recognised principle of non-discrimination, especially to those persons on the ground that they are victims of trafficking in persons.

Article 2
Use of Terms

For the purposes of this Convention:

a.   "Trafficking in persons" shall mean the recruitment, transportation, transfer, harbouring or receipt of persons, by means of the threat or use of force or other forms of coercion, of abduction, of fraud, of deception, of the abuse of power or of a position of vulnerability or of the giving or receiving of payments or benefits to achieve the consent of a person having control over another person, for the purpose of exploitation. Exploitation shall include, at a minimum, the exploitation of the prostitution of others or other forms of sexual exploitation, forced labour or services, slavery or practices similar to slavery, servitude or the removal of organs;

b.   The consent of a victim of trafficking in persons to the intended exploitation set forth in Paragraph (a) of this Article shall be irrelevant where any of the means set forth in Paragraph (a) have been used;

c.   The recruitment, transportation, transfer, harbouring or receipt of a child for the purpose of exploitation shall be considered "trafficking in persons" even if this does not involve any of the means set forth in Paragraph (a) of this Article;

d.   "Child" shall mean any person under eighteen (18) years of age;

e.   "Victim" shall mean any natural person who is subject to an act of trafficking in persons as defined in this Convention;

f.   "Organised criminal group" shall mean a structured group of three or more persons existing for a period of time and acting in concert with the aim of committing one or more serious crimes or offences established in accordance with this Convention, in order to obtain, directly or indirectly, a financial or other material benefit;

g.   "Serious crime", as stated in Paragraph (f) of this Article, shall mean conduct constituting an offence punishable by a maximum deprivation of liberty of at least four years or a more serious penalty;

h.   "Transnational Crime" shall mean an offence that is transnational in nature. An offence is transnational in nature if:

  (i)   It is committed in more than one State;

  (ii)   It is committed in one State but a substantial part of its preparation, planning, direction or control takes place in another State;

  (iii) It is committed in one State but involves an organised criminal group that engages in criminal activities in more than one State; or

  (iv) It is committed in one State but has substantial effects in another State.

i.   "Public official" shall mean:

  (i)   any person holding a legislative, executive, administrative or judicial office of a Party, whether appointed or elected, whether permanent or temporary, whether paid or unpaid, irrespective of that person's seniority;

(ii) any other person who performs a public function, including for a public agency or public enterprise, or provides a public service, as defined in the domestic laws of the Party and as applied in the pertinent area of law of that Party;

(iii) any other person defined as a "public official" in the domestic laws of that Party.

j.   "Property" shall mean assets of every kind, whether corporeal or incorporeal, movable or immovable, tangible or intangible, and legal documents or instruments evidencing title to, or interest in, such assets;

k.   "Proceeds of crime" shall mean any property derived from or obtained, directly or indirectly, through the commission of an offence;

l.   "Freezing" or "seizure" shall mean temporarily prohibiting the transfer, conversion, disposition or movement of property or temporarily assuming custody or control of property on the basis of an order issued by a court or other competent authority;

m.   "Confiscation", which includes forfeiture where applicable, shall mean the permanent deprivation of property by order of a court or other competent authority;

n.   "Predicate offence" shall mean any offence as a result of which proceeds have been generated that may become the subject of an offence as defined in Article 7 of this Convention.

Article 3
Scope of Application

This Convention shall apply to the prevention, investigation and prosecution of the offences established in accordance with Article 5 of this Convention, where the offences are transnational in nature, including those committed by organised criminal groups, as well as to the protection of and assistance to victims of trafficking in persons.

Article 4
Protection of Sovereignty

1.   The Parties shall carry out their obligations under this Convention in a manner consistent with the principles of sovereign equality and territorial integrity of States and that of non-intervention in the domestic affairs of other States.

2.   Nothing in this Convention entitles a Party to undertake in the territory of another Party the exercise of jurisdiction and performance of functions that are reserved exclusively for the authorities of that other Party by its domestic laws.

Chapter II
Criminalisation

Article 5
Criminalisation of Trafficking in Persons

1.   Each Party shall adopt such legislative and other measures as may be necessary to establish as criminal offences the conduct set forth in Article 2 of this Convention, when committed intentionally.

2.   Each Party shall also adopt such legislative and other measures as may be necessary to establish as criminal offences:

   a. Subject to the basic concepts of its legal systems, attempting to commit an offence established In accordance with Paragraph 1 of this Article;

   b. Participating as an accomplice in an offence established in accordance with Paragraph 1 of this Article;

c. Organising or directing other persons to commit an offence established in accordance with Paragraph 1 of this Article.

3. Each Party shall adopt such legislative or other measures as may be appropriate so that offenders are liable to higher penalties than usual if any of the following aggravating circumstances are present:

a. Where the offence involves serious injury or death of the victim or another person, including death as a result of suicide;

b. Where the offence involves a victim who is particularly vulnerable such as a child or a person who is unable to fully take care of or protect himself or herself because of a physical or mental disability or condition;

c. Where the offence exposed the victim to a life threatening illness, including HIV/AIDS;

d. Where the offence involves more than one victim;

e. Where the crime was committed as part of the activity of an organised criminal group;

f. Where the offender has been previously convicted for the same or similar offences;

g. Where the offence was committed by a public official in the performance of his or her public duties.

Article 6
Criminalisation of Participation in an
Organised Criminal Group

1. Each Party shall, in relation to offences covered by this Convention as provided in Article 3, adopt such legislative and other measures as may be necessary to establish as criminal offences, when trafficking in persons is committed intentionally:

a. Either or both of the following as criminal offences distinct from those involving the attempt or completion of the criminal activity:

(i) Agreeing with one or more other persons to commit a serious crime for a purpose relating directly or indirectly to the obtaining of a financial or other material benefit and, where required by domestic law, involving an act undertaken by one of the participants in furtherance of the agreement or involving an organised criminal group;

(ii) Conduct by a person who, with knowledge of either the aim and general criminal activity of an organised criminal group or its intention to commit the crimes in question, takes an active part in:

(a) Criminal activities of the organised criminal group;

(b) Other activities of the organised criminal group in the knowledge that his or her participation will contribute to the achievement of the above-described criminal aim;

b. Organising, directing, aiding, abetting, facilitating or counselling the commission of serious crime involving an organised criminal group.

2. The knowledge, intent, aim, purpose or agreement referred to in Paragraph 1 of this Article may be inferred from objective factual circumstances.

Article 7
Criminalisation of the Laundering of
Proceeds of Crime

Each Party shall, in relation to offences covered by this Convention as provided in Article 3, adopt, in accordance with fundamental principles of its domestic law, such legislative and other measures as may be necessary to establish as criminal offences, when committed intentionally:

a. (i) The conversion or transfer of property, knowing that such property is the proceeds of crime, for the purpose of concealing or disguising the illicit origin of the property or of helping any person who is involved in the commission of the predicate offence to evade the legal consequences of his or her action;

  (ii) The concealment or disguise of the true nature, source, location, disposition, movement or owner-ship of or rights with respect to property, knowing that such property is the proceeds of crime;

b. Subject to the basic concepts of its legal system:

  (iii) The acquisition, possession or use of property, knowing, at the time of receipt, that such property is the proceeds of crime;

  (iv) Participation in, association with or conspiracy to commit, attempts to commit and aiding, abetting, facilitating and counselling the commission of any of the offences established in accordance with this Article.

Article 8
Criminalisation of Corruption

1.   Each Party shall, in relation to offences covered by this Convention as provided in Article 3, adopt such legislative and other measures as may be necessary to establish as criminal offences, when committed intentionally:

a. The promise, offering or giving to a public official, directly or indirectly, of an undue advantage, for the official himself or herself or another person or entity, in order that the official act or refrain from acting in the exercise of his or her official duties;

b. The solicitation or acceptance by a public official, directly or indirectly, of an undue advantage, for the official himself or herself or another person or entity, in order that the official act or refrain from acting in the exercise of his or her official duties.

2.   Each Party shall also consider establishing as criminal offences other forms of corruption.

3.   Each Party shall also adopt such measures as may be necessary to establish as a criminal offence participation as an accomplice in an offence established in accordance with this Article.

Article 9
Criminalisation of Obstruction of Justice

Each Party shall, in relation to offences covered by this Convention as provided in Article 3, adopt such legislative and other measures as may be necessary to establish as criminal offences, when committed intentionally:

a.   The use of physical force, threats or intimidation or the promise, offering or giving of an undue advantage to induce false testimony or to interfere in the giving of testimony or the production of evidence in a proceeding in relation to the commission of offences covered by this Convention;

b.   The use of physical force, threats or intimidation to interfere with the exercise of official duties by a justice or law enforcement official in relation to the commission of offences covered by this Convention. Nothing in this Paragraph shall prejudice the right of Parties to have legislation that protects other categories of public officials.

Article 10
Jurisdiction

1.   Each Party shall adopt such measures as may be necessary to establish its jurisdiction over the offences established in accordance with Article 5, Article 6, Article 7, Article 8, and Article 9 of this Convention when:

a. The offence is committed in the territory of that Party; or

b. The offence is committed on board a vessel that is flying the flag of that Party or an aircraft that is registered under the laws of that Party at the time that the offence is committed.

2.   Subject to Article 4 of this Convention, a Party may also establish its jurisdiction over any such offence when:

a. The offence is committed against a national of that Party;

b. The offence is committed by a national of that Party or a stateless person who has his or her habitual residence in its territory; or

c. The offence is:

(v) One of those established in accordance with Article 6, Paragraph 1, of this Convention and is committed outside its territory with a view to the commission of a serious crime within its territory;

(i) One of those established in accordance with Article 7, Paragraph (b) (ii), of this Convention and is committed outside its territory with a view to the commission of an offence established in accordance with Article 7, Paragraph (a) (i) or (ii) or (b) (i), of this Convention within its territory.

3.   For the purposes of Article 19 of this Convention, each Party shall adopt such measures as may be necessary to establish its jurisdiction over the offences covered by this Convention when the alleged offender is present in its territory and it does not extradite such person solely on the ground that he or she is one of its nationals.

4.   Each Party may also adopt such measures as may be necessary to establish its jurisdiction over the offences covered by this Convention when the alleged offender is present in its territory and it does not extradite him or her.

5.   If a Party exercising its jurisdiction under Paragraph 1 or 2 of this Article has been notified, or has otherwise learned, that one or more other Parties are conducting an investigation, prosecution or judicial proceeding in respect of the same conduct, the competent authorities of those Parties shall, as appropriate, consult one another with a view to coordinating their actions.

6.   Without prejudice to norms of general international law, this Convention does not exclude the exercise of any criminal jurisdiction established by a Party in accordance with its domestic laws.

Chapter III
Prevention

Article 11
Prevention of Trafficking in Persons

1.   The Parties shall establish comprehensive policies, programmes and other measures:

   a. To prevent and combat trafficking in persons; and

b. To protect victims of trafficking in persons, especially women and children, from revictimisation.

2. The Parties shall endeavour to undertake measures such as research, information and mass media campaigns and social and economic initiatives to prevent and combat trafficking in persons.

3. Policies, programmes and other measures established in accordance with this Article shall, as appropriate, include cooperation with non-governmental organisations, other relevant organisations and other elements of civil society.

4. The Parties shall take or strengthen measures, including through bilateral or multilateral cooperation, to alleviate the factors that make persons, especially women and children, vulnerable to trafficking, such as poverty, underdevelopment and lack of equal opportunity.

5. The Parties shall adopt or strengthen legislative or other measures, such as educational, social or cultural measures, including through bilateral and multilateral cooperation, to discourage the demand that fosters all forms of exploitation of persons, especially women and children, that leads to trafficking.

Article 12
Areas of Cooperation

The areas of cooperation under this Convention on prevention of trafficking in persons may, in conformity with the domestic laws of the respective Parties, include appropriate measures, among others:

a. To discourage the demand that fosters all forms of exploitation of persons, especially women and children, that leads to trafficking;

b.   To take or strengthen measures where appropriate, such as through bilateral, multilateral or regional cooperation to prevent and combat trafficking in persons, so as to alleviate the factors that make persons, especially women and children, vulnerable to trafficking, such as poverty, underdevelopment and lack of education and equal opportunity;

c.   To strengthen policies and programmes to prevent trafficking in persons through research, information, awareness-raising and education campaigns, social and economic initiatives and training programmes, in particular for persons vulnerable to trafficking;

d.   To further strengthen regional cooperation in the investigation and prosecution of trafficking in persons cases;

e.   To enable free movement of people to take place legally, and to ensure that immigration requirements are adhered to, by disseminating accurate information on the requirements and conditions enabling the legal entry into, exit from, and stay in their respective territories;

f.   To exchange and share information on measures to reduce children's vulnerability to trafficking in persons, so that they can grow up and live in a safe environment;

g.   To promote capacity-building, including trainings, technical cooperation, and the holding of regional coordination meetings;

h.   To ensure that any person who perpetrates or supports trafficking in persons is brought to justice.

Article 13
Cross-border Cooperation, Control and Validity of Documents

1.   The Parties shall endeavour to undertake cross-border cooperation, in order to prevent and detect trafficking in

persons, as appropriate, among border control agencies by, *inter alia*:

a. Establishing and maintaining direct channels of communication;

b. Enhancing intelligence exchange and sharing of information including through establishing, developing or utilising appropriate databases.

2. The Parties shall prevent the movement of traffickers and victims of trafficking in persons by effective border control and controls on the issuance of identity papers and travel documents, and through effective measures to prevent counterfeiting, forgery or fraudulent use of identity papers and travel documents.

Chapter IV
Protection

Article 14
Protection of Victims of Trafficking in Persons

1. Each Party shall establish national guidelines or procedures for the proper identification of victims of trafficking in persons, and where appropriate, may collaborate with relevant non-governmental victim assistance organisations.

2. In a case where the trafficking takes place in more than one country, each Party shall respect and recognise the identification of victims of trafficking in person made by the competent authorities of the receiving Party.

3. Unless the victim otherwise informs, such identification shall be notified to the sending Party without unreasonable delay by the receiving Party.

4.   Each Party shall consider adopting legislative or other appropriate measures that permit victims of trafficking in persons to remain in its territory, temporarily or permanently, in appropriate cases. Each Party shall give appropriate consideration to humanitarian and compassionate factors to this end.

5.   Each Party shall endeavour to provide for the physical safety of victims of trafficking in persons while they are within its territory.

6.   In appropriate cases and to the extent possible under its domestic laws, each Party shall protect the privacy and identity of victims of trafficking in persons, including, *inter alia,* by making legal proceedings relating to such trafficking confidential.

7.   Each Party shall, subject to its domestic laws, rules, regulations and policies, and in appropriate cases, consider not holding victims of trafficking in persons criminally or administratively liable, for unlawful acts committed by them, if such acts are directly related to the acts of trafficking.

8.   Each Party shall not unreasonably hold persons who have been identified by its competent authorities as victims of trafficking in persons in detention or in prison, prior to, during, or after civil, criminal, or administrative proceedings for trafficking in persons.

9.   Each Party shall communicate to identified victims of trafficking in persons within a reasonable period, information on the nature of protection, assistance and support to which they are entitled to under domestic laws, and under this Convention.

10. Each Party shall, where applicable, provide care and support to victims of trafficking in persons, including in appropriate cases,

in cooperation with relevant non-governmental organisations, other organisations, and other elements of civil society, in the following:

  a. Appropriate housing;

  b. Counselling and information, in particular as regards their legal rights, in a language that the victims of trafficking in persons can understand;

  c. Medical, psychological and material assistance; and

  d. Employment, educational and training opportunities.

11. Each Party shall make its best effort to assist in the reintegration of victims of trafficking in persons into the society of the sending Party.

12. Each Party shall, take into account, in applying the provisions of this Article, the age, gender and special needs of victims of trafficking in persons, in particular the special needs of children.

13. Each Party shall ensure that its domestic legal system contains measures that offer victims of trafficking in persons the possibility of obtaining compensation for damage suffered.

14. Each Party shall make provisions for appropriate funds to be allocated, including where applicable, establishing national trust funds, for the care and support of victims of trafficking in persons.

Article 15
Repatriation and Return of Victims

1.   The Party of which a victim of trafficking in persons is a national or in which the person had the right of permanent residence at the time of entry into the territory of the receiving Party shall facilitate and accept, with due regard for the safety

of that person, the return of that person without undue or unreasonable delay.

2.   When a Party returns a victim in accordance with Paragraph 1 of this Article, such return shall be with due regard for the safety of that person and for the status of any legal proceedings related to the fact that the person is a victim of trafficking in persons.

3.   In accordance with Paragraphs 1 and 2 of this Article, at the request of a receiving Party, a requested Party shall, without undue or unreasonable delay, verify whether a person is its national or permanent resident, whichever is applicable, at the time of entry into the territory of the receiving Party.

4.   In order to facilitate the return of a victim of trafficking in persons who is without proper documentation, the Party of which that person is a national or in which he or she had the right of permanent residence at the time of entry into the territory of the receiving Party shall agree to issue, at the request of the receiving Party, such travel documents or other authorisation as may be necessary to enable the person to travel to and re-enter its territory.

5.   Each Party shall adopt such legislative or other measures as may be necessary to establish repatriation programmes where appropriate, and if necessary, involving relevant national or international institutions and non-governmental organisations.

6.   This Article shall be without prejudice to any rights afforded to victims of trafficking in persons by any domestic laws of the receiving Party.

7.   This Article shall be without prejudice to the provisions of any applicable bilateral or multilateral agreement or immigration arrangements that provide for more favourable rights and privileges to victims of trafficking in persons.

Chapter V
Law Enforcement

Article 16
Law Enforcement and Prosecution

1. Each Party shall adopt such measures as may be necessary to ensure that competent authorities dealing with trafficking in persons cases are equipped with appropriate skills or knowledge in the fight against trafficking in persons and the protection of victims of trafficking in persons, and where appropriate, designate specialised units or authorities for this purpose.

2. Each Party shall take effective and active steps to detect, deter and punish corruption, money laundering, participation in an organised criminal group and obstruction of justice that contributes to trafficking in persons.

3. Each Party shall ensure that its legal system is efficient to deal with trafficking in persons cases.

4. Each Party shall adopt such measures as may be necessary to ensure coordination of the policies and actions of its government's departments and other public agencies against trafficking in persons, and where appropriate, set up coordinating bodies to combat organised crimes such as trafficking in persons, corruption, money laundering and obstruction of justice.

5. Each Party shall, consistent with the domestic laws of the sending and the receiving Parties, through informal cooperation or mutual legal assistance where appropriate, encourage the victims of trafficking in persons to voluntarily enter and stay temporarily in the territory of the receiving Party for purposes of testifying or otherwise cooperating in the prosecution of

their traffickers, with due regard for the safety of the victims of trafficking in persons.

6.   Each Party shall provide or strengthen training programmes for relevant officials in the prevention of and fight against trafficking in persons, with focus on methods used in preventing trafficking, investigating and prosecuting the traffickers, and protecting the rights of the victims, including protecting the victims and their families from the traffickers, and the privacy of the victims.

7.   Each Party shall take all necessary steps to preserve the integrity of the criminal justice process including through protecting victims and witnesses from intimidation and harassment, where necessary, and punishing perpetrators of such acts, in appropriate cases.

8.   Each Party shall, where appropriate, establish under its domestic laws a long statute of limitations period in which to commence proceedings for any offence covered by this Convention and a longer period where the alleged offender has evaded the administration of justice.

9.   Nothing contained in this Convention shall affect the principle that the description of the offences established in accordance with this Convention and of the applicable legal defences or other legal principles controlling the lawfulness of conduct is reserved to the domestic laws of a Party and that such offences shall be prosecuted and punished in accordance with that law.

Article 17
Confiscation and Seizure

1.   Each Party shall adopt, to the greatest extent possible within its domestic legal system, such measures as may be necessary to enable confiscation of:

a. Proceeds of crime derived from offences covered by this Convention or property the value of which corresponds to that of such proceeds;

b. Property, equipment or other instrumentalities used in or destined for use in offences covered by this Convention.

2.   Each Party shall adopt such measures as may be necessary to enable the identification, tracing, freezing or seizure of any item referred to in Paragraph 1 of this Article for the purpose of eventual confiscation.

3.   If proceeds of crime have been transformed or converted, in part or in full, into other property, such property shall be liable to the measures referred to in this Article instead of the proceeds.

4.   If proceeds of crime have been intermingled with property acquired from legitimate sources, such property shall, without prejudice to any powers relating to freezing or seizure, be liable to confiscation up to the assessed value of the intermingled proceeds.

5.   Income or other benefits derived from proceeds of crime, from property into which proceeds of crime have been transformed or converted or from property with which proceeds of crime have been intermingled shall also be liable to the measures referred to in this Article, in the same manner and to the same extent as proceeds of crime.

6.   For the purposes of this Article and Article 21 of this Convention, each Party shall empower its courts or other competent authorities to order that bank, financial or commercial records be made available or be seized. Each Party shall not decline to act under the provisions of this Paragraph on the ground of bank secrecy.

7.   Each Party may consider the possibility of requiring that an offender demonstrate the lawful origin of alleged proceeds of crime or other property liable to confiscation, to the extent that such a requirement is consistent with the principles of its domestic laws and with the nature of the judicial and other proceedings.

8.   The provisions of this Article shall not be construed to prejudice the rights of *bona fide* third parties.

9.   Nothing contained in this Article shall affect the principle that the measures to which it refers shall be defined and implemented in accordance with and subject to the provisions of the domestic laws of a Party.

Chapter VI
International Cooperation

Article 18
Mutual Legal Assistance in Criminal Matters

1.   In order to combat offences of trafficking in persons which are transnational in nature, the Parties shall, subject to their respective domestic laws, afford one another the widest measure of mutual legal assistance in criminal investigations or criminal proceedings in relation to such offences established in accordance with Article 5 of this Convention.

2.   The Parties shall carry out their obligations under Paragraph 1 of this Article in accordance with the Treaty on Mutual Legal Assistance in Criminal Matters.

Article 19
Extradition

1.   Each of the offences established in accordance with Article 5 of this Convention shall be deemed to be included as an extraditable offence in any extradition treaty existing between Parties. The Parties undertake to include such offences as extraditable offences in every extradition treaty to be concluded between them.

2.   If a Party that makes extradition conditional on the existence of a treaty receives a request for extradition from another Party with which it has no extradition treaty, it may consider this Convention the legal basis for extradition in respect of any offence established in accordance with Article 5 of this Convention.

3.   Subject to the provisions of its domestic laws and its extradition treaties, the requested Party may, upon being satisfied that the circumstances so warrant and are urgent and at the request of the requesting Party, take a person whose extradition is sought and who is present in its territory into custody or take other appropriate measures to ensure his or her presence at extradition proceedings.

4.   A Party in whose territory an alleged offender is found, if it does not extradite such person in respect of an offence established in accordance with Article 5 of this Convention applies solely on the ground that he or she is one of its nationals, shall, at the request of the Party seeking extradition, be obliged to submit the case without undue delay to its competent authorities for the purpose of prosecution. Those authorities shall take their decision and conduct their proceedings in the same manner as in the case of any other offence of a grave nature under the domestic law of that Party. The Parties concerned shall cooperate with each other, in particular on

procedural and evidentiary aspects, to ensure the efficiency of such prosecution.

5.   For the purpose of this Article, each Party shall designate a central authority to be notified to the depositary of this Convention.

Article 20
Law Enforcement Cooperation

1.   The Parties shall cooperate closely with one another, consistent with their respective domestic legal and administrative systems, to enhance the effectiveness of law enforcement action to combat the offences covered by this Convention. Each Party shall, in particular, adopt effective measures:

   a. To enhance and, where necessary, to establish as well as utilise existing channels of communication between their competent authorities, agencies and services in order to facilitate the secure and rapid exchange of information concerning all aspects of the offences covered by this Convention, including, if the Parties concerned deem it appropriate, links with other criminal activities;

   b. To cooperate with other Parties in conducting inquiries with respect to offences covered by this Convention concerning:

   (i)   The identity, whereabouts and activities of persons suspected of involvement in such offences or the location of other persons concerned;

   (ii)   The movement of proceeds of crime or property derived from the commission of such offences;

   (iii) The movement of property, equipment or other instrumentalities used or intended for use in the commission of such offences;

c. To provide, when appropriate, necessary items or quantities of substances for analytical or investigative purposes;

d. To facilitate effective coordination between their competent authorities, agencies and services and to promote the exchange of personnel and other experts, including, subject to bilateral agreements or arrangements between the Parties concerned, the posting of liaison officers;

e. To exchange information with other Parties on specific means and methods used by traffickers, including, where applicable, routes and conveyances and the use of false identities, altered or false documents or other means of concealing their activities;

f. To exchange information and coordinate administrative and other measures taken as appropriate for the purpose of early identification of the offences covered by this Convention.

2.   With a view to giving effect to this Convention, the Parties shall consider entering into bilateral or multilateral agreements or arrangements on direct cooperation between their law enforcement agencies and, where such agreements or arrangements already exist, amending them. In the absence of such agreements or arrangements between the Parties concerned, the Parties may consider this Convention as the basis for mutual law enforcement cooperation in respect of the offences covered by this Convention. Whenever appropriate, the Parties shall make full use of agreements or arrangements, including international or regional organisations, to enhance the cooperation between their law enforcement agencies.

3.   The Parties shall endeavour to cooperate within their means to respond to trafficking in persons and other offences

covered by this Convention committed through the use of modern technology.

Article 21
International Cooperation for Purposes
of Confiscation

1.   A Party that has received a request from another Party having jurisdiction over an offence covered by this Convention for confiscation of proceeds of crime, property, equipment or other instrumentalities referred to in Article 17, Paragraph 1 of this Convention situated in its territory shall, to the greatest extent possible within its domestic legal system:

   a. Submit the request to its competent authorities for the purpose of obtaining an order of confiscation and, if such an order is granted, give effect to it; or

   b. Submit to its competent authorities, with a view to giving effect to it to the extent requested, an order of confiscation issued by a court in the territory of the requesting Party in accordance with Article 17, Paragraph 1 of this Convention insofar as it relates to proceeds of crime, property, equipment or other instrumentalities referred to in Article 17, Paragraph 1, situated in the territory of the requested Party.

2.   Following a request made by another Party having jurisdiction over an offence covered by this Convention, the requested Party shall take measures to identify, trace and freeze or seize proceeds of crime, property, equipment or other instrumentalities referred to in Article 17, Paragraph 1 of this Convention for the purpose of eventual confiscation to be ordered either by the requesting Party or, pursuant to a request under Paragraph 1 of this Article, by the requested Party.

3. The provisions of Article 18 of this Convention are applicable, *mutatis mutandis,* to this Article. In addition to the information specified in Article 18, requests made pursuant to this Article shall contain:

a. In the case of a request pertaining to Paragraph 1 (a) of this Article, a description of the property to be confiscated and a statement of the facts relied upon by the requesting Party sufficient to enable the requested Party to seek the order under its domestic laws;

b. In the case of a request pertaining to Paragraph 1(b) of this Article, a legally admissible copy of an order of confiscation upon which the request is based issued by the requesting Party, a statement of the facts and information as to the extent to which execution of the order is requested;

c. In the case of a request pertaining to Paragraph 2 of this Article, a statement of the facts relied upon by the requesting Party and a description of the actions requested.

4. The decisions or actions provided for in Paragraphs 1 and 2 of this Article shall be taken by the requested Party in accordance with and subject to the provisions of its domestic laws and its procedural rules, any bilateral or multilateral treaty, agreement or arrangement to which it is bound in relation to the requesting Party, and the Treaty on Mutual Legal Assistance in Criminal Matters.

5. If a Party elects to make the taking of the measures referred to in Paragraphs 1 and 2 of this Article conditional on the existence of a relevant treaty, that Party shall consider this Convention the necessary and sufficient treaty basis.

6.   The provisions of this Article shall not be construed to prejudice the rights of *bona fide* third parties.

7.   The Parties shall consider concluding bilateral or multilateral treaties, agreements or arrangements to enhance the effectiveness of international cooperation undertaken pursuant to this Article.

Article 22
Disposal of Confiscated Proceeds of Crime or Property

1.   Proceeds of crime or property confiscated by a Party pursuant to Article 17 or Article 21, Paragraph 1 of this Convention shall be disposed of by that Party in accordance with its domestic laws and administrative procedures.

2.   When acting on the request made by another Party in accordance with Article 21 of this Convention, Parties shall, to the extent permitted by domestic laws and if so requested, give priority consideration to returning the confiscated proceeds of crime or property to the requesting Party so that it can give compensation and assistance to the victims of trafficking in persons or return such proceeds of crime or property to their legitimate owners.

3.   When acting on the request made by another Party in accordance with Article 17 and Article 21 of this Convention, a Party may give special consideration to concluding agreements or arrangements on sharing with other Parties, on a regular or case-by-case basis, such proceeds of crime or property, or funds derived from the sale of such proceeds of crime or property, in accordance with its domestic laws or administrative procedures.

Chapter VII
Final Provisions

Article 23
Establishment of Coordinating Structures

Each Party shall consider establishing coordinating structures in the fight against trafficking in persons, including enhancing cooperation under all areas of this Convention.

Article 24
Monitoring, Reviewing and Reporting

1.   The ASEAN Senior Officials Meeting on Transnational Crime (SOMTC) shall be responsible for promoting, monitoring, reviewing and reporting periodically to the ASEAN Ministerial Meeting on Transnational Crime (AMMTC) on the effective implementation of this Convention.

2.   The ASEAN Secretariat shall provide the support for supervising and coordinating the implementation of this Convention and assist the SOMTC in all matters relating thereto.

Article 25
Confidentiality of Documents, Records and Information

1.   Each Party shall preserve the confidentiality and secrecy of documents, records and other information received from any other Party, including the source thereof.

2.   No document, record or other information obtained pursuant to this Convention shall be disclosed to or shared with any other Party, State or person except with the prior written consent of the Party which provided such document, record or information.

Article 26
Relationship with Other International Instruments

This Convention shall not derogate from obligations subsisting between the Parties pursuant to other international agreements nor, where the Parties agree, shall it prevent the Parties from providing assistance to each other pursuant to other international agreements or the provisions of their respective domestic laws.

Article 27
Settlement of Disputes

Any difference or dispute between the Parties arising from the interpretation or application of the provisions of this Convention shall be settled amicably through consultation and negotiation between the Parties through diplomatic channels or any other peaceful means for the settlement of disputes as agreed upon between the Parties.

Article 28
Ratification, Approval and Depositary

1.   This Convention shall be subject to ratification or approval in accordance with the internal procedures of the Parties.

2.   The instruments of ratification or approval shall be deposited with the Secretary-General of ASEAN who shall promptly inform the other Parties of such deposit.

Article 29
Entry into Force and Amendment

a.   This Convention shall enter into force on the thirtieth (30th) day following the date of the deposit of the sixth (6th) instrument of ratification or approval with the Secretary-General of ASEAN in respect of those Parties that have submitted their instruments of ratification or approval.

b.   For any Party ratifying or approving this Convention after the deposit of the sixth (6th) instrument of ratification or approval, but before the day the Convention enters into force, the Convention shall also apply to that Party on the date the Convention enters into force. In respect of a Party ratifying or approving this Convention subsequent to its entry into force pursuant to Paragraph 1, it shall enter into force for that Party on the date its instrument of ratification or approval is deposited.

c.   This Convention may be modified or amended at any time by mutual written consent of the Parties. Such modification or amendment shall enter into force on such date as shall be mutually agreed upon by Parties and shall form part of this Convention.

d.   Any modification or amendment shall not affect the rights and obligations of the Parties arising from or based on the provisions of this Convention before the entry into force of such modification or amendment.

Article 30
Withdrawal

1.   Any Party may withdraw from this Convention at any time after the date of the entry into force of this Convention for that Party.

2.   The withdrawal shall be notified by an instrument of withdrawal to the Secretary-General of ASEAN.

3.   The withdrawal shall take effect one hundred and eighty (180) days after the receipt of the instrument of withdrawal by the Secretary-General of ASEAN.

4.   The Secretary-General of ASEAN shall promptly notify all the other Parties of any withdrawal.

Article 31
Registration

This Convention shall be registered by the Secretary-General of ASEAN to the United Nations Secretariat pursuant to Article 102 of the Charter of the United Nations.

DONE at Kuala Lumpur, Malaysia, this Twenty-First Day of November in the Year Two Thousand and Fifteen, in a single original copy in the English language.

For Brunei Darussalam:

HAJI HASSANAL BOLKIAH
Sultan of Brunei Darussalam

For the Kingdom of Cambodia:

SAMDECH AKKA MOHA SENA PADEI TECHO HUN SEN
Prime Minister

For the Republic of Indonesia:

JOKO WIDODO
President

For the Lao People's Democratic Republic:

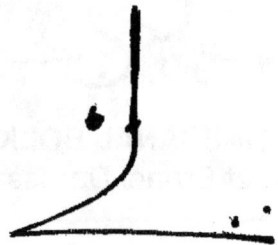

THONGSING THAMMAVONG
Prime Minister

For Malaysia:

DATO' SRI MOHD NAJIB TUN ABDUL RAZAK
Prime Minister

For the Republic of the Union of Myanmar:

THEIN SEIN
President

For the Republic of the Philippines:

BENIGNO S. AQUINO III
President

For the Republic of Singapore:

LEE HSIEN LOONG
Prime Minister

For the Kingdom of Thailand:

GENERAL PRAYUT CHAN-O-CHA (RET.)
Prime Minister

For the Socialist Republic of Viet Nam:

NGUYEN TAN DUNG
Prime Minister

FINAL

EAST ASIA SUMMIT LEADERS' STATEMENT ON COMBATING MARINE PLASTIC DEBRIS

WE, the Heads of State and Government of the Member States of the Association of Southeast Asian Nations (ASEAN), Australia, the People's Republic of China, Republic of India, Japan, Republic of Korea, New Zealand, the Russian Federation, and the United States of America on the occasion of the 13th East Asia Summit (EAS) in Singapore, on 15 November 2018;

EMPHASISING that the East Asia Summit, with ASEAN as the driving force, will continue to be a Leaders-led forum for dialogue on broad strategic, political, and economic issues of common interest and concern, with the aim of promoting peace, stability and prosperity in East Asia;

NOTING the common aspiration to achieve the 2030 Agenda for Sustainable Development and its focus on people, planet, and prosperity, peace and partnership, not only for this generation but for generations to come, with concern over the health of oceans and marine biodiversity which form an integrated and essential component of the Earth's ecosystem and are critical to sustaining it;

NOTING with concern the high and rapidly increasing levels of marine plastic litter and the expected increase in negative effects on marine biodiversity, ecosystems, animal well-being, fisheries, maritime transport, recreation and tourism, local societies and economies, and the urgent need for strengthened knowledge of the levels and effects of microplastics and nanoplastics on marine ecosystems, seafood and human health;

RECOGNISING the adverse impact of climate change, ecological changes and natural disasters, among other factors, and the importance of ensuring the integrity of all ecosystems, including oceans, and in this effort, recognising the importance of relevant multilateral environmental agreements;

WELCOMING the 5th Our Ocean Conference which was held in Bali, Indonesia, on 29-30 October 2018 which recognised the urgent need for collective and coordinated actions to address the challenge of marine debris in the region;

EMPHASISING the importance of sustainable lifestyle, consumption and production patterns to advance the reduction of marine plastic debris;

FURTHER EMPHASISING the importance of measures of resource efficiency, including circular economy, product lifecycle management, sustainable materials management, and reduce, reuse, recycle ("3R") approaches, as appropriate;

RECOGNISING that the efforts on environmentally sound plastic waste management contribute to the prevention and reduction of marine plastic debris;

CONVINCED that EAS participating countries should enhance cooperation to respond to maritime challenges and promote the sustainable development of the seas and oceans;

COMMITTED to enhance the conservation and sustainable use of oceans and their resources by implementing international law as reflected in the 1982 United Nations Convention on the Law of the Seas (UNCLOS), which provides the legal framework for the conservation and sustainable use of oceans and their resources;

FURTHER RECOGNISING that the seas and oceans connect our region and link it to other regions of the globe, and that the stability of this maritime area anchors our growth and our future;

RECALLING the United Nations General Assembly Resolution Oceans and the Law of the Sea in the General Assembly, adopted 5 December 2017, which called for national, regional and sub-regional actions to address the problem of marine plastic debris, as well as the commitment we made in the 2015 EAS Statement on Enhancing Regional Maritime Cooperation, to enhance our cooperation in sustainable marine economic development, in protecting and preserving the marine and coastal environment, marine biodiversity, ecosystem and resources, as well as in protecting people who depend on them for their livelihood from harmful activities, such as land-based and sea-based pollution;

RECALLING the International Maritime Organisation's commitment to the "Development of an action plan to address marine plastic litter from ships" with a target completion date of 2020;

RECALLING the Food and Agriculture Organisation of the United Nations' (FAO) commitment to develop a global strategy to address Abandoned, Lost or Otherwise Discarded Fishing Gear (ALDFG), as part of the FAO's work to address marine plastic debris issues;

RECALLING further the EAS Conference on Combating Marine Plastic Debris held in Bali, Indonesia, in September 2017, which highlighted the importance of regional action in order to prevent and reduce marine plastic debris, and the ASEAN Conference on Reducing Marine Plastic Debris in ASEAN Region held in Thailand in November 2017, which reviewed the status of marine plastic debris in ASEAN region from the global, regional and legal perspectives, and exchanged information on the existing national policies, initiatives and technology solutions to the issue;

CONVINCED that the EAS could play a significant role to reduce the incidence and impact of such pollution on marine ecosystems, including through the effective implementation of relevant initiatives such as ASEAN Community Vision 2025 and the UN 2030 Agenda for Sustainable Development, particularly its target to, by 2025, prevent and significantly reduce marine pollution of all kinds, in particular from land-based activities, including marine debris and nutrient pollution;

FURTHER RECALLING our commitments as outlined in the Manila Plan of Action to Advance the Phnom Penh Declaration on the East Asia Summit Development Initiative (2018-2022) to promote cooperation on combating marine plastic pollution, to effectively establish and implement a coherent and coordinated regional approach, focused on prevention and management of waste and litter and promotion of investments in waste management infrastructure, also through cooperation with the private sector;

DESIRING to have further cooperation and collaboration among multiple authorities and agencies at the local, national, regional and international levels, including governmental, non-governmental, civil society, the private sector and the public to combat marine plastic debris;

EMPHASISING the importance of promoting maritime cooperation through dialogue and cooperation and optimising ASEAN-led mechanisms to address common challenges on maritime issues, including utilising the role of the Expanded ASEAN Maritime Forum as an effective platform to constructively engage in open and substantive dialogue;

DO HEREBY DECLARE that maritime cooperation especially in the area of marine plastic debris, merits further consideration, and **DETERMINED** to take concrete actions in combating marine plastic debris, namely to:

1. **IMPROVE** and promote environmentally sound management of plastic waste and resource efficiency, including circular economy, product life-cycle management, sustainable materials management, and "3R" approaches, as appropriate, and including by involving producers and manufacturers of plastics and related products, as well as recycling and waste management stakeholders; through activities such as improving relevant programmes on reducing plastic waste from land-based and sea-based activities; and through developing sustainable, quality and resilient infrastructure;

2. **PROMOTE** awareness, research and education on marine plastic debris by

    a) Promoting public information campaigns for citizens and businesses to prevent and reduce marine plastic debris;

    b) Increasing awareness of the threat of marine plastic debris among all relevant stakeholders, including by reaching out to schools and the community, especially fishing and coastal communities;

    c) Supporting research efforts to evaluate the status of marine plastic debris, including by, where possible and appropriate, collecting relevant information on plastic entering the marine environment and assessing their impact on ecosystems and human health;

    d) Involving research institutions and academia to improve future waste management on land as well as offshore waste reduction;

e) Promoting knowledge sharing, including by expert exchanges, sharing of technological solutions and best practices on mutually determined terms;

f) Encouraging innovation or new technology shaped by government institutions, private sector and/or civil society in order to prevent and reduce marine plastic debris, including by exploring environmentally sound alternatives to conventional plastics;

3. **ENHANCE** cooperation in policy reform and law enforcement where appropriate, including by stepping up capacity building involved in preventing and reducing marine plastic debris.

4. **IMPLEMENT** policies that incentivise the private sector and end-user in reducing and combating marine plastic debris.

5. **STRENGTHEN** regional and international cooperation by

a) Strengthening the coordination and cooperation among EAS participating countries in preventing and reducing marine plastic debris, in accordance with their domestic laws and bilateral or multilateral agreements that they are party to;

b) Promoting international collaboration to prevent and reduce marine plastic debris in relevant ASEAN-led mechanisms and other relevant international, regional and sub-regional forums, such as the United Nations Environment Programme (UNEP), G-20, Asia Pacific Economic Cooperation (APEC), and Partnerships in Environmental Management for the Seas of East Asia (PEMSEA);

c) Improving capacity building in preventing and reducing marine plastic debris and enhance coordination among EAS participating countries;

d) Promoting multi-stakeholder cooperation, and engagement among governmental institutions, civil society organisations, private sector, media, and all relevant stakeholders, to strengthen efforts in prevention and reduction of marine plastic debris;

e) Exploring the possible development of a regional plan of action and guidelines, to prevent and reduce marine plastic debris;

f) Encouraging prevention and management of marine plastic debris, including buoys for aquaculture and ghost nets;

g) Promoting efforts to support the development of national action plans, in accordance with national circumstances and applicable international and domestic laws to prevent, reduce and manage marine plastic debris.

******

INDEX

Note: Page numbers followed by "n" refer to endnotes.